The Tradition of Non-Use of Nuclear Weapons

The Tradition of Non-Use of Nuclear Weapons

T. V. Paul

STANFORD SECURITY STUDIES
An Imprint of Stanford University Press
Stanford, California

Stanford University Press

Stanford, California

Library of Congress Cataloging-in-Publication Data

Paul, T. V.
    The tradition of non-use of nuclear weapons / T. V. Paul.
        p. cm.
    Includes bibliographical references and index.
    ISBN 978-0-8047-6131-4 (cloth : alk. paper)—ISBN 978-0-8047-6132-1 (pbk. : alk. paper)

    1. Nuclear weapons—Government policy. 2. Nuclear nonproliferation—Government
policy. 3. Nuclear weapons—Moral and ethical aspects. 4. Nuclear warfare—Psychological
aspects. 5. Deterrence (Strategy) I. Title.

    U264.P38 2009
    355.02'17—dc22

                                        2008025300

Typeset by Thompson Type in 10/14 Minion

Special discounts for bulk quantities of Stanford Security Studies are available to
corporations, professional associations, and other organizations. For details and discount
information, contact the special sales department of Stanford University Press.
Tel: (650) 736-1783, Fax: (650) 736-1784

CONTENTS

ACKNOWLEDGMENTS

THE IDEA OF WRITING A BOOK on nuclear non-use first occurred to me in 1990 when as a doctoral student at the University of California, Los Angeles (UCLA), I attended a presentation on the subject by Thomas Schelling. The eminent strategic scholar had discussed this subject briefly in several of his writings, but a book-length study was missing in the literature. Since then, scholars, especially of the Constructivist vein, have written on the subject of the nuclear taboo, but they tend to undervalue the material dimensions of the issue. In this book, I have developed an argument for the rise and persistence of the tradition of non-use based on reputation and image concerns while linking these factors to normative considerations. The work is partially motivated by a concern for the preservation of the tradition in light of changes taking place in the nuclear policies of the United States and other nuclear powers, as this tradition serves many cherished goals of the international community, especially in the areas of nuclear nonproliferation and prevention of nuclear war.

My work has been immensely helped by a wide array of scholars and graduate student assistants over the years. I am especially thankful to Timothy Crawford, Jeffrey Knopf, and Patrick Morgan, who made extensive comments on my full draft manuscript. Others who read and commented various chapters include the late Hayward Alker, William Bain, Rajesh Basrur, Avner Cohen, Richard Harknett, Patrick James, Paul Kapur, Hiro Katsumata, Peter Katzenstein, Christopher Layne, Michael Lipson, Mark Manger, Terry McNamee, Vincent Pouliot, Richard Price, Norrin Ripsman, T. P. Sreenivasan, John Vasquez, and Christopher Way. Special praise goes to Theodore McLauchlin and Mahesh Shankar for reading and copy-editing the manuscript. Theodore also made many constructive suggestions for improving the manuscript. Over the years, Simon Collard-Wexler and William Hogg collected a considerable amount of material for this project.

Others who helped me in some way or other in making this book possible include Bahar Akman, John Hall, Izumi Kawaskai, Christopher Manfredi, Imad Mansour, Carman Miller, Douglas Porch, Lawrence Prabhakar, Richard Schultz, Nina Tannenwald, Stéfanie Von Hlatky, and James Wirtz. Presentations at the University of British Columbia, the University of Cincinnati, Cornell University, the University of Hong Kong, the University of Southern California, the George Bush School at Texas A&M University, Jawaharlal Nehru University (New Delhi), Loyola College (Chennai), Mahatma Gandhi University (Kottayam), S. Rajaratnam School of International Studies (Singapore), the Indian Institute of Science (Bangalore), Kerala University (Trivandrum), the Royal United Services Institute for Defense Studies (London), and the University of Wales at Aberystwyth, and several conference panels at the American Political Science Association, International Studies Association, and British International Studies Association, all have provided me opportunities for examining the validity of my ideas. Generous funding from the Social Sciences and Humanities Research Council of Canada (SSHRC), Fonds québécois de la recherche sur la société et la culture (FQRSC), James McGill Chair, Naval Postgraduate School, and the Security and Defense Forum (SDF) helped me tremendously in undertaking travel, research, and writing. Geoffrey Burn, Editor and Director of Stanford University Press, showed keen interest in the book project. I also acknowledge that portions of Chapters 1 and 7 are drawn from my article, "Nuclear Taboo and War Initiation: Nuclear Weapons in Regional Conflicts," *Journal of Conflict Resolution* 39(4) (December 1995), 696–717 (with permission from Sage Publications). It has taken many years for me to complete this book as other projects intervened. My family members frequently bore with my absences for field research and conferences, and I lovingly dedicate this book to them—my wife, Rachel, and my daughters, Kavya and Leah.

Montreal
August 2008

The Tradition of Non-Use of Nuclear Weapons

1 INTRODUCTION

IN AUGUST 2008, the world observed the sixty-third anniversary of the atomic bombings of Hiroshima and Nagasaki, history's first and only instances of nuclear attack. Since 1945, the nuclear age has generated considerable debate on the utility, morality, and legitimacy of the acquisition, possession, control, and use of nuclear weapons. Buried in the global discourse on the nuclear dilemma is the fact that atomic weapons have not been used militarily by any nuclear state since 1945. While their non-use between nuclear states may largely be explained by the operation of mutual deterrence, it remains a puzzle as to why these weapons have not been used against nonnuclear opponents, who could not retaliate in kind. In some cases, nuclear weapon states (NWS) have lost the wars they fought against nonnuclear weapon states (NNWS). Occasionally, NWS have experienced the temptation to use their atomic arms, yet desisted from doing so. In other instances, nonnuclear states initiated crises or wars, anticipating non-use of atomic weapons by the defending nuclear state. In some other cases, NNWS continued fighting with NWS, and thereby imposed enormous costs on the latter in personnel and resources, even though the NWS had the capability to retaliate with nuclear weapons and thus terminate the war expeditiously.

I argue that the unwillingness to use nuclear weapons can be partially attributed to an informal norm inherent in *the tradition of non-use*, which has gradually emerged since 1945. A tradition in this sense is a time-honored practice of non-use that has been followed by nuclear states since 1945 as an "accustomed obligation."[1] This tradition has largely been shaped by two dominant factors: first, an appreciation of the material character of the weapon concerned (i.e., the horrendous short- and long-term impact its use would create), beginning with Hiroshima and Nagasaki, but more powerfully entrenched following the hydrogen bomb tests in the early 1950s; second, the negative reputational effects its use would generate, especially in terms of projecting poor images, signaling wrong intentions, and setting bad precedents. The awareness among nuclear states that the unpredictability and enormity of nuclear weapons use actually reduced their utility for most strategic purposes involving nonnuclear states caused them to practice self-deterrence. Over time, the iterated non-use of nuclear weapons became self-perpetuating through the establishment of an informal norm: that is, later decisions to refrain from nuclear use were based, in part, on previous decisions to desist and a desire to continue the practice.

Tactical/strategic constraints also need to be examined in order to understand why nuclear arms have not been used since 1945. However, an explanation solely based on the tactical and strategic unsuitability of the weapon is unlikely to show us the larger picture of non-use for over sixty years as these considerations are context-dependent. The non-use of nuclear weapons under varying strategic/tactical circumstances suggests that other causal mechanisms might be operating more powerfully or alongside strategy and tactics in the choices of nuclear states. In other words, the story of non-use of nuclear arms is much larger than what a pure strategic/tactical account can offer. This book provides a larger discussion of the politics of nuclear non-use, not only in terms of the crisis decisions made by nuclear powers involving nonnuclear states but also from the perspectives of different states on the usability or non-usability of nuclear weapons in world politics at large.

Although previous works on the subject locate the reasons for non-use largely in either rationalist/materialistic or in normative/ideational considerations, I argue that both sets of factors need to be examined in order to get a comprehensive and more accurate view of the phenomenon of non-use. In that sense, this book approaches the subject on the basis of analytical eclecticism that has been proposed by some social scientists.[2] This approach also combines the *logic of consequences* and the *logic of appropriateness* as presented by James March and Johan Olsen. The reputational argument developed in Chapter 2 is based on a rational logic of consequences, while the normative argument inherent in the tradition of non-use relies on a logic of appropriateness. I argue that the reputational variables linked to the logic of consequences are the primary causal factors for understanding the continued non-use of nuclear weapons, but the logic of appropriateness in the form of a normative prohibition inherent in the tradition of non-use has intermingled with the former, especially as the nuclear age has advanced.[3] First, reputation arbiters such as scientists, strategists, peace movements, and developing-country leaders helped increase the reputational costs of nuclear use through compelling arguments using a logic of appropriateness as well as a logic of consequences. Second, the practice of non-use became reinforced through iteration over time, through mechanisms that included both the entrenchment of costs for using nuclear weapons (consequences) and the development of ideas about responsible state behavior (appropriateness).

This book approaches the subject from a puzzle-driven perspective as opposed to a purely paradigm-driven approach. While paradigms offer disciplinary coherence, allowing scholars to devote their energies to research programs that share common assumptions, premises, dominant variables, and units of analysis, they also limit the prospects for answering pressing policy issues or intellectual puzzles that do not have black-or-white answers. Further, when analysts attempt to pigeonhole explanations to fit one paradigm or another, they tend to leave out the nuances involved in the explanation for the phenomenon they study. The effort in this book is to offer a richer analysis and not to create a grand theory but an intermediate theory, in order to explain the puzzle of nuclear non-use.[4]

The tradition seems to have emerged due to the realizations that nuclear weapons are radically different from conventional weapons and that their use would show the user in an excessively bad light in international public opinion. However, beyond reputation, there exists a practical value of non-use to the NWS, especially for the United States and the Soviet Union. The reputation for non-use served the twin goals of U.S. international security policy during the Cold War, that is, preserving peace through mutual deterrence but at the same time preventing the spread of nuclear weapons. The Soviet Union had similar objectives vis-à-vis the West and the developing world. In this sense, this has been a partially "invented tradition" (a practice that is deliberately constructed) in order to impart legitimacy for the major powers' monopoly over nuclear weapons.[5] Moral, ethical, and legal factors are important to the extent that they enter into reputational considerations. Since it is not a formal, enforceable legal norm, but a practice followed by the nuclear states, I use the term *informal norm* to denote the normative restraint inherent in the tradition of non-use. Moreover, most nuclear states proclaim that they intend to use their weapons only under certain circumstances—for example, to deter or retaliate against challenges to the vital interests of their nation-state, including survival. In contrast, when it comes to the use of chemical or biological weapons, most of these states have made legal commitments, and tend to deny any deterrence or retaliatory intent. In that respect, the nuclear non-use norm is legally less enshrined than the norms against the use of chemical and biological weapons (although, ironically, these norms have been more widely violated). Therefore, until it becomes a full-fledged legal prohibition, the nuclear non-use norm will remain an informal norm rooted in a tradition.

In order to gain a broader understanding of the tradition of non-use, this book examines several interrelated questions. First, what have been the reasons for the unwillingness of nuclear weapons states, both new and old, to use their capability against nonnuclear adversaries in war? Second, what have been the calculations of nonnuclear states that confronted nuclear powers on the battlefield? Third, if nuclear use is constrained by reputational considerations, what are the implications for theories of deterrence and compellence, as well as for the political utility of these weapons as instruments of power? Fourth, does the existence of the unequal nuclear nonproliferation regime partially depend on the maintenance of this tradition? Specifically, what role did it play in the bargain between nuclear haves and have-nots, especially in the conclusion of the Nuclear Nonproliferation Treaty (NPT) and its continued existence? Fifth, how resilient or fragile is this informal norm? Do new political and technological developments have the potential to unravel the restraining power of the tradition? If so, what precisely are these forces in the contemporary and emerging international system? Finally, does the preservation of the tradition of non-use serve any fundamental interests of the global community (involving both nuclear and nonnuclear states)? If yes, what are they?

TABOO OR TRADITION?

Many analysts explain the non-use of nuclear weapons by referring to a "taboo" that arose against their use.[6] Others refer to the practice of non-use as a "tradition." The terms are often used interchangeably, although they have different meanings. The presence of a taboo-like prohibition against nuclear use has been noted by important scholars and policy makers such as Thomas Schelling, McGeorge Bundy, and Robert McNamara. Former American Secretary of State John Foster Dulles initially used the term *taboo* to describe the unwritten prohibition against the use of nuclear weapons. On October 7, 1953, Dulles was reported to have said: "Somehow or other we must manage to remove the taboo from the use of these weapons."[7] Dulles was in favor of developing usable nuclear weapons to obtain the key battlefield military objectives of the United States in Korea. George Ball presented a stringent prohibition when he contended that the revulsion against nuclear use "has enveloped nuclear weapons in a rigid taboo," and that the nation that first broke it "would suffer universal condemnation."[8]

While scholars such as Bernard Brodie saw no purpose in nuclear weapons other than deterrence, Thomas Schelling popularized the concept of a "tradition of non-use" in his writings in the 1960s. In his words, what makes atomic weapons different is a powerful tradition for their non-use, "a jointly recognized expectation that they may not be used in spite of declarations of readiness to use them, even in spite of tactical advantages in their use."[9] A tradition in this respect is based on a habit or disposition that prevents the use of nuclear weapons as a serious option for consideration by decision makers.[10] Schelling argues that the main reason for the non-use of nuclear weapons is the perception that they are unique and that once introduced into combat they could not be "contained, restrained, confined, or limited."[11] Although prolonged conventional war can also cause somewhat similar levels of casualties, the difference is in the perception of the impact.[12] The swiftness with which widespread destruction can take place and the lingering aftereffects in the form of radiation hazards are the distinguishing marks of nuclear weapon use vis-à-vis attacks relying on conventional weapons.

Social Taboos

While it is possible that some elements of a taboo-like prohibition might exist, the tradition of non-use does not contain a strict prohibitionary norm. Let us explore what a taboo means in order to assess whether the literal use of the term is justified in this instance. The term *taboo* is derived from the Polynesian word *tabu* or *tapu* which means "prohibition." In its sociological aspects, it refers to "a system of prohibitions observed as customs."[13] A taboo arises from the fear of something "mystically dangerous," and generally its authority is based on custom. As Webster states: "The authority of a taboo is unmatched by that of any other prohibition. There is no reflection on it, no reasoning about it, no discussion of it. A taboo amounts simply to an imperative thou-shalt-not in the presence of the danger apprehended."[14] Taboo denotes the prohibitions arising from the mysterious attributes of a person, thing, or place, or a transitory condition. To Freud, it connotes attributes such as "sacred," "consecrated," "above the ordinary," "dangerous," "forbidden," "unclean," and "uncanny."[15] It thus refers to a social prohibition on a human activity considered as forbidden or sacred.

According to the *Encyclopedia Britannica,* a taboo is a "prohibition of an action or the use of an object based on ritualistic distinctions of them either as being sacred and consecrated or as being dangerous, unclean, and accursed." Taboos "include prohibitions on fishing or picking fruits at certain seasons; food taboos that restrict the diet of pregnant women; prohibitions on talking to or touching chiefs or members of other high social classes; taboos on walking or traveling in certain areas, such as forests; and various taboos that function during important life events such as birth, marriage, and death."[16] Assumptions of danger and fear of repercussions of the particular act committed characterize most social taboos. For some social taboos, the anticipated repercussions could be in the form of disease or death or an incalculable trauma to the victim, the violator, and his or her associates, while for others, it could be shame, embarrassment, and social isolation.[17] For some social taboos, the violator is stigmatized as "eccentric" and "abnormal," although the level of punishment and redemption could vary from one social taboo to another.[18]

In modern societies, there are a number of well-established social taboos in evidence. They include restrictions on diets, sexual activities, and exposure of particular body parts. Two of the most significant ones are the taboos against incest and cannibalism.[19] These two acts are not only forbidden by law, but people rarely discuss them in regular conversations. In other words, ordinarily people do not wish to talk about them, and when they hear that transgressions have occurred, reactions are usually those of horror and disgust; the transgressor is characterized as a "psychopath" who is in need of urgent psychiatric intervention. People in general observe these and other social taboos not simply because of the legal prohibitions against them, but because of the socially accepted understanding of their prohibition. Taboos are also powerful instruments of social order, although some of them may not have a clear rational basis.

Why Is Nuclear Non-Use a Tradition?

As discussed above, the tradition of non-use of nuclear weapons has been characterized as equivalent to a taboo, although many scholars and practitioners use the term *taboo* in a figurative and a loose sense, as an unwritten and uncodified prohibitory norm against nuclear use. The term is also used to the extent that both social and nuclear taboos are based on the fear of consequences of a given course of action. Similarly, both may be reinforced by legal and nonlegal restraints and considerations as well. Thus, like social taboos, the nuclear taboo is likely to have been influenced by a number of considerations—moral and legal norms and rational calculations in particular. The nuclear taboo might have arisen as a response to a realization of the danger or the unforeseeable consequences of a nuclear war. The mysterious attributes of the weapon might have played a role in the creation and persistence of the taboo. States George Quester: "The very notion of a 'taboo' involves a ban on human behavior that is not subjected continuously to a rational balancing of costs and benefits, but that settles in, through wide-spread social acceptance, as an axiomatic redefinition of what constitutes legitimate behavior."[20]

But the differences between well-entrenched social taboos and the nuclear taboo are many. Most social taboos are punishable acts—punishable either by the community (through customs) or the state (through law), each expecting observance by its members. The legal and moral opprobria are so strong that transgressors of powerful social taboos, if caught, would be punished seriously, and their fundamental rights could be curtailed drastically. This is also the case with many social taboos practiced in tribal societies. Some such societies imposed the death penalty on transgressors of deeply held taboos.

In contrast, the prohibition against nuclear use is not as absolute as in the case of many social taboos. International law does not explicitly prohibit the use of nuclear weapons, especially if it is in retribution or in the protection of a state in danger of being overrun. This is clear in the judgment on the legality of nuclear weapons offered by the International Court of Justice (ICJ) in July 1996, holding that neither customary nor conventional international law explicitly prohibits the use of nuclear weapons, although nuclear use could be considered to be a violation of international humanitarian law under most circumstances. The majority opinion stated: "The threat or use of nuclear weapons would generally be contrary to the rules of international law applicable in armed conflict, and in particular the principles and rules of humanitarian law." It continued: "However, in view of the current state of international law, and of the elements of fact at its disposal, the Court cannot conclude definitively whether the threat or use of nuclear weapons would be lawful or unlawful in an extreme circumstance of self-defense, in which the very survival of a State would be at stake."[21] The court did not clarify what constitutes an extreme circumstance of self-defense, thereby leaving its judgment open to interpretation by the national leadership during times of crisis. Moreover, the court did not "address the status of self-defence claims in circumstances where no nuclear weapons are threatened, used or even possessed by an aggressor state that has put the survival of its adversary at risk."[22] Despite the apparent lack of stringent legal sanctions, nuclear states still have been reluctant to use these weapons, and this has been viewed as due to a taboo-like prohibition.[23] However, the regulatory aspect in this respect is ambiguous, as there is no formal punishment mechanism for violation of the nuclear taboo, while the effects of informal punishments such as shame and humiliation are at best uncertain. Social taboos will not persist without expectations of severe punishments if the taboo is broken.[24]

In some other aspects as well, the tradition of non-use of nuclear weapons is not as powerful as social taboos such as the ones against incest or cannibalism. The difference is that nation-states have contingency plans to use nuclear weapons under certain circumstances. Individuals do not even consider breaking deeply held social taboos (as the concept implies no rational consideration of performing a forbidden act), such as those against incest or cannibalism—unless the perpetrator is a psychopath or is facing extreme circumstances such as extinction. In contrast, supposedly rational military planners of responsible states have considered and continue to assess the possibility of nuclear use. The doctrines and strategies, especially those of the United States, Russia, the United Kingdom, and France, have kept open the option of nuclear use against nonnuclear states under certain contingencies. The procurement and deployment of nuclear weapons by rational military organizations suggest that they envision nuclear use. Deterrence against conventional and nonconventional attacks prompts most nuclear states to keep the first-use option open, but the expansion of possible use for purposes beyond deterrence, including maintaining the credibility of power status, compellence, prevention, preemption, signaling resolve, getting allies and adversaries to intervene on one's side, and domestic political calculations, suggests the wide range of uses for nuclear weapons perceived by decision makers of nuclear states. For most nuclear states, the redlines for nuclear use have been changing, especially in the post–Cold War era as deterrence against nuclear attack is no longer the only consideration for the threat of nuclear retaliation. The chance of use, however improbable, lies beneath the threat of use, even when the threatening party, in reality, does not want to consummate the threat. Even if, in the first instance, there is no intention to carry out a threat, such an intention can change if the target does not comply and the sender perceives high credibility costs in not following the threat through. Therefore, the threat of use also is a form of violation of the taboo against nuclear use. Using a strict definition of the term *taboo,* a leader is not supposed to even contemplate the option.

Given the fact that some nuclear states maintain the option of nuclear first use, I argue that the tradition of non-use is not yet a taboo or a fully developed formal norm. Rather it is an informal social norm. Conceptually, norms are characterized by "regularities of behavior" containing "sanctions for failing to follow them."[25] Social norms are "widely internalized patterns of behavior, deviation from which is likely to meet with social disapproval . . . law often indirectly influences such action by shaping social norms."[26] Martha Finnemore defines norms as "shared expectations about appropriate behavior held by a community of actors. Unlike ideas which may be held privately, norms are shared and social; they are not subjective, but inter-subjective. Ideas may or may not have behavioral implications; norms by definition concern behavior."[27] But different social norms have varying strengths, and hence have different impacts on national choices in disparate realms. Legal support may be necessary for a norm to be called a hard or formal norm. Those norms that lack a strong legal basis are soft or intermediate norms derived from informal customs and practices. Legal norms, even though they can also be violated, nevertheless raise the bar for infringement.

If fully developed as a hard legal norm, the practice of non-use would be treaty-based, and the principal norm in this regard would read: "nuclear states shall not use their nuclear weapons against nonnuclear states," under circumstances in which survival is not immediately threatened. No nuclear state has made an unequivocal legally binding commitment to this effect. They have made partial assurances to NPT signatories, but in recent years have changed those pledges to allow for nuclear weapons use against nonnuclear states holding and threatening to use chemical and biological weapons. They have opposed any formal agreement on non-use. In fact, nuclear states do not want to accept the formal existence of such a norm, lest the credibility of their policies of nuclear deterrence and compellence suffer. Their unwillingness may also result from a fear of further raising the bar for nuclear use, suggesting that legality does have an impact in their calculations. However, they have made limited pledges of no first use toward members of the NPT in good standing.

If the tradition of non-use were a full-fledged norm, an associated proposition would read: "nuclear states shall not make loose nuclear threats against non-nuclear states." Threats, by their very nature, presume a contingent use. This dimension of the norm has been violated, especially by the United States and Israel, in the context of conflicts in the Persian Gulf and the Middle East. Further, if it is a full-fledged taboo-like prohibition, a third associated norm would read: "nuclear states shall not introduce nuclear weapons into theaters of conflict with non-nuclear states." Such introduction implies a potential willingness to use, however improbable it may be. This norm has also been violated in the Korean, Falklands, and Gulf conflict zones. In other words, the norm needs to be unconditional in order for it to qualify as a hard norm. For the norm of non-use of nuclear weapons to be robust, resembling a taboo-like prohibition, the above-mentioned three components should be observed continuously by nuclear states.

The discussions by legal scholars of formal and informal laws are useful here in clarifying the concept of the tradition of non-use even further. Formal laws are equivalent to hard laws that are "created using precise constitutional processes," as opposed to "norms that are not produced through specific sources or processes." Hard law is assumed to be more "precise," "inevitably more effective,"[28] and binding, whereas informal law is "based upon the premise that certain principles are important, and should ideally shape international law and policy even if they are not binding."[29] International lawyers also "speak of a progression along a continuum from soft to hard law, though this progression is by no means inevitable or invariably desirable," and "identifying the point on the continuum where the 'soft norm' becomes a 'hard' is notoriously challenging."[30] Some scholars also believe that social norms, by definition, are different from legal norms. Legal norms are "created by design—usually through some kind of deliberative process, precisely specified in written texts, linked to particular sanctions, and enforced by a specialized bureaucracy. Social norms, by contrast, often are spontaneous rather than deliberately planned (hence, of uncertain origin), unwritten (hence, their content and rules for application are often imprecise), and enforced informally."[31] This does not mean states cannot break norms enshrined in international law. But breaking a legal norm becomes harder (but not impossible) as a norm is enshrined in precise legal terms. Legal texts add another layer to the strength of a norm, and in that sense legal norms are superior to social norms that do not have legality attached to them. However, even informal social norms have restraining power on states, as in the nuclear area, the main theme of this book.

The tradition of non-use of nuclear weapons has not made the progression from an informal norm to a legal norm because of the desire of nuclear states to maintain ambiguity in their nuclear policies for deterrence and compellence purposes. The key test for the robustness of the non-use norm is whether it has only limited declaratory or rhetorical value or whether states observe it in the face of compelling circumstances. Are nonnuclear states fairly confident that the threat of use of nuclear weapons is not going to be executed due to the presence of the norm? Historically, how has the norm affected the choices of the concerned states, both nuclear and nonnuclear, in crisis and noncrisis situations? Is it possible that the ambiguity inherent in the informal norm of non-use is both a weakness and a strength, because it allows a certain amount of malleability for deterrence purposes? Does it offer partial legitimacy to the unequal nuclear possession allowed by the NPT, since the permanent five (P-5) major powers of the United Nations (UN) Security Council are permitted to keep their weapons as custodians of international security while assuring other states that they would not be attacked with nuclear weapons and that they do not need to possess nuclear weapons in order to deter NWS? In this sense, can the preservation of the informal norm be explained by the considerable strategic advantages that it offers to nuclear and nonnuclear states?

Although it is not a fully developed legal norm, the non-use of nuclear weapons has been a standard expected behavior of nuclear states over an extended period of time. The non-use of nuclear weapons due to deterrent threats is to be excluded from the purview of the tradition, as it is often difficult to distinguish whether nuclear weapons were not used because of the tradition or because of a fear of retaliation. This study therefore strictly limits the tradition to the non-use of nuclear weapons by nuclear states against nonnuclear states. In addition, nuclear states have so far desisted from using their nuclear weapons for preventive purposes (i.e., the rise of a new nuclear state) despite threatening to do so, suggesting that the tradition may have broader relevance.

As I demonstrate in Chapter 2, the tradition of non-use has developed due to both rational-materialistic and reputational considerations, and has emerged as a key source of self-deterrence practiced by nuclear states vis-à-vis nonnuclear powers. Historical examples, largely drawn from U.S. policy, suggest that nuclear use has been considered but rejected. At times, this was due to instrumental strategic and tactical reasons, that is, nuclear attack would not have achieved stated strategic and tactical objectives. However, the empirical evidence, as presented in Chapters 3 and 4, demonstrates that the larger reasons appear to be reputational and norm-driven, as self-deterrence was practiced by leaders even in contexts where they perceived tactical suitability of nuclear use.

The awesome destructive power of nuclear weapons gave the basic impetus to the rise of the tradition of non-use, as the potential for total destruction gives nuclear weapons an all-or-nothing character unlike any other weapon invented so far. This means a nuclear state may not use its ultimate capability unless a threshold is crossed, for example, when a vital issue, such as the survival of the state itself, is threatened. The notion of a "weapon of last resort" is crucial here. Decision makers and the public at large in most NWS believe that there is great danger in the use of nuclear weapons with respect to casualties and aftereffects, in both psychological and physical terms. Breaking the tradition would elicit the revulsion of generations to come, unless it was for a question of extremely vital importance, such as the physical existence of the nuclear state or its key allies. It would bring severe reputational costs to the user and result in an extremely bad precedent. Nuclear use could also push some of the hitherto nonnuclear states to attempt to acquire nuclear weapons capability as their own independent national deterrent.

The tradition has been observed by all established and new nuclear states thus far. Nations with different ideological and political systems and military traditions—the United States, Russia, the United Kingdom, France, China, India, Pakistan, and Israel—have not used them in conflict, pointing toward the emergence of a global "recognition that nuclear weapons are unusable across much of the range of traditional military and political interests."[32] The unwillingness of the United States to use them in Korea and Vietnam to obtain a decisive military victory, and the Soviet demurral from using them to avert defeat in Afghanistan (although it would have been difficult in the context of the guerilla resistance they were facing),[33] suggest the entrenchment of the tradition among the superpowers even during the peak years of the Cold War era. Paradoxically, both the United States and the Soviet Union used chemical weapons (in Vietnam and Afghanistan, respectively) even though they were waging war against guerilla forces.[34] The Chinese aversion to using nuclear weapons against Vietnam to obtain victory in the 1979 Sino-Vietnamese War indicates that other nuclear powers have observed the tradition of non-use as well.

THE CHAPTERS

In Chapter 2, two perspectives are presented, one that rejects the tradition and the other that views nuclear non-use as a strict taboo-like prohibition. The former is based on *realpolitik* skepticism, while the latter is developed by Constructivist scholars. After looking at the strengths and weaknesses of both perspectives, I develop an eclectic model of non-use, combining reputational and normative factors that cause the practice of self-deterrence among nuclear states. This rationalist-normative analysis attempts to capture how and why the tradition emerged and became acceptable to a wide variety of states of different ideological coloration, while elucidating its rational/instrumental value for both nuclear and nonnuclear states. Chapters 3 and 4 look at how the tradition developed in the United States and how it was sustained, despite pressures on or temptations for successive American presidents to use nuclear weapons in different regional conflicts. Chapter 5 focuses on the other P-5 powers—Russia, Britain, France, and China—and examines their policies toward nuclear use and their contributions toward the development and sustenance of the informal norm. Chapter 6 explores the nuclear policies of India and Pakistan and the undeclared nuclear state, Israel, and their approaches toward nuclear use in general and the tradition of non-use in particular. Chapter 7 focuses on NNWS and their perceptions of the tradition while engaging in wars with nuclear powers. It probes the calculations of NNWS that initiated wars against NWS and the unwillingness of NNWS to give up their conflicts once they were well underway, even when their opponents held nuclear weapons. In Chapter 8, the relationship between the tradition and the nonproliferation regime is discussed. Of particular interest are the efforts by the NNWS to convert the informal norm into a formal enforceable legal norm by demanding negative security guarantees, and through their efforts at the UN General Assembly, the NPT bargaining table, and the World Court (on a decision on the legality of nuclear use). With respect to nonproliferation, it is crucial to see why 184 NNWSs (of whom several are technologically capable) have, by signing the NPT, given up their option to acquire nuclear weapons, while allowing the five declared states to possess them. Are they assured that there exists a normative prohibition against nuclear use and that these weapons are only intended for deterrence? If so, why do NNWS then constantly demand a formal no-first-use commitment from nuclear weapon states? Is this demand a reflection of a lack of complete faith in the tradition? It appears that they are eagerly pursuing a formal norm through the creation of a legal instrument because of their desire to make the tradition of non-use a robust legal norm.

Chapter 9 analyzes the changing nuclear policy of the United States in response to the complex security environment since the end of the Cold War, and especially after the terrorist attacks of September 11, 2001. It is argued that the current U.S. nuclear policy and possible development of new weapons may undermine the tradition. The concluding chapter presents the findings of the study and implications of the tradition of non-use. The key implications are for deterrence theory and policy, as well as for compellence and coercive diplomacy. There are other implications as well, both for the prospects of nuclear war and for nuclear disarmament. The chapter concludes with a cost/benefit assessment of the preservation of the tradition and its utility in a wide range of areas of national and international security interests. I conclude that the informal norm's survival in perpetuity is highly desirable, but is contingent on several factors, including the specific destructive character of the nuclear weapons available today and in the foreseeable future. The policy implication is that if the informal norm is to achieve higher potency, unambiguous legal sanctions will have to be developed and decision makers will have to internalize the norm fully and nurture it so that nuclear weapons, be they small or large, will never again be used as an instrument of interstate war and intimidation.

2 BASES OF THE TRADITION OF NON-USE

FROM A SOCIAL SCIENCE PERSPECTIVE, it is crucial to explain the sources of the tradition of non-use of nuclear weapons and the reasons for its persistence today. Social scientists have not yet fully unpacked the rise, persistence, or weakening of an informal social norm similar to the one inherent in the tradition of non-use. Understanding the mechanisms by which the tradition emerged is important in order to know the causes of its persistence and the conditions of its potential demise. In this chapter, I outline the plausible sources of the tradition of non-use and assess their relative significance.

To begin with, is there a normative prohibition on nuclear use? Only a few scholars have delved into this question directly. But they differ significantly on the existence of the norm and its importance. Here I look at two perspectives. One comes from realpolitik skeptics who reject the existence of a taboo or a tradition on the non-use of nuclear weapons. The other is developed by Constructivist scholars who treat the norm of non-use as a powerful, taboo-like prohibition, with both regulative and constitutive effects over the choices of nuclear states. Some scholars who do not identify themselves as belonging to any particular theoretical paradigm have discussed the tradition as a powerful force in international politics. They include Thomas Schelling, John Lewis Gaddis, George Quester, and McGeorge Bundy; their writings, although containing many realist assumptions and theoretical components, nevertheless accept the existence of a normative tradition.

THE SKEPTICS

Skepticism on the presence of a taboo or a tradition has been raised by realpolitik-oriented scholars, although realists in general have not paid much attention to this issue. Skeptics base their arguments about the non-use of nuclear weapons on: (1) deterrence—either mutual or extended; (2) tactical/strategic unsuitability; and (3) power politics considerations—for example Cold War calculations preventing the nuclear powers from using nuclear weapons against nonnuclear states for fear of escalation in the central strategic theater, that is, Europe. Accordingly, nuclear weapons have not been used against nonnuclear states because of: (a) fear of retaliation by the other nuclear powers; (b) lack of military utility; (c) dearth of good targets for nuclear attacks; (d) the possibility of using conventional weapons to destroy the targets that existed; and (e) complication and contamination of the battlefield by nuclear attacks. States Colin Gray, a critic of the taboo argument: "Policy makers in the eight nuclear weapon states do not equate such stigmatization—or singularization, for a less pejorative rendering—with unusability. Nuclear weapons may be weapons of last resort—for us, at least—but last resort should not be confused with 'no resort.'"[1] To Gray, "the postulate of a nuclear taboo is an ethnocentric delusion on the part of Western theorists."[2]

More nuanced realist explanations base the non-use of nuclear weapons on concerns of prudence, inappropriateness for achieving political or strategic goals, fear of negative impact on national goals (especially in a limited war situation), adverse impact on great power relationships and power structures (e.g., the Cold War-era bipolar strategic relationship between the superpowers), and a high estimation of the value of nuclear weapons for deterrence—which by its very nature would fail if nuclear weapons were ever used in anger or in retribution. These concerns do not necessarily have any connection to morality, ethics, law, or culture, as these are the products of power and power relationships in the first place, under realist logic.[3]

IDEATIONAL AND CULTURAL BASES:
CONSTRUCTIVIST EXPLANATIONS

While the skeptics reject the presence of a normative prohibition, Constructivist scholars have argued that the tradition is indeed a stringent, taboo-like prohibition; that it is a socially constructed, intersubjective norm; and that the origins of this norm go beyond material/rationalist factors.[4] For instance, Richard Price and Nina Tannenwald argue that a rationalist-materialist explanation, based on the intrinsic characteristics of the weapon, or on deterrence grounded in cost-benefit calculations deriving from the possibility of retaliatory threat, cannot account for the origins of the norm of non-use of nuclear weapons. They draw on both domestic structures and a genealogical approach in explaining the origin and persistence of a nuclear weapons taboo in U.S. policy. The former argument suggests that the democratic nature of the United States and its interest and identity helped the creation of a prohibitionary norm. As for the latter, the evolution of the nuclear non-use norm occurred gradually in a nonlinear fashion and it was not inevitable: "it owes much to the combined workings of contingency and the iterated practice of non-use over time, as well as to self-conscious efforts on the part of some to foster a normative stigma."[5] In subsequent work, Tannenwald explores the intersubjective nature of the taboo and the pathways through which it originated. These pathways include societal pressure, especially by domestic and transnational social groups; strategic social construction; the acceptance of the taboo by individual leaders; and finally, iterated behavior over time, "similar to the notion of custom in international law, where obligation arises out of convention."[6] Tannenwald, in her book-length study on the nuclear taboo, modifies the position to include material factors, although the thrust of her argument still remains ideational as opposed to material. She argues that the taboo has "delegitimize[d] nuclear weapons as weapons of war," and has embedded "deterrence practices in a set of norms, both regulative (regulating behavior) and constitutive (defining roles and identities), that stabilize and restrain the self-help behavior of states."[7] To Tannenwald, nuclear non-use is "not simply a tradition both because people believe it is a taboo (with associated taboo-like qualities) and because, as it strengthens over time, it becomes decreasingly based on reciprocity."[8]

CRITIQUE

I examine the problems with both these positions before introducing my eclectic framework, which gives importance to rational and normative considerations, presented in terms of *logic of consequences* and *logic of appropriateness*, respectively.

Problems with Realpolitik Claims

The claim by realpolitik scholars that there is never a tradition of non-use nor a normative prohibition against nuclear use in existence is belied by the fact that the weapon has not been used since August 1945, even though highly realpolitik-oriented leaders (e.g., Eisenhower, Dulles, Nixon, and Kissinger) considered their use (for detailed analysis, see Chapters 3 and 4). Although issues of tactical and strategic unsuitability come to the fore on some such occasions, the empirical evidence strongly suggests that considerations beyond tactical/ strategic constraints entered decision-makers' calculations when nuclear use was considered. A pure realpolitik explanation has difficulty answering several questions. First, why would countries stop using a weapon for such a long period of time after two early instances of use, all the while building newer and more lethal weapons of that same category, expending massive amounts of resources toward their development, acquisition, and maintenance? Second, nuclear superpowers lost wars with minor powers; these defeats diminished their credibility, status, and prestige, causing great internal and external changes (e.g., Vietnam for the United States, and Afghanistan for the Soviet Union). Yet these same nuclear superpowers refrained from using all their capabilities, including nuclear weapons, in order to avert such an outcome. Despite the limitations of nuclear weapons in confronting guerilla warfare, the use of tactical nuclear weapons could have probably decapitated leaders of resistance and revolutionary movements and averted the possibility of failure for the superpower concerned, a consideration that was given substantial prominence in U.S. thinking during the Johnson and Nixon eras. Moreover, the superpowers used chemical weapons (napalm and Agent Orange in the case of Vietnam and yellow rain in the case of Afghanistan), suggesting that they were not waging simple counterinsurgency wars in those countries.[9] As I discuss in Chapters 3 and 4, the United States did indeed consider nuclear use against China, North Korea, and Vietnam, whose forces were waging asymmetric wars partially based on guerilla principles. Third, archival materials now available suggest that it was more than crude realpolitik calculations that entered the minds of many of these leaders; they did not view nuclear weapons as just like other weapons, but saw them as possessing uniquely destructive qualities that placed them beyond simple war-winning instruments. This unique attribute of nuclear weapons as perceived by decision makers is not captured by simple realpolitik explanations of their non-use.[10]

However, a broadened interest-based explanation can incorporate elements of some of the realist logic, while drawing on factors from other nonrealist perspectives such as morality/ethics and international law.

Problems with the Constructivist Position

Although I see much merit in the ideational arguments of Constructivists, their dominant focus on ideas and national culture and their tendency to undervalue material factors, especially the brute physical characteristics of the bomb and the self-interests of states in non-use, seem to make their case an overstated one. Even while stating the need to link material and nonmaterial variables, and while acknowledging the presence of material factors in explaining the origins of the taboo, they tend to underplay the latter in accounting for the persistence of a norm. Tannenwald's works acknowledge material factors, but she provides very little, if any, discussion of what material factors contribute to the creation and persistence of the taboo-like prohibition. It is true that Constructivists have come a long way from their earlier either/or arguments, but the analytical purchase of ideas and national culture are still overdetermined in these perspectives, ironically similar to a criticism they make against material approaches. Although Constructivists are currently doing much work on creating eclectic models, they have yet to fully tease out the linkage between ideas and material factors so as to get a clearer understanding of how the two intermesh.[11] This seems necessary for us to obtain a convincing handle on a complex subject such as nuclear non-use. In addition, Constructivist accounts of nuclear taboo give considerable weight to actor identity and culture, which I do not find very valuable in my explanation.

A critical test for the ideational argument is to find out if the norm of non-use has been in the security interests of nuclear weapons states, especially the United States and the Soviet Union, given that one of their key aims in the Cold War was to obtain the allegiance of states in the developing world, with a secondary goal being the prevention of the spread of nuclear weapons to additional states. The Constructivist scholars' claim that the tradition originated in the United States also needs further verification. Even on the Western Bloc side, it seems that the British, as well as other European allies, were major opponents of U.S. plans to use nuclear weapons in Korea.

In addition, the nondemocratic Soviet Union and China have contributed powerfully to the rise of the tradition, especially by declaring no-first-use policies and by refraining from the use of nuclear weapons against nonnuclear states. Appreciating their contribution is highly important for an understanding of norms like the non-use of nuclear weapons in a divided international system. Though these two Communist states cared little about acceptable behavior in internal repression of dissidents, their words and actions still helped to reinforce a vital norm of international conduct in the nuclear area. In part, this contribution originated from a Cold War environment of competition in reputation, with the Third World as audience. In China's case, the norm has more recently been perpetuated by Beijing's weaknesses in the number of nuclear weapons it possesses and a desire to appear as a responsible great power.

The Soviet and Chinese contributions also help to demonstrate that non-use does not necessarily have a close relationship with domestically driven political culture. Although in the post–Cold War era, Russia has backed off from its no-first-use policy, nondemocratic China has continued to profess it, while democratic America, Britain, and France have been making plans to use nuclear weapons in possible preemptive and preventive situations vis-à-vis regional challengers and terrorist groups pursuing weapons of mass destruction. The Western powers, along with democratic Israel, have been the most prone to making loose nuclear threats in crisis and noncrisis situations involving nonnuclear states. Although the Soviets and Chinese had fewer occasions to threaten the use of nuclear weapons against nonnuclear states, and although their archives are yet to be open to public access on this issue, going by available historical record, it is possible to make a contention that it has been the democratic United States that has most often contemplated nuclear use on occasions of threat to less-than-vital interests. Democracies also have a tendency to use unlimited conventional force against nondemocracies (unlike their behavior toward fellow democracies). In recent years, it has been democracies that have engaged in threats of nuclear and conventional strikes against nondemocracies such as Iraq (under Saddam Hussein), North Korea, and Iran, in order to prevent them from acquiring nuclear weapons.[12]

Despite these criticisms, I agree with Constructivists that the non-use of nuclear weapons cannot be purely explained by material or power politics considerations and that there is a certain amount of normative prohibition (based on considerations of a logic of appropriateness). Self-deterrence in the area of nuclear weapons use is explainable not by tactical or strategic considerations alone, but by a normative tradition against nuclear use that has emerged over the past several decades. I also concur with Constructivists on the role of norm entrepreneurs who appear to be intermediaries in the creation and diffusion of a norm of non-use.

In this book, however, I differentiate my arguments from Constructivist perspectives on the following grounds. First, I give national culture or regime type no significant role, as the tradition has been observed by nuclear weapon states of all political cultures. Second, I treat the tradition as an informal and intermediate norm; its regulatory and constitutive effects are not as powerful or absolute as a taboo-like prohibition. Third, states' self-interest, partially driven by a logic of consequences, has underpinned the creation and sustenance of the tradition. Self-interest and the logic of consequences go beyond the emergence of the tradition (a role that Constructivists sometimes acknowledge), and are also prominent factors in its maintenance. Rational calculations, that is, Cold War concerns regarding reputation and image, maintenance of alliance relationships, allegiance of nonallied states, and nonproliferation, all were important factors behind the maintenance of the tradition, and these are largely self-interest-driven concerns even if they are reinforced by norms. During the Cold War, the superpowers' competition for the allegiance of developing countries was intense, as is evident in the immense resources they spent on propaganda and public diplomacy in those countries. Similarly, the United States especially feared that alliance cohesion among Western countries would be loosened if nuclear weapons were used against nonnuclear states.

Finally, I argue that the informal norm is contingent on changing technological and political conditions that are material, and not necessarily ideational, in nature. It could degrade if new weapons that have low collateral damage are developed and are deployed for use. Further, if political conditions change such that several nonnuclear states seek nuclear weapons and the potential for their use by state and nonstate actors increases in different parts of the world, the tradition could weaken and break down. The efforts by the United States and Russia to develop mininukes are indeed attempts to overcome the reputational constraints inherent in the tradition of non-use. In my perspective, although the tradition has strengthened over the years, there appears to be no linear progression toward a world of robust nuclear non-use; active human action is necessary in order to preserve this tradition. I foresee a mixed pattern in the tradition's future: at some level the tradition is embedded, but at another level, ongoing efforts are being made by political, scientific, and bureaucratic elites in many nuclear states to transcend the tradition and make nuclear weapons useable by devising new weapons and strategies. Through these efforts, these elites are implicitly accepting the presence of the tradition and are seeking to overcome it one way or another.

The explanation below lies between material and normative perspectives, respectively giving importance to the logic of consequences and logic of appropriateness (although I weigh in favor of the former over the latter). It rejects arguments of both a powerful taboo-like prohibition and simple realpolitik skepticism. I give much more weight to the tradition than realpolitik skeptics do, but not as much as Constructivists make of it. Elements of the explanation draw on the analyses offered by John Lewis Gaddis, Thomas Schelling, George Quester, and McGeorge Bundy. However, these scholars have not yet developed a powerful causal argument for the rise and persistence of the tradition. This is where I hope to make my contribution to the understanding of this subject.

EXPLAINING NUCLEAR NON-USE

In this book, I develop an explanation for the emergence and persistence of the tradition of non-use of nuclear weapons, based on material factors and reputation. This reflects eclecticism as an approach to the study of international relations. Unlike pure realist arguments, this explanation does not reject the moral and legal logic completely. The relevant material concerns, especially the intrinsic physical effects of nuclear weapons, have moral, legal, and normative as well as rational connotations. Further, the reputation of a state is partly based on other states' views of morality and law and whether the former is adhering to these in its security and foreign policy behavior.

This approach also reflects a strong preference for a problem- or puzzle-based international relations research as opposed to paradigm-driven work. While there are many reasons for paradigm-driven scholarship, I contend that important puzzles should also form the second leg of any discipline. When scholars try hard to place analytical phenomena in one paradigm or the other, they tend to miss considerable nuances. I believe that in a problem- or puzzle-driven analysis, variables from different paradigms can be used to explain a phenomenon more accurately. The effort here is not creating a grand theory but developing a puzzle-driven intermediate theory and explanation for a significant intellectual and policy problem.[13]

In Figure 2.1 and the following text, I show the working of an eclectic model that treats both the material and nonmaterial considerations in the origins and maintenance of a tradition of non-use and its impact on actual practice.

The Material Bases

The informal norm inherent in the tradition of non-use arose and persisted partially from the material bases of the weapon concerned and the consequences of its use as understood by decision makers over the past half century.

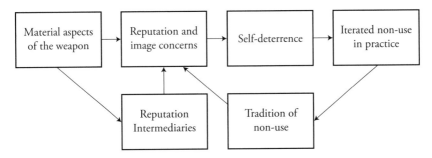

Figure 2.1. Causal Linkage of Non-Use.

In that sense, it is a prudential or rational norm developed or partially "invented" in view of the enlightened self-interest of nuclear states—and its future depends on the evolving character of the weapon and its utility as an instrument of deterrence as well as compellence.

The material bases of the tradition pertains to the fact that nuclear arms are "absolute" or "uncontestable" weapons, in that they are unique in their destructiveness while their use generates several consequences that decision makers cannot fathom or calculate.[14] They are qualitatively different from conventional weapons in terms of their short- and long-term impact. As Thomas Schelling argues, nuclear weapons are unique because once introduced into combat they cannot be "contained, restrained, confined, or limited."[15] In many respects, the destructive power of nuclear weapons is so awesome that it belies the fundamental Clausewitzian dictum that war is politics by other means. As Mandelbaum argues, the use of nuclear weapons would jeopardize "both the natural limits on violence, and the prospects for imposing further, political controls, that Clausewitz believed kept all actual wars from mounting to horrible, senseless, 'absolute' extremes."[16] Although a prolonged conventional war can also cause horrendous levels of destruction, the difference is in the decision makers' perception of control of events and the impact of a given course of action in the military realm. Decision makers tend to engage in conventional wars believing that they can control events and that victory is possible with limited costs. They tend to enter wars hoping military conflict will be short and costs not prohibitive. In the nuclear context, this expectation of victory and control over events disappears altogether, making leaders unsure of the consequences of their actions. The swiftness with which destruction takes place and the long-term lingering effects of an attack are the two distinguishing points in this respect. Moral concerns enter the picture to the point that, once unleashed, a leader loses control of the weapon, making it impossible to scale down the destruction and its possible unimaginable effects; thus, he or she may be entering a morally unacceptable realm of human action.

The perception of the uniqueness of nuclear weapons arose because the potential for total destruction gives them an all-or-nothing character unlike any other weapon invented thus far. This perception is based on a real material fact, and it is not largely an idea developed due to cultural factors. The perception that nuclear weapons are different arose largely as a result of the impact of the Hiroshima and Nagasaki attacks and the thermonuclear tests in the South Pacific in the 1950s; as a result, even "ordinary people have come to see such weapons as different, and so destructive that they can never be treated as 'just another weapon.'"[17] Though other weapons such as submarines and mustard gas had been subjected to international condemnation and norms against their use,[18] the immense destructiveness of nuclear weapons activated global concern and focused international attention more than any previous weapon. In the United States, it was President Harry Truman who took away the custody of the weapon from the military and gave it to the civilian Atomic Energy Agency, in appreciation of the unique destructive nature of the weapon vis-à-vis conventional weapons and hence the need for civilian control over its use. The uniqueness of the weapon means that a nuclear state may not use its ultimate capability unless a threshold is crossed (e.g., when a vital interest, such as the survival of the state itself, is threatened).

State leaders seem to calculate that military victory following a nuclear attack may not be materially, politically, psychologically, or morally worth obtaining if it involves the destruction of the total, or a sizable segment, of an enemy's population and results in the contamination of a large portion of its territory with radioactive debris. Thus, the tradition seems to have emerged plausibly from the realization by nuclear states that there are severe limits to what they can accomplish by actually using a nuclear weapon.[19] It also implies that after a certain point the capacity to destroy may not be useful, as the relationship between the power to harm and the power to modify the behavior of others is not linear.[20]

Additionally, the effects of even a limited nuclear attack may extend beyond the local area of attack, spatially and temporally.[21] There exists no guarantee that the aftereffects, such as the spread of radioactive debris, can be confined to the target state's territory. Neighboring states that may be neutral or aligned with the nuclear state could be the victims of the nuclear fallout as well. The fear that, once unleashed, nuclear terror will escape meaningful political and military control and physical limitation seems to have influenced decision-makers' choices in this regard. Thus, a norm (defined as "collective expectations about proper behavior for a given identity," in this case as a responsible nuclear power)[22] seems to have arisen partially as a function of the perception of the awesome destructive power of atomic weapons. It is also based on the self-interests of actors concerned, a point that is not often given due prominence in norm analysis.[23] This perception did not arise suddenly. It was evolutionary; the Hiroshima and Nagasaki attacks and their consequences were the initial military and political shocks that gave birth to this perception. These were later compounded by the increase in lethality and numbers of different types of nuclear weapons that were introduced by the nuclear powers, and the open testing in the atmosphere of powerful hydrogen bombs, especially in the 1950s.

Reputational Factors

The argument based on the physical character of a nuclear weapon can take us only up to a point, because their retaliatory use is a cardinal feature of deterrence theory and policy, implying that the use of nuclear weapons is envisaged under at least some conditions; if the character of nuclear weapons were sufficient to explain their non-use, then their use should *never* be contemplated. This means that a convincing explanation needs to bring in nonmaterial factors also. This is where reputational considerations enter the picture. I argue that the unique material character of the weapon leads to reputational costs involved in its use. Leaders often tend to worry about the costs in terms of reputation and image of their nation and themselves when they undertake a particular course of action in the military realm.[24] The chief concern here may be that the use of nuclear weapons would be condemned worldwide and can bring the revulsion of generations to come. The leader who orders the use of such a weapon could suffer incredible reputational costs. The reputational costs can also be very high among allies who may abandon the power that used such a weapon in anger. Positive reputation, on the other hand, can attract the allegiance of allies and additional members or sympathizers to one's side. The Cold War competition for allies was also a contest between the superpowers for positive reputation to attract nonaligned states to their side.

Reputation connotes a shared expectation which in turn is reinforced through time by iterated practice. The tradition of non-use, therefore, has a strong dimension of temporal reinforcement. Thomas Schelling puts it cogently:

> What makes atomic weapons different is a powerful tradition that they *are* different. The reason—in answer to the usual rhetorical question—why we do not ban bows and arrows on the grounds that they too, like nuclear weapons, kill and maim people, is that there is a tradition for the use of bows and arrows, a jointly recognized expectation that they will be used if it is expedient to use them. There is no such tradition for the use of atomic weapons. There is instead a tradition for their nonuse—a jointly recognized expectation that they may not be used in spite of declarations of readiness to use them, even in spite of tactical advantages in their use.[25]

As shown in Figure 2.1, the temporal dynamics operate in the following way. First, the material character of the weapon gives rise to reputation concerns through a logic of consequences, that is, in the calculations of decision makers. Reputation concerns are highlighted due to the efforts of norm entrepreneurs or reputation intermediaries, who make arguments based on the logic of consequences and the logic of appropriateness. These reputation concerns lead to self-deterrence on the part of the nuclear states, as evident during the crises/wars of the 1950s and 1960s. Second, when self-deterrence is practiced over a period of time, it becomes a tradition which in turn helps to self-deter in contexts of potential nuclear use vis-à-vis nonnuclear states. This feedback loop becomes stronger over the passage of time; as more years go by without use, the more times an opportunity for use is not taken, the harder it becomes to cross the threshold. The tradition thus affects self-deterrence in a feedback loop effect. This does not mean that the progression of the tradition is linear and that it will automatically get stronger over time, however, since material changes to the character of the weapon could undermine the tradition. If the absolute destructive nature of the weapon changes radically, the reputation costs will decrease and hence the probability will increase for use. This seems to be the hope of those who favor developing "usable" mininuclear weapons which indeed could create a new risk of eroding the tradition.

Theorists of international law have used the concept of reputation to refer to (a) "the extent to which a state is considered to be an honorable member of the international community," and (b) "the degree to which a state reliably upholds its international commitments."[26] Fear of international opprobrium is a motivating factor for compliance.[27] According to Downs and Jones, the rational-choice meaning of reputation—"the reliability with which a state abides by its commitments determines its value as a prospective partner and what others are willing to commit in return"—is the most important dimension of the concept. According to them, "a state might be interested in maintaining different reputations in different areas."[28] Similarly, Beth Simmons argues that international legal commitment is a means by which "governments seek to raise the reputational costs of reneging," and that "governments make commitments to further their interests and comply with them to preserve their reputation for predictable behavior" in a given area.[29]

Reputation has emerged as an important factor in the study of the behavior of firms, especially in the marketing of products and services. Firms spend a considerable amount of resources and efforts to obtain, retain, and improve their reputations and brand names, lest their product become outdated or they lose customer base and eventually go out of business.[30] Although nations are unlikely to go out of business due to a loss of reputation, states can also be driven by reputation considerations in order to achieve the support of public opinion for their policies, both nationally and internationally. This is why countries, similar to firms, spend enormous amounts of money on public diplomacy and propaganda, especially in other states. In addition, individual leaders may also be driven by reputation considerations. They may want to protect their personal reputation; translating this consideration to the international realm would mean avoidance of a certain kind of warfare that may simply make them and their nation look like immoral and unlawful actors. Nuclear arms fall into the category of a weapon that, if used, could elicit considerable negative reputation to the leader who ordered it.

In the nuclear area, reputation and image thus work at three levels—international, nation-state, and decision maker. At the international level, key state leaders could make a national interest calculation that the reactions of third parties would impose costs for the state that outweigh the benefits of nuclear use. At the nation-state level, a leader could fear losing power or public confidence if there is a public opinion backlash against nuclear use. At the decision-maker level, a leader could be self-deterred from nuclear use as a result of worries about the opinion of others, the judgment of history, his or her legacy, and his or her desire to maintain a self-image as a morally good person.[31] It is often a combination of these three levels that enters the reputation calculations of leaders, although empirical work could establish which dimension dominates in a given decision-maker's choices in a particular situation.

Reputation considerations at the international level could be based on the fear that the use of nuclear weapons would be condemned worldwide, upsetting the reputation and image of the user, with the demand for global nuclear disarmament becoming an issue of highest salience. The expected possible aftereffects of a nuclear attack generate fears among decision makers that, if they break the tradition, they could become political pariahs at home and abroad, and that their use of nuclear weapons could establish a bad precedent for others to follow. From this perspective, the moral factors might be mixing with the fear of consequences in generating the tradition of non-use.[32] The innocent victims of a nuclear attack, and the possibility of aftereffects lasting for generations, could make the leader who casually ordered a nuclear attack a permanent immoral figure in history books, and thus could act partially as a deterrent against nuclear use by decision makers.[33]

In this perspective, legal and moral/ethical considerations are not totally irrelevant in explaining the tradition of non-use. Just like morality, leaders may consider legality as part of their overall cost-benefit calculations. They may view that an act like nuclear use does necessitate legal justification, and if perceived by others as a totally illegal act, their reputation, image, prestige, and legitimacy would suffer irreparable damage, nationally and internationally. According to legal positivists, international legal norms are generally not enforced by coercive state action but "by fear on the part of nations . . . of provoking general hostility, and incurring its probable evils, in case they shall violate maxims generally received and respected."[34] Leaders, especially in democracies, tend to view legality as part of their choices in the military realm, often for reputational and domestic and international legitimacy reasons.

A secondary dimension of reputation is related to the nonproliferation objectives of nuclear powers. Of the nuclear states, five are both permanent members of the UN Security Council (P-5) and have their nuclear possession enshrined in the Nuclear Nonproliferation Treaty (NPT). These five states want to preserve both deterrent and nonproliferation goals. First, it is likely that the actual use of nuclear weapons would mean that deterrence had failed. Second, if nuclear weapons were used against a nonnuclear state, it would also break the nonproliferation commitment by the nuclear states vis-à-vis nonnuclear states made during and after the conclusion of the NPT. It would also set a bad precedent for other nuclear powers to follow. The tradition could have

been strengthened partially because of its value in preserving the nonproliferation objectives of the nuclear weapon states (NWS), especially the United
States. The informal norm is an assurance to the nonnuclear weapon states
(NNWS) that they need not acquire independent nuclear weapons capability
for deterrence purposes. The NWS justify their nuclear monopoly by arguing
that their nuclear weapons are primarily meant for mutual deterrence and not
for use against NNWS. The NNWS also see benefit in the informal norm, as it
lowers the attractiveness of nuclear weapons as instruments of deterrence or
coercion against them. In fact, several NNWS have confronted NWS in wars
and crises, apparently believing that nuclear weapons would not be used in
retaliation (as I discuss in Chapter 7).

The nonproliferation regime is built around legitimacy and exchange
power. Legitimacy in this respect is the general acceptance of the nuclear
order by most nations, even though the regime is unequal and sovereignty-
limiting for some actors. The regime gives partial legitimacy to the P-5 states
to maintain their monopoly rights and offers legal grounds for coercive action
against those nonnuclear states attempting to violate the regime's rules and
principles. Legitimacy in this regard is based on the principle of "serving the
larger good" as the regime has been "duly constituted by the international
community."[35] It is based on an acceptance by states that the nuclear order,
even though it is unequal, ought to be respected as an instrument of collective good and as a way to manage a complex security problem. This mutu-
ally rewarding aspect is the crux of exchange theory, which is relevant to the
nonproliferation regime. Nuclear have-nots are exchanging their sovereign
right to build nuclear weapons in return for a normative order that implicitly
prohibits nuclear use on them by the nuclear haves.[36] The exchange also included a pledge by the NWS that they would pursue disarmament in earnest,
as stated in Article VI of the NPT. Without legitimacy and exchange power,
the regime would collapse, as neither coercive sanctions nor brute force is
likely to keep it intact for long.

The NWS have in general attempted to preserve the nuclear status quo,
which allows a limited number of states the right to hold these weapons. The
use of nuclear weapons, especially since the 1960s, would have prompted the
unraveling of the nuclear nonproliferation regime, as additional countries
would seek nuclear weapons in their effort to acquire countervailing deterrent capabilities. Once used, the uniqueness surrounding nuclear weapons
would have been lost. Country studies in subsequent chapters will explore

the extent to which these considerations entered into the creation and sustenance of the tradition of non-use.

Deterrence Reputation Versus Non-Use Reputation   This discussion suggests that the NWS have been driven by two types of reputation concerns. First, they have been motivated to maintain a reputation for resolve in signaling retaliatory threats, for deterrence vis-à-vis other nuclear states. Second, toward NNWS, the reverse becomes the case; they have been driven by a desire to signal non-use so as to obtain their allegiance in Cold War competition (through projecting an image as good states and reliable partners) and secondarily to prevent NNWS from seeking nuclear weapons to deter nuclear states.

The nuclear arena shows that a nation can hold different and competing reputational concerns. For instance, during the Cold War, both superpowers were keen on developing reputations for peace and order and as promoters of nuclear nonproliferation and eventual nuclear disarmament. They spent an enormous amount of resources on public diplomacy by producing and distributing propaganda materials and operating information centers in different countries.[37] Simultaneously, they wanted to cultivate a reputation for resolve so that their nuclear capability would be valued as instruments of deterrence by other nuclear powers and as a currency of power in the international system by all states, especially in the context of extended deterrence covering nonnuclear protégés.

Deterrence theorists developed the widely used meaning of reputation in international relations.[38] Reputation in the deterrence context is very much part of the three building blocks of the theory and policy: capability, credibility, and communication. The deterrer should have sufficient capability to inflict unacceptable punishment on the deteree, the threat of retaliation should be credible or believable, and the threat should be meaningfully communicated to the target state. Credibility is assumed to be very much dependent on the state's reputation for use of force in the past.[39] If, in the past, the state wavered, a challenger would believe that the commitment to use of force was shaky and the threat of retaliation noncredible. Therefore, for deterrence to succeed, an opponent should believe that the deterrer will fight rather than back down. With nuclear weapons, the components of deterrence are not simple or straightforward. From an existential deterrence perspective, a nuclear state may be able to show resolve when confronting another nuclear state even without much communication of retaliatory intent, as the fear of nuclear escalation could act as a deterrent from direct attack. However, resolve to use nuclear weapons is difficult to communicate to a nonnuclear adversary, especially if it is not for something as important as the survival of the threatened state itself. It is thus virtually impossible to develop a reputation for nuclear use around past conflict behavior, when that behavior invariably precluded nuclear use. Furthermore, states tend not to make extremely explicit threats or promises, because of the fear of cost to the "actor's reputation if he defaults."[40] This problem is particularly manifest in the case of nuclear threats that a state can make vis-à-vis a nonnuclear state. The constraint of this nature may be termed *self-deterrence*.

It is problematic to suggest that reputation only matters in terms of resolve in the deterrence context, as reputation can also be built around the non-use of force. In other words, a nuclear state can create an expectation that for anything other than a real challenge to its survival, it will not use its nuclear weapons, as the threat of use of nuclear weapons will not be taken seriously. Credibility for nuclear deterrence will decrease if all and sundry threats are to be deterred with nuclear weapons. If all threats are deterrable with nuclear weapons and they are equivalent to a panacea for all diseases, then the tendency on the part of the nonnuclear state would be to disregard the threat, thereby raising considerable questions about credibility or believability.[41] The credibility of a threat can also decline if threats are not carried out for a long period of time. States Kenneth Boulding: "credibility, as it were, is a commodity which depreciates with the mere passage of time."[42]

Reputation for unwillingness to use nuclear weapons may be driven by a desire to dissuade future use of nuclear weapons by other nuclear states, that is, extend the shadow of the future in order to achieve reciprocity in non-use. Reputation concerns operate as self-deterrents here. The understanding of reputation as used in neoliberal institutionalist theory is useful in this context. The theory of decentralized cooperation gives reputation a central role. According to this school, a key reason for states to comply with commitments is their "fear that any evidence of unreliability will damage their current cooperative relationships and lead other states to reduce their willingness to enter into future agreements."[43] Axelrod contends that cooperation can occur without a central authority on the basis of reciprocity and if the "shadow of the future" is long enough for future interactions. However, a reputation for cooperation is vital in order to sustain cooperation in the long run.[44] Similarly, Robert Keohane argues that states want to maintain a good reputation so as to enter into advantageous agreements with other states. Rule violation could establish bad precedents, which could, in the end, produce a "collective bad."[45]

Reputation affects how an international regime is formed and sustained. It is assumed that if states believe in the implicit promises that other states make, they will reciprocate. Thus the successful maintenance of the nonproliferation regime depends on the belief that nuclear states hold a reputation for non-use for anything other than existential threat.[46] Game theorists pay special attention to reputation, and their findings are relevant for understanding regime formation and maintenance. Positive reputation seems to help efficiency and cooperation as actors receive information "on their partner's behavior in interactions with third parties."[47]

Reputation Intermediaries   Reputation at the interstate level becomes salient in part when particular groups succeed in propagating certain adverse effects of choices that decision makers may have to make in an issue area. These norm entrepreneurs frame the issues, and "are critical for norm emergence because they call attention to issues . . . by using language that names, interprets, and dramatizes them."[48] They are indeed agents of the socialization of a norm. Without their active work, the public might not know much about the ramifications of issues, and, as a result, governments could ignore adverse public reactions and reputation costs. These norm entrepreneurs are reputation intermediaries and facilitators. The tradition of non-use of nuclear weapons that emerged over a period of time is owed, to a large extent, to the works of these reputation intermediaries or norm entrepreneurs who propagate the dangers of nuclear war, a point that Constructivist scholars have rightly highlighted. Different groups of norm entrepreneurs were necessary to bring forth the rational/material and reputational dimensions of nuclear weapons to worldwide attention.[49] Four groups of norm entrepreneurs played a role in the creation and sustenance of the tradition. They are atomic scientists, peace groups, nuclear strategists, and nonnuclear nonaligned states.

The first groups of norm entrepreneurs were *atomic scientists* involved in the Manhattan project. Scientists such as Leo Szilard, Niels Bohr, and J. Robert Oppenheimer argued that unless an international authority was created to control the atom, nuclear weapons would spread to various countries, and aggressive powers could use them for aggressive purposes.[50] President Truman partially agreed with them. The Acheson/Lilienthal proposals and the Baruch Plan of 1946, which called for an international body to conduct nuclear research and development while removing such controls from national hands, resulted to a great extent from the views of nuclear scientists, especially Niels Bohr. These scientists engaged in intense lobbying of the Truman administration and disseminated their views through a series of memoranda. Prior to the end of World War II, Vannevar Bush, chairman of the Manhattan Project's Military Committee and his deputy, James Conant, had urged Secretary of War Henry Stimson to turn over atomic weapons to an international agency once the war ended.[51] Both Bush and Conant were members of the Acheson/Lilienthal Panel, appointed by President Truman to enquire about the possibility of international control, and the Panel's recommendations were adopted under the Baruch Plan.[52] The Federation of Atomic Scientists began publishing the *Bulletin of the Atomic Scientists* in 1945, and its famous Doomsday Clock played a considerable role in the propagation of the dangers of nuclear war.[53] However, the early influence of scientists waned and the idea of international control of the atom was virtually dead by 1947. The McMahon Act of 1946 enshrined secrecy as the key characteristic of U.S. nuclear policy, banning all international cooperation at sharing nuclear technology, including with its close wartime ally Britain.[54] Many scientists continued to play a critical role in highlighting the ill effects of nuclear weapons, while others were creating deadlier and deadlier nuclear weapons in national laboratories.

Peace movements constituted a second group of reputation intermediaries. Starting from the early 1950s, these groups played an important role in raising the world's consciousness about the dangers of nuclear weapons testing and the nuclear arms race, while they called for effective arms control and disarmament.[55] There have been hundreds of peace groups that have clamored for nuclear disarmament, but the most prominent ones included the Campaign for Nuclear Disarmament (CND), the National Committee for a Sane Nuclear Policy (SANE), the World Peace Council, the World Federation of Churches, Pugwash, and Greenpeace. Prominent intellectuals and scientists such as Bertrand Russell, Albert Schweitzer, Irène and Frédéric Joliot-Curie, Norman Cousins, Eugine Rabinowitch, and Joseph Rotblat, played key roles during the 1950s in the international peace movements.[56] However, the role of peace groups waxed and waned according to the urgency of issues relating to the nuclear arms race. For instance, these groups were very active during the atmospheric tests in the 1950s and the post–Cuban Missile Crisis and Vietnam War eras. They would emerge as important norm defenders during the 1980s in response to the loose talk by Reagan administration officials of a winnable nuclear war. They also received a fillip when Soviet President Mikhail Gorbachev accepted their logic on the dangers of the unbridled nuclear arms race. However, in the post–Cold War era, many peace movements have re-ceded in prominence as nuclear issues have become less newsworthy, partly because, in the public perception, nuclear war between old nuclear powers is unlikely, but also because the focus has turned to new nuclear states and nonstate actors.

The third critical group of reputation intermediaries consisted of *military strategists*, led by Bernard Brodie. In his edited collection, *The Absolute Weapon: Atomic Power and World Order*, Brodie argued that "[e]verything about the bomb is overshadowed by the twin facts that it exists and that its de-structive power is fantastically great," and that "[n]o adequate defense against the atomic bomb exists, and the possibilities of its existence in the future are exceedingly remote."[57] Brodie's most influential statement read: "Thus far the chief purpose of our military establishment has been to win wars. From now on its chief purpose must be to avert them. It can have almost no other useful purpose."[58] This group included Arnold Wolfers, Jacob Viner, and William T. R. Fox.[59] Some of these strategists thus helped to project the uniqueness of nuclear weapons and their unsuitability to wage regular war. Their intellectual efforts influenced future scholarly works on nuclear weapons and deterrence theory. However, leading strategists also devised theories and policies on de-terrence and nuclear use if deterrence failed.[60] Hence, like scientists, the role of strategic analysts is a mixed one in the creation of the tradition of non-use.

The final group of reputation intermediaries consisted of *developing states*, under the aegis of the Non-Aligned Movement. The movement had its ori-gins in the 1955 Afro-Asian Conference in Bandung, the declaration of which stated that "disarmament and the prohibition of the production, experimen-tation, and use of nuclear and thermonuclear weapons of war are imperative to save mankind and civilization from . . . wholesale destruction."[61] At every summit meeting that followed its founding, nuclear disarmament would emerge as a key theme for the group. Non-aligned leaders, especially India's Jawaharlal Nehru and Yugoslavia's Josip Broz Tito, actively participated in promoting peace movements by throwing the support of their governments behind them. As nonnuclear states, the nonaligned states made substantial contributions at the UN disarmament forums, especially the Eighteen Na-tion Disarmament Committee, and the NPT negotiations and five-year NPT review conferences.[62] As I discuss in Chapter 8, they also were in the forefront of creating nuclear-weapon-free zones and consulting the International Court of Justice (ICJ) for its opinion on the legality of nuclear use.

These four groups of norm intermediaries played different roles, some-times coordinated but often independently, in helping to generate high repu-tation costs for nuclear use. Each decade saw ups and downs in their role as well as that of the tradition itself. During the 1950s and 1960s, with the de-velopment of even larger nuclear weapons, the bombs dropped on Hiroshima and Nagasaki paled in comparison; consequently, the powerful aura sur-rounding nuclear weapons increased. The latter part of 1950s saw some seri-ous efforts to control the spread of nuclear weapons (such as with the Atoms for Peace proposal). This decade also witnessed the arrival of the Soviet Union as a nuclear weapon state, and the U.S.-Soviet arms race accelerated to new levels. Nuclear testing of ever more destructive weapons took place, generat-ing strong international protests. The most significant protests were mounted against atmospheric nuclear testing by the superpowers over the Pacific in the first half of the 1950s and its larger implications for health. In the United States, a national movement against nuclear testing emerged, supported by the 1956 presidential campaign of Adlai Stevenson, which included peace groups such as "Leo Szilard's Council for a Livable World; Bernard Lown's Physicians for Social Responsibility; and SANE, the National Committee for a SANE Nuclear Policy."[63]

The decade of the 1960s witnessed the development of high-yield nuclear weapons, an intensified discourse on deterrence and mutual assured destruc-tion (MAD), and criticisms of deterrence theory and policy as "abstract" and "potentially catastrophic" for a variety of reasons, including irrationality among decision makers.[64] The civil defense programs and the national drills initiated by the Kennedy administration further galvanized international at-tention on the dangers of nuclear war.[65] The Cuban Missile Crisis was a piv-otal turning point for the tradition. The crisis brought the world to the brink of nuclear war, and made clear the dangers of an uncontrolled arms race and political brinkmanship. Following the crisis, peace movements played a sig-nificant role in publicizing the dangers of nuclear arms races, testing, and use. Particularly in the U.S. context, these movements helped to strengthen the call for arms control agreements.[66] However, the conclusion of the Partial Test Ban Treaty (PTBT) in 1963 and the ending of atmospheric testing removed the issue from the American public's radar screen for over a decade, even as the superpowers accelerated their arms buildup and underground testing of new and lethal nuclear arms. The conflict in Vietnam, the loss of the imme-diacy of the nuclear threat, and the promise of cheaper nuclear power, helped the issue to fade from the U.S. public's perceptions; it emerged again only with the arrival of the Reagan administration in 1980.[67]

Despite the escalation of the U.S.-Soviet nuclear rivalry, international efforts at nonproliferation became intense in the 1960s. The NPT negotiations and the hard bargaining that led to the conclusion of the treaty appeared to have strengthened the non-use principle. No explicit non-use convention was signed as part of the NPT, but one of the key demands of the nonnuclear states has been a concrete legal convention to that effect. They have maintained that demand in almost all review conferences since 1968. There was thus an understanding that the NPT implicitly forbids nuclear use and eventually will lead to nuclear disarmament. The NNWS signed on to the unequal treaty with the expectation that the NPT would become a forerunner of general and complete nuclear disarmament. However, following the signing of the NPT, the United States under the Nixon administration considered nuclear use in Vietnam, so it is not clear how serious the U.S. commitment was on the non-use issue. Despite efforts by some weapon makers and hard-core military planners to break the tradition and treat nuclear weapons like any other weapon, the conventionalization of nuclear weapons has failed to occur.

In the post–Cold War world, the tradition has shown some resilience, with U.S. leaders choosing not to exercise the nuclear option even prior to the start of the 1991 and 2003 Gulf wars. However, they also stepped up a policy of "calculated ambiguity" in order to create uncertainty in the minds of the so-called "rogue leaders," thus dissuading them from developing and using weapons of mass destruction. The United States also changed its policy on nuclear weapons by considering nuclear weapons use as a possible tool for prevention and preemption. Together, these policy changes have raised questions about the robustness of the tradition in the United States. Second-generation nuclear states such as Israel, India, Pakistan, and North Korea have entered the nuclear club, while others, such as Iran, have stepped up their efforts to acquire nuclear weapons. It is yet to be seen how strongly these states have internalized the tradition of non-use in their national security calculations.

CONCLUSION

The tradition of non-use of nuclear weapons emerged over several decades. I have argued that there is an informal normative prohibition against nuclear use and that different nuclear actors have behaved as if they have a responsibility not to use nuclear weapons vis-à-vis nonnuclear states. The intrinsic destructive characteristics of nuclear weapons have been part of the reason for the tradition's rise and persistence. The destabilizing and absolute character of nuclear weapons has limited their strategic utility. With the passage of time, these characteristics also fed the reputational considerations that helped to sustain the informal norm. The reputation costs associated with use and the reputation benefits for refraining from use both played a significant role in leaders' calculations regarding nuclear weapons in crisis contexts. Reputational interests thus became the leading reason for the non-use of nuclear weapons over the past sixty-three years. The next chapter addresses the evolution of the tradition in the United States and explores how the various factors presented here operated in determining U.S. policy with respect to the non-use of nuclear weapons.

3 THE UNITED STATES AND THE TRADITION I: THE TRUMAN AND EISENHOWER YEARS (1945–1961)

It is a terrible thing to order the use of something that . . . is so terribly destructive, destructive beyond anything we have ever had. You have got to understand that this isn't a military weapon . . . It is used to wipe out women and children and unarmed people, and not for military uses. So we have got to treat this differently from rifles and cannon and ordinary things like that.

—President Harry S. Truman, April 1948

You boys must be crazy. We can't use those awful things against Asians for a second time in less than ten years. My God.

—President Dwight Eisenhower, April 1954

AS THE FIRST NATION TO DEVELOP, test, and acquire nuclear weapons, and most significantly as the one and only state ever to use an atomic weapon, the United States has played a crucial role in the evolution and sustenance of the tradition of non-use. Much of the discourse on the tradition has occurred in the United States. This is not surprising given that the intellectual foundations of nuclear deterrence theory came out of American policy and academic worlds. However, based on available historical records, among all the nuclear powers, it has been the United States that has most often pondered the possibility of nuclear use against nonnuclear adversaries.[1]

It is important to trace the evolution of the tradition of non-use of nuclear weapons for the United States by looking at the key turning points and events that shaped its path. What contributed to the rise and persistence of the tradition in the U.S. case? What role did reputation, strategic/tactical calculations, and moral considerations play in this process? This chapter goes through the historical record under presidents Truman and Eisenhower, by exploring the key events that marked significant turning points in the evolution of the nascent tradition. It will also see if the tradition itself constrained these presidents in any meaningful way.

THE TRUMAN YEARS (1945–1953)

Harry Truman was president during the most critical formative years of the tradition of nuclear non-use. He was the first and only American president ever to order the use of atomic weapons, on the Japanese cities of Hiroshima and Nagasaki in August 1945. The Hiroshima bombing on August 6 killed over 70,000 people instantly and another 130,000 over five years, while the Nagasaki attacks on August 9 ended nearly 70,000 lives instantaneously and another 70,000 within five years of the attack.[2] A large number of survivors would suffer permanently due to cancer and other diseases caused by atomic radiation as well as burn injuries. Truman justified these attacks as necessary to end the war expeditiously and thereby save the lives of half a million U.S. soldiers and thousands of Japanese citizens, who, he claimed, would have been casualties of any U.S. invasion to obtain Japan's unconditional surrender.[3] Controversy surrounds the decision to use the bombs and Truman's justification of it, especially regarding the Nagasaki attack, which some historians argue was intended as a warning shot to Soviet leader Joseph Stalin not to enter the Japanese theater.[4] Others contend that Truman did not make a serious effort to gain Japan's surrender until he was able to use the bomb.[5] Truman has also been criticized for exaggerating the number of U.S. casualties likely to result from a land invasion of Japan.[6] It may well be possible that given the differences of opinion the Western Allies and the Soviets had over territorial demarcations and control of postwar Europe, and the Soviet declaration of war on Japan two days after the Hiroshima bombing, Truman felt compelled to order the Nagasaki attack. Obviously, three days were not sufficient for Japan to agree on an unconditional surrender. A desire to deny Russia any territorial claims in Manchuria and postwar power sharing in Japan thus seems a plausible explanation for the second nuclear attack.[7] The attacks prompted a powerful international response, although it can be argued that neither Truman nor the scientists involved in the Manhattan Project fully grasped beforehand the potential impact in both human toll and political ramifications.

The Hiroshima/Nagasaki Experience and the
International Control of the Atom

The Hiroshima and Nagasaki episodes seem to have exerted a profound impact on American foreign policy. In a fundamental sense, the idealist tradition in America came to the forefront temporarily as a result of the Hiroshima/Nagasaki experiences.[8] Truman himself stated: "the destruction of Hiroshima and Nagasaki was lesson enough for me. The world could not afford to risk war with atomic weapons."[9] Truman was successfully (though temporarily) persuaded by leading American scientists to control and eventually eliminate all nuclear weapons under an international authority. These scientists, led by Vannevar Bush, James Conant, and Robert Oppenheimer, would become the first group of norm intermediaries at this point. During the war, they had recommended to Secretary of War Henry L. Stimson the sharing of atomic technology with the Soviet Union in collaboration with Britain as a way to achieve international control of the atom.[10] They expressed the concern that many other countries would eventually acquire the bomb, and that aggressive states would use them to pursue their offensive goals, especially in a surprise fashion. Therefore, before the genie got fully out of the bottle, an international mechanism was needed to control the spread of the atom and achieve eventual elimination of the weapon.[11] Those hopes motivated the Acheson-Lilienthal Report of 1946, which was later adopted by Bernard Baruch in his proposals contained in the Baruch Plan.[12]

The Acheson-Lilienthal Report recommended the creation of an international atomic development authority with complete control over world supplies of uranium and thorium, as well as the power to lease such materials to national facilities and offer a workable system of safeguards to remove from individual nations' "intrinsically dangerous" nuclear activities. The international authority would leave as much freedom as possible to national establishments to conduct peaceful nuclear activities. The report cited three reasons for international control: first, atomic energy and atomic weapons "have placed at the disposal of mankind 'means of destruction hitherto unknown'"; second, "there can be no adequate military defense against atomic weapons"; and third, "no single nation can in fact have a monopoly" in the employment of these weapons.[13] Remarkably, the proposal assumed that nations would not allow any single power to get control of civilian atomic materials dispersed in their territories and start building nuclear weapons.[14]

The Baruch Plan, which followed the Acheson-Lilienthal proposals, was even more ambitious. Bernard Baruch, the chief U.S. delegate to the UN Atomic Energy Commission (UNAEC), advocated international control with a veto-proof system of "swift and assured penalties" on violators. However, a critical part of the Baruch Plan was to allow the United States to retain its nuclear monopoly until all countries had signed on to the plan and a proper international control mechanism was developed.[15] This plan was rejected by the Soviets, who formulated their own proposals for a convention prohibiting the production, stockpile, and use of nuclear weapons by all states. The signatories of the convention would destroy all existing stockpiles of nuclear weapons within three months of its coming into force, a measure aimed at the United States, which was the only atomic power at that time. However, there was no enforcement or control mechanism attached to the proposed convention.[16] The United States opposed this proposal while the Soviets refused to accept the Baruch Plan, thus dooming early efforts at international control of the atom. Whether genuinely committed or not, during the first three years of the atomic age, Truman became an advocate of international control, as a result of the devastation of Hiroshima/Nagasaki and the arguments presented by influential scientists and other peace activists, while his advisors came out with plans for eventual nuclear disarmament.

Nuclear Preponderance and Plans for War with the Soviet Union

The Truman administration, while pursuing an international control agenda, also wished to retain America's military preponderance, especially in the nuclear area.[17] Although the international control issue was being considered, the question of a preventive war against the Soviet Union in view of its impending nuclear acquisition was very much on top of the administration's agenda. The military was in favor of a preventive attack on the Soviet Union. Three war plans produced by military planners between 1945 and 1950, drawing heavily on the lessons of air power in World War II, proposed that the United States engage in a preventive attack on Soviet industrial and military targets in order to stop it from becoming a nuclear weapon power. These plans, *Pincher* (1946), *Broiler* (November 1947), and *Crankshaft* (1948), all called for nuclear air offensives against Soviet war-making capabilities as the best way to prevent a future war with the Communist nation.[18]

The *Pincher Plan*, prepared by the Joint War Planning Committee of the Joint Chiefs of Staff (JCS), proposed the use of nuclear weapons against the Soviet Union in the event of a war in Europe. With the rapid decline of U.S.-Soviet relations, especially in the wake of the Communist coup in Czechoslovakia and the June 1948 Berlin Blockade by the Soviets, air offensives relying on nuclear weapons became a crucial part of U.S. war plans against the Soviet Union.[19] However, immediately prior to the Blockade crisis, Truman had rejected the "Joint Emergency War Plan," prepared by the JCS, which had called for a "powerful air offensive designed to exploit the destructive and psychological power of atomic weapons against the vital elements of the Soviet war making capacity."[20] Truman asked for an alternative plan relying on conventional capability, as he was still hoping for the outlawing of nuclear weapons through international convention, and thinking also that "the American people might not permit the government to use atomic weapons for 'aggressive purposes.'"[21] As Truman put it:

> I don't think we ought to use this thing unless we absolutely have to. It is a terrible thing to order the use of something that . . . is so terribly destructive, destructive beyond anything we have ever had. You have got to understand that this isn't a military weapon . . . It is used to wipe out women and children and unarmed people, and not for military uses. So we have got to treat this differently from rifles and cannon and ordinary things like that.[22]

Reputation and disarmament concerns come to the forefront in Truman's choice at this time.

However, the efforts at finding a conventional alternative to confront the Soviet Union were jettisoned in July 1948.[23] Truman dispatched three squadrons of nuclear-capable B-29 aircraft to Europe, the same type of aircraft that was used in the bombings of Hiroshima and Nagasaki, without revealing that they were only conventionally armed. According to Defense Secretary James Forrestal, there was a consensus among Western leaders that in the event of a war, nuclear weapons would be used.[24] However, during the crisis Truman rejected a request made by Forrestal to transfer nuclear weapons from civilian to military control, stating that he did not want "to have some dashing lieutenant colonel decide when would be the proper time to drop one." Forrestal had argued that "there was a very serious question as to the wisdom of relying upon an agency other than the user of such a weapon, to assure the integrity and usability of such a weapon."[25] Truman, in his *Memoirs*, contends that he opposed preventive war as "there is nothing more foolish than to think that war can be stopped by war. You don't 'prevent' anything by war except peace."[26] Secretary of War Henry Stimson presented the reputational concerns powerfully, calling preventive war "worse than nonsense," arguing that it "results from a cynical incomprehension of what the people of the world will tolerate from any nation," and adding that "we could not possibly take that opportunity without deserting our inheritance. Americans as conquerors would be tragically miscast."[27]

It has been argued that the United States only had fifty or so unassembled weapons and that operational constraints actually prevented their use in the Berlin Crisis.[28] However, the available evidence suggests that Truman's military advisors were generally confident that nuclear weapons would be used, but the president hesitated and made little effort to openly play the atomic card as an instrument of blackmail. What is remarkable is that it was not deterrence (i.e., fear of Soviet retaliation in kind) that prevented nuclear use, as the United States had an atomic monopoly during this period. Truman was still hoping for international control, and was not confident of the implications of nuclear use in that regard. He was also concerned about domestic and international opinion on the use of nuclear weapons.

In May 1949, the report of the Harmon Committee (headed by Lt. General Hubert Harmon of the Air Force) studied the likely effects of atomic attacks on seventy Soviet cities and concluded that nuclear attack would destroy 30 to 40 percent of Soviet industrial capabilities, kill 2.7 million and injure 4 million Russians, and leave 28 million homeless, while inflicting serious damage to Soviet war-making capacity. However, it warned that the use of atomic weapons would not "bring about capitulation, destroy the roots of Communism or critically weaken the power of Soviet leadership to dominate the people." Instead, "it would validate Soviet propaganda against the United States, unify the people, and increase their will to fight."[29] This report reinforced the position of critics, especially in the U.S. Navy, who were skeptical of the efficacy of atomic air offensives. But it also encouraged a substantial expansion of U.S. nuclear forces so as to achieve dominance vis-à-vis the Soviets in Europe.[30]

The early enthusiasm of the scientists and others for international control did not last long. By 1947, many scientists had returned to laboratories in pursuit of careers in the cutting edge of atomic research. Moreover, the McMahon Act of July 1946 ended all international cooperation in atomic sharing, including with America's wartime ally Britain, and placed nuclear weapons development in the hands of a civilian agency, the Atomic Energy Commission (AEC). This did not mean that the military gave up all control over atomic weapons. A military liaison committee was given the authority to review all AEC decisions.[31] American leaders were determined to retain the U.S. atomic monopoly as long as they could. By July 1949, Truman had given up hopes of achieving meaningful international control, since the conflict with the Soviets had intensified, and he ordered the strengthening of U.S. nuclear capability.[32] After a period of intense internal debate in 1949, Truman finally approved the hydrogen bomb project, despite the opposition of the General Advisory Committee of the AEC, led by J. Robert Oppenheimer, father of the atomic bomb.[33] The committee had argued that "the moral opprobrium associated with building such a weapon, together with the possibilities of international control and the poor state of Soviet thermonuclear research ... outweighed any political or strategic use the superbomb might provide."[34] However, this argument did not dissuade Truman from launching the hydrogen bomb project.

The Truman administration's thinking on atomic use against the Soviet Union was contained in National Security Council Document 68 (NSC-68), which was approved in April 1950. It called for a massive increase in arms spending, but contended that the threat the United States faced was of "piecemeal aggression," and that "excessive reliance on nuclear weapons would leave the United States, in such situations, with 'no better choice than to capitulate or precipitate a global war.'"[35] The document contained sections that discussed the benefits and disadvantages of a preventive nuclear strike on the Soviet Union. It concluded that preventive war was "generally unacceptable to Americans" and that it would be "repugnant" and "morally corrosive."[36] An annex to NSC-68 proposed that in order to maintain its leadership role in the global arena, the United States must act with "patience and self-restraint," "avoid being arbitrary, domineering and condescending," and convince other nations that war with the Soviet Union was not inevitable and that it was not in the American "character to wage aggressive or preventive war."[37] Reputation and image considerations thus come to the fore in the calculations of the authors of NSC-68 and its annexes.

The Truman administration rejected another proposal, contained in NSC-100, that before the United States lost its nuclear advantage, it should mount an atomic offensive against the Soviet Union (especially if Moscow engaged in further acts of aggression in vital U.S. areas of interest) as well as a combined air and sea campaign using nuclear weapons against China in order to stop Chinese advances in Korea. The plan was submitted by Stuart Symington, chairman of the National Security Resources Board, in January 1951, as an alternative to NSC-68. Its rationale was that the use of atomic weapons was morally justified as it would offer "a measure of moral freedom for the United States."[38] Despite the rejection of NSC-100 and the adoption of the more cautious NSC-68, U.S. plans for war with the Soviet Union relied heavily on nuclear weapons. According to one historian, "Truman was never happy with this emphasis on atomic weaponry, but he neither spent much time pondering options nor asked his subordinates to study alternatives. Comparatively, atomic weapons were cheap, and Truman accepted plans and approved budgets that made the United States dependent on their use should war erupt."[39]

Despite the urgings of many in the military, Truman avoided a preventive nuclear strike on the Soviet Union, thus helping to create a nascent tradition of non-use of nuclear weapons, even when the United States held a nuclear monopoly. Truman's stated reasons for non-use of nuclear weapons in Korea were moral reputation and projection of America's image as a peaceful nation. In his farewell radio address, Truman declared "Now, once in a while, I get a letter from some impatient person asking, why don't we get it over with? Why don't we issue an ultimatum—make all out war, drop the atomic bomb? For most Americans, the answer is quite simple: We are not made that way. We are a moral people. Peace is our goal, with justice and freedom. We cannot, of our own free will, violate the very principles that we are striving to defend."[40] The non-use at this time was remarkable to an extent, but the test of such a policy of non-use would be in Korea, where the first major war since the end of World War II occurred.

The Korean War: 1950–53

The U.S. intervention in Korea, under the UN banner, to defend its South Korean ally against invasion and occupation by North Korea, was the first critical test of the emerging tradition of non-use. It is also an interesting case given that the U.S. decision makers considered nuclear use to prevent a Chinese invasion in support of North Korea. It is reported that on June 25, 1950, the first day of the war, President Truman "asked whether we could knock out [Russian] bases in the Far East," as it was assumed that Moscow was behind the policies of its Communist allies, China and North Korea. After hearing that this was possible if nuclear weapons were employed, President Truman ordered the Air Force to prepare a plan to wipe out all Soviet air bases in the Far East without a specific order for action.[41]

Two weeks into the war, on July 9, 1950, General Douglas MacArthur, the commander in charge of the UN operations in Korea, sent the JCS a "hot message" in which he requested the dispatch of twenty or so nuclear bombs to the Korean theater for tactical use. This was agreeable to Assistant Chief of Staff for Operations General Charles Bolte, who thought that "some 10 to 20 bombs could be spared for the Korean theater." The JCS rejected the use of nuclear weapons at this point in the war, "because targets sufficiently large to require atomic bombs were lacking, because of concerns about world opinion 5 years after Hiroshima, and because the JCS expected the tide of battle to be reversed by conventional military means."[42] The military's opposition was driven by concerns of depreciation of the weapon's deterrent value if it was used in a theater like Korea,[43] but the political elite, especially Secretary Acheson, cited fears that it would "frighten our allies to death."[44] Reputational considerations, in the form of fears of adverse world opinion, formed a large part of the mix of reasons for the abandonment of proposals to use nuclear weapons in Korea, or against China or the Soviet Union, at this stage.

Despite this earlier rejection of the use of atomic weapons, Truman threatened to use nuclear weapons in response to the intervention of Chinese troops, who were pushing the UN troops from North Korea. At a press conference on November 30, 1950, he stated that "every weapon that we have," including the atomic bomb, might be used, and that "always there has been active consideration of its use."[45] This led British Prime Minister Attlee to undertake a hasty trip to the United States to urge the president not to use nuclear weapons in Korea, as he thought "American threats to use the bomb would suggest that 'Europeans and Americans have a low regard for the value of Asiatic lives,' and that such weapons should be reserved only for times when 'desperate measures were warranted'—'certainly not [in] a conflict in which the U.S. were confronted with a Power like Korea."[46] Strong opposition came from other European countries such as France, which believed that the conflict in Korea did not warrant the use of atomic weapons and that an American use of such weapons in East Asia would result in a Soviet attack on Western Europe.[47]

Bruce Cumings, in his major historical work on the Korean War, narrates the efforts by General Douglas MacArthur, the commander of the UN forces in Korea, to obtain approval by Truman for the use of nuclear weapons in order to relieve beleaguered UN forces. On several occasions, MacArthur made requests to the president for the release of nuclear weapons to his command for use. On December 9, 1950, he reportedly asked for commander's discretion for atomic use, and on December 24, he made another request for twenty-six nuclear bombs to be used against twenty-four "retardation targets" and Manchurian bases of the Chinese People's Liberation Army (PLA). Again, on March 10, 1951, MacArthur asked for atomic weapons to gain superiority against the large Chinese forces assembled near the Korean border, ready to intervene. Partially in support of the general's position, the JCS ordered atomic retaliation against Chinese bases in Manchuria in the event that a large number of forces entered the battle against UN forces.[48] But this large Chinese entry did not occur.

However, in April 1951, as a result of the worsening military situation in Korea and reports of troop movements by the Soviets, Truman approved the military's request for the transfer of nine Mark IV nuclear bombs from AEC custody to Strategic Air Command (SAC) bases in Guam and Okinawa. AEC Chairman Gordon Dean wrote in his diary that he was told by Truman that there was a heavy concentration of Russian and Chinese forces in the region, "all of which indicates that not only are the Reds [Chinese and the North Koreans] and the Russians ready to push us out of Korea, but [that they] may attempt to take the Japanese islands and with their submarines cut our supply lines to Japan and Korea." He had a request from the JCS for weapons, but stated that "no decision had been made to use these weapons and he hoped very much that there would be no necessity for using them."[49]

Gordon was concerned about placing the bombs in the vicinity of MacArthur, and Truman agreed to discuss the matter thoroughly at the NSC in case the bomb was to be used. However, JCS Chairman General Omar Bradley did not inform MacArthur of Truman's decision or the availability of the bomb for use.[50] According to Cumings, the president's order was never sent because Truman wanted to remove MacArthur and appoint a reliable commander before a decision to use atomic bombs was made. Further, contrary to expectations of U.S. leaders, "the Chinese and the Soviets did not escalate the war." However, according to Cumings, the nine Mark IVs did not go back to the AEC, but remained in SAC custody in Guam after their transfer on April 11, 1951.[51] Truman apparently wanted the new commander of the UN forces, General Matthew Ridgway, to be able to use nuclear weapons in the event that the Communists attacked U.S. forces outside Korea.[52] While relieving MacArthur on "confidence grounds," Truman used the argument that he needed a reliable commander in case nuclear use was decided.[53]

U.S. contemplation of the use of nuclear weapons in Korea continued throughout the year. In September and October 1951, the United States conducted *Operation Hudson Harbor,* an exercise involving dummy warheads dropped by a B-29 bomber, to test the utility of actual nuclear use in North Korea. However, the results showed that atomic bombs would not be effective, as the "identification of a large number of enemy troops was extremely difficult in a timely manner."[54]

A State Department official in the Bureau of Far Eastern Affairs, John K. Emmerson, captured the difficulties of using nuclear weapons in Korea in his secret memo to the administration, presented in November 1950. He warned that atomic use would be deplored by a large number of states, even by allies who were participating in the U.S.-led operations in Korea. To him, the nuclear weapon "has the status of a peculiar monster conceived by American cunning, and its use by us, in whatever situation, would be exploited to our serious detriment." It could result in the "breaking apart the United Nations Coalition then fighting in Korea and possibly the United Nations itself," a "disastrous loss of confidence on the part of Western Europe" and "irreparable damage to the moral position of the United States." In addition, the Soviet Union would be likely to intervene in the war, and it would receive less global condemnation than the United States if the latter resorted to nuclear use. Moreover, in Asia, another atomic use would cause a "revulsion of feeling," and would confirm fears that "we reserve atomic weapons exclusively for Japanese and Chinese," with the result that "our influence in non-Communist nations of Asia would deteriorate to an almost non-existent quantity."[55] We do not know the precise impact the report had on the administration's decisions, but it powerfully reflects the unease among U.S. officials on nuclear use.

Truman's statement in November 1950 did evoke considerable opposition in Asia. India's Prime Minister Jawaharlal Nehru warned of the "widespread feeling in Asia that the atomic bomb is a weapon used only against Asiatics," and Attlee told his French counterpart, René Pleven, "any action [regarding the use of the bomb] must be thought of in relation to its effect on Asiatic opinion."[56] In his *Memoirs,* Truman wrote: "Europeans generally assumed that a new war would be a battle of atomic weapons, and the slightest mention of atomic bombs was enough to make them jittery." Referring to his remark on possible atomic use in Korea, he stated, "just how sensitive and on edge the world has become was demonstrated when the words 'atomic bomb' were mentioned at my press conference on November 30."[57] Truman's reluctance to use nuclear weapons in Korea was thus caused largely by two fundamental factors: the concerns regarding creating a bad reputation worldwide if Washington used nuclear weapons again in Asia, and the tactical/strategic unsuitability of the weapon for the particular military goal. A close reading of the documents and statements, however, show that the reputation concerns were more prominent than tactical considerations.

Truman is also notable for his decision to keep atomic weapons and conventional weapons separate in the U.S. arsenal, thereby showing the uniqueness of the former. Equally important was his decision to leave the control of atomic weapons to the AEC, as opposed to the military. Notes one historian: "by denying the military control over atomic weapons, he reasserted civilian authority over how wars were to be fought."[58] The civilian control of atomic weapons was justified by Truman thus: "because of the power and world significance of atomic energy, I was convinced that it had to be placed under civilian control."[59] States Gaddis: "In this way, Truman took the first step toward building what has turned out to be one of the most important principles of postwar international relations: the idea that nuclear weapons differ emphatically from all other weapons, and should be treated with corresponding respect."[60]

The Truman presidency thus saw the beginning of a tradition of non-use. As discussed above, Truman also initially hoped for an international mechanism to control nuclear energy and thus prevent the spread of weapons and materials to other countries. This goal of international control and nonproliferation of the atom partially prevented him from seriously considering the preventive use of atomic weapons against the Soviet Union before it acquired nuclear arms in 1949. However, in the later years of his presidency, Truman presided over a massive expansion of the U.S. arsenal. In that process, he made the fateful decision to acquire the more powerful hydrogen bomb. In addition, he considered using nuclear weapons in the Korean theater, only to back down in the end. This restraint emerged largely for reputational reasons, that is, fear of adverse domestic and international opinion, especially among the U.S. allies. His reluctance to use nuclear weapons prevented an early conclusion of the Korean War, dragging the war on for three years, resulting in over fifty thousand battlefield deaths for the United States, over a quarter of a million for South Korea, one hundred and thirty thousand for the People's Republic of China (PRC), and an undetermined number for North Korea, in addition to the several hundred thousand injured.[61]

The Truman-era reluctance to use nuclear weapons despite pressures and urgings by the military, and the assertion of civilian control over the weapon, helped to generate the embryonic tradition of non-use, but it was not at all apparent that it would be observed by the next president, Dwight Eisenhower, who considered the threat of nuclear use against nonnuclear adversaries a legitimate means to achieve U.S. strategic and war aims.

THE EISENHOWER YEARS (1953–61)

Testing the Tradition of Non-Use in Crisis

The Eisenhower era faced considerable pressures on the nascent tradition, as his administration toyed with the idea of nuclear use to end the Korean War. Eisenhower had a different approach toward nuclear weapons from Truman. He entered the White House with a strategic mind-set developed during his World War II experience in commanding the U.S. forces in Europe to victory, in the process relying on massive use of force, especially air power. He was determined to gain an advantage in the Cold War competition with the Soviet bloc, even if it meant a nuclear war.[62] Eisenhower came to power in 1953 with the determination to end the Korean War, which had been going on for over two and a half years at great human and material costs for all sides involved. In his *Memoirs,* Eisenhower discusses his plans to threaten the use of nuclear weapons in order to expedite the armistice agreement with China in North Korea. To Eisenhower:

> to keep the attack from becoming overly costly, it was clear that we would have to use atomic weapons . . . If we decided upon a major, new type of offensive, the present policies would have to be changed and the new ones agreed to by our allies. Foremost would be the proposed use of atomic weapons. In this respect American views have always differed somewhat from those of some of our allies. For the British, for example, the use of atomic weapons in war at that time would have been a decision of the gravest kind. My feeling was then, and still remains, that it would be impossible for the United States to maintain the military commitments which it now sustains around the world (without turning into a garrison state) did we not possess atomic weapons and the will to use them when necessary. But an American decision to use them at that time would have created strong disrupting feelings between ourselves and our allies.[63]

In addition to the fear of adverse reactions from allies, Eisenhower was worried about the possibility of the Soviet Union entering the war, and he was concerned about the "unprotected cities of Japan" becoming Soviet nuclear targets.[64] Here he was concerned about setting a bad precedent for the Soviets to follow suit.

Eisenhower decided to "let the Communist authorities understand that, in the absence of satisfactory progress, we intended to move decisively without inhibition in our use of weapons, and would no longer be responsible for confining hostilities to the Korean peninsula. We would not be limited by any world-wide gentlemen's agreement."[65] Eisenhower, in his memoirs as well as in conversations with his special assistant Sherman Adams, claims that it was the danger of nuclear war that compelled the Communists to end the Korean War quickly.[66] In its nuclear brinkmanship policy, the administration made specific nuclear threats to China. After moving atomic weapons to Okinawa, Secretary of State John Foster Dulles told Indian Prime Minister Nehru in May 1953 that the United States "could not be held responsible for failing to use atomic weapons if a truce could not be arranged. This message was planted deliberately in India so that it would get to the Chinese Communists, as it did," claims Adams.[67] Through lower-ranking U.S. officials at the Panmunjom talks, the administration sent covert messages to the Chinese that if the armistice was not concluded, the United States would "remove the restrictions of area and weapons," meaning an expansion of the war to mainland China involving nuclear weapons.[68]

However, doubts have been raised over the Eisenhower/Dulles claim that it was the nuclear threat that compelled the Chinese and North Koreans to agree to the Armistice Agreement in July 1953 despite the nonresolution of issues such as the repatriation of prisoners of war. It is argued that the main Chinese concessions were announced before the nuclear threats were made and that the U.S.-led conventional attacks had already created sufficient devastation for the Chinese and the North Koreans to rethink their strategy. Moreover, Stalin's death increased the sense of vulnerability among the Communist allies.[69] There is also doubt whether the Chinese Communist leaders received the threat, and, according to Richard Immerman, "Mao was convinced that because it enhanced PRC security and respect for his regime and military, the draw with the United States constituted a great victory."[70]

In May 1953, the administration had appointed a working committee of the National Security Council (NSC) under Robert Cutler, special assistant for National Security Affairs, to reassess U.S. national security policy. It was called *Project Solarium,* and involved three task forces assessing various dimensions of U.S. policy, including nuclear use. The military-led task forces recommended active policies to roll back Communism, relying on U.S. military superiority, while others proposed a comprehensive approach to deal with the Soviet threat so as to avoid a nuclear war, showing a lack of consensus among the planners on the questions of containment or nuclear coercion.[71]

At an NSC meeting on October 7, 1953, Secretary of Defense Charles E. Wilson and JCS Chairman Admiral Arthur Radford pressed the president for a decision on nuclear use, as the United States was spending enormous amounts of money on the building and maintenance of its nuclear weapons capability. Radford argued that the United States must not be paralyzed by American and world opinion and that the "administration must not grant the Europeans a veto." Radford was supported by Dulles, who made his now famous statement: "Somehow or other we must manage to remove the taboo from the use of nuclear weapons." Eisenhower responded by saying that securing allies' understanding must precede the use of nuclear weapons as "nothing would so upset the whole world as an announcement at this time by the United States of a decision to use these weapons."[72] Despite this position of Eisenhower, NSC-162/2 states that "in the event of hostilities, the United States will consider nuclear weapons to be available for use as other munitions."[73]

The nuclear option came up again during the crisis in Indochina. The administration seriously considered nuclear use as an option to relieve the besieged French fortress in Dien Bien Phu in 1954. The Viet Minh attack on the fortress began on March 13, 1954, and ended on July 21 with the surrender of the French forces and disastrous consequences for French colonial rule in Indochina. The contingency plan *Operation Vulture* involved U.S. air strikes including nuclear weapons, but it was not executed. Two studies, prepared by the army operations staff, had recommended using "one to six 31-kiloton bombs, to be delivered by Navy carrier aircraft during daylight against Viet Minh positions around Dien Bien Phu," and concluded that "the use of atomic weapons was technically and militarily feasible and could produce a major alteration in the military situation in favor of the French" and to "the U.S. advantage." They also proposed disguising the aircraft with French markings to reduce the reactions from other countries. These studies provoked intense debate among other staff divisions, especially U.S. Air Force intelligence, which contended that suitable targets did not exist; it would not only provoke a serious risk of all-out war, but also would:

completely alienate Asian nations such as India, Burma, and Indonesia and furnish a rationale for overt Chinese intervention in Southeast Asia. The Psychological Warfare Office dismissed the idea that U.S. involvement could somehow be disguised. World opinion would certainly attribute a nuclear strike to the United States regardless of the cover plan employed. Communist propaganda would depict the United States as unstable, barbaric, and impatient. The chief of psychological warfare concluded that the damage to America's reputation arising from use of atomic weapons "would outweigh the psychological disadvantages which would follow the loss of Dien Bien Phu."[74]

On April 20, 1954, Dulles and Radford discussed the possibility of nuclear use to relieve the French forces. To Radford, the proper use of three tactical nuclear weapons could "smash the Viet Minh."[75] A State Department Counselor, Douglas MacArthur II, raised the major challenge to Radford's proposals. To him, the proposal would prompt "very serious questions affecting the whole position of U.S. leadership in the world," raising "great hue and cry throughout the parliaments of the free world," and giving the Russians and other critics an opportunity to declare "that we were testing out weapons on native peoples and were in fact preparing to act irresponsibly and drop weapons of mass destruction on the Soviet Union whenever we believed it was necessary."[76] At the end of April, at an NSC meeting, military planners brought up the idea once again, to which Eisenhower responded: "You boys must be crazy. We can't use those awful things against Asians for a second time in less than ten years. My God."[77] This implies that the United States did not want to look racist by hitting Asians again. It also places reputation at the center of Truman's reasons for refusing to use nuclear weapons.

The First Taiwan Straits Crisis of 1954–55 offers another incident when the nascent tradition of non-use was tested. The crisis, which lasted for nine months, erupted in September 1954, as a result of the heavy shelling by Chinese Communist troops of the Republic of China (ROC)-held islands of Quemoy and Matsu. In response, the United States began to ponder a strategy of intervention. The administration had secretly committed to Chiang Kai-shek to defend the islands in the event of a major attack by the PRC, and, in April 1955, promised Chiang that in case the nationalists were forced to evacuate the islands, the "United States would establish a 500-mile blockade of China's coastal waters until the Communists renounced their intention to liberate Taiwan."[78] The administration's thinking on nuclear use came out when Dulles proclaimed: "If we defend Quemoy and Matsu, we'll have to use atomic weapons. They alone will be effective against the mainland airfields." Eisenhower himself replied in the affirmative to a reporter's question, on March 16, 1955, on whether the United States would use tactical nuclear weapons in East Asia.[79] However, Dulles also acknowledged that a decision to defend the islands, which were not critical to Taiwan's security, "would alienate world opinion and gravely strain our alliances . . . because it would probably lead to initiating the use of atomic weapons."[80]

However, during this crisis, Dulles pressed hard to abandon the distinction between conventional and nuclear weapons and consider a nuclear attack on China in response to the PRC's occupation of the small Tachen islands and the military buildup opposite Quemoy and Matsu. In his view, "it does not seem to make much sense," "if you have one bomb—one artillery shot— which will do the business, but use a hundred others which are most costly and the result is just the same."[81] Dulles spoke on March 12, 1955, of "new and powerful weapons of precision which can utterly destroy military targets without endangering unrelated civilian centers," adding that "if the United States became engaged in a major military activity anywhere in the world that those weapons would come into use."[82] Dulles was even more emphatic when he stated three days later that the "United States was prepared to use tactical atomic weapons in case of war in the Formosa Straits."[83] Vice President Richard Nixon stated: "tactical atomic explosives are now conventional and will be used against the targets of any aggressive force."[84] In Eisenhower's words, "in any combat where these things can be used on strictly military targets and for strictly for military purposes, I see no reason why they shouldn't be used just exactly as you would use a bullet or anything else."[85] This episode showed that tactical/strategic constraints were not as prominent in the non-use of nuclear weapons against China.

Eisenhower and Dulles decided to educate the public that there was no major distinction between conventional and nuclear weapons. Eisenhower encouraged Dulles to add a paragraph in a speech he was going to make that "we would use atomic weapons as interchangeable with conventional weapons," but not as "weapons of mass destruction."[86] The effort was to show people that tactical nuclear weapons were qualitatively different from strategic nuclear weapons: that the former would not cause as much destruction as the latter and were hence acceptable as a battlefield weapon. However, a Central Intelligence Agency (CIA) estimate, on March 16, 1955, warned that if atomic weapons were to be used, "the predominant world reaction would be one of shock. These reactions would be particularly adverse if these weapons were used to defend the offshore islands or destroy military concentrations prior to an all-out Chinese Communist attempt to take the offshore islands."[87] In another report, the CIA chief had warned of dangerous levels of radioactive fallout on Quemoy itself and the possibility of thousands of casualties on the islands from radiation if nuclear bombs were used on mainland China.[88]

The crisis de-escalated in April 1955 after Chinese premier Chou En-lai made conciliatory moves toward the United States. The Chinese backing off under nuclear threat thus bolstered the case of hardliners in the administration. Eisenhower, however, was much more cautious than Radford and Dulles were during this crisis. Despite his caution, the crisis showed the willingness of the administration to go to the extreme of nuclear brinkmanship supposedly to protect worthless islands, but more importantly to bolster the credibility of its *New Look* policy contained in NSC-162/2.[89] This policy sought to balance the economic resources and options available to the United States to confront conventional and nuclear threats from Communist countries through massive reliance on nuclear weapons forces.

The Taiwan Straits witnessed another crisis in August 1958, when Communist forces resumed shelling Quemoy and Matsu again. This crisis unfolded in a very similar fashion to the first crisis. The administration was bent on defending the islands, even if it meant nuclear escalation. Reportedly, the air and naval vessels and howitzers that were assembled by the United States on the islands were nuclear armed. Strong warnings by Dulles seem to have influenced the Chinese to back down from full-scale invasion of the islands, and on September 6 Chou En-lai expressed the desire to settle the conflict peacefully.[90] Thus the two Taiwan Straits Crises brought the United States very close to nuclear use against a nonnuclear China. The crises escalated as a result of the administration's get-tough policy with the Communist regime, which it perceived as a test case for the credibility of the massive retaliation strategy. In these crises, the non-use norm was marginalized while the compellent aspect of nuclear policy was highlighted.

The ongoing conflict with China and the Soviet Union would push the administration to ponder nuclear use in limited wars involving the Communist countries. Administration officials debated the feasibility of nuclear use in limited wars at NSC meetings in 1956. At a meeting in February 1956, in response to Radford, who had "called for greater flexibility in the employment of nuclear weapons for small wars," Eisenhower replied that "the use of nuclear weapons would raise serious political problems in view of the current state of world opinion as to the use of such weapons." Although the president did not think "world opinion was right in its views about the use of nuclear weapons in small wars . . . [it] was nevertheless a fact" and "it would be some considerable time before the United States reaches a point where it can adopt any military course of action it regards as appropriate without regard for the political repercussions of such a course of action."[91] Harold Stassen, special assistant to the president on disarmament policy, warned of the "terrible repercussions which we would experience if we had recourse to the use of nuclear weapons aginst the colored peoples of Asia."[92] On the issue of waging a war with China, Eisenhower himself told Dulles, "it is oftentimes necessary to take heavy liabilities from a purely military standpoint, in order to avoid being in the position of being an aggressor and the initiator of war."[93] At another NSC meeting in May 1957, the president said that the allies "do not wish to be defended by nuclear weapons. They all regard these weapons as essentially offensive in character, and our allies are absolutely scared to death that we will use such weapons."[94]

During another meeting, Dulles said, "world public opinion was not yet ready to accept the general use of nuclear weapons in local conflicts. If we resort to such a use of nuclear weapons we will in the eyes of the world, be cast as ruthless military power, as was Germany." He added that each of the assistant secretaries of state was strongly opposed to nuclear use, "because of the disastrous effect of such a policy on public opinion in the areas for which" they were responsible.[95] In fact, Dulles appeared to have been taking a very contradictory position on nuclear weapons. Initially, Dulles opposed the use of nuclear weapons against Japan on moral and reputation grounds, arguing that it would create a dangerous precedent and that he favored international control of the atom. However, he also became the chief advocate of massive retaliation and worked hard to remove the "taboo" against nuclear use and the distinction between conventional and nuclear weapons. He favored the creation of so-called small, "clean," useable weapons, and encouraged their use in several crisis situations.[96]

The discussion above and the statements by U.S. policy makers powerfully attest to the argument that reputation and image concerns were a primary reason for the Eisenhower administration's reluctance to use nuclear weapons in East Asia. Based on available evidence, tactical and strategic considerations appear in some discussions among U.S. officials, but they were at most secondary in the final decision not to resort to the use of nuclear weapons. Despite its strident rhetoric otherwise, the administration was hamstrung by fear of adverse world public opinion, especially in allied countries. The president overruled the advice of some of his key officials on the question of nuclear use in an effort to maintain the distinction between conventional and nuclear weapons. Yet he also showed a determination to engage in nuclear brinkmanship and crisis management in order to obtain political and diplomatic goals, that is, reap the benefits of nuclear possession without actually using the weapon. Eisenhower's brinkmanship policy was partly driven by the desire to prevent the outbreak of war by raising the stakes so high that the fear of an automatic thermonuclear war would engender caution among the Soviets and their allies. The administration claimed that compromise on the part of the Chinese and Soviet Communist powers, as in the Quemoy-Matsu crises in 1954–55 and 1958 and the Berlin Crisis in 1958–59, was driven largely by their fear of war and the U.S. willingness to employ nuclear coercion.[97]

Diplomacy, Domestic Control, and Weapons Development

While pondering the possibility of nuclear use, the Eisenhower administration was also concerned about nuclear proliferation, or the "fourth country problem," as it was referred to at that time.[98] International control of the atom reemerged as a major theme during the Eisenhower administration, alongside defense, deterrence, and arms control. However, the solution was no longer based on an international control mechanism, as had been proposed in the Baruch Plan in 1946. The *Atoms for Peace* proposal was put forward by Eisenhower in a speech at the UN General Assembly on December 8, 1953. In the proposal, Eisenhower called upon the nuclear powers to make "joint contributions from their stockpiles of normal uranium and fissionable materials to an International Atomic Energy Agency" to be "set up under the aegis of the United Nations." He added: "The Atomic Energy Agency would be made responsible for the impounding, storage, and protection of the contributed fissionable and other materials," and the agency would devise methods to allocate the fissionable materials for peaceful purposes such as generation of electrical energy and addressing the needs of agriculture and medicine. He pledged that the United States would undertake its contributions in good faith.[99]

The administration's aim was to encourage states to abandon nuclear weapons plans in return for civilian energy benefits through international cooperation.[100] More importantly, the United States was attempting to elicit cooperation from the Soviet Union in the matter of nuclear control. It served the administration's many goals, was "an excellent public diplomacy," was attractive to domestic opinion, supported "U.S. commercial interests," and was useful to the "cohesion and defense of the Atlantic Alliance."[101] In hindsight, it can be argued that *Atoms for Peace* perhaps accentuated the proliferation problem, as states such as Israel, India, and Pakistan acquired much of their early civilian capabilities under this program but later on were able to convert them to the development of nuclear weapons. Both France and China increased their nuclear efforts during this period and would test their weapons subsequently. However, it has been argued that without *Atoms for Peace*, nuclear proliferation would have occurred more rapidly through the unregulated international market, absent any restraining framework or safeguards by an international agency.[102]

Despite its efforts at stemming horizontal proliferation, the Eisenhower administration was notable for its massive expansion of U.S. nuclear forces and the testing of hydrogen bombs over the Pacific, which drew major international protests. The atmospheric testing of the hydrogen bomb (code-named *Bravo*) on March 1, 1954, produced a fifteen megaton yield—seven hundred fifty times that of the Hiroshima bomb, and three times more than expected. Unparalleled radiation levels spread across a large area of the Pacific, affecting nearby Japanese fishermen (one of whom died) and Marshall Islanders (many of whom developed radiation-related illnesses).[103] The radiation was detected worldwide, and a general fear spread through the globe: "if a single thermonuclear blast could have global ecological consequences, what would be the effects of using tens, hundreds, or even thousands of nuclear weapons?"[104]

Soviet leader Georgii Malenkov warned of the "end of world civilization," while Winston Churchill, who had until then urged the United States to engage in a preventive nuclear war on the Soviet Union, made a complete u-turn, warning that a "few such explosions on British soil would leave his country uninhabitable."[105] Despite these expressions of concern, the United States, the Soviet Union, and the United Kingdom conducted 231 atmospheric nuclear tests between 1953 and 1958. These tests and their fallout increased global awareness of the escalating nuclear arms race. The visit of thirty-four female victims of Hiroshima (Hiroshima Maidens) in June 1952 and May 1955 to the United States for medical treatment received considerable media coverage.[106] Witnessing, first-hand, the material effects of nuclear weapon use and testing was essential for increased global opposition to nuclear arms and the strengthening of the tradition at this stage.

Worldwide calls for a test ban emerged, and the Eisenhower administration was forced to engage in a public relations campaign in order to quell the opposition, which it did by proposing a partial test ban agreement with the Soviet Union. Among the chorus of those protesting were different peace movements and newly emerging Asian and African states. Indian Prime Minister Nehru called for a "standstill agreement" on nuclear testing as a prelude to an international treaty banning nuclear tests. British philosopher Bertrand Russell took a leadership role, along with Albert Einstein, Albert Schweitzer, and Soviet-supported peace movements such as the World Peace Council, in questioning the nuclear arms race while arguing for a world government. Groups such as Pugwash emerged in the 1950s as a result of the tests, and a worldwide movement favoring nuclear disarmament and a test ban remained active for the next several years.[107] In the United States, the 1952 and 1956 Democratic presidential candidate, Adlai Stevenson, argued in favor of a test ban. President Eisenhower was somewhat favorable but his powerful chief of the AEC, Lewis Strauss, was fervently opposed to any such proposal.[108]

The efforts by various groups in promoting a test ban did not succeed immediately and had to wait until President Kennedy's arrival to fructify.[109] Administration officials resisted calls for a test ban, fearing Soviet unreliability. Eisenhower, mindful of Washington's international reputation, stated: "everybody seems to think that we're skunks, saber-rattlers and war mongers. We ought not to miss any chance to make clear our peaceful objectives."[110] Even Strauss felt that the hydrogen bomb tests were creating a major embarrassment for the United States in the propaganda war with the Soviets, even driving the allies away. "They think we are getting ready for a war of this kind."[111] At an NSC meeting in May 1954, Dulles proposed a test moratorium, which would place the United States "in a much better position from the point of view of propaganda and our posture vis-à-vis the free world. It would certainly help us to meet the vicious attacks on us as warmongers by Soviet propaganda." Vice President Nixon supported the idea, arguing that the "United States was taking a 'hell of a licking' on the propaganda front." The president agreed that "the world is much more terrified now than it was in 1946. The long list of Russian violations of agreements wasn't as physically terrifying to people as was the prospect of atomic warfare."[112]

The administration engaged in some serious negotiations with the Soviets on a test ban and disarmament in the latter half of the 1950s. In his meeting with his disarmament advisors on April 26, 1958, Secretary of State Dulles stated that:

> it was urgent that we do something to erase the picture which people abroad hold of the United States as a militaristic nation . . . In this respect the Soviet Union, with its ability to control what is known about it, has an advantage over

a free society like that of the United States. This picture of continued military emphasis in the United States hurts us and probably causes us to lose more than we gain from small technical military advances . . . It is thus imperative that actions be taken which will make evident the United States interest in peace and in controlling armaments.[113]

Serious negotiations on a draft test ban treaty were held in Geneva in October 1958 and March 1959 and continued until December 1960, but had to be postponed due to the technical difficulties in verification and the worsening East-West relations during this period.[114] Reputation concerns emerge as a primary reason for the administration's test ban and nonproliferation proposals.

The Eisenhower era also saw some major changes in the civilian control of nuclear weapons that the Truman administration had established. The changes included the transfer of control of nuclear weapons from the AEC to the military and the dispersal of the weapons onto bases around the world. In addition, an attempt was made to blur the distinction between nuclear and conventional arms. For instance, NSC-162/1 stated: "in the event of hostilities, the United States will consider nuclear weapons to be as available for use as other munitions."[115] Accordingly, "nuclear weapons were integrated to all aspects of force procurement, deployment and war planning."[116]

It was also the Eisenhower administration that approved "pre-delegation" authority to commanders in the field. This authorized them to launch a nuclear attack on the Soviet Union if a Soviet attack destroyed the U.S. command and killed the president and there was no time for consultation after the enemy had launched a nuclear attack on U.S. territory.[117] Further, it was under Eisenhower that the United States created the Single Integrated Operation Plan (SIOP) for nuclear war, which involved targeting, weapons delivery systems, flight paths, nuclear detonation, measurements of devastation, defensive measures, and other planning concerns. The plan included preemptive and retaliatory strikes on thousands of targets in Russia, China, and other Warsaw Pact states, including their nuclear weapon facilities, command and control centers, and at least one hundred thirty of their cities. Eisenhower unsuccessfully tried to place limits on the war plans prepared by his military planners, and had reportedly stated when he received SIOP for 1962 that "it frighten[ed] the devil out of me."[118] Yet the president himself was aware of the dangers of atmospheric testing and the unbridled arms race. His parting words in 1961, warning of the undue influence of the "military-industrial complex" and the need for societal vigilance, suggest that he was concerned about the internal implications of the uncontrolled arms race.[119] However, he had done very little to curb the power of the military-industrial complex in the system when he was in power.

In terms of the tradition of nuclear non-use, Eisenhower's legacy is a mixed one, and to some extent negative, as he toyed with the idea of nuclear use against nonnuclear China on a few occasions. He also presided over the massive growth of nuclear weaponry under the *New Look* policy, and the launching of the doctrine of *massive retaliation* which called for use of nuclear weapons against any major threat posed by the Soviet Union. Deterrence based on massive retaliation became the cardinal feature of American policy, which was "designed to promote caution in Soviet foreign policy, to restrain what the Americans regarded as the Soviet's natural aggressive impulses."[120] The massive retaliation doctrine was based on an "undiscriminating threat to respond to any communist-inspired aggression, however marginal the confrontation, by means of a massive nuclear strike against the centers of the Soviet Union and China."[121] However, many nuclear strategists opposed massive retaliation while seeking a more flexible strategy to confront both strategic and substrategic conventional challenges. The Communist doctrines relied on flexible tactics, making them able to launch "many different kinds of challenges," and the United States "needed to prepare for many types of nonnuclear or 'limited' war," which meant "outfitting the American land, sea, and air forces with 'conventional' armaments."[122] Massive retaliation appeared to be an incredible strategy for the opponents, and it was later rejected by the Kennedy administration in favor of a *flexible response* strategy. Eisenhower's efforts at a nuclear test ban and for containing the proliferation problem did not go too far either, due largely to disagreement among administration officials, Cold War suspicions, and lack of presidential leadership.[123]

Some historians have argued that Eisenhower was not as bellicose as some of his policies might have suggested. Although he had engaged in a calculated policy of brinkmanship, he had no intention of using nuclear weapons.[124] Others contend that Eisenhower was willing to use nuclear weapons more readily than argued by previous scholars.[125] This debate is the result of the contradictory nuclear policies that Eisenhower pursued. At times he talked about winning an all-out nuclear war against the Soviet Union and its allies, but at other times, he pondered the possibilities for nuclear disarmament. He also showed a tendency to threaten nuclear war in order to protect less-than-vital interests, such as the Quemoy and Matsu islands, in order to shore up U.S. credibility and resolve. Gaddis summarizes the predicament: "The Eisenhower record on nuclear weapons is, in short, riddled with apparent inconsistencies, and as a result historians have had great difficulty deciding what his strategy really was. He himself, despite the remarkably full record he left behind, did remarkably little to clarify the matter."[126]

Despite the administrative changes to nuclear control, the nascent tradition of non-use survived during the Eisenhower era, as the United States refrained from engaging in a nuclear war with both nuclear and nonnuclear adversaries. The non-use of nuclear weapons, especially in the Far East, helped to preserve and strengthen the embryonic tradition of non-use. Whatever the merits of the debate on Eisenhower's nuclear brinkmanship policies, fortunately the tradition survived despite the intense Cold War competition the United States was waging with the Soviet Union and China during the 1950s.

CONCLUSION

This discussion of the nuclear policies of the Truman and Eisenhower administrations shows that different factors—reputational, strategic/tactical, and moral—appear to have influenced these administrations' choices regarding the non-use of atomic weapons against nonnuclear states in the crises in which they were involved. However, the documentary evidence powerfully suggests that tactical or strategic considerations were not as significant for them as reputational and image considerations were. Although they talked about possible Russian military reactions, American leaders were cognizant that the Soviet Union had no nuclear weapons until 1949 and had only a handful of them and limited delivery capacities for another half decade, which gave the United States overwhelming preponderance and a near monopoly.[127] In August 1958, Eisenhower himself acknowledged, while discussing the need for a test ban that "the new thermonuclear weapons are tremendously powerful," but they "are not, in many ways, as powerful as is world opinion today in obliging the United States to follow certain lines of policy."[128] The vast number of documents these administrations left behind all show that reputational consideration in terms of adverse world public opinion acted as a major self-deterrent to the United States to using nuclear weapons during these two presidencies. Although the Nth-country problem (that is, additional states acquiring nuclear weapons) was an issue, nonproliferation considerations were not pivotal, at least in the first two presidencies, for the rise of the tradition. *Atoms for Peace* and the test ban initiatives were driven partially by the U.S. desire to mollify world public opinion and to regain Washington's reputation as a peace-loving nation in the face of worldwide opposition to nuclear testing.

The nascent tradition of non-use began during the presidencies of Truman and Eisenhower. The reluctance to use nuclear weapons in wars and crises during these administrations gave rise to the tradition in the U.S. case. By the time Eisenhower came to power, the reputational concerns inherent in the tradition were already acting as a constraint, as evident in the several discussions at NSC meetings. The United States faced two forms of reputational considerations with respect to nuclear weapons since the first decades of the atomic age. First, it wanted to keep the threat of nuclear use vis-à-vis adversaries credible for deterrence and compellence purposes. Second, the desire to maintain a reputation as a peace-loving nation and the fear of adverse world opinion prevented Truman and Eisenhower from using nuclear weapons, even when the United States possessed tremendous nuclear advantages over its adversaries.

4 THE UNITED STATES AND THE TRADITION II: KENNEDY TO CLINTON (1961–2001)

Make no mistake . . . There is no such thing as a conventional nuclear weapon. For 19 peril-filled years no nation has loosed the atom against another. To do so now is a political decision of the highest order. And it would lead us down an uncertain path of blows and counterblows whose outcome none may know. No President of the United States of America can divest himself of the responsibility for such a decision.

—President Lyndon B. Johnson, September 1964

AS DISCUSSED IN THE PREVIOUS CHAPTER, the embryonic tradition of non-use emerged and survived during the key formative years of 1945 to 1960, under the Truman and Eisenhower administrations. Eisenhower left office with a huge nuclear arsenal in place, and with the notion of massive retaliation well ingrained in the U.S. strategic doctrine. A state of Mutual Assured Destruction (MAD) was in operation, as the Soviet Union had developed its own matching nuclear capabilities during this period. The Cuban Missile Crisis, which occurred under the Kennedy administration, was a pivotal event which further embedded the fear of nuclear weapons globally and, consequently, solidified the non-use tradition. This chapter addresses U.S. nuclear policy, and, in particular, the approach toward non-use against nonnuclear states from the Kennedy era to the Clinton years.

THE KENNEDY YEARS (1961–63)

John F. Kennedy began his presidency in January 1961 opposed to the *massive retaliation* policy of the Eisenhower administration. Instead, his administration instituted a strategy of *flexible response* which would rely on multiple options to respond to a Soviet attack, beginning with a conventional response and then escalating to nuclear retaliation, if warranted. This was aimed at creating firebreaks on conflicts, preventing them from going nuclear instantaneously, which would have been the consequence of massive retaliation. However, according to critics, "from the military perspective, there was no fundamental change in strategy" under the Kennedy administration, as political and bureaucratic factors prevented it from making radical changes. Despite their skepticism of battlefield nuclear weapons, "many within the administration believed that the United States had to be able to credibly threaten the first use of U.S. strategic forces."[1]

The Kennedy administration witnessed two major crises in which nuclear war with the Soviet Union was of high probability. During the intense Second Berlin Crisis in September 1961, the administration considered proposals for a limited nuclear first strike against Soviet military targets in case the Berlin crisis turned violent. According to Fred Kaplan, officials from the Pentagon and the White House "had worked out a plan for a first strike that would virtually wipe out the Soviets' nuclear arsenal, minimizing the chance of retaliation."[2] However, Kennedy realized that his options were not very good in view of the Soviet ultimatum on a peace treaty between East and West Germany. The U.S. demand for a "free city" or "neutral status" for West Berlin was not met, and the U.S.S.R. built the Berlin Wall in August 1961. Despite the intensification of the conflict relationship with the Soviets, and despite the gung-ho attitude of many of his military officials, it is apparent from his decisions that Kennedy wanted to prevent a nuclear war by all means.[3]

The Cuban Missile Crisis was the second key crisis and the closest the superpowers ever came to a nuclear war. The crisis engendered a great fear of nuclear war and the possibility of both calculated and inadvertent nuclear escalation as the Kennedy administration upped the ante and attempted to compel the Soviet leader, Nikita Khrushchev, to withdraw Soviet missiles from Cuba. Although critics have contended that Kennedy's aggressive policies toward Cuba (such as the Bay of Pigs invasion in 1961) led to the Soviet decision to bring nuclear missiles to the island nation, it is now well-documented that Kennedy played a decisive role in preventing a disastrous nuclear war, despite being urged by many of his advisors, military commanders, and congressional leaders to resort to the most dangerous military option, a surgical strike.[4] Such an attack could certainly have prompted Khrushchev to respond, possibly by launching a war in Europe. It can be argued that the fear of nuclear war was now embedded, and that deterrence based on MAD and the tradition of non-use both became stronger as a result of the Cuban Missile Crisis.

Though it bolstered the credibility of mutual deterrence, the Cuban Missile Crisis showed that a miscalculation on either side could have resulted in a catastrophic war. Kennedy was concerned about the dangers of relying on the chain of command from the president to the field commander and the dual-key arrangements attached to nuclear launch facilities. Bundy argues that the most powerful impact of the crisis was that "neither side want[ed] to run such risk again."[5] The crisis was followed by efforts both at horizontal arms control and at a vertical arms race, a contradictory outcome. The vertical arms race took off largely because of a Soviet recognition of weaknesses vis-à-vis the United States.[6] Further, it helped to remove the "stereotypical cold war images," especially in Europe, helping to generate support for a détente and more concrete arms control measures such as the Hot Line and test ban talks.[7]

In the aftermath of the Cuban Missile Crisis, the United States and the Soviet Union began to take an active interest in preventing the spread of nuclear weapons to additional countries.[8] President Kennedy had warned of the arrival of fifteen to twenty-five nuclear weapon states if the international community did not do something urgently.[9] The Partial Test Ban Treaty (PTBT), which prohibited nuclear testing in the atmosphere, space, and underwater— but allowed underground testing—was signed in August 1963. It was a result of consistent demands by nonnuclear states and peace movements, who were appalled by the effects of uncontrolled atmospheric nuclear tests, especially in the Pacific.[10] In addition, the negotiations for the Nuclear Nonproliferation Treaty (NPT) began during this period.

The PTBT was part of intense efforts made by the Kennedy administration to arrest the spread of nuclear weapons, especially to China. Kennedy was alarmed by the possibility of Chinese acquisition of nuclear weapons, and his administration made plans to use all possible avenues, such as coercive force if necessary, to stop the Chinese from going nuclear and adhere to the PTBT. Kennedy sought Soviet cooperation in order to launch a preventive attack on Chinese nuclear facilities, which the Russian leader Khrushchev rejected.[11] Kennedy and his advisors initiated extensive spying of China's nuclear activities and considered military action with or without Soviet support. These discussions for preventive action intensified during the Johnson presidency, which I will discuss below.

It is also now revealed that Kennedy was uncertain of the utility of building massive numbers of nuclear weapons. In conversations with his advisors in December 1962, Kennedy stated, "You can't use them as a first weapon

yourself, they are only good for deterring . . . I don't see quite why we're building as many as we're building."[12]

Despite these considerations, the possibility of use of nuclear weapons by
the Kennedy administration appeared in some crisis situations. Recently declassified official documents suggest that the issue of nuclear use appeared
in the conversations of Kennedy and his advisors in the National Security
Council (NSC) in May 1963, when they discussed the possibility of the United
States using nuclear weapons to prevent China from invading India a second
time. To Kennedy, the fall of India would be tantamount to the fall of another
significant domino to Communism, and must be stopped. At the meeting,
Secretary of Defense Robert McNamara stated: "Before any substantial commitment to defend India against China is given, we should recognize that in
order to carry out that commitment against any substantial Chinese attack,
we would have to use nuclear weapons. Any large Chinese Communist attack on any part of that area would require the use of nuclear weapons by the
U.S. and this is to be preferred over the introduction of large numbers of U.S.
soldiers." General Maxwell D. Taylor, then Chairman of the Joint Chiefs of
Staff (JCS), stated: "This is just one spectacular aspect of the overall problem
of how to cope with Red China politically and militarily in the next decade.
I would hate to think that we would fight this on the ground in a non-nuclear
way." In response, Kennedy said, "[w]e should defend India, and therefore, we
will defend India" if it was attacked, without mentioning the nuclear option.

The important dimension of these discussions for the tradition of non-
use is the opinion of two of the other members of the NSC. Secretary of State
Dean Rusk cautioned that a nuclear attack on China should only occur with
the support of critical allies, while then-Undersecretary of State George Ball
warned of the negative reputational effects of using weapons against East
Asians. According to Ball: "If there is a general appearance of a shift in strategy to the dependence on a nuclear defense against the Chinese in the Far
East, we are going to inject into the whole world opinion the old bugaboo of
being willing to use nuclear weapons against Asians . . . This is going to create
great problems with the Japanese—with all the yellow people."[13]

THE JOHNSON ERA (1963–69)

The Johnson period witnessed the strengthening of the tradition, manifested
in the administration's opposition to using nuclear weapons to win the Vietnam War, its refusal to use nuclear weapons against China to prevent that
country from becoming nuclear, and its active efforts in concluding the NPT.

During the 1964 Presidential campaign, Johnson fiercely opposed Republican candidate Barry Goldwater's call for victory in the Cold War using nuclear weapons, especially in Vietnam. In one of his speeches, at Detroit in September 1964, Johnson described nuclear war as a great catastrophe, with "hundreds of millions dead, cities in ashes, fields gone barren, and industry destroyed." He stated:

> Make no mistake. There is no such thing as a conventional nuclear weapon. For 19 peril-filled years no nation has loosed the atom against another. To do so now is a political decision of the highest order. And it would lead us down an uncertain path of blows and counterblows whose outcome none may know. No President of the United States of America can divest himself of the responsibility for such a decision.[14]

The logic of consequences appears powerfully in this statement. This statement was perhaps the first by a U.S. leader showing the power of the tradition of non-use, and it attests that the tradition had entered the calculations of the U.S. president. To Johnson, nuclear use was not a viable option because it would break a tradition that was maintained by his predecessors, and if he violated it, it would set a bad precedent for others to follow. In that sense, the reverse loop shown in my model in Chapter 2 is present in the calculations of U.S. decision makers here.

Reputational reasons were powerful factors presented by other administration officials in their opposition to the use of nuclear weapons in Vietnam. Undersecretary of State George Ball, in a memo presented to the administration in October 1964, argued that it would be difficult to maintain a distinction between tactical and strategic weapons for public opinion, and that U.S. nuclear use would create a "profound shock" not only in Japan but also "among the non-white nations on every continent." Ball contended that the use of even one nuclear weapon would cause a "loss of prestige" for the United States among the nonaligned developing countries, and would "liberate the Soviet Union from the inhibitions that world sentiments had imposed on it," as the United States would have "provided a justification for their use." "The Communists would certainly point out that we were the only nation that had ever employed nuclear weapons in anger. And the Soviet Union would emphasize its position of relative virtue in having a nuclear arsenal which it had never used."[15] Surprisingly, in his memo, Ball devotes only one sentence to the military consequences of nuclear use.[16] Ball was presenting powerfully the concerns about the negative impact on reputation, prestige, and image as well as the dangers of precedent-setting behavior if the United States used nuclear weapons. What is noticeable is the relatively limited concerns about nuclear retribution by the Soviet Union as a source of restraint.

McGeorge Bundy, who was Special Assistant for National Security Affairs to Presidents Kennedy and Johnson, contends that no one close to Johnson proposed nuclear use in Vietnam, as the anticipated consequences of such an attack deterred them from doing so. This was not due to the absence of suitable targets, as there were plenty of ports, landing places, supply lines, and so forth that could have been attacked by low-yield nuclear weapons. He also discounts the probability of Russian and Chinese intervention as a cause for restraint. Bundy locates the causes of non-use solely on reputational concerns:

> We may begin to get an answer when we think of the effect of any such use of nuclear weapons on the Vietnamese. What kind of reaction would there have been, on both sides in divided Vietnam, to such attacks? Would what was decisive in a military sense have had terrible consequences not only in human terms but in the minds of the survivors? Could you, in that reaction, lose the war by winning it? And what would have been the reputation of the United States elsewhere—in the nearby countries whose future was so large a part of what had led the American government to persist, or in the rest of the newly independent world, or in Latin America, or in the Atlantic Alliance?[17]

Despite the reputational problems inherent in nuclear use as outlined by Bundy, during the war senior military leaders and the U.S. ambassador to South Vietnam, Henry Cabot Lodge, Jr., raised the possibility of nuclear use, which was rejected by Johnson and his senior advisors. Instead, Johnson did escalate the conventional bombing of North Vietnam. Massive bombing operations such as "Rolling Thunder" were meant to break the will of the North Vietnamese and force them to give up their resistance. The use of nuclear weapons in Vietnam was considered by the administration, especially to destroy targets such as tunnels that the Vietcong used to transport weapons and men, but McNamara and other officials such as Rusk and Bundy all opposed such proposals, and Johnson concurred with their positions.[18]

In 1966, in response to rumors of proposals for the use of nuclear weapons in Vietnam, a four-member team of scientists under the name *JASON Group* conducted a study on the impact of tactical nuclear use in Vietnam.[19] The group was responding to discussions within the Defense Department regarding the use of tactical nuclear weapons to destroy the mountain passes between North Vietnam and Laos that the Vietcong were using as a route for large-scale troop reinforcement and supply of materials. The Pentagon-funded group concluded that the use of tactical nuclear weapons in Southeast Asia would offer the United States no decisive military advantage. These weapons may have been effective in "stopping the enemy from moving large masses of men in concentrated formations," but were of "little use against troops moving in small groups under forest cover." In addition, they argued that the political and military costs of nuclear use would outweigh any possible benefits. Politically, crossing the nuclear threshold could "greatly weaken the barriers to proliferation and general use of nuclear weapons." They also argued that the "effect on world opinion, and on the opinion of U.S. allies in particular, would be extremely unfavorable," while its effect on domestic opinion in the United States "would be extremely divisive." Militarily, nuclear weapons would not be effective unless used in large quantities, but the U.S. staging areas in South Vietnam could become targets of nuclear retaliation by Communist guerillas, who might gain nuclear arms from China or the Soviet Union.[20] It is not clear if this report had any direct effect on U.S. decision making at that time, but it is assumed that McNamara decided to put an end to discussions of nuclear use in the Defense Department, calling them irrelevant.[21] The scientists were emphasizing the general problems with breaking the tradition of non-use, and the reasons they cited most prominently included both reputational and tactical considerations.

During the Johnson era, Chinese acquisition of nuclear weapons became a major concern again. Many studies by U.S. military planners proposed preventive attacks, as Chinese nuclear acquisition was perceived as a major threat not only to the United States, but also to its allies and other states in East, South, and Southeast Asia.[22] The administration continued Kennedy's efforts to stop China from going nuclear, in the end deciding only to refrain from concrete military action. The reasons for inaction in the military realm were both political and military related. According to a State Department official, Robert Johnson, who had prepared a report on the costs and benefits of preventive action against China, a military attack would be dangerous and could fail; "it could hurt the United States' image and weaken its prestige, the intangible assets of world power."[23]

The Johnson memorandum, which became the basis for U.S. policy, rejected military action to prevent China from acquiring nuclear weapons on the grounds that the effect of any successful attack would last only four to five years, as China would rebuild its capabilities, and the United States would have to resort to another round of attacks. Most prominently, the memorandum listed the following adverse international political reaction as grounds for desisting from military action:

> (a) It is an illustration of the U.S. unwillingness to accept the existence of Communist China as a major world actor; (b) it conflicts with U.S. efforts to argue the limited military significance of Chicom [Chinese Communist] nuclear capability; (c) it is an action with strong racialist overtones—the white man (including the French) can develop the bomb, but it is not considered safe for colored people to possess them; (d) it is highly dangerous, involving grave risk of precipitating war (or escalation of existing conflict) in Asia and even of bringing the Soviets to the support of the Chinese; and (e) it is another illustration of the U.S. preoccupation with military considerations.[24]

According to Burr and Richelson, the U.S. decision not to pursue a preventive military option was influenced by uncertainties in intelligence analysis, probable adverse "overseas reactions," and a negative effect on U.S. nuclear deterrent capabilities.[25]

The Chinese nuclear tests in October 1964 prompted major efforts by the Johnson administration on the issue of stemming nuclear proliferation.[26] The Gilpatric Report, named after the chairman of the taskforce appointed by Johnson in November 1964, former Deputy Secretary of Defense Roswell Gilpatric, became the basis of much of this newfound enthusiasm for nuclear nonproliferation. The report proposed that the United States "greatly intensify" nonproliferation efforts by concluding an international treaty for the "non-dissemination and non-acquisition of nuclear weapons," and pursue a carrot-and-stick policy to halt the spread of nuclear weapons.[27] President Johnson carried through the NPT negotiations, along with the Soviet Union and Britain, and it was during his term that the treaty was finally concluded in 1968. It came into force in 1970. Although the United States and the other nuclear powers did not commit a formal non-use guarantee to the nonnuclear states under the Treaty, the implicit understanding was that those states that gave up their nuclear weapons option would not be targeted or attacked with nuclear weapons, and that they would be offered the civilian benefits of the atom under international safeguards.[28] In Chapter 8, this subject is discussed more elaborately.

The Johnson era showed the power of the tradition of non-use, as the administration refused to use nuclear weapons even when it was facing enormous difficulties in Vietnam. Though active in the nonproliferation arena,

Johnson rejected proposals for a nuclear attack on China to prevent it from becoming a nuclear power. Nuclear use would have seriously hampered the administration's nonproliferation efforts as well as other arms control goals that it wanted to pursue with the Soviet Union.

THE NIXON YEARS (1969–74)

The Nixon era is known for several attempts by the United States to threaten the use of nuclear weapons for political and strategic purposes. These attempts show that the tradition was not progressing in a linear fashion and that it could be challenged if leaders who did not believe in its value gained control of the government. In fact, an active effort was made by the administration, especially Nixon's National Security Advisor Henry Kissinger, to use nuclear weapons as a coercive instrument in order to achieve U.S. foreign policy goals vis-à-vis Communist and some other developing nations. These included a nuclear alert in October 1969; several efforts to use the nuclear threat, including *Operation Duck Hook* in 1969, to compel the North Vietnamese to agree to U.S. war terms; and the nuclear alerts during the 1971 India-Pakistan and the 1973 Middle East wars. Nixon believed that by pretending to act irrationally in terms of nuclear use, he could manipulate the Soviets and their allies to modify their behavior in the developing world. To some extent, Nixon and Kissinger were attempting to imitate the brinkmanship strategy of Eisenhower, but in the end their efforts at nuclear coercion showed little if any success. Their war policies in Vietnam were not popular domestically or internationally, as evident in widespread protest rallies, constraining the nuclear use option even further than in the Eisenhower years. However, the Nixon/Kissinger team valiantly continued to use nuclear threat as the key means of achieving U.S. strategic goals. Although these were bluffs in some instances, a conditional intent to use lies beneath a threat if it has any meaning to an adversary's calculations. In that sense, these were affronts to the tradition of non-use.

The most prominent efforts by the Nixon administration at nuclear coercion occurred in Vietnam. In March 1969, the administration considered an escalation strategy in order to end the intransigence of the North Vietnamese in the Paris peace negotiations. The strategy included the potential use of nuclear weapons. Joint Chiefs of Staff (JCS) position papers and memoranda studying progressive escalation from conventional to nuclear means were forwarded to Kissinger. One such paper suggested that "a team of Pentagon technical experts in atomic and chemical warfare [make] an extended visit of the Far East, stopping off at CINCPAC [office of the Commander-in-Chief, Pacific], Okinawa, Saigon and Bangkok" as a feigned way to show an American willingness to use nuclear weapons if the Communists did not compromise. However, these reports had rejected the actual "use of atomic, biological or lethal chemical weapons in Vietnam" as "it would excite very strong public and congressional reaction." In addition, "the predictable reaction worldwide, particularly in Japan and Okinawa, upon the surfacing of this scenario, militates against its employment."[29]

Despite these negative assessments, the administration launched a worldwide nuclear alert in 1969, which was couched as a "Joint Chiefs of Staff Readiness Test."

> The alert began on October 13, 1969, when U.S. tactical and strategic air forces in the United States, Europe, and East Asia began a stand-down of training flights to raise operational readiness; Strategic Air Command [SAC] increased the numbers of bombers and tankers on ground alert; and the readiness posture of selected overseas units was heightened. On October 25, SAC took the additional step of increasing the readiness of nuclear bombers, and two days later SAC B-52s undertook a nuclear-armed "Show of Force" alert over Alaska, code-name "Giant Lance."[30]

By the end of October 1969 the alert was rescinded. The purpose of this alert was to convince the Soviets to persuade their Vietnamese allies to end the war. However, these alerts had no palpable effects on the Soviets or their Vietnamese allies, suggesting that they did not view the U.S. threat as credible.[31]

President Nixon began his term in 1969 with a secret plan to win the Vietnam War. Nixon believed that the reason why the Chinese and the North Koreans agreed to negotiate the Armistice Agreement in 1953 was President Eisenhower's threat to use nuclear weapons. Prior to the Republican National Convention of 1969, Nixon told Richard J. Whalen, his speech writer, that if elected president, "I would use nuclear weapons," and would be willing "to threaten their use in appropriate circumstances."[32]

Nixon's strategy was to act like a "madman" to induce cooperation from Communist adversaries, akin to the strategy in a game of chicken. Nixon told White House Chief of Staff H. R. Haldeman that Eisenhower's nuclear threats were responsible for the ending of the Korean War in 1953. "I call it the madman theory, Bob," he said. "I want the North Vietnamese to believe I've reached the point where I might do *anything* to stop the war. We'll just slip the word to them that 'for God's sake, you know Nixon is obsessed about Communists. We can't restrain him when he's angry—and he has his hand on the nuclear button'—and Ho Chi Minh himself will be in Paris in two days begging for peace."[33] The threat was incredible to the Vietnamese because of the possible retaliation by Russia and China and the difficulty of mounting it in secrecy, without which it would have provoked further peace demonstrations against the war in the United States and abroad.

Kissinger did indeed work on a plan to use nuclear weapons in order to expedite the end of the war. The plan, code-named *Operation Duck Hook,* had called for:

> massive bombing of Hanoi, Haiphong, and other key areas in North Vietnam; the mining of harbors and rivers; the bombing of the dike system; a ground invasion of North Vietnam; the destruction—possibly with nuclear devices— of the main north–south passes along the Ho Chi Minh Trail; and the bombing of North Vietnam's main railroad links with China. There was a separate, even more secret study dealing with the implications of using tactical nuclear weapons on the rail lines, the main funnel for supplies from the Soviet Union as well as China. In all, twenty-nine major targets in North Vietnam were targeted for destruction in a series of air attacks planned to last four days and be renewed, if necessary, until Hanoi capitulated.[34]

Kissinger told Roger Morris, a senior NSC staff member, in response to a question on nuclear use, "it is the policy of this administration not to use nuclear weapons and we shall not, so these options exclude that one thing. But you are not to exclude the possibility of a nuclear device being used for purposes of a blockade in the pass to China if that seems to be the only way to close the pass," referring to the railroad between North Vietnam and China. The plan was never carried out due to fears of increased domestic violence and the possibility that it would cost Nixon re-election.[35] Reputational costs at the domestic political level are central in explaining this decision of non-use.

Tapes released by the U.S. National Archives in March 2002 reveal that, a few weeks before escalating the conventional bombing, President Nixon matter-of-factly raised the idea of using a nuclear bomb. During a conversation with Nixon on April 25, 1972, Kissinger presented various options to compel the Vietnamese to agree to peace, including attacking power plants and docks. Nixon responded by saying "I'd rather use the nuclear bomb." Kissinger replied: "That, I think, will just be too much," and in response, Nixon quipped: "The nuclear bomb. Does that bother you?" adding, "I just want you to think big."[36] However, in an interview with *Time* Magazine in 1985, Nixon said he rejected the bombing of the dikes because it "would have drowned 1 million people, for the same reason that I rejected the nuclear option. Because the targets presented were not military targets." In addition, Nixon feared that massive retaliation including nuclear use would have destroyed "any chances for moving forward with the Soviets and China."[37]

McGeorge Bundy argues that the use of nuclear weapons would have provoked the opponents of the war both at home and abroad even further, making the American position untenable.[38] Even a realist like Kissinger found that nuclear nations, although capable of destroying each other, would not be able to impose their will. He states: "the capacity to destroy proved difficult to translate into a plausible threat even against countries with no capacity for retaliation. The margin of the superpowers over non-nuclear states had been widening; yet the awesomeness of their power had increased their inhibitions. As power had grown more awesome, it had also turned abstract, intangible, elusive."[39] Later on Nixon himself stated that if the United States had "chosen to go for a knockout blow by bombing the dikes or using tactical nuclear weapons, the resulting domestic and international uproar would have damaged our foreign policy on all fronts."[40] At a meeting in May 1972, in response to Nixon's comment that he did not care about civilian casualties, Kissinger stated: "I'm concerned about the civilians because I don't want the world to be mobilized against you as a butcher."[41] Self-deterrence appears a very powerful check on nuclear use against nonnuclear states even for a hard realist such as Kissinger.

Going by Nixon's statement, both reputational and tactical concerns appear significant in his decision not to execute the nuclear threats that he and his advisors considered on different occasions. If the United States used nuclear weapons in Vietnam, there was recognition that American and world opinion would have turned much more oppositional as the anti-Vietnam protests were surging nationally and internationally.[42] In addition, the weapon conceived was inappropriate due to its immense destructive capability against nonmilitary targets. The massive destruction of those targets would have cost too much in terms of reputational considerations. A disproportionate destruction would have resulted in the deaths of hundreds of thousands of Vietnamese and contaminated vast areas of that country with radioactive debris.

Moral concerns, albeit to a limited extent, appear to be entering the calculations even for leaders who did not want to be concerned about them.

The Nixon period also saw efforts by the United States to develop plans for waging limited nuclear war with the Soviet Union, both in the European and regional contexts. Nixon was appalled by the prospects of an all-out nuclear war and was interested in the United States developing less damaging limited-war options. Kissinger was an early proponent of such a strategy and was instrumental in developing some plans for limited war.[43] Kissinger sought to identify targets for limited nuclear strikes in the Middle East in order to signal the Soviets not to escalate the conflict.[44] The so-called Schlesinger Doctrine (named after Secretary of Defense James Schlesinger) called for developing new targeting plans, based on smaller, more limited nuclear strike options, to retaliate against Soviet aggression without causing major dangers to Soviet cities. The intent was to deter both conventional and nuclear conflict; if deterrence failed, the policy was to "terminate nuclear hostilities at the lowest level of conflict possible," and if war escalated, the United States "would seek to secure the best possible outcome for itself and its allies."[45] In January 1974, Nixon signed National Security Decision Memorandum (NSDM) 242, which directed the preparation of a "wide range of limited nuclear employment options," to demonstrate the seriousness of the United States' intent to use nuclear weapons if necessary.[46]

The Nixon-Kissinger strategy was to make nuclear weapons a key instrument to deter Soviet involvement in regional theaters. "Yet, the civilian-military consensus for limited options remained relatively shallow. For example, nuclear planners at the Pentagon dragged their feet, even questioning whether civilians should be involved in such sensitive issues as nuclear targeting or whether limited strategic options even made sense."[47] Skeptics argued that it would not be possible to limit nuclear war; such a policy might undermine deterrence in Europe, "damage relations with Western Europe, and lower the threshold for nuclear weapons use."[48]

The Nixon administration also engaged in nuclear saber rattling in the Indian subcontinent in 1971. The war between India and Pakistan in December 1971 saw the liberation of East Pakistan as the new state of Bangladesh, partly the result of military intervention by neighboring India. As the Pakistani military position began to crumble, on December 10, 1971 the Nixon administration decided to dispatch the nuclear-armed Seventh Fleet (a ten-ship naval force spearheaded by USS *Enterprise*) from the Pacific to the Bay of Bengal with the intention of coercing India not to escalate the war on West Pakistan. The task force carried seventy-five nuclear-armed fighter-bombers on board and included a nuclear attack submarine. "Nixon and Kissinger believed that coercive diplomacy worked. India offered an unconditional ceasefire in the West, removing the threat there."[49]

Nixon, in a subsequent interview, claimed that the United States considered the nuclear option in 1971 because of the fear that the Soviets would intervene in support of India if China invaded India.[50] His aim appeared to be more to deter India than to deter a Soviet intervention. However, there is little evidence that Indian Prime Minister Indira Gandhi was planning an escalation in the West, as she had obtained her strategic objective of bifurcating Pakistan. By the time the task force reached the Bay of Bengal on December 15, 1971, "India had already eliminated Pakistani military resistance in the East, established an air and sea blockade isolating East Pakistan, and unilaterally chosen to confine its attention in the West to the long-disputed territory of Kashmir" and not Pakistan proper.[51] This episode of nuclear coercion of a nonnuclear state added to India's determination to acquire nuclear weapons capability, and it subsequently tested its first device in May 1974.

The Nixon administration once again raised the nuclear alert in the 1973 Middle East War. On October 23, Israeli advancing forces broke the ceasefire agreement and surrounded Egypt's Third Army in Suez City. In the face of the Egyptian Army's imminent collapse, Soviet leader Leonid Brezhnev put on alert two Warsaw pact divisions in Bulgaria. On October 24, Brezhnev sent a message to Kissinger threatening unilateral action. In response, on October 25, the Nixon administration ordered U.S. nuclear forces to raise their alert status from DEFCON 4 to DEFCON 3. The U.S. claim that Moscow was delivering SCUD nuclear armed missiles to Egypt was proven incorrect later on.[52] States Nixon: "We could not allow Israel to go down the tube. We could not allow the Soviets to have a predominant position in the region. That had to be the bottom line. I wanted to send that message, and putting the weapons on alert did that."[53]

In both the India-Pakistan and Middle East wars, the Nixon administration saw regional wars as Soviet-inspired, and threatened nuclear escalation as a way to end the wars in a manner favorable to the United States. By exaggerating the Soviet role in these conflicts, the administration courted possible global war as a result of escalating regional conflicts which had their own regional causes. The threats of nuclear use against India and Egypt constituted cases of disregard of the tradition of non-use of nuclear weapons against non-nuclear states. Even if its actions in the Middle East were intended primarily to coerce Moscow to refrain from intervention in favor of Cairo, the Nixon administration was disregarding the spirit of the tradition. Further, although each state had limited alliance relationships with Moscow, neither Egypt nor India was under the Soviet nuclear umbrella as the East European states were, or taking its orders from Moscow.

The tradition of non-use survived the Nixon/Kissinger era, although it faced some major challenges during this period. The United States retreated from Vietnam without achieving victory, and its unwillingness or inability to use nuclear weapons to defeat North Vietnam gave a new fillip to the tradition. Nixon and Kissinger attempted to use nuclear weapons as devices for compellence and had very little positive results to show at the end. Their reluctance to use nuclear weapons was influenced by both tactical/strategic considerations and reputational concerns (especially at the domestic level). However, it is clear that their efforts to break the tradition did not succeed and that the tradition persisted through those crucial years.

The end of the Nixon era brought an end to the possibility of nuclear use against nonnuclear states for at least another two decades. There were hardly any occasions during the presidencies of Ford, Carter, or Reagan to threaten the use of nuclear weapons against nonnuclear states.

THE CARTER YEARS (1977–81)

The Carter years were significant for the tradition to the extent that there was considerable discussion about developing the neutron bomb, a "usable" nuclear weapon that would not destroy material assets or contaminate the environment, but would kill living beings. Carter decided to suspend the plans to develop the neutron bomb (an enhanced radiation weapon) after considerable national and international protests, especially in Europe, and partially due to his own personal beliefs about the inappropriateness of the weapon.[54] James Schlesinger, who served as Secretary of Energy under Carter, argues that Carter decided not to proceed with the neutron bomb, despite disagreement of all his advisors with that decision, by "exercising his moral judgment."[55] The proposed plan was to install neutron bombs on Lance missiles and artillery shells which were to be deployed in Europe. However, Carter "kept open the option of proceeding with production at a later date so he [could] use it as a 'bargaining chip' with the Russians in arms reduction negotiations."[56] The "ban the neutron bomb" campaign, which started in Europe, also had a major impact on Carter's decision.[57] The outcry was also driven by the argument that the neutron bomb would kill people as opposed to property, thereby privileging the latter over the former. However, the strong opposition of allies and the worldwide outcry were the primary reasons for the cancellation.[58]

Arguments against developing the neutron bomb included: (1) that it was important not to blur the distinction—the firebreak, as it was called—between nuclear and conventional weapons; (2) that either because of its low yield or because of its "benign" kind of lethality, there would be a strong temptation to use this type of weapon where other kinds of nuclear weapons were otherwise not allowed; and (3) that the "use of neutron weapons would pave the way for nuclear escalation."[59] These arguments suggest that the fear of breaking the tradition of non-use underlay the opponents' views, and that Carter accepted it as a legitimate concern in canceling the plan to develop the new bomb.[60]

Despite the importance of moral considerations in his approach to international politics in the nuclear weapons area, Carter's legacy is a mixed one. In July 1980, he issued Presidential Directive PD-59, which called for U.S. forces, in the event of deterrence failure, to be "capable of fighting successfully so that the adversary would not achieve his war aims and would suffer costs that are unacceptable, or in any event greater than his gains, from having initiated an attack."[61] Moreover, the Carter Doctrine, promulgated in the aftermath of the Soviet invasion of Afghanistan in 1979, declared that "an attempt by an outside force to gain control of the Persian Gulf region will be regarded as an assault on the vital interests of the United States" and "will be repelled by any means necessary including military force."[62] This doctrine, if implemented verbatim, would not have precluded the use of nuclear weapons against Soviet troops or regional states which offered the Soviets military assistance.[63]

PD-59 "set as the center of U.S. policy a countervailing strategy, defined as a strategy that denies an enemy the possibility of winning a nuclear war," and the basis for denying such a victory was the U.S. capability to attack the political leadership's control of the Soviet Union and the Soviet military leadership's control of its military forces. Thus PD-59 directed the U.S. armed forces to prepare for fighting a prolonged but limited nuclear war, targeting what "the Soviet leadership values most—its military forces and its own ability to maintain control after a war starts."[64] According to one analyst, "in the four years of the Carter administration, options for nuclear war-fighting were set in policy more firmly than ever before. Carter's switch was popularly explained, at the time, as a product of his campaign to appease the hawkish right wing of the Senate so that its most influential members would vote to ratify the SALT II arms control treaty that he had negotiated with the Soviets."[65]

Despite the talk of nuclear war with the Soviets, in the context of policy vis-à-vis nonnuclear states, the administration made some positive steps toward a more formal non-use pledge. This was largely because of the activism of the administration in the nonproliferation arena. And in that context it made a qualified commitment to non-use of nuclear weapons against nonnuclear states. At a Special Session of the UN General Assembly on Disarmament in 1978, the administration pledged:

> The United States will not use nuclear weapons against any non-nuclear states party to the NPT or any comparable internationally binding commitment not to acquire nuclear explosive devices, except in the case of an attack on the United States, its territories or armed forces, or its allies, by such state allied to a nuclear weapon-state or associated with a nuclear weapon state in carrying out or sustaining the attack.[66]

The Carter administration had adopted nuclear nonproliferation, along with human rights, as one of its core global agenda items, but in the end had limited success in each area. Carter made serious efforts with countries such as India, which had exploded a nuclear bomb in 1974, to persuade them to sign on to the NPT. The Nonproliferation Act of 1978 was brought forward by the Carter administration, further tightening the U.S. nonproliferation policy. In general, his efforts had limited success, but during his presidency the tradition of non-use received limited legal status through the United States making a qualified negative security assurance toward nonnuclear states at the United Nations.

THE REAGAN ERA (1981–89)

Ronald Reagan became president in 1981, after defeating Jimmy Carter, with the avowed intention of dramatically increasing U.S. military spending and defeating the Soviet Union in the nuclear arms race. Nuclear weapons fitted well in the administration's newly bellicose strategy toward the Soviet bloc. The intellectual basis of the Reagan approach was enunciated by a group of conservative strategic analysts who believed in "peace through strength." The *Committee on Present Danger* (composed of hard-line strategists and officials such as Richard Pipes, William R. Van Cleave, General Daniel O. Graham, Thomas W. Wolfe, John Vogt, Foy Kohler, Paul Nitze, Seymour Weiss, Jasper Welch, and Paul Wolfowitz) had warned of a "window of vulnerability" in which the Soviets had amassed a massive nuclear advantage over the United States and could threaten a nuclear war. They questioned the official U.S. intelligence estimates by arguing that the Soviets were bent on developing an offensive nuclear capability and pursuing a war-fighting doctrine. In response to this projected threat, they proposed substantial increases in U.S. military spending, which President Reagan accepted as official policy. One of their proposals was that the United States should be prepared to fight and win a nuclear war with the Soviet Union.[67]

In its pursuit of strategic superiority over the Soviet Union, the administration launched a massive arms modernization program in addition to adopting a war-fighting counterforce strategy. The idea behind the buildup was that the Soviet Union would not be able to match U.S. capabilities and that it would give the United States political and diplomatic advantages, but more importantly the ability to fight and win a long nuclear war.[68] The Reagan-era buildup of nuclear weaponry included ten-warhead MX missiles, Trident II missiles, B-1B bombers carrying air-launched cruise missiles, stealth bombers, and ballistic-missile-defense systems that would undercut the Anti-Ballistic Missile (ABM) Treaty. Under Reagan, strategic long-range nuclear weapons in U.S. possession increased by twenty-five hundred warheads, although nonstrategic weapons declined by three thousand due to the retirement of older systems.[69]

The administration also launched a program to improve the rapid deployment capabilities of the United States in order to ensure that Washington could intervene in theaters in the developing world, which the Soviet Union was attempting to incorporate into its sphere of influence. Although the doctrinal change did not include direct nuclear use in such theaters, if the superpowers collided in nonnuclear state theaters, escalation to nuclear war was possible. However, the intensified U.S.-Soviet conflict in Afghanistan, Africa, and Latin America remained nonnuclear as the superpowers avoided direct confrontation while pursuing active proxy wars wordwide.[70] This arms race gave rise to the *Freeze Now* movement, which called for an end to U.S. buildup and for strategic arms negotiations with the Soviets. Reagan acceded to those calls in 1982 when his administration began negotiations on a Strategic Arms Reduction Treaty (START).[71] The 1987 Intermediate-Range Nuclear Forces

Treaty (INF) with Soviet leader Mikhail Gorbachev was a major capstone in Reagan's success in the nuclear arms control area.

The Reagan administration is notable for launching the Strategic Defense Initiative (SDI), popularly known as "Star Wars." In his speech on March 23, 1983, Reagan called upon U.S. nuclear scientists "to turn their great talents now to the cause of mankind and world peace, to give us the means of rendering these nuclear weapons impotent and obsolete."[72] The multilayered system was expected to protect the United States against incoming Soviet missiles at different stages—the launch phase, passage through the atmosphere, flight outside the atmosphere, and the terminal phase. Other than the technical difficulties of attaining a foolproof system, it has been argued that the deployment of SDI "would increase Soviet fears that the United States was preparing for a preventive war or for the unfettered use of nuclear coercion. These fears might lead the Soviet Union to launch its own preemptive strike."[73] It is possible that SDI, if successfully developed, would have resulted in the destruction of U.S.-Soviet strategic stability built around MAD.

The tradition of non-use was reinforced in the 1980s when, in the face of the Reagan administration's talk of limited nuclear war, an international front emerged forcing the administration officials to withdraw their war-fighting doctrines. *Freeze Now* and the worldwide protests against nuclear tests helped to reinforce further the perception that nuclear weapons were different from conventional weapons and that no state could use them casually in anger or retribution.[74] The public was also deeply opposed to Reagan administration efforts to revive civil defense, showing that public opinion rejected the idea of nuclear use. The antinuclear front was galvanized by the leak of the Pentagon's May 1982 Draft Defense Planning Guidance on fighting a long nuclear war with the Soviet Union. It stated that "should deterrence fail and strategic nuclear war with the USSR occur, the United States must prevail and be able to force the Soviet Union to seek earliest termination of the hostilities on terms favorable to the United States."[75] The plan was partially the basis of the administration's stress on the modernization of strategic weapons as opposed to initiating major quantitative increases in the U.S. nuclear arsenal.

President Reagan offers a good example of how competing moral, political, and reputational considerations came into play in making hard national security decisions. Despite his hard-nosed approach toward the Soviet Union, Reagan apparently was appalled by the horrendous aftereffects of a nuclear war. Some suggest that after getting a briefing on how he should be ordering the use of nuclear weapons, Reagan became very worried and began to talk about nuclear abolition.[76] In fact, at the Reykjavik summit with Gorbachev in October 1986, President Reagan abruptly proposed a treaty to abolish nuclear weapons.[77] This generated considerable anxiety among his advisors, who attempted to persuade him to abandon the proposal. Reagan also seemed to have genuinely believed that SDI would make nuclear abolition possible. This pro-SDI position would kill any chances of nuclear abolition, however, as Gorbachev refused to abandon his opposition to the SDI.[78]

The end of the Cold War in 1991 inaugurated a brief period of enthusiasm for nuclear disarmament and even nuclear abolition. Gorbachev's far-reaching arms control initiatives as well as successes in nonproliferation—for example, the rolling back of the South African nuclear capability—all gave support to the tradition of non-use. However, rising concerns about Iraq's attempts at nuclear acquisition and its invasion of Kuwait changed the discourse on nuclear weapons. The 1991 Gulf War offered an opportunity to test the vitality and robustness of the tradition in a changed global strategic environment.

THE BUSH (SENIOR) PERIOD (1989–93)

The presidency of George H. W. Bush witnessed the fall of the Berlin Wall, the dismantling of the Warsaw Pact alliance, the end of the Cold War, and the collapse of the Soviet Union as a state. Along with Gorbachev, President Bush pursued far-reaching arms control initiatives such as the first Strategic Arms Reduction Treaty (START I) and the removal of tactical nuclear weapons worldwide. The September 1991 Bush arms control proposals included the elimination of 2,150 land-based tactical weapons in Lance missiles and nuclear artillery; the withdrawal of 700 air-based and 2,175 sea-based tactical missiles and 360 submarine-launched cruise missiles (SLCMs); the elimination of all strategic bombers, 450 minuteman II missiles, and 1,600 Poseidon C3 submarine-launched ballistic missile (SLBM) warheads; and the cancellation of the Rail-Mobile MX and Road-Mobile Midgetman.[79] The reduction of tactical nuclear forces, in particular, has had major implications for the tradition of non-use, as these are weapons that could be used in theaters of conflict against nonnuclear states if ever such an option was considered.

The Bush presidency saw a major opportunity to test the robustness of the nuclear non-use tradition. This occurred during the Persian Gulf War against Iraq, waged by the United States and its coalition partners to eject Iraq from Kuwait in 1990–91. The President and his officials warned Iraqi leader Saddam Hussein not to carry out "unconscionable acts" like "the use of chemical or biological weapons," and deliberately made ambiguous threats of retaliation. On the eve of the war, in a letter sent to Hussein through Secretary of State James Baker via Saddam's Foreign Minister Tariq Aziz, President Bush warned that the "American people would demand the strongest possible response. You and your country will pay a terrible price if you order unconscionable acts of this sort."[80] According to Baker, although Bush did not state that the "unconscionable act" would produce an American nuclear attack, he "used words that were clearly designed not to exclude the possibility" of nuclear use.[81]

The president avoided directly answering the question whether the United States would retaliate with nuclear weapons if Iraq used chemical weapons, at a press conference on February 5, 1991. He stated: "I think it's better never to say what option you may be considering," since he wanted the Iraqi leader to "think very carefully" about launching a chemical attack and since the United States "would like to have every possible chance that he decides not to do this."[82]

Despite the contradictory messages the administration sent out to Baghdad, "before the start of the war, President Bush privately ruled out the use of nuclear weapons even if Iraq used chemical weapons (although this decision was never communicated to the Defense Department or the military leaders planning the war). Baker called this policy of secretly planning not to use nuclear weapons, yet publicly threatening just the opposite, "calculated ambiguity."[83] At a meeting with his advisers at Camp David in December 1990, Bush had decided that the United States would not retaliate with nuclear weapons in the event of a chemical or biological attack, but it would go after the regime.[84] The threat of regime removal was viewed as more of an effective deterrent than nuclear retaliation, although U.S. officials outwardly kept open the possibility of nuclear retaliation in order to gain deterrent value from a policy of "calculated ambiguity."

With respect to the tradition of non-use, the interesting dimension here is that no formal guidelines on the presidential decision were ever given to the Pentagon with respect to the use or non-use of nuclear weapons. Although postwar statements by then-Secretary of Defense Dick Cheney and General H. Norman Schwarzkopf suggest that they would have considered using nuclear weapons in response to an Iraqi chemical attack, their behavior during the war suggested that nuclear weapons would not have been used even in response to chemical weapons attack. Then-JCS Chairman General Colin Powell declares that he asked to destroy JCS nuclear strike analysis, and Schwarzkopf has said he would never have recommended a nuclear strike, contradicting his own previous statement on the issue.[85] On nuclear use, President Bush himself stated in a postwar interview: "I will stay with that view, that it would be extremely difficult. I suppose you could conjure up some horrible scenario that would call for the use of battlefield tactical nuclear weapons or something, but it was not something we really contemplated at all."[86]

Following the war, in response to Iraq's clandestine nuclear program, Cheney issued a top-secret "Nuclear Weapons Employment Policy," which detailed the use of nuclear weapons against proliferators. "In response, the United States Strategic Command (STRATCOM) began developing targeting scenarios for military strikes against command and control facilities and nuclear, chemical, and biological weapons facilities in 'rogue nations' (including Iran, Iraq, Libya, and North Korea)."[87]

The Gulf War, according to some, helped to preserve the tradition of non-use. More than that, the tradition itself appeared to have influenced the choices of top U.S. decision makers, as they were reluctant to break it, fearing adverse consequences. To McGeorge Bundy, "the Gulf War has in fact reinforced that tradition, and in ways more remarkable than the simple fact that no nuclear weapon was exploded."[88] To Bundy, it was very unlikely that President Bush would have ordered a nuclear attack in response to a gas attack by Saddam Hussein, and his motive in the war appeared to be to "help moderate the behavior" of Saddam Hussein.[89] This unwillingness to consider the nuclear option, unlike in Korea and Vietnam, suggests, on the one hand the deepening of the tradition of non-use. On the other hand, the policy of "calculated ambiguity" and the public hinting of a response that might include nuclear weapons in retaliation to chemical and biological attacks suggest a weakening of the tradition (at least rhetorically) in the changed international security context. During Gulf War I, there was an increasing willingness on the part of U.S. leaders to use the nuclear threat (a threat they were not willing to follow through) with the intent of deterring chemical and biological weapon use by a weaker opponent.[90]

An argument against the use of nuclear weapons made by Newt Gingrich, then-Republican whip in the U.S. House of Representatives, is useful for understanding the role of the tradition in the calculations of U.S. decision makers. Fellow Republican Dan Burton of Indiana had argued that "if the alternative was bloody ground warfare, tactical nuclear weapons should be used to save American lives." Gingrich responded that "if the United States should establish a pattern out there that it is legitimate to use those kinds of weapons, our children and grandchildren are going to rue the day." On a more immediate note he added: "we would not want to live in a world in which we had sent a signal to every country on the planet to get nuclear weapons as fast as we can."[91] Gingrich, although not a direct decision maker with respect to the war, was echoing a widely held belief that the United States should not establish a bad precedent. He did not want to legitimize the use of nuclear weapons for the sake of the next generation, and he did not want to encourage nuclear proliferation as a result of U.S. policy.

The fact that President Bush decided against nuclear use early on suggests the power of the tradition on his calculations. He was cognizant that the U.S.-led coalition was waging a war against Saddam Hussein's regime and that he did not want to alienate the Iraqi people completely. In addition, this was a war waged with UN approval and the support of many Arab nations and any disproportionate use of force, especially nuclear weapons, on innocent Iraqis would have thrown away the international legitimacy that the United States wanted to maintain in the war.

THE CLINTON ERA (1993–2001)

The Bill Clinton presidency was notable for renewed U.S. efforts at nonproliferation. Most elements of the Bush approach with regard to the extension of the potential use of nuclear weapons against chemical and biological weapons use were accepted, with some concrete additions. Since July 1993, the Clinton administration openly suggested that the United States would use force to prevent "rogue states" from developing nuclear, biological, and chemical (NBC) weapons, and it launched the Counterproliferation Initiative in 1994 in support of this aim. The administration's plans also included the development of a theater missile defense system to protect the United States and its allies from weapons of mass destruction (WMD) attacks by regional states.[92]

The 1994 Nuclear Posture Review (NPR) confirmed the targeting policy vis-à-vis potential proliferators developed by the Bush administration. The United States has, since then, expanded the target list for nuclear use to include developing countries possessing or seeking WMD. In February 1996, the United States adopted the Doctrine for Joint Theater Nuclear Operations, "which 'translated' overall doctrine for use in regional scenarios in Europe, the Middle East, and the Korean peninsula. Third World proliferation dangers had been transformed to 'the preeminent threat.' The targets of deterrence were to be short-, medium-, and intermediate-range missiles capable of carrying nuclear, biological, or chemical warheads."[93] This JCS doctrine also allowed the United States to use nuclear weapons against terrorist groups such as al-Qaeda if they possess WMD capabilities. Furthermore, regional and local U.S. commanders do not necessarily have to wait to be attacked with NBC weapons before retaliating. Rather they are told that both active and passive defense measures should be taken against this possibility, "which may include nuclear first strike."[94]

The administration enlarged the Bush policy of "calculated ambiguity," to include preventive attacks against nonnuclear enemies. During his Senate testimony, on March 28, 1996, Defense Secretary William Perry declared that "as we stated during the Gulf War, if any country were foolish enough to use chemical weapons against the United States, the response would be absolutely overwhelming and devastating."[95] Perry once again stated (in response to the possibility of a chemical attack by Libya), "if some nation were to attack the United States with chemical weapons, then they would have to fear the consequences of a response from any weapon in our inventory . . . We could make a devastating response without the use of nuclear weapons, but we would not forswear the possibility."[96]

The Clinton administration was also sympathetic to developing earth-penetrating nuclear weapons and mini-nukes. For instance, the administration's budget for the 1994 fiscal year included funding for research and development of weapons such as the High Power Radio Frequency Warhead, the Precision Low Yield Warhead, the Cruise Missile Warhead, and the B-61 Diameter Bomb, all purported to be used against WMD targets in the so-called "rogue states."[97]

However, in the larger nuclear policy, the administration initiated some changes. The major change was Presidential Decision Directive (PDD) 60 in November 1997, which reversed the Reagan-era U.S. policy to fight and win a protracted nuclear war. The framework also made a change to the procedures for launch-on-warning, although Bush's expansion of nuclear use against chemical and biological weapons use was maintained. According to administration officials, the United States reserved the right to the first use of nuclear weapons against a state which is "not in good standing under the Nonproliferation Treaty or an equivalent International Convention," and "if a state attacks the United States, its allies or its forces 'in alliance' with a nuclear capable state."[98] This document also contained "language that would permit US nuclear strikes after enemy attacks using chemical or biological weapons."[99] Perry's successor, William Cohen, also reaffirmed the administration's policy in 1998 when he stated that keeping the nuclear first-use option open would serve to deter, as it would keep "any potential adversary who might use chemical or biological [weapons] unsure of what our response would be."[100]

North Korea's nuclear program became a key anti-proliferation issue during the Clinton era. In 1994, Clinton's military advisors and political leaders from both parties proposed a preventive strike on North Korean nuclear facilities. It is not clear that the attack ever was supposed to include a nuclear component, but it is possible that if the war escalated to North Korean attacks on South Korea and Japan, by treaty commitments, the United States would have had to come to the defense of those allied states, a posture which included nuclear retaliation as well. According to one analyst, by the time the Clinton era arrived, the norm against preventive war had virtually been marginalized by an "anti-proliferation imperative," as the "administration explicitly considered the preventive attack option to destroy North Korea's nuclear infrastructure without the slightest hint of normative hesitation. The most outspoken members of Congress and opinion leaders, those who dominated the public discussion of North Korea's nuclear program in 1993 and 1994, urged the administration to take a tougher line, including the use of preventive military force."[101]

In the summer of 1993, the administration's approach included "graduated coercive diplomacy, using sanction and military deployment to pressure Pyongyang," which included air strikes and covert operations. The Pentagon opposed those measures because of the difficulties of destroying deeply buried facilities and the likely high casualties during the first 90 days of war—in the range of 300,000 to 500,000, especially given the forward deployment of North Korean forces near the demilitarized zone and their artillery reach to Seoul.[102] Two meetings in May and June involving the president and top civilian and military advisors discussed the Osiraq option, referring to the preventive strike by Israel of Iraq's Osiraq reactor in 1981, but concluded that while an attack could delay the North Korean program, it would not stop it. More importantly, they assessed the possible North Korean military response on South Korea and the conflict's impact in terms of high casualties and economic devastation and concluded then to proceed with sanctions with the support of other countries. The crisis ended in 1994 following diplomatic intervention by Jimmy Carter, who brokered an agreement called the Agreed Framework, under which North Korea concurred to freeze its nuclear activities in return for food and energy aid.[103] Defense Secretary William Perry told an interviewer on the question of nuclear weapons use against North Korea, "I can't envision the circumstances in which the use of nuclear weapons would be a reasonable or prudent military action."[104]

During its tenure, the Clinton administration focused intensely on the question of nuclear nonproliferation and counterproliferation. It was active in extending the NPT in perpetuity in 1995 and in the conclusion of the Comprehensive Test Ban Treaty in 1996, although the latter has yet to receive the mandated number of adherents or ratification by the U.S. Senate. In 1995, prior to the indefinite extension of the NPT, the administration renewed this U.S. commitment by declaring:

> The United States reaffirms that it will not use nuclear weapons against non-nuclear weapon States Parties to the Treaty on the Non-Proliferation of Nuclear Weapons except in the case of an invasion or any other attack on the United States, its territories, its armed forces or other troops, its allies, or on a State towards which it has a security commitment, carried out or sustained by such a non-nuclear weapon state in association or alliance with a nuclear-weapon state."[105]

The UN Security Council in 1995 acknowledged this and similar commitments by the United States and other nuclear weapons states and incorporated them in the final document relating to the permanent extension of the NPT. In addition, the United States had also signed and ratified the non-use clause in the Africa Nuclear-Free Zone (Pelindaba) Treaty, and had given a similar bilateral assurance to Ukraine in 1994 in order for Kiev to abandon its nuclear weapons. However, despite these pledges, U.S. officials had "enunciated purposefully ambiguous qualifications" in response to specific perceived threats from chemical and biological weapons of regional states, and repeatedly state that Washington's pledge is political and not legal.[106]

The Clinton legacy in terms of the tradition of non-use is a mixed one. The Clinton era witnessed efforts by the United States to transcend the tradition in U.S. official policy even while making some serious efforts in the area of nonproliferation. The efforts at developing "useable" nuclear weapons, the decision to enlarge nuclear response in order to deter chemical and biological weapons use, and the enunciation of "calculated ambiguity" as part of official policy, all affected the way nuclear weapons were perceived, as against the previous four decades. None of this means that the tradition was violated, as the administration did not engage in intense military conflicts, although it threatened and engaged in limited crisis behavior that could have resulted in nuclear use with regional adversaries possessing WMD. But the policy expansion regarding the use of nuclear weapons against nonnuclear states is a significant aberration to the tradition of non-use and perhaps its continued robustness.

President Clinton's departure from office was followed by the arrival of the George W. Bush administration, which included proponents of the potential use of nuclear weapons against states and non-state actors possessing or attempting to acquire NBC weapons. In Chapter 9, I continue the discussion on the nuclear use policies of the Bush (Junior) administration, especially since the September 11 terrorist attacks.

CONCLUSION

The presidents under consideration in this chapter—especially Kennedy, Johnson, Carter, and Reagan—engaged in massive nuclear arms buildups in their quest to achieve superiority over the Soviet bloc. Three presidents, Kennedy, Johnson, and Nixon, considered the use of nuclear weapons against nonnuclear states during periods of crises and wars. The historical survey presented in this chapter suggests that the tradition was maintained over the years under different administrations, despite impulses toward breaking it. Evidence presented here strongly supports the contention that reputational considerations were the primary factor for the entrenchment of the tradition in the U.S. case. Each time a president or his advisors thought about using nuclear weapons, they were discouraged by these considerations. While Johnson was concerned about both internal and external reputations, Nixon was more worried about domestic reputation costs. The Nixon administration attempted to ignore the reputational considerations but was in the end hamstrung by fears of adverse domestic repercussions.

The Kennedy and Johnson administrations were constrained by reputational and strategic considerations in their decisions not to pursue preventive war with a nonnuclear China. Nixon was eager to follow Eisenhower's brinkmanship policies, especially in Vietnam and the Middle East, but could not carry it further. Carter was morally constrained, as evident in his abandonment of the neutron bomb, although the peace movements also had an impact on his policies. During Carter's tenure, a formal commitment on negative assurances was made, which added a quasi-legal dimension to the tradition of non-use, although U.S. officials insist that it was a "political" and not a "legal" commitment. Reagan had no occasion to threaten a nonnuclear state with nuclear weapons. Bush had such an opportunity in the 1991 Persian Gulf War, when the United States began to subtly change its nuclear deterrence policy to include retaliation against chemical and biological attacks. The administration used ambiguous nuclear threats to prevent Saddam Hussein from using WMD, especially chemical and biological weapons. But the fact that nuclear use was discounted before the war started suggests the vitality of the tradition in the United States. The Clinton era saw the restatement of the negative security assurances to nonnuclear states. However, the official change to include chemical and biological weapons use and development as possible reason for the United States using nuclear weapons has perhaps weakened the foundations of the tradition. The "calculated ambiguity" policy which began under Bush (Senior) was enlarged by the Clinton administration, and would further become part of the Bush (Junior) administration's preemptive and preventive doctrines (see Chapter 9).

One important conclusion that emerges from this historical assessment is the high propensity of some U.S. presidents to raise the threat of nuclear use against nonnuclear adversaries, in some cases states aligned with the Soviet Union or China. Unlike the claims of previous studies that portray the United States as the lead originator and supporter of the tradition, it seems that Washington considered nuclear use or threat of use on many occasions. Desperate military situations, as in Korea and Vietnam, and relative inferiority in conventional troop levels, plausibly compelled U.S. presidents to seek quick fixes involving nuclear use, but the threats were never executed. Part of the explanation for this dual nature of American policy lies in the competing reputational concerns that its defense and foreign policies sought to address; on the one hand, U.S. administrations wanted to retain high levels of credibility for deterrence and compellence purposes, but on the other hand, they were constrained by fear of high reputational costs in the event of nuclear use and by the apprehension that the disproportionate effects for nuclear use nullified any particular tactical gains nuclear use would have produced.

5 RUSSIA, BRITAIN, FRANCE, CHINA, AND THE TRADITION

WHILE THE UNITED STATES IS THE PIVOTAL CASE in examining the tradition of non-use, a brief survey of the nuclear policies of the other four core nuclear weapon states (Russia, Britain, France, and China) is important in order to understand whether they have contributed to the rise and observance of the tradition of non-use. It is vital also to explore whether these other major nuclear powers have been affected by the tradition with respect to the potential use of nuclear weapons against nonnuclear states. This chapter seeks to answer the following additional questions: How have these other declared nuclear weapons states perceived the utility of nuclear weapons vis-à-vis nonnuclear states, especially in the crises/wars in which they have been involved? How have their evolving positions on nuclear first use affected the tradition of non-use? The discussion here is amplified in Chapter 7's examination of some of the key wars that these states have fought with their nonnuclear rivals.

THE SOVIET UNION/RUSSIA

The Soviet Union's contribution to the tradition is not well understood because of the dearth of released archival materials. The actual behavior of the Soviet Union during its crises and wars involving nonnuclear states indicates that Moscow rarely—if at all—brandished its nuclear weapons against nonnuclear states. This apparent restraint suggests that the Soviet Union and its successor, Russia, have clearly observed the tradition of non-use and have played a crucial role in the emergence and sustenance of the tradition over half a century.[1] However, in the post–Cold War era, due to the decline of its conventional capabilities, Russia has been increasingly relying on nuclear weapons for its security and has revised its no-first-use policy. This means that under some extreme circumstances, the tradition of non-use may be broken by Russia in a future crisis involving nonnuclear states.

In general, the Soviet policy toward nuclear weapons was motivated by a combination of strategic and reputational considerations. Strategically, the Soviet Union was concerned that the United States would consolidate and expand its early advantage in nuclear arms. The Soviet Union was a proponent of international control of nuclear weapons, as well as of an international ban on nuclear use against nuclear and nonnuclear states anywhere in the world.[2] The measures it advanced during the late 1940s were aimed at causing the United States to abandon its nuclear capability. Later, it also supported a ban on nuclear testing, and proposals for the setting up of nuclear-free zones in different parts of the world, such as the Rapacki Plan of 1957, introduced by Poland to denuclearize Central Europe, involving East and West Germany, Poland, and Czechoslovakia.[3] These nonproliferation proposals were specifically intended to prevent Germany from acquiring nuclear weapons. With regard to reputation, Soviet proposals were also aimed at gaining an upper hand in the propaganda war with the United States during the Cold War.[4] The chief concern of Moscow was with gaining support among the nonnuclear states of the developing world. In addition, the record indicates the importance of norm entrepreneurs in the development of reputation concerns for the Soviet Union. The World Peace Council received strong backing from the Soviet Union, and Moscow vigorously supported meetings of the Pugwash movement. Soviet leaders such as Nikita Khrushchev "sent repeated, fulsome messages to these gatherings."[5] The peace movements seem also to have influenced Soviet positions partially on nuclear disarmament issues. This influence was most clearly manifest during the Khrushchev and Mikhail Gorbachev eras. Possible ulterior motives that the Soviet Union held do not detract from the contribution that it made to the tradition of non-use and its emergence as an informal norm. Throughout the Cold War, Moscow did not use or threaten to use nuclear weapons against nonnuclear states and its propaganda position—though aimed at securing a strategic advantage—had, it seems, the result of constraining policy in a significant way.

Stalin: Responses to the U.S. Nuclear Monopoly and the Beginning of the Cold War

The Soviets began the post–World War II era as a disadvantaged power in the nuclear arena. Their response to this imbalance was to seek, in international organizations, to limit the U.S. upper hand, while continuing to rely on its advantage in conventional forces in military planning, as it simultaneously developed its own nuclear capability. In June 1946, in response to the U.S.-initiated Baruch Plan, which had envisioned international control of the atom, the Soviet Union proposed to the United Nations a draft international Convention on the Prohibition of the Production and Use of Nuclear Weapons Under All Circumstances, and the destruction—within a three-month period of the date on which the convention went into effect—of all stockpiles of complete and incomplete atomic weapons. This Plan, proposed by Soviet representative Andrei Gromyko, also contained a provision that within six months of its conclusion, "the signatory states were to enact legislation providing for punishment of any breach of the Convention," premised on the 1925 Geneva Convention against the use of chemical weapons. However, the Soviet proposal relied on national governments to enforce the agreement and lacked international inspection and control provisions.[6] The Soviets wanted the United States to get rid of its weapons while the United States desired to preserve its monopoly until the Russians gave up their plans to acquire nuclear weapons. Other Soviet proposals in this area during the 1940s and 1950s included the creation of the UN Atomic Energy Commission in June 1947; a proposal to the UN General Assembly in September 1948 to ban the production and utilization of atomic energy for military purposes and reduce by one-third the armed forces of the Permanent Five members of the UN Security Council (P-5); a draft declaration submitted to the U.S. Secretary of State in January 1954, urging the P-5 nations to pledge unconditionally not to use atomic, hydrogen, or other kinds of weapons of mass destruction (WMD); and the September 1959 and March 1962 treaty proposals on general and complete disarmament submitted to the 18-Nation Geneva Disarmament Committee.[7] The 1954 draft declaration is perhaps one of the first formal contributions of the Soviet Union to the emergence of the tradition of non-use.

During the period of U.S. atomic monopoly, 1945–49, the Soviet Union played down the role of atomic weapons in its war plans. The Soviet leadership relied on bravado and its experience during World War II against Germany, when the Soviet forces could withdraw to their vast interior against the advancing German troops, who failed to defeat Russia despite massive air bombing by the Luftwaffe. The Soviet military claimed that its air defenses and Soviet counterattacks on U.S. air bases would limit any major U.S. nuclear assault. Although Soviet Premier Josef Stalin did not ignore the bomb, he believed that the impact of an American use of nuclear weapons could be nullified by effective ground forces and sea power. The presumed Soviet ability to conquer Western Europe conventionally was viewed as a strong deterrent against the United States resorting to nuclear attack. The loss of Europe would also deprive the United States of the staging ground for airbases for the B-29, its chief delivery system for nuclear weapons.[8]

According to David Holloway, there is no evidence that Soviet behavior in Europe or the Middle East (e.g., Iran in 1946) was influenced by the U.S. monopoly on nuclear weapons. The Soviet policy on nuclear weapons under Stalin "was guided by two principles: the concept of the war of nerves, and the idea of limits." According to the first, the Soviets anticipated that the United States would attempt to intimidate Moscow with nuclear threats; the Soviet response would be to appear not frightened, and to raise international tensions occasionally. The concept of "limits" was a policy approach that meant no escalation or major war with the West, despite increased tensions with their erstwhile allies.[9] Stalin tested these propositions during the 1948 Berlin Blockade, when the United States could not derive much advantage from its atomic monopoly.[10]

Soviet testing of the atomic bomb in 1949 altered Moscow's approach toward nuclear weapons. In 1951, Stalin declared that nuclear weapons were acquired only to deter an American nuclear attack, and not to deter conventional strikes.[11] Although the Soviets accepted deterrence as the basis for its nuclear relationship with the West early on, a belief that nuclear war with the West could be fought and won was also part of Soviet strategic thinking in the 1950s and 1960s. The Soviet regime kept on asserting the notion that "it must continue to believe in survival and victory of some form" in the event of a nuclear war with the United States.[12] However, by the 1970s, deterrence, based on retaliatory strikes, was acknowledged as the basis for Soviet security, and by the end of 1980s, second-strike threats were accepted as the foundation of Soviet nuclear strategy, suggesting that a war-fighting strategy was abandoned.[13]

Khrushchev: Confrontation and Coexistence

Stalin's immediate successor, Premier Georgii Malenkov, believed that "nuclear war would likely mean the death of civilization" and hence "war was not inevitable." He was also "unwilling to invest heavily in nuclear weapons."[14] In February 1955, Malenkov was replaced by Nikita Khrushchev, whose nuclear policy, like his general approach toward the West, was complicated. Khrushchev could be confrontational, as part of a general "anti-imperialist" policy, while at the same time advocating *peaceful coexistence*. On nuclear policy, he attempted to control nuclear proliferation, while at the same time presiding over an enormous increase in the Soviet arsenal, and engaged in preparing for a winnable nuclear war.

After presenting Malenkov's antinuclear approach as a reason for his ouster, the new leader engaged in an active foreign policy, vigorously backing liberation wars against colonial rule through economic, political, and, in some instances, military support to newly emerging states. However, nuclear weapons had no role to play in this process, "except to serve as symbols of Soviet prestige and scientific ability."[15] Khrushchev was aware of the dangers of nuclear war as he initiated a policy of peaceful coexistence with the West. Paradoxically, he was also instrumental in the massive expansion of Soviet intercontinental ballistic missile (ICBM) forces, which generated prospects for "preemption by surprise" and increased the conflict with the West.[16] His goal was to "use the nuclear stalemate to undermine NATO [North Atlantic Treaty Organization], make the United States acknowledge the USSR as an equal power, and facilitate the dismantling of 'imperialism' in the Third World."[17]

Despite his bellicose rhetoric and efforts at raising the level of nuclear confrontation with the West, Khrushchev was perhaps more antinuclear than is generally understood. In 1953, upon his assumption of the position of the General Secretary of the Communist Party, Khrushchev received his first briefing on nuclear weapons. According to Khrushchev, when he learned all the facts about nuclear weapons, he could not sleep for several days. He states: "Then I became convinced that we could never possibly use these weapons, and when I realized that I was able to sleep again. But all the same we must be prepared. Our understanding is not sufficient answer to the arrogance of the imperialists."[18]

Khrushchev's policy of peaceful coexistence with the West, his offer of a moratorium on atmospheric tests in 1958, and his unwillingness to hand over a prototype nuclear bomb to China, were all partially motivated by his desire to avoid a nuclear war and develop a "cooperative-conflictual" relationship with the West. The idea behind this policy was to conduct competition with the West in the areas of ideology and economic affairs, in which he believed the Soviet Union would emerge as the victor.[19] Khrushchev believed that "fear of nuclear war in a country's leader can paralyze that country's defenses," making war inevitable; hence, while pursuing efforts to avoid war, the nation should not reveal that it is "frightened of it."[20]

The peaceful coexistence policy was opposed by Communist party stalwart Vyacheslav Molotov and his supporters, but Khrushchev emerged victorious in inner-party conflict. This policy, and his opposition to China's developing nuclear weapons, also led to a gradual estrangement with Mao and to the onset of Sino-Soviet rivalry. Khrushchev was concerned that once "irresponsible powers" (e.g., West Germany and China) acquired nuclear capability, they "might use nuclear weapons to trigger a U.S.-Soviet war."[21] The Soviet proposal for a test ban was thus motivated by the desire to arrest nuclear proliferation to additional countries such as Germany and China.[22] Khrushchev's policy on nonproliferation led to bitter conflict with China, as Beijing did not share concerns about the spread of the bomb to additional countries, or the "enemy-partner" image of the United States held by the Soviet Union.[23] In June 1959, the USSR unilaterally abrogated an agreement that it had signed in October 1957 to transfer nuclear technology and materials to China. This occurred in the aftermath of the Chinese efforts to acquire Quemoy and Matsu from Taiwan, when Moscow feared that it would be dragged into a conflict between China and the United States. This event was a crucial watershed for both the Sino-Soviet split and the Soviet Union's evolving position on nuclear nonproliferation.[24]

The Berlin Crisis of 1961 was an intense interchange which saw the erection of a wall dividing East and West Berlin. The Soviet perception of events was that under Kennedy, the United States raised the threat of nuclear attack, but Khrushchev stood his ground.[25] The 1962 Cuban Missile Crisis, which was prompted by Khrushchev's policy of deploying medium- and intermediate-range nuclear missiles in Cuba, influenced Soviet perceptions on nuclear brinkmanship. Although the stated goal for the deployment was to protect the island from the United States, and to force Washington to withdraw Jupiter missiles from Turkey, it has been argued that Khrushchev was concerned about a closer Cuba-China relationship.[26] The escalation of the crisis, especially the U.S. decision to quarantine Soviet vessels, forced Khrushchev to concede, as he began to realize the possibility of a nuclear war and the limits of his own brinkmanship policies.[27] Soviet inferiority in nuclear capability was revealed in the crisis, and henceforth the policy shifted to achieving strategic parity, and later superiority, driven by a "never again" determination on the part of the Soviet military to avoid humiliation. While the political leadership was thinking of war avoidance, the military was planning to fight preemptively and win a nuclear war, in case the West unleashed one.[28] New data suggest that starting in the early 1960s, the Soviets and their Warsaw pact allies, after realizing strategic inferiority, had a plan to initiate a nuclear first strike deep into Western Europe in order to preempt a Western nuclear strike so that the Pact could "fight" and "win" a nuclear war.[29]

Brezhnev: From Détente to the Second Cold War

The regime of Khrushchev's successor, Leonid Brezhnev, was an active participant in the Nuclear Nonproliferation Treaty (NPT) negotiations as Moscow accepted arms control as a major part of its post–Cuban Missile Crisis diplomatic approach towards the West. In order to make the NPT acceptable to nonnuclear states, in 1966 the Soviet Union proposed to conclude a no-first-use convention at the United Nations. Prime Minister Alexei Kosygin proposed a ban on nuclear attacks on states that did not deploy nuclear weapons on their territory. This was a move aimed at mollifying the concerns of the nonnuclear states, but also partially intended to prompt West Germany to abandon NATO nuclear weapons deployed on its territory. The United States and its Western allies rejected the plan.[30] The Soviet Union again proposed, in September 1967, a draft convention on the prohibition of the use of nuclear weapons. In September 1972, Foreign Minister Gromyko proposed permanent prohibition of the use of nuclear weapons, and in September 1980, Moscow presented a draft Resolution to the UN General Assembly, urging nuclear states to offer "guarantees to non-nuclear states against the use or threat of use of nuclear weapons, [and] to make efforts for the speedy elaboration and conclusion of an international convention on this matter."[31]

In response to the persistent demands of the developing world, Moscow offered a more formal commitment not to be the first to use nuclear weapons. On June 16, 1982, while addressing a UN Special Session on disarmament, Brezhnev declared that the USSR "assume[d] an obligation not to be the first to use nuclear weapons." This commitment came into effect immediately, as "should a nuclear war start, it could mean the destruction of human civilization and perhaps the end of life itself on earth."[32] The Soviet armed forces were given orders to plan nuclear war only in response to a first strike by nuclear opponents, although some questioned the counterforce potential of the Soviet military. However, the pledge was made in the context of seeking to influence world public opinion, and in response especially to the NATO decision to deploy new missiles in Europe. Further, the geographic and strategic contiguity of Eastern Europe to its territory made a no-first-use policy strategically viable to the Soviet Union.[33] Geographic contiguity meant that it did not need to offer extended deterrence; instead "it could rely on direct conventional defense . . . While the U.S. first-use policy risks Soviet nuclear retaliation in the event of a European war, the Soviet Union can at least put the onus to escalate on U.S. decisionmakers by forswearing first use."[34]

The Soviet Union maintained its no-use policy during the Afghan War (1979–89), despite the major reverses its forces suffered and their eventual withdrawal without achieving any war objectives. Based on the information available, it is not clear whether the Soviet leaders ever contemplated using nuclear weapons against the Afghan resistance. Although tactical weapons might have been useful against some supply routes and possible chokepoints, it is unclear how such strikes would have contributed to the Soviet political aims in Afghanistan. Soviet occupation was not meant to decimate Afghanistan (although it had that result), but to establish a pro-Soviet regime there. This would have meant achieving some semblance of popular support for the Soviet-installed regime.

Tactical considerations might have also played a role in Moscow's desistence from considering nuclear use against the Afghan resistance. Given the nature of the terrain and the asymmetric war method employed by the resistance, the Soviets would have only achieved limited gains by the introduction of nuclear weapons in combat. The Mujahedin resistance to Soviet occupation was both urban and rural, and the war was prosecuted by loose networks, often based on norms of reciprocity in a tribal context, rather than by a trained, professional military with a central leadership.[35] The Afghan resistance pursued localized objectives, and "this made the resistance difficult to decapitate or coopt."[36] Thus, it is unlikely that the Soviets would have achieved anything more by using nuclear weapons. But tactical explanations may not fully capture the wider causes of Soviet non-use.

In a larger political/strategic perspective, the Afghan resistance was waging the war with the active participation of the United States and Pakistan, and any use of nuclear weapons would also have resulted in stronger U.S. countermeasures. The Soviet invasion ended the superpower détente and initiated the Second Cold War with the West. Soviet use of nuclear weaponry would have heightened the rivalry and intensified the East-West conflict. However, despite their reluctance to use nuclear weapons, the Soviets were reported to have used chemical weapons against the Afghan resistance. The U.S. State Department reported that between 1980 and 1982, there were thirty-six incidents of chemical weapon use by the Soviet Union, which resulted in over 3,000 deaths.[37] This, however, is not fully verified. What is anomalous is the fact that the nuclear-armed superpower gave up the conflict (which subsequently hastened its demise as a global power and considerably shrunk its territory) without threatening or even considering all the capabilities under its command, including nuclear weapons. The answer may lie partially in the nonnuclear reputation that the Soviets had assiduously built up in the developing world over four decades.

During the 1970s, Soviet strategic thinking very much revolved around the notion of *correlation of forces,* which was measured in terms of the ideological, political, economic, industrial, and military strength of the Soviet Union vis-à-vis the capitalist countries led by the United States. It had a larger ideological focus than pure balance of power as obtained strictly through military capabilities or countervailing alliance blocs. The Soviet assessment that the correlation of forces had shifted in its favor led to an active intervention policy in the Third World as adopted by Brezhnev in the 1970s, even alongside détente. This reading of the favorable correlation of forces gave incentives to the Soviets to consolidate the position of world socialism, supporting national liberation struggles and increasing camaraderie with the Socialist countries on the basis of the principle of nonintervention. This new assertiveness was very much evident in Soviet policy shifts in Angola, the Horn of Africa, South Yemen, and Afghanistan.[38] Soviet interventions to shore up the support of friendly regimes meant that Moscow placed enormous importance on reputation in the developing world vis-à-vis the United States and its Western allies. Any use or threat of use of nuclear weapons for these purposes would have dealt a severe blow to its reputation as a friend of the developing world and the Socialist countries.

In fact there seems to be no instance, including the Afghan case, in which the Soviets considered nuclear use against nonnuclear states. To Moscow, the Cold War was also a war of ideologies and over world public opinion. Although the Cold War competition was conducted most ferociously in the realm of arms buildup and external interventions, both superpowers, especially the Soviet Union, expended a considerable amount of resources to propagandize their pro-peace agendas and pro-developing world policies. The Soviet Union was a major cosponsor of peace initiatives along with developing countries at the UN and associated agencies, such as the Geneva Disarmament Forum. It co-sponsored the NPT and the London Suppliers Club, and eventually joined the Missile Technology Control Regime (MTCR) to arrest the spread of nuclear weapons and missiles to other countries. In that sense, the Soviet use or threat of nuclear weapons against a nonnuclear state would have adversely affected Moscow's reputation and image in the developing world. After expending so much on goodwill in the Third World, it was unlikely that the Soviet Union could have easily given up what it regarded as its moral high ground in the propaganda war with the West. Soviet prestige would have been dealt a severe blow had it used a nuclear weapon against a nonnuclear state. The Soviet example shows that states could become compliant with the normative views inherent in their propaganda and rhetoric, as violating them could cause considerable damage to their reputation, image, and global power position.

Gorbachev: Nuclear Perestroika

The arrival of Mikhail Gorbachev as Soviet Communist Party general secretary in March 1985 catapulted the Soviet approach toward nuclear arms to a larger significance in world politics. Gorbachev came to power with the intention of radically changing the Soviet position in the world. Preventing a nuclear war became a pivotal policy plank of the Gorbachev team.[39] His *Glasnost* (openness) and *Perestroika* (restructuring) policies were driven by the desire to prevent Soviet decline and find an accommodation with the West. Nuclear disarmament, based on "reasonable sufficiency," was crucial to Gorbachev's plans for rapprochement with the West and reduction in Soviet military spending. Gorbachev relentlessly pushed the idea of restructuring Soviet forces from an offensive to a defensive posture and was willing to make radical changes to the organization, doctrine, and training of the Soviet military establishment.[40] Gorbachev was heavily influenced by President Ronald Reagan's announcement, in March 1983, launching a strategic defense initiative (SDI) or Star Wars program, and by the Chernobyl accident of April 1986. Chernobyl, especially, had a tremendous influence on Gorbachev and his team, and they used the tragedy in Ukraine to question orthodoxy in Soviet nuclear beliefs.[41] At the Reykjavik summit in 1986, Gorbachev proposed, and Reagan accepted, the elimination of all nuclear weapons by 1996. However, Gorbachev's insistence that the United States abandon the SDI program evoked the total opposition of U.S. officials, which doomed the proposal. In any event, most U.S. officials were not supportive of the Reagan initiative. Gorbachev, his team, and many leading Soviet scientists were influenced by the nuclear protest movements such as *Freeze Now* that were engulfing Western Europe and other parts of the world in response to Reagan's nuclear buildup and the American decision to deploy new missiles in Western Europe.[42]

Gorbachev and his key advisors believed that nuclear war was the primary challenge to global security, and he was willing to make several unilateral disarmament proposals that changed the Western perception of the Soviet threat. Both the United States and the Soviet Union, during the 1991–92 period, took unilateral initiatives to reduce their tactical nuclear weapons. In October 1991, Gorbachev announced tactical nuclear weapons reductions, and in January 1992, his successor Boris Yeltsin confirmed these initiatives. When Gorbachev ended his term, several arms control treaties had been signed, such as the Intermediate-Range Nuclear Forces Treaty (INF) in 1987; the first Strategic Arms Reduction Treaty (START I) in 1991; the Conventional Armed Forces in Europe treaty (CFE); and the Ballistic Missile Notification Agreement in 1988.[43] At the global level, the end of the Cold War, the dissolution of the Warsaw Pact, and the breakup of the Soviet Union all reduced the nuclear threat tremendously. However, after the fall of the Soviet Union, Russia did not fully embrace the Gorbachev approach to nuclear arms, and began to count on these weapons for its security in the post–Cold War era. The Russian government, especially under Vladimir Putin, also failed to dismantle the tactical weapons that Russia had agreed to abolish under Gorbachev.

Post–Cold War Changes

The dismantling of the Warsaw Pact and the collapse of the Soviet Union compelled Russia to revisit its nuclear policy. The steady decline in Russia's conventional forces encouraged Russian military planners to assign new roles to nuclear weapons, such as deterrence against conventional attacks. Accordingly, a new draft military doctrine was adopted in November 1993, which proposed that "Russia could use nuclear weapons not only in response to a nuclear attack but also in case of a conventional attack against nuclear weapons or the early-warning system, which would be classified as a nuclear attack. No-first-use was seen as a policy that could be adopted in the future on a multilateral basis." In November 1993, the final version was adopted, which mentioned that nuclear weapons would not be used "against any state-party to the Nuclear Non-proliferation Treaty of 1968 that does not have nuclear weapons," but with these caveats: "nuclear weapons could be used against non-nuclear weapons states that were allies of a nuclear weapon state or acted together with a nuclear weapon state; in both cases, nuclear weapons could be used only in response to an attack against Russia, its armed forces, or its allies."[44] These changes brought Russia's nuclear doctrine somewhat closer to the doctrines of NATO and the United States. Despite these changes, in 1993,

Moscow made a formal non-use commitment to Ukraine, Belarus, and Kazakhstan as part of their denuclearization program.[45]

Russia increased the role of nuclear weapons for its security policy in its January 2000 *New National Security Concept* and April 2000 military doctrine. The military doctrine stated:

> The Russian Federation reserves the right to use nuclear weapons in response to the use of nuclear and other types of weapons of mass destruction against it and (or) its allies, as well as in response to large-scale aggression utilizing conventional weapons in situations critical to the national security of the Russian Federation. The Russian Federation will not use nuclear weapons against states party to the Nonproliferation Treaty that do not possess nuclear weapons except in the event of an attack on the Russian Federation, the Russian Federation armed forces or other troops, its allies, or a state to which it has security commitments that is carried out or supported by a state without nuclear weapons jointly or in the context of allied commitments with a state with nuclear weapons.[46]

These documents suggest that Russia could use nuclear weapons in retaliation against conventional, chemical, or biological attacks by smaller powers on its periphery. Russia thus sees nuclear weapons as usable not only in conflict with other major powers, but also "in conflicts on Russia's periphery" if the Russian leadership decided that it had no other option to counter a WMD attack involving chemical or biological weapons. "They might also be used to counter attacks by small-scale but capable conventional forces impacting targets that Russia considers to be of strategic importance."[47]

The 2000 Doctrine made a couple of crucial changes to the 1993 Doctrine. It permits Russia to use nuclear weapons "in response to the use of other weapons of mass destruction," such as chemical weapons (provision similar to the one adopted by the United States) and against any country or coalition—not necessarily one that includes a nuclear state—if the situation is critical to Russian national security.[48] The key events that led to the changes to the Russian military doctrine in the area of nuclear first use were NATO's military operations in Kosovo in 1999 against strident Russian opposition to an attack on its Serb allies, and the continued violence in Chechnya, the Muslim-dominated Russian republic attempting to break away from the Russian Federation.[49] The 2003 Defense White Paper assigned additional functions to nuclear weapons, "to prevent political pressure against Russia and her allies; to be able to de-escalate aggression; to be in a position to use certain components of the forces incrementally; and to demonstrate resolve by raising alert status, holding exercises and redeployments," all making it possible for Russia to wage a limited nuclear war.[50]

According to a critic of the Russian nuclear policy:

> Russia's persistent emphasis on nuclear deterrence limits Russia's maneuver in local and regional wars (in the spectrum from low-intensity operations to nuclear warfare). Limited or demonstrative use of nuclear weapons in armed conflict is unacceptable for the world public opinion. The threat or use of nuclear weapons, when there is no threat or use of such weapons against Russia, mean the breach of the limits of acceptable use of military force.[51]

The nuclear doctrine has also been criticized for the reasons that none of Russia's neighbors holds military assets capable of challenging Russia militarily without outside help; that "it would be senseless to use nuclear weapons against the territory and population, which Russia hypothetically might want to occupy"; and that "[i]n most cases if military conflict occurs Moscow may face only guerrilla-type warfare, for which nuclear force is neither required, nor effective."[52]

Russia has, however, denied any role for nuclear weapons in a preventive or preemptive strike against terrorists.[53] In response to the U.S. initiatives to develop bunker-buster mini-nukes, Russian generals expressed concerns that these were highly destabilizing weapons, but also suggested that Russia should develop them as well. Col. Gen. Yuri Baluyevsky, a senior Russian military official, described the U.S. plans as "very destabilizing" and "extremely scary," and said that "nuclear weapons, which have served as a political deterrent, are being transformed into a battlefield instrument." In his view, Russia should review its military strategy and hold on to its tactical nuclear weapons.[54] Russia has also shown interest in developing low-yield nuclear weapons. In February 2004, Viktor Mikhailov, a former Russian nuclear minister and, at the time, head of the Nuclear Research Institute, conceded that Russia was also conducting research on low-yield weapons, but it would take at least 10–15 years to create such a weapon. He also claimed Russia was ahead of the United States in the research.[55] More importantly, Russia has kept a large arsenal of nonstrategic weapons, including tactical nuclear weapons, despite its 1991–92 commitments to dismantle them.[56]

Russia's main security concern is with Western encroachment in its spheres of influence. The United States has expanded its military facilities into ex-Soviet republics, such as Kazakhstan and Tajikistan. Further, the March

2004 expansion of NATO to include the Baltic states (Estonia, Latvia, and Lithuania) and several Eastern European states (Bulgaria, Romania, Slovenia, and Slovakia) and the potential inclusion of Georgia and Ukraine in the Western alliance also worry Russian strategists. They fear that these states, in collusion with Western countries, could challenge Russian dominance of the region and endanger Russian security interests. However, unlike the United States, Russia's relations with countries in the Middle East, including Iran, are not adversarial, making it improbable that it would be in a position to violate the tradition of non-use of nuclear weapons. Further, none of the states in the Russian periphery has nuclear weapons, and all are conventionally inferior to Russia.[57] The major security challenge to Russia is posed by nonstate actors such as the Chechen insurgent groups, but nuclear weapons do not have much value in waging that type of asymmetric warfare. Thus the Russian policy change in the area of nuclear doctrine may have little practical application.

Soviet and Russian Contributions

The discussion suggests that the Soviet Union played a crucial role in the rise and persistence of the tradition of non-use of nuclear weapons by making many efforts to give it legal standing through its proposals on non-use and declaration of a no-first-use policy. The Soviet Union was also an active participant at world peace movements, which often carried anti-U.S. connotations, and this weakened Soviet ability to promote non-use ideas, because their motives were suspected in the West. Soviet actions vis-à-vis nonnuclear states during the Cold War suggest a respect for the tradition of non-use of nuclear weapons. The historical record indicates that the USSR was motivated primarily by reputational concerns, including its doctrine of the correlation of forces in the ongoing struggle with the West. Since the end of the Cold War, the successor state, Russia, has changed the official policy to include nuclear use against nonnuclear states. Even with this policy change, it is highly unlikely that Russia would confront a security challenge vis-à-vis nonnuclear states in the near term that can be met with nuclear weapons. Thus, the tradition might be more significant in Russia's foreign policy posture than acknowledged by Moscow's contemporary security planners.

BRITAIN

The attitudes of successive British governments toward the question of nuclear use present evidence that the tradition has had multiple sources for its origin and persistence. Britain decided to develop nuclear weapons on its own following the passage of the McMahon Act of 1946 by the U.S. Congress, which prohibited the sharing of nuclear materials and technology with any other state, including Britain—notwithstanding their wartime alliance. The British focus on nuclear weapons was aimed at obtaining a seat at the great power table. To many in the British political elite, "a nuclear capability seemed the perfect response to the problems facing Britain in the aftermath of the Second World War, namely an uncertain relationship with the United States, the threat of the Soviet Union, an unstable Empire, a shattered economy and a new strategic environment dominated by the bomb."[58] Subsequently, in response to Cold War competition with the Soviet Union, the United States changed its policy, and in January 1948, Anglo-American nuclear cooperation resumed.[59] Some of the British attitude toward nuclear use mirrored American policies. However, there was an active antinuclear movement in Britain, which, in a limited way, influenced the country's discourse on nuclear weapons and nuclear use.

The British antipathy toward nuclear use was most prominently evident in Prime Minister Clement Attlee's dash to Washington in December 1950 to urge President Harry Truman not to use nuclear weapons in Korea without prior consultation with countries involved in the UN force stationed in the peninsula. Truman, at a press conference on November 30, 1950, had declared that UN sanction was not necessary for him to authorize use of nuclear weapons in Korea. A communiqué was issued after the British-American meeting, on December 8, 1950, which read: "The President stated that it was his hope that world conditions would never call for the use of the atomic bomb. The President told the Prime Minister that it was also his desire to keep the Prime Minister at all times informed of developments which might bring about a change in the situation."[60] This did not imply that the U.S. president would obtain prior concurrence of Britain before a decision to use the bomb was made. Attlee expressed his reason for seeking such a commitment in his statement to the French prime minister that an attack on China might lead to an impression that "European and Americans have a low regard for the value of Asiatic lives."[61] He was also of the opinion that such weapons should be reserved only for times when "'desperate measures' were warranted—certainly not [in] conflicts in which the U.S. were confronted with a power like Korea."[62]

Despite Attlee's antipathy toward nuclear use, it appears that many British military planners:

regarded nuclear weapons as on a continuum with conventional weapons, albeit a much more powerful weapon. The armed forces were therefore taught to regard them as just another category of weapon. Public opinion, on the other hand, tended to perceive nuclear weapons as of a *qualitatively* different order, special instruments of awesome mass annihilation, the use of which would cross moral and political thresholds.[63]

Attlee, especially, presided over the early buildup of nuclear weapons. But he was concerned about the dangers of nuclear war and hoped for a world where war would be ruled out.[64] Winston Churchill, while in opposition (1945–51), proposed preventive war on the Soviet Union. He urged the West to make use of its advantage in atomic weapons to refashion the European order and use the bomb, if necessary, to prevent Soviet expansionism into areas considered the spheres of Western influence. However, his peace-through-strength approach changed after the Soviets acquired a nuclear capability. After returning to power in 1951, Churchill proposed a much more conciliatory policy of intensified superpower negotiations to avoid a catastrophic war.[65] The atmospheric tests in the Pacific by the United States altered Churchill's perception of war as he recognized that nuclear weapons could destroy humanity as a whole.[66]

The Suez War of 1956, involving Britain, France, and Israel, was an opportunity for Britain to use its newly acquired nuclear capability—first tested in October 1952—as an instrument of compellence. Egyptian President Gamal Abdel Nasser, despite confronting a formidable coalition of three states, one of them a nuclear power, refused to abandon his policy of nationalizing the Suez Canal. In response, the three states began an attack on Egypt in October 1956. However, the war had to be called off as a result of U.S. pressures as well as Soviet threats to intervene. Even though Britain did not directly threaten nuclear use, the general lack of effectiveness of nuclear weapons against nonnuclear adversaries as a potential instrument of compellence was revealed in this crisis. Despite this episode, Britain expanded its nuclear arsenal under Prime Minister Harold Wilson, who was opposed to Britain's agreeing to a test ban before building a substantial nuclear arsenal. Britain tested its first hydrogen bomb under Wilson in May 1957. However, the British government also was sensitive to the rising tide of protest movements across the world in the second half of 1950s demanding a test ban treaty.[67] There was also an active "ban the bomb" movement in Britain which was much stronger than its U.S. counterparts.

During the 1960s, nonproliferation concerns became dominant in British policy. Britain attempted to act as an intermediary between nuclear and non-nuclear states in order to accomplish the conclusion of the NPT. London attempted unsuccessfully to allay the fears of many nonnuclear states, especially India, regarding possible nuclear use by nuclear weapon states. In the aftermath of the Chinese nuclear tests in 1964, Indian Prime Minister Lal Bahadur Shastri visited London and sought Britain's assistance in providing "a nuclear umbrella to protect the non-nuclear powers from nuclear blackmail by third parties."[68] Britain was not able to persuade the nuclear powers, as the non-aligned policy of India precluded such an umbrella, while neither the Soviet Union nor the United States was willing to offer anything other than vague diplomatic commitments.

During the 1960s, British leaders tied nonproliferation to the future use of nuclear weapons. To Prime Minister Harold Macmillan, "nuclear weapons are so barbarous as to be almost incredible. If nuclear proliferation continued unabated, the great crime against humanity would eventually be committed."[69] However, in 1963, Britain committed its nuclear forces to NATO as a second pillar of the alliance's deterrence against the Soviet Union, agreeing to be involved in the defense of Europe, based on a flexible response strategy.[70]

Nuclear weapons again became a crucial part of British defense policy under Margaret Thatcher. The Conservative prime minister was a strong supporter of the Reagan administration, which ardently believed in the need for a strong defense buildup in order to defeat Communism. However, later on she supported partial disarmament, as a result of the Gorbachev revolution. But she also sanctioned the purchase of Trident II missiles from the United States as a replacement for the aging Polaris system.[71]

Thatcher's conduct of the Falklands War raises questions about Britain's commitment to the non-use tradition. The British task force that sailed to the South Atlantic carried nuclear weapons on its ships, an action that has been attributed to the lack of time required for offloading. However, this also carried with it a great danger of nuclear accidents, as Argentina could have destroyed some of the nuclear weapon-carrying vessels, leaving the possibility of radioactive materials spread around the South Atlantic region.[72] (Chapter Seven discusses the Falklands War in greater detail.) French President François Mitterrand seemed to have revealed that Thatcher threatened to use nuclear weapons against Buenos Aires if France, which had supplied Argentina with Exocet missiles before the war, did not disclose the secret codes for their operation. In confidential discussions, Mitterrand told his psychoanalyst, Ali Magoudi: "With her four nuclear submarines on mission in the Southern Atlantic, she threatens to launch the atomic weapon against Argentina—unless I supply her with the secret codes that render deaf and blind the missiles we have sold to the Argentines. Margaret has given me very precise instructions on the telephone."[73] This conversation is still difficult to verify given that no other accounts have surfaced on it.

In the post–Cold War era, questions began to be aired on the utility of British nuclear forces and its policy toward nuclear disarmament, including the no-first-use issue. The changes in the East-West competition affected British nuclear policy as well. "In 1990, NATO decided that with the end of the Cold War, nuclear weapons were to be regarded solely as 'weapons of last resort.'"[74] Together with the removal of most U.S. and British tactical nuclear weapons from Europe, this doctrinal shift represented a departure from European warfighting scenarios. It is likely that the continued public perception of nuclear arms as qualitatively different, more destructive, and higher-threshold weapons has contributed to the diminished utility of tactical nuclear weapons. Although military planners have been prepared to contemplate their use in a range of regional conflict scenarios, political calculations about anticipated adverse reactions from allies or from the general public might have acted as decisive inhibitors. To one analyst, "[i]t is also clear from the terms and language employed that the policy-makers are aware that to the extent that there is public consent for British nuclear weapons, it is almost entirely for an instrument of international prestige that will never be used: a deterrent, not a weapon of war."[75] The public perception of the weapons as a last resort was evident in many polls before and after the end of the Cold War. According to one survey, conducted between 1979 and 1984, only 3 percent of the respondents agreed to the proposition that Britain would have been justified in using nuclear weapons if it were losing the Falklands War. While 34 percent would use the weapons only if the opponent used them first, 49 percent wanted to keep them as a deterrent but never actually use them.[76]

With the fall of Communism, Britain also changed its nuclear weapons policy. The focus shifted from the Soviet threat to challenges coming from aspiring nuclear states in the developing world. Under the Conservative government of John Major, Britain changed its policy on its no-first-use pledge, along with the United States, when, on the eve of and during the Persian Gulf War of 1991, it threatened Saddam Hussein that it would use nuclear weapons if Iraq employed chemical or biological weapons against the coalition forces or their regional allies.[77]

Following its electoral victory in 1997, the Labour government of Tony Blair launched a Strategic Defense Review in May 1997 and published it as a White Paper which presented British defense needs until 2015. The results of the review were announced in July 1998. According to the review, Britain would have the smallest number of nuclear weapons of any declared nuclear state; it proclaimed the eventual goal of "global elimination of nuclear weapons."[78] In the meantime, the major change in this review has been the expansion of a possible substrategic role for the Trident nuclear missile system. It stated: "The credibility of deterrence also depends on retaining an option for a limited strike that would not automatically lead to a full scale nuclear exchange. Unlike Polaris and Chevaline, Trident must also be capable of performing this 'sub-strategic' role."[79] The implication here is that Britain could use Trident to deter or to retaliate against chemical and biological attacks from a state or a regional rogue actor. According to a critic, by expanding the role of nuclear weapons to deter the use of other WMD, "sub-strategic weapons themselves help promote complex games of micro-deterrence in regional crises, the complexities of which make the deterrence of the Cold War appear very simple indeed."[80]

British policy again underwent changes in the wake of the September 11, 2001, terrorist attacks on U.S. targets. In the run-up to the 2003 attack on Iraq, Britain upped the ante regarding nuclear retaliation in response to chemical or biological attacks by Iraq. Defence Secretary Geoff Hoon told a Parliamentary defense committee in March 2002 that dictators such as Saddam Hussein could "be absolutely confident that in the right conditions we would be willing to use our nuclear weapons." The states of concern at that time included Iraq, Libya, North Korea, and Iran. However, Hoon was less confident that such a threat would be sufficient to deter some states of concern, such as Iraq, from using WMD.[81] Hoon restated this threat in an interview with the BBC in February 2003, when he stated that "Saddam Hussein 'can be absolutely confident' that the UK is willing to use nuclear weapons 'in the right conditions.'"[82] The discussion suggests that although Britain contributed to the tradition of nonuse and observed it, on occasions it engaged in making loose nuclear threats vis-à-vis nonnuclear states. Most British prime ministers advocated nuclear disarmament even when presiding over the buildup of British nuclear forces.[83]

Its introduction of nuclear weapons to the Falklands War zone, its threat of use against Iraq in both Gulf wars, and its possible plans for converting Trident missiles for substrategic purposes, suggest that Britain, along with the United States, has challenged the tradition that it has helped to create and that its current and prospective strategic plans could, in the future, help undermine the tradition even further.

FRANCE

France became the fourth nuclear weapon state on February 13, 1960, when it conducted a large atmospheric test in Algeria. France had decided to pursue the nuclear path after its withdrawal from the Suez in 1956, following the aborted Anglo-French-Israeli invasion of Egypt. U.S. opposition and the British decision to abandon the invasion gave incentives to President Charles de Gaulle to further pursue an independent foreign policy and withdraw from NATO. As part of this push toward strategic independence, including a self-supporting approach to defense against the Soviet Union, France acquired a nuclear force— the *Force de frappe*—to support its great-power goals.[84] Although France was not forthcoming with a no-first-use policy, given that the French nuclear capability was small and meant to offer deterrence by punishment to a potential invader, it seems such a policy was implicit in the French nuclear posture.

According to France's policy of *dissuasion* (deterrence), strategic weapons were meant to threaten severe reprisal should an opponent decide to strike. It was also based on the notion of "proportional deterrence," which would mean that the adversary would suffer more than France in a war.[85] The limited tactical nuclear weapons in the French arsenal were not meant for waging a limited nuclear war, but "to deliver a single 'ultimate warning' (*ultime avertissement*), before the possible all-out strategic strike. To fulfill these first roles, France needs only a limited nuclear capability, which follows the principle of 'reasonable sufficiency' (*suffisance raisonnable*)."[86] The independent nuclear capability was maintained under Presidents de Gaulle, Georges Pompidou, and Valéry Giscard d'Estaing, and claimed to offer France a greater deterrent and more weight in intra-alliance matters, although France was not a formal member of NATO.[87]

Six years before it acquired an independent nuclear capability, in 1954, France was in favor of using nuclear weapons in Indochina. In the Dien Ben Phu debacle of May 1954, when the French garrison was overrun by Vietminh forces under General Vo Nguyen Giap, France requested that the United States use nuclear weapons to relieve the besieged French forces. A U.S. war plan for Indochina, called *Operation Vulture,* seemed to have both nuclear and conventional components. A U.S. nuclear attack would have involved three bombs. When U.S. Secretary of State John Foster Dulles told President Dwight Eisenhower that the French leadership expected the United States to drop two or three atomic bombs against the Vietminh, Eisenhower responded to tell the French that "they must have misunderstood [Chairman of the Joint Chiefs of Staff Admiral Arthur] Radford."[88] Eisenhower turned down the request.[89] It is unclear how the besieged fort and the French soldiers in it could have been saved by the use of nuclear weapons, as radiation effects would have probably killed French soldiers themselves. However, its defeat in Indochina increased the French resolve to acquire nuclear weapons.

France conducted its first nuclear tests in February 1960 in the Algerian Sahara Desert, continued atmospheric testing there until April 1961, and then carried out underground testing up to February 1966. The last of the atmospheric tests was a "low yield 'scuttle' of the test device to prevent it from falling into the hands of mutineers during the 'Revolt of the Generals,' set in motion three days earlier by General Maurice Challe."[90] As a result of intense condemnation by African nations, the tests were finally ended in 1966 when France moved its testing site to the Mururoa Atoll in the South Pacific. In response to its difficulties in fighting the Algerian war of independence (which relied mainly on guerrilla warfare), there is no indication that France under President de Gaulle ever considered using nuclear weapons to keep its North African colony. In fact, France made every effort to prevent the army mutineers who opposed French withdrawal from Algeria from gaining access to nuclear weapons, due to concerns that they would use or threaten to use nuclear weapons in order to further their objective of preventing Algerian independence.[91]

The direct French contribution to the tradition of non-use has been minimal, although during the past forty-three years as a nuclear weapon state, France has never used or threatened to use its weapon against a nonnuclear state. Despite this record, at times France engaged in activities that contributed to nuclear proliferation. France was also a persistent opponent of a ban on atmospheric and underground testing until the mid-1990s, and it refused to sign the NPT until 1992. The reasons for the opposition were a desire on the part of France to retain autonomy from the United States and Britain and its hope to engage in nuclear commerce with developing countries, which it feared would be affected by the NPT restrictions.[92] It contributed to the development of Israel's nuclear capability by giving its first nuclear reactor at

Dimona and then supplying nuclear materials for its operation. France was also willing to provide nuclear reactors to Pakistan in 1990, only to withdraw under intense U.S. pressure.

As a result of considerable international opposition and in view of the end of the Cold War, France modified its long-standing independent nuclear policy in the early 1990s when it joined the NPT and other supplier-led export control regimes. It stopped nuclear testing in February 1996, just before the Comprehensive Test Ban Treaty (CTBT) was approved by the United Nations. In addition, it signed the additional protocols of the South Pacific Nuclear-Free Zone and other nuclear-free zones, which legally made it incumbent upon France not to use nuclear weapons against states that were parties to the zonal arrangements. However, simultaneously, France changed its policy on nuclear use in ways that would affect the tradition of non-use.

These changes were undertaken in the post–Cold War era, along with the alterations in nuclear policies of the United States and Britain. During the early 1990s, French strategists debated the need to refashion nuclear strategy to mirror the U.S. counterproliferation strategy and to change the French prevention-deterrent strategy from a *weak to the strong* to a *strong to the weak* or *strong to the crazy* war-fighting strategy. The 1994 Defense White Paper had rejected a war-fighting strategy in response to challenges from the Third World "as [a] dangerous mistake."[93] However, the White Paper acknowledged for the first time that French vital interests could be threatened by regional powers. The core vital interests were defined as "integrity of the national territory, including the mainland as well as overseas departments and territories, the free exercise of our sovereignty, and the protection of the population."[94] This White Paper generated a limited debate, which, however, ended in a stalemate as President Mitterrand and his successor, Jacques Chirac, agreed to maintain ambiguity in nuclear policy, but not to radically change the French deterrent strategy.

France also offered qualified negative security assurances somewhat similar to the ones made by other nuclear weapon states—the United States, Russia, and Britain. According to a letter sent to the UN Secretary General and a statement presented to the Conference on Disarmament in Geneva, France reaffirmed its 1982 commitment that "it will not use nuclear weapons against non-nuclear weapon States Parties to the NPT, except in the case of an invasion or any other attack on France, its territory, its armed forces or other troops, or against its allies or a State toward which it has a security commitment, carried out or sustained by such a State in alliance or association with a nuclear-weapon State."[95] During the 1991 Gulf War, President Mitterrand declared that France would not use nuclear weapons in retaliation against chemical or biological attacks, a move that was criticized by opposition leader Jacques Chirac.[96] In addition, France joined the NPT in 1992 and committed itself to most of the nonproliferation commitments as a nuclear weapon state and a supplier country.

Despite this commitment, France had changed its position on nuclear use in an effort to deter possible chemical or biological attacks by the mid-1990s. In August 1995, new President Chirac declared: "Only the [nuclear] deterrent force guarantees France against the possible use of weapons of mass destruction, of whatever type they may be."[97] In September 1995, Foreign Minister Alain Juppé stated that the use of WMD could justify a French response with nuclear weapons. This declaration was made despite the negative security assurance that was offered at the time of the NPT renewal conference in May 1995 that France would not use nuclear weapons against nonnuclear states, parties to the NPT, that were also not aligned with a nuclear weapon state.[98] The purpose of the policy change was that France wanted to keep its response to possible WMD attacks uncertain so as to enhance the credibility of its deterrent threats.[99]

In the wake of the September 11, 2001, terrorist strikes in the United States, the nuclear use issue became even more critical for France and other Western nuclear powers. According to reports in October 2003, President Chirac signed an order according to which France could use nuclear weapons to "meet the threat of a chemical attack," implying that France could use nuclear weapons against a nonnuclear state and just not in retaliation, but also in a preventive mode. The French newspaper *Libération* said in an editorial that, in contrast to the previous French doctrine of "the weak facing down the strong" (*du faible au fort*), which refrained from spelling out when France would use nuclear weapons, the new doctrine was described as "the strong facing down the mad" (*du fort au fou*), and that this change had been effected without public debate.[100] France thus has been emulating the other two Western nuclear powers, the United States and Britain, on the nuclear use issue.

In January 2006, President Chirac made a radical announcement regarding the use of nuclear weapons against a nonnuclear state. For the first time, unlike any other nuclear state, France declared that it would be willing to use nuclear retaliation against a state sponsoring a major terrorist attack on the country, even if it did not involve a WMD. While addressing the crew

RUSSIA, BRITAIN, FRANCE, AND CHINA 115

of *Vigilant,* a submarine that carries French nuclear weapons, Chirac stated: "The leaders of states who use terrorist methods against us, as well as those who consider using in one way or another weapons of mass destruction, must understand that they would expose themselves to a firm and appropriate response on our part," and "this response could be a conventional one. It might also be a different kind." He added that "all our nuclear forces have been reconfigured accordingly. To this end, the number of warheads has been reduced on some missiles on our submarines," so as to achieve precision in striking selected targets.[101] Some consider the decision as a way to justify the enormous amount of money spent on nuclear weapons and to position Chirac as a tough fighter on terrorism for domestic public opinion purposes.[102] But the rhetoric has consequences for the French commitment to the tradition of non-use of nuclear weapons.

France, however, is constrained by possible consequences in view of adverse public opinion in case it resorted to nuclear use. A substantial majority of the French public (69 percent in 1999) supported the maintenance of a nuclear capability only for deterrence purposes. According to a French analyst, Pascal Boniface, only the extreme Right political party, the National Front, has argued in favor of a nuclear use strategy. Boniface warns that if France alters its policy on nuclear use, it "would be playing into the hands of its antinuclear foes, by associating itself with the idea that such [a] weapon can be used to fight, and not to preserve the peace. In so doing, France would have squandered any further prospect of maintaining the political legitimacy it has fought so hard to gain for its arsenal." It would also give a fillip to antinuclear public opinion in both France and Germany.[103] Other French military analysts have argued that France should not break the tradition against the use of nuclear weapons because that is the "basis of their peace-preserving effect"; the "banalization of nuclear weapons would not fail to lead to their use and then to the end of their peace-preserving effect."[104]

During the Cold War, in many respects, France was a unique nuclear weapon state, as its *Force de frappe* was developed both to deter Soviet invasion and to maintain a currency of power in the international system. France also refrained from using or threatening to use nuclear weapons against non-nuclear states, even though it was not a full member of the NPT or other nuclear supplier-led regimes. In the post–Cold War era, Paris has changed its nuclear use policy in line with the United States and Britain, thereby undermining the strength of the tradition of non-use. Further, France has raised the possibility of the use of nuclear weapons against a state that sponsors a major terrorist attack on French territory, even if it did not involve WMD. The vitality of the tradition may be under challenge due to France's new nuclear policy, but it is difficult to see when and where France would ever get an opportunity to use nuclear weapons against nonnuclear states.

CHINA

The nuclear policy of the People's Republic of China (PRC), the fifth official nuclear state, from the early days of its nuclear acquisition, has been in support of the tradition of nuclear non-use. In fact, among all the P-5 nuclear states, China has been the only power to consistently maintain a no-first-use policy and has made proposals for a multilateral treaty formalizing that position among the nuclear powers. China acquired nuclear weapons in reaction to U.S. threats of nuclear use during conflicts in Korea and the Taiwan Straits in the 1950s. China obtained the necessary skills, technology, and materials while it was in alliance with the Soviet Union. The first nuclear test was conducted in October 1964, and a hydrogen bomb was tested in June 1967. After the test, the Chinese government made a statement that it "solemnly declares that China will never at any time or under any circumstances be the first to use nuclear weapons."[105]

Subsequently, it made an unconditional commitment toward nonnuclear states of non-use of its weapons in the event of a conflict with them.[106] In a 1964 statement, China also proposed that:

> a summit conference of all the countries of the world be convened to discuss the question of the complete prohibition and thorough destruction of the nuclear weapons, and that as the first step, the summit conference conclude an agreement to the effect that the nuclear powers and those countries which may soon become nuclear powers undertake not to use nuclear weapons either against non-nuclear countries and nuclear-free zones or against each other.[107]

China repeated this commitment in 1971, after assuming its seat on the UN Security Council, when it called on the nuclear states to "undertake the obligation not to be the first to use nuclear weapons against each other; particularly the obligation not to use nuclear weapons against non-nuclear weapon states, nor against nuclear-free zones."[108] During the June 1982 UN General Assembly session on disarmament, it called on all nuclear states "to reach an agreement on the non-use of nuclear weapons. Pending this, the nuclear states should each undertake unconditionally not to use or threaten to use nuclear weapons against non-nuclear weapon states or nuclear free-zones and not to be the first to use nuclear weapons against each other at any time or under any circumstances."[109]

The 2002 National Defense White Paper reiterated the Chinese position that China consistently upholds the policy of no first use of nuclear weapons, and adopts an extremely restrained attitude toward the development of nuclear weapons. The White Paper repeated the earlier commitment that "under no circumstances would it be the first to use nuclear weapons," and that it has undertaken "unconditionally not to use or threaten to use nuclear weapons against non-nuclear weapon states or nuclear-weapon-free zones, and has consistently urged all nuclear weapon states to enshrine these commitments in a legal form."[110] Consistent with its declaratory position of no first use, China developed only a small nuclear arsenal, and its nuclear missiles have been liquid-fuelled, making them slow to assemble. They are also low in accuracy due to their limited circular error probable (CEP). Beijing also claimed to have not deployed tactical nuclear weapons, although there are some questions surrounding this claim.

The ideological basis of China's position on nuclear weapons may be part of the reason for its long adherence to a no-first-use policy. In the 1950s, in public statements Mao Zedong underrated the effectiveness of nuclear weapons. In August 1946, Mao stated: "The atom bomb is a paper tiger with which the U.S. reactionaries try to terrify the people. It looks terrible, but in fact is not. Of course, the atom bomb is a weapon of mass destruction, but the outcome of war is decided by the people, not by one or two new weapons."[111] His decision to intervene in Korea in October 1950 in support of North Korean allies was partially driven by these calculations.[112] Chinese statements during that time argued that nuclear weapons could be defended against and that the United States was vulnerable to Soviet intervention in the event of a nuclear strike on China. In international forums, however, China repeatedly argued that "the nation that first used nuclear weapons should be condemned and punished for war criminality."[113] This suggests that the Chinese were calculating the normative restraints on the United States, as well as considering strategic and tactical concerns in preventing a U.S. nuclear strike while intervening in Korea.

Despite this public posture, Mao sanctioned China's nuclear program in 1956 in order to avoid being "bullied" by others, especially the United States.[114]

China initiated a nuclear weapons program in response to U.S. nuclear threats in Korea and in the Quemoy-Matsu crises, and as such wanted to show to the developing world that it was not acquiring nuclear weapons for anything other than for defense or minimum deterrence.[115] Nuclear weapons did not fit well into Mao's guerrilla strategy or into the war strategies and doctrines adopted by the People's Liberation Army (PLA) later on. "The Maoist military discourse about 'people's war' and active defense was designed in part deliberately to portray China as defensively-oriented, a non-traditional major power that defended the interests of the military have-nots in the international system."[116] Notably, "Chinese strategists were unable to reconcile nuclear weapons and Mao's doctrine of people's war . . . until the early 80s there was no strategic research in China and no direct linkage of nuclear weapons to foreign policy. Earnest efforts to come up with a nuclear strategy suitable to China, a medium sized nuclear power like . . . Britain and France began in the mid-80s."[117] The lingering Maoist influence on strategy may partially explain the Chinese aversion toward developing and deploying a large nuclear force or a first-use policy, which would definitely raise the stakes in its relationship with other great powers, especially the United States.

The Chinese strategists initially adopted a minimum deterrence strategy, which, according to them, "requires only the ability to carry out a simple, undifferentiated countervalue second strike. The adversary's people and social wealth are held hostage, and the fear of unacceptable damage deters any first strike. Any measures that might reduce the destructiveness of nuclear war are destabilizing." China only needs a handful of warheads to achieve its deterrence objectives.[118] This strategy is based on a "delayed second strike (DSS): China will retaliate after withstanding a nuclear strike rather than attempting either a launch under attack (LUA) or a launch-on-warning (LOW)-type strategy, where missiles are launched after detection of an attack but before impact. China arguably does not possess the requisite early warning capabilities in order to move toward a LOW-type policy."[119]

However, by the 1980s many strategists had started questioning this strategy, arguing that "minimum deterrence capabilities are too vulnerable to a disarming first strike, and thus have little deterrent value."[120] They began to discuss more openly the idea of "limited deterrence," giving it:

[a] distinctly limited counterforce-war-fighting flavor. A number of Chinese strategists now argue that a limited deterrent means having enough capabilities to deter conventional, theater, and strategic nuclear war, and control

and suppress escalation during a nuclear war. That is, a limited deterrent should be able to respond to any level or type of attack from tactical to strategic, and the initial response should be calibrated to the scope of the initial attack.[121]

Accordingly, Chinese strategists have developed a list of both countervalue and counterforce targets in order to engage in a flexible strategy, departures from the earlier thinking favoring a "single counter-value punitive strike" and limited deterrence. This also meant abandoning the no-first-use pledge, as striking first may be essential given the inferiority of the Chinese nuclear forces.[122] However, the "bulk of China's aging missile force is liquid-fueled, the missiles are on a low state of alert, with fuel, warheads, and missiles all stored separately," and "Beijing has no ability to launch 'on warning' that is, at short notice or once an attack has already begun." But this situation "will change once it deploys more advanced missiles in years to come."[123]

China's rethinking of nuclear strategy is partially the result of changes in U.S. nuclear policy, especially under the George W. Bush administration. The administration's withdrawal from the Anti-Ballistic Missile (ABM) Treaty; its pursuit of national and theater missile defenses and their possible deployment in East Asia in the protection of Taiwan, Korea, and Japan; its inclusion of China as a potential target for a nuclear strike in the Nuclear Posture Review (NPR) of 2002; and the increased role of nuclear weapons in U.S. strategy and doctrine are factors in this regard. With respect to the NPR, the Chinese policymakers were:

> disturbed because the document directly contradicts several tenets that are strongly held in the Chinese security community: that nuclear weapons are becoming less relevant in the modern world; that nuclear weapons can never be used; and that a conflict with the United States over Taiwan would not involve nuclear weapons. Chinese analysts are particularly focused on two sections of the NPR: the specific mention of the conditions for the use of nuclear weapons over a conflict in the Taiwan Strait and the possible pursuit of earth-penetrating tactical nuclear weapons.[124]

Over the years, questions have been raised about the redlines for China's use of nuclear weapons given its track record in military confrontations with smaller neighbors. China's use of coercive diplomacy against Taiwan and its use of force against India and Vietnam suggested that the Chinese position on the use of force against smaller adversaries is less than benign. However, China withdrew from Vietnam after failing to achieve its goals, and there was no indication that China used the threat of nuclear weapons in any way to achieve its strategic or battlefield objectives vis-à-vis Hanoi. The main purpose of the intervention was Deng Xiaoping's desire to "teach Vietnam a lesson" and show the Soviets that China did not fear Moscow. Vietnam resisted valiantly, as the Vietnamese had experience in fighting the United States and French forces for two decades. The offensive "failed to halt Hanoi's joining with Moscow in an implicit anti-China alliance, and coercive diplomacy failed to accomplish anything substantive."[125]

Taiwan is a theater where China could slide into a situation of nuclear use even though it does not correspond with China's ultimate aim to reincorporate the territory it considers a renegade province. In March 2005, China passed a law which effectively preauthorized the use of force in the event of Taiwan taking steps toward formal independence. The legislation declared that:

> in the event that the "Taiwan independence" forces should act under any name or by any means to cause the fact of Taiwan's secession from China, or that major incidents entailing Taiwan's secession from China should occur, or that possibilities for a peaceful reunification should be completely exhausted, that state shall employ non-peaceful means and other necessary measures to protect China's sovereignty and territorial integrity . . . The law stipulates that the State Council, China's cabinet, and the Central Military Commission, the top military body, "are authorized to decide on and execute" military action with no more than a notice provided to the legislature.[126]

However, Chinese strategists had already added a caveat by stating that China does not consider it a violation of the no-first-use pledge if it uses nuclear weapons on its own territory, which presumably includes Taiwan.[127]

In July 2005, a Chinese general raised the possibility of abandoning the no-first-use policy and resorting to nuclear use against the United States in order to defend its claim over Taiwan. Major General Zhu Chenghu stated that China had "no capability to fight a conventional war against the United States," and that "war logic" dictated that the weaker state employ all it can, which involves the use of nuclear weapons in the event that the United States intervened in a conflict over Taiwan.[128] Although no formal announcements preceded this individual statement, it showed that Chinese military leaders are beginning to question the feasibility of no-first-use in the event of a conflict over Taiwan.[129] Military action need not mean that China would succeed in defeating the Taiwanese, given the qualitatively superior conventional weaponry that Taiwan holds and the strong possibility of U.S. intervention in support of the Taiwanese forces. China could be compelled to up the ante, including issuing nuclear threats, if the situation turned against it in a major way. China's deployment of short- and intermediate-range missiles in the Fujian province, across the strait from Taiwan, adds credence to the concern about a potential scenario of nuclear use.[130] However, this may be nothing more than a way to deter U.S. intervention; the credibility of Chinese nuclear use is questionable given the massively disproportionate nuclear response the United States can inflict on China in the event of a nuclear exchange. In September 1999, China issued a pledge stating that it "will not be the first to use nuclear weapons and will not use nuclear weapons against non-nuclear weapon countries and regions, let alone against our Taiwan compatriots." This pledge was made by Chinese foreign ministry spokesman Sun Yuxi, who was responding to China's claim that it had developed neutron bomb "and did nothing to damp speculation that the announcement was a warning to Taiwan." Taiwan President Lee Teng-hui provoked a crisis when he stated that the "two sides should deal with each other as separate states."[131]

Despite China's consistent position on nuclear no-first-use, its behavior has been contradictory on the question of other nuclear norms, such as the transfer of weapons technology and materials to nonnuclear states aspiring to become nuclear powers. China, despite joining the NPT, has continued to supply Pakistan with nuclear and fissile materials for some years.[132]

On the positive side, China has been reluctant to increase its nuclear weapon capability despite pressures to do so, largely as a result of U.S. missile defense policies. Even with the planned modernization of China's aging DF-5 ICBMs with DF-31 missiles and the submarine-launched version JL-2, the number of missiles still range between eighty to one hundred thirty warheads, although some estimates put it around four hundred. China also reportedly stopped production of fissile materials in 1990. It is also reported that China can produce a larger number of weapons and missiles, but has deliberately chosen not to do so due to fears of an arms race with the United States and unintended use by its own officers. The deliberate ambiguity has generated different estimates by Western sources and much confusion in strategic circles over the years.[133]

China's non-use pledge is also somewhat challenged by its deployment of short-range nuclear missiles toward Taiwan and India, even before the latter became a declared nuclear weapon state in 1998. According to some studies, China has deployed two to three brigades of DF-15 missiles targeted toward Taiwan, two DF-3 and DF-21 missile brigades in Kunming and Yunnan provinces, targeted toward Southeast Asia and India, and three DF-3/DF-4 brigades of missiles in Xining and Qinghai provinces, targeted toward Russia and India. It is possible that some of these missiles were targeted toward India even before it conducted its nuclear tests in 1998 and developed an operational nuclear capability.[134] The likely targeting of Southeast Asian states, especially Vietnam and the Philippines from Kunming, also suggests China's not-so-immutable position in this regard.[135] Both Tibet's Dalai Lama and George Fernandes, India's Defense Minister in 1998, have stated that China has been deploying nuclear missiles and other nuclear weapons systems in Tibet aimed at India.[136]

Despite these aberrations toward Taiwan and India, the significant contribution of China to the tradition of non-use has to be recognized. China is the only nuclear state that has consistently maintained a no-first-use policy and expressed a willingness to sign a no-first-use convention. China has also proposed to the United Nations the conclusion of a no-first-use treaty and has supported the creation of nuclear-free zones, with an undertaking by nuclear states of non-use against parties to the zonal treaties.[137] China has also signed the additional protocols of all nuclear-free zones that are open to signature.[138]

Image and reputation (conceived in terms of world public opinion, especially among the developing countries) seem to be significant variables in the Chinese approach toward nuclear non-use. The no-first-use policy has "significant political value for China in the international community"; to Chinese scholars "it shows China is a responsible partner in terms of enhancing global security."[139] China has maintained the position that it acquired nuclear weapons as a last resort to deter American pressures and that its position is consistent with nonnuclear states, especially in the developing world. China's use or threat of use of nuclear weapons against nonnuclear powers would tarnish the image and reputation that China has built with considerable difficulty over several decades. Despite China's not-so-impeccable credentials in the nonproliferation arena, in the development of the tradition of non-use and its persistence China has played a critical role.

CONCLUSION

This chapter discussed the nuclear policies of the Soviet Union/Russia and the three second-tier nuclear powers, Britain, France, and China, in the context of their approach on the question of nuclear non-use against nonnuclear powers. All four nuclear powers, despite possessing different political systems and strategic cultures, contributed to the rise and persistence of the tradition of non-use. Of these states, the Soviet Union and China perhaps contributed most to the tradition by making formal non-use commitments and adhering to them. Post-1991 Russia, Britain, and France have also refrained from using their weapons, although they have made no firm commitments regarding their non-use as the Soviet Union and China did, and have modified their nuclear use policies during the post–Cold War era to encompass nuclear use against rogue states and nontraditional threats. Britain also contributed to the tradition by nudging its ally, the United States, not to use nuclear weapons during some early critical turning points in the evolution of the tradition. The formal contribution of France is ambiguous, although its non-use in conflicts such as in Algeria is commendable.

In the post-September 11, 2001, international environment, France, by widening the role of nuclear use has probably raised the most significant challenge to the tradition, although the new nuclear policies of Russia and Britain have also questioned its basis to an extent. It is, however, quite possible that the newfound uses for nuclear weapons have been articulated by these states in view of the elusive security challenges they face from terrorism and WMD threats from regional states. Expectations of residual deterrence that may result from the threat of nuclear retaliation against WMD attacks seem to be the main reason for these policy changes. The new policy pronouncements are also meant to satisfy domestic constituencies who question the rationale and high expenditures for nuclear weapons maintenance and modernization after the end of the Cold War.

6 THE SECOND-GENERATION NUCLEAR STATES: ISRAEL, INDIA, PAKISTAN, AND THE TRADITION

IN THIS CHAPTER, the nuclear policies of three second-generation nuclear states—Israel, India, and Pakistan—are analyzed. The effort is to see how their nuclear policies have supported or diminished the tradition of non-use, the reasons for their particular approaches to nuclear weapons, and the future implications of their policies for the tradition. In particular, an analysis of their behavior in crises and wars involving nuclear and nonnuclear powers is useful for understanding the robustness of the tradition as far as these states are concerned. In terms of the tradition of non-use, the Israeli nuclear policy is the most significant of the three, as it confronted nonnuclear Arab states in several crises and wars since it became a de facto nuclear state in 1966, and made ambiguous threats of nuclear use in case its opponents crossed certain redlines. The discussion will also illuminate how these states—India and Pakistan in particular—plan to use nuclear weapons in a future conflict situation. India has announced its commitment to a non-use policy toward nonnuclear states and a no-first-use policy toward nuclear states. Pakistan has not articulated an explicit non-use policy vis-à-vis nonnuclear states, as its main focus is on a first-use threat with the intent of deterring any conventional attacks by India. Therefore, the discussion on Pakistan will largely center on its nuclear doctrines vis-à-vis India, another nuclear state, although the tradition as I study here is focused on nuclear versus nonnuclear states. However, Pakistani supply of nuclear materials to other countries and terrorist groups that are more likely to use nuclear weapons suggests that the tradition has been indirectly challenged by Islamabad and its officials involved in such transfers.

A fourth nuclear state, North Korea, is excluded from the analysis, as it is impossible to obtain reliable information on its national security policy, especially its nuclear posture. Further, it has agreed to give up nuclear weapons following the six-party talks led by the United States in February 2007 in return for normalization of relations, security guarantees, and economic assistance.[1] In the future, Iran is likely to emerge with nuclear weapons, and its commitment to the tradition is yet to be determined. Going by the fears that the Iranian program has caused among the United States and fellow Gulf and Arab states such as Saudi Arabia and Egypt, at least for these countries, Iran cannot be trusted with nuclear weapons, as its policy may be unpredictable.

ISRAEL

Israel is believed to be the world's fifth largest nuclear power, behind the United States, Russia, China, and France, with an arsenal comparable in size to Britain's. In 2006, it was estimated that Israel possessed about two hundred weapons of all sizes.[2] The ambiguity (*amimut* in Hebrew) that characterizes Israel's nuclear posture is referred to by a leading scholar of Israeli nuclear policy as "Israel's last taboo." The taboo, according to Anver Cohen, is observed by a "code of secrecy, non-acknowledgment," and censorship, both at the official and the societal levels. Israel has rarely made explicit its capability or strategy/doctrine with respect to nuclear use.[3] The ambiguity was first developed in the 1960s in response to U.S. pressures to abandon the bomb project, but later it was viewed as a way to give Arab states less reason to go nuclear by reducing domestic pressures for nuclear weapons. Israeli policy makers also found ambiguity useful for maintaining domestic consensus, arresting public debate on nuclear policy, and preventing the Israeli forces from relying excessively on nuclear deterrence.[4] Finally, opacity has also been a reason for the tacit U.S. approval of the Israeli nuclear program.[5] In December 2006, Israeli Prime Minister Ehud Olmert inadvertently stated that Israel had nuclear weapons, which led to a furor, and he retracted his statement.[6]

Israeli governments have, on several occasions, maintained that they will not be the first to introduce nuclear weapons in the region, and that they would sign the Nuclear Nonproliferation Treaty (NPT) after a comprehensive peace settlement was concluded with all Arab states.[7] Despite this ambiguous formula, Israel is believed to possess nuclear weapons as a last resort or as an existential insurance against a combined assault by Arab states. The superiority that Israel possesses in conventional capability and the politico-military support it enjoys from the United States have made the probability of an Arab assault unlikely, especially since the mid-1970s. With the settlement of its border dispute with Egypt in 1978, Israel's main adversarial relationship also eased. Moreover, political changes within the Arab states have made it improbable that a coordinated all-out assault could occur in the near or medium terms. However, the efforts by Iran to acquire nuclear weapons, the possession of chemical and biological weapons by Israel's principal foes, Syria and Iran, and the possibility that, in the future, terrorist groups might acquire and use nuclear weapons or dirty bombs—crude radiological weapons made from nuclear material—all create uncertainty for Israeli strategic planning and its approach toward the use of nuclear weapons.[8] In the twenty-first century, Israel may well emerge as a leading candidate for the use of nuclear weapons, especially if it is attacked with chemical and biological weapons by its enemy states in conjunction with networks of terrorist groups and nonstate actors such as Hezbollah.

It would be illuminating to look briefly at the four major crises involving Israel and nonnuclear states since it became a de facto nuclear state around 1966.[9] These cases are the 1967 War, the 1973 War, the 1991 Gulf War, and the 2003 Iraq War. Some of these cases are further discussed in Chapter 7. According to Cohen, Israel had assembled two rudimentary nuclear devices on the eve of the 1967 war with Egypt and other Arab states for use in case Israel's national existence were in peril.[10] To Cohen, Israeli nuclear weapons were conceived of as a "national insurance policy" and "national safety valve," in the event of "a colossal failure of the IDF [Israel Defense Forces] and decisive strategic surprise by Egypt,"[11] Arab states acquiring nuclear weapons, or its adversaries' resorting to an attack that would destroy the Israeli state itself. According to Cohen, on the eve of the 1967 War, Israel had taken steps to weaponize the capability and had made contingency plans to test it behind enemy lines, east of Sinai.[12] Michael Karpin also contends that during the second half of 1966, Israel had acquired a nuclear weapon capability, and that it had conducted a cold nuclear test in November 1966.[13] In 1966, the Israeli military establishment had developed four redlines whose crossing would lead to the use of nuclear weapons. These were: "(a) a successful Arab military penetration into populated areas within Israel's post-1949 borders; (b) the destruction of the Israeli Air Force; (c) the exposure of Israeli cities to massive and devastating air attacks or to possible chemical or biological attacks; (d) the use of nuclear weapons against Israeli territory."[14]

However, Cohen argues that nuclear use in 1967 for anything other than for maintaining Israel's existence as a sovereign state would not have had any political or military benefits and "would have added a huge element of uncertainty" and "created shock waves with unanticipated consequences." To him, "the situation in May 1967 demonstrated the unsettled nature of the Israeli nuclear dilemma: Israel could not afford not to realize its nuclear option (as a weapon of last resort), but it could also not afford to make any use of it (in circumstances short of last resort)."[15] Since Israel won the war and the existence of the state was not in question during it, a demonstration test was not necessary. The high level of secrecy and the unwillingness to brandish the weapon, other than for a supreme emergency, suggest that the Israeli leaders were treating these weapons differently from conventional weapons and that their use could not be sanctioned under any ordinary circumstances.

What considerations went into the Israeli leadership's decision not to use nuclear weapons during the three subsequent military crises/conflicts? In 1973, Israel was the target of a limited war, launched by Egypt and Syria, while in the 1991 Gulf War, it sustained missile attacks from Iraq. In the 2003 Gulf War, it was feared that Iraq would attack Israel, possibly with chemical weapons, but that contingency failed to materialize; indeed, it is doubtful that Iraq had the weapons or the capability for delivering them. In terms of nuclear non-use, all three wars are important, as Israel considered or threatened to use nuclear weapons in response to the opponent's military attacks or provocation.

Several studies suggest that in 1973, in the face of Egyptian and Syrian advances, the Israeli leadership considered a nuclear response. Seymour Hersh contends that at an October 8, 1973, meeting of the Israeli kitchen cabinet, consisting of Prime Minister Golda Meir, Chief of Army Staff Moshe Dayan, Army Chief General David Elazar, military aide General Israel Leor, and minister without portfolio Israel Galili, three decisions were made. The first was to make operational the nuclear missile launchers at Hirbat Zachariah and put on alert eight specially marked F-4 aircraft. "The initial target list included the Egyptian and Syrian military headquarters near Cairo and Damascus. It could not be learned how many weapons were armed, although Dimona was known to have manufactured twenty warheads by 1973."[16] There were two purposes behind these nuclear moves. First, Israel aimed to compel the Soviets, who would come to know about this deployment, to "urge their allies in Egypt and Syria to limit their offensive and not attempt to advance beyond the pre-1967 borders." The second, more significant, purpose was to "force the United States to begin an immediate and massive resupply of the Israeli military" as there was a strong perception among the Israeli elite that the Nixon-Kissinger White House was trying to let the Arabs win some ground in order to compel Israel to negotiate a peace treaty later on.[17]

Reports published in later years have suggested that nuclear use was a possibility in 1973. According to a report in the *Washington Times* in April 2003, Israel came dangerously close to nuclear use during the 1973 War. Quoting a senior U.S. state department official involved in the crisis, the paper said that on October 8, "Israel's northern front commander, Maj. Gen. Yitzak Hoffi . . . informed Israeli Defense Minister Moshe Dayan that he could not hold out much longer against the 1,400 Syrian tanks rolling through Israeli defenses on the Golan Heights." Dayan was "attacked by acute panic" and declared to advisors: "This is the end of the Third Temple." But he also resolved that "if Israel was to perish, it would take Damascus and Cairo with it." Dayan secured Prime Minister Golda Meir's approval for arming "13 intermediate range Jericho missiles with nuclear weapons. Eight F-4 Phantom fighter aircraft were also to be given nuclear arms." "Over the next 3 days, the launchers were armed at Hirbat Zachariah while the F-4s, on 24-hour alert, based at Tel Nof Rehovot, were also prepared, according to former Pentagon officials." The nuclear attack did not take place, as the United States began an air bridge to replenish Israeli capability, aiding its subsequent victory over Egypt.[18]

It is also reported that the idea of using nuclear weapons was presented by Israeli military leaders on October 9, when "Israel had lost 50 combat planes and more than 500 tanks." Golda Meir rejected Dayan's gloom-and-doom scenario but instead decided to approach Washington. The nuclear card was used to gain Washington's immediate military support.[19] Some believe that Israel used the threat of nuclear escalation in order to compel President Nixon to order an airlift of arms and ammunition to replenish the dwindling Israeli conventional arsenal.[20] One could conclude that in this instance, Israel's subsequent victories, and the Egyptian/Syrian failure to advance further prevented nuclear use.

The key point here is the Israeli leadership's efforts to raise the nuclear threat to gain political objectives that are not directly related to the redlines mentioned previously, especially survival as a state. The purpose of the alert appeared to be to persuade the Soviets not to intervene in the war in support of Egypt and Syria, while encouraging the United States to offer superior conventional capability in order to mount a counteroffensive. There was certainly a sense among Israeli decision makers that nuclear weapons were a class apart and meant for the protection of the Third Temple (a metaphorical reference for Israel itself).[21] But there was an inclination to resort to nuclear threat for purposes other than deterrence, as exemplified in the 1973 instance of bringing out nuclear missiles to elicit cooperation from the United States. This belies the uniqueness of nuclear weapons as a deterrent-only weapon, and suggests that the attitude of the Israeli leadership towards nuclear weapons use has been ambivalent over the years.

In the Israeli case, there has been no proper debate on nuclear weapons possession or use, and leadership perceptions mattered in particular choices that the country has made in this realm. For instance, in 1973, Moshe Dayan was sure of Israel's imminent collapse and the need for nuclear retaliation, while Prime Minister Meir and her confidants, especially Army Chief Elazar, were less convinced. Had it not been for Meir's powerful presence, it is likely that nuclear weapons would have been brought out and used as a tool for political leverage as well as for deterrence and compellence purposes. It also shows a modest impact of the tradition of non-use on Meir, who appears to have been reluctant to resort to the absolute weapon even when great uncertainty existed about the course of the war and Israel's chances of success. However, although Israel did not use nuclear weapons, it remains an open question if the tradition of non-use or even Meir's personal opposition would have been sufficient to deter Israel had the United States not supplied weapons and spare parts and especially if an Israeli military collapse seemed likely.

In the post–Cold War era, Israel also appears to have taken a leaf from U.S. policy with regard to the threat of use of nuclear weapons to deter the use of chemical and biological weapons by opponents. The Israeli response during the 1991 Persian Gulf War suggests that the tradition of non-use does exist for Israel, albeit in a weakened form. This crisis implies that by 1991, Israel had expanded the role of nuclear weapons to deter the use of chemical and biological weapons by its adversaries. Israel desisted from responding militarily to Iraqi aggression due to a combination of factors. First, the United States pressured it not to intervene, as the Israeli intervention would have broken the coalition against Saddam Hussein, which involved many Arab states. Second, Israel would not have done a better job in locating and destroying the Scud missiles than the United States did. Third, the Iraqi Scud attacks resulted in low fatalities, reducing the pressure to counterattack disproportionately. Despite these constraints, Israel was reported to have rolled out a Jericho missile, capable of carrying nuclear weapons, a week after the first Scud missile attack, before pulling it back. The objectives appear to have been to encourage Moscow to exert pressure on Saddam Hussein to stop the attacks and demonstrate to the United States that "Israel's patience was wearing thin." Others believe this was intended "primarily as a sign of Israeli frustration."[22]

Prior to the 2003 Gulf War, there were calls on Israel to threaten or use nuclear weapons if Saddam Hussein used chemical or biological weapons against Israel. It was argued that in order to make Israel's nuclear deterrent credible, such a threat was necessary. However, such proposals generated some amount of debate within Israel. According to a critic of this policy, if Israel broke the tradition of non-use, "it might lose its international legitimacy," and "violating the nuclear taboo without facing a clear and immediate threat to our existence is one of the worst possible crimes against humanity."[23]

Although the nuclear weapons issue is a prohibited subject for the Israeli public and officials, public opinion consistently and increasingly supported Israel's possession and possible use of nuclear arms. According to one annual survey, the support for nuclear use in the face of a major security threat increased steadily from 36 percent in 1986 to 80 percent in 1998. On a separate question on the possible contingencies in which Israel could use nuclear weapons, the answers in 1998 were: 99 percent in response to nuclear attack, 86 percent in response to gas or biological attack, 45 percent to avoid defeat in a conventional war, and 25 percent to save many lives. In 1986, 91 percent agreed with the idea of use of nuclear weapons in a desperate military situation.[24] Further, it was reported that Israel had developed low-yield neutron bombs which could destroy troops but not property, and in 1990 it was suggested that Israel might already be developing mini-nukes to destroy hardened command-and-control centers in enemy states.[25]

The discussion above suggests that although Israel has observed the tradition of non-use and has been partially influenced by it, the country remains perhaps one of the leading candidates to use nuclear weapons against a non-nuclear state and thereby break the tradition of non-use. The fact that none of its opponents among the Arab and Gulf states hold nuclear weapons precludes the mutual nuclear deterrent scenario (until Iran obtains the capability). Israel made ambiguous nuclear threats in 1973, 1991, and 2002–03. Israel is also a likely target of future weapons of mass destruction (WMD) attacks by nonstate actors, raising the possibility of Israel resorting to preventive or preemptive attacks on countries that harbor such groups. However, the reluctance of Israel to use its nuclear weapons in past crises and wars involving nonnuclear states offers some comfort that the tradition of non-use may have reasonably entrenched itself even in this hard test case. One can also argue that many of their nuclear threats have been meant to deter adversaries or to elicit cooperation from the United States, but this kind of situation could give rise to a "commitment trap"—a temptation to resort to nuclear use to lend credibility to the declared policy—in a severe crisis situation, a problem identified by Scott Sagan.[26]

INDIA

India became a nuclear-capable state in 1974, when it tested its first device in the Rajasthan desert. However, for over two decades it kept an ambivalent position on weaponization and decided to pursue a full-fledged program only in the late 1980s, largely in response to Pakistan's nuclear weapons acquisition and India's frustration with the slow pace of global nuclear disarmament. The tests themselves were prompted by a mixture of systemic and domestic factors, such as the extension of the NPT in perpetuity; the pressure on India to sign the Comprehensive Test Ban Treaty (CTBT), which would have foreclosed a nuclear weapons option; and, above all, the arrival of the nationalistic Bharatiya Janata Party (BJP)-led coalition government into power.[27] Since the nuclear tests in 1998, India has openly made a no-first-use pledge and has incorporated this policy into its nuclear doctrine. However, in response to a growing fear of nuclear weapons falling into the hands of terrorist groups, and of such actors using chemical and biological weapons with or without the connivance of its enemy states, India has modified its no-first-use policy. It now includes the contingency of nuclear attack in retaliation against chemical or biological attacks by adversaries.

India's attitude toward nuclear weapons offers a major test case for morality-based arguments about nuclear weapons possession and use. The possession of the bomb was early on perceived as against the peaceful ideals that India's father of the nation, Mohandas Gandhi, stood for. His political heir apparent, Jawaharlal Nehru, also outwardly showed great antipathy toward nuclear weapons. However, it is argued that Nehru implicitly laid the foundations of a nuclear weapons program when he initiated the civilian program, which was used in subsequent years for developing a nuclear bomb.[28]

However, to a certain extent, it was India's lack of trust in the robustness of the tradition of non-use and of negative security assurances that encouraged New Delhi to initiate a nuclear weapons program. After the Chinese nuclear tests in 1962, India approached the Western powers for nuclear protection. Later on, it opposed joining the NPT, partly due to the treaty's failure to fully guarantee nonnuclear states protection against nuclear first use.[29] India's decision to conduct a nuclear test in 1974 was to some extent influenced by its experience during the 1971 Bangladesh War, when the Nixon administration dispatched the nuclear-armed USS *Enterprise* to deter India from attacking West Pakistan.[30] India justified its May 1998 Pokhran tests by the absence of decisive steps by nuclear states toward a "nuclear-weapon-free world," and by the fact that some nuclear states had "doctrines that permit the first use of nuclear weapons." Thus India had decided to exercise its nuclear option and forgo its self-imposed restraint.[31] In his statement in the Indian Parliament, Prime Minister Atal Bihari Vajpayee stated that India does not "intend to use" nuclear weapons for "aggression or for mounting threats against any country; these are weapons of self-defense, to ensure that India is not subjected to nuclear threats or coercion."[32] An authoritative study on Indian nuclear policy states:

> By refusing to treat deterrence as an outcome that is best assured by developing various strategies of defense, such as preemptive attacks, limited nuclear options, or robust strategic defenses, New Delhi has adhered to the traditional opposition that theorists like [Glenn] Snyder have postulated to exist between deterrence and defense, coming down strongly in favor of the former and rejecting the latter, at least at the level of declaratory policy.[33]

However, the tradition seems to have played a role in the formulation of India's nuclear doctrine. India, similarly to China, has a policy of no first use and non-use against nonnuclear states, which is enshrined in its official nuclear doctrine. The nuclear doctrine approved by the Indian government on January 2003 consists of eight components. They are: (1) "[b]uilding and maintaining a credible minimum deterrent"; (2) "[a] posture of 'No-first Use,'" that is, "[n]uclear weapons will only be used in retaliation against a nuclear attack on Indian territory or on Indian forces anywhere"; (3) "[n]uclear retaliation to a first strike will be massive and designed to inflict unacceptable damage"; (4) "[n]uclear retaliatory attacks can only be authorized by the civilian political leadership through the Nuclear Command Authority"; (5) "[n]on-use of nuclear weapons against non-nuclear weapon states"; (6) "[h]owever, in the event of a major attack against India, or Indian forces anywhere, by biological or chemical weapons, India will retain the option of retaliating with nuclear weapons"; (7) a continuance of strict controls on export of nuclear and missile related materials and technologies, participation in the Fissile Material Cutoff Treaty negotiations, and continued observance of the moratorium on nuclear tests; and (8) "[c]ontinued commitment to the goal of a nuclear-free world, through global, verifiable, and non-discriminatory nuclear disarmament."[34] These elements suggest that along with deterrence, non-use and nonproliferation calculations also figure in Indian policy toward nuclear weapons.

India's policy of no first use is derived from both normative and instrumental calculations. India has been a major advocate of nuclear disarmament and the conclusion of a legal treaty on non-use by nuclear weapon states since the early days of the nuclear age. The Indian nuclear doctrine is a continuation of that policy. It shows that India as of now wants to limit nuclear weapons solely to deterrence and prestige/power purposes, and has no intention of using them as an instrument for fighting or winning wars. It also shows that India does not seek to obtain territorial goals by using or threatening to use nuclear weapons. By incorporating a no-use policy against nonnuclear states in its nuclear doctrine, India is signaling to different categories of states its adherence to a more robust tradition of non-use, of which it has been an early and active advocate.

In an instrumental sense, the minimum-deterrent posture based on a no-first-use policy precludes building an operational system on a hair-trigger alert, or the amassing of large quantities of weapons or delivery systems beyond what is needed for a minimum deterrent capability. It is based on the assumption that India does not need to match its adversaries in terms of number or yield of weapons. Moreover, it rejects battlefield nuclear weapons, a brinkmanship strategy, and nuclear blackmail of any kind.[35] Foreign Minister Jaswant Singh stated on May 9, 2000, that although India was not a party to the NPT, it was a nuclear weapons state bound by the NPT provisions for nuclear states and that it supported demands for "unqualified negative security assurances raised by a large majority of non-nuclear states" and was willing to "'provide requisite assurances to the nuclear weapon free zones in existence or being negotiated,' except in South Asia."[36]

However, there is evidence that after its nuclear tests India has slowly moved away from its normative position on complete global nuclear disarmament to more modest arms control aims. This is the result of changes taking place at the domestic, regional, and international levels. Domestically, the BJP-led government was more interested in realpolitik uses of nuclear capability for obtaining great power status. Regionally, the intensification of conflict with Pakistan following the nuclear tests, and globally, the changing nuclear policies of the United States and other nuclear states contributed to this transformation. India is eager to acquire theater missile defenses while expressing willingness to join a whole host of arms control agreements that it had opposed in the past.[37] In its 2005–06 agreement with the United States, India also agreed to bifurcate its civilian and military nuclear facilities and place the former under the International Atomic Energy Agency (IAEA) safeguards. This willingness is also partly derived from the need to lift the international sanctions against India, imposed under various supplier regimes in the civilian energy sector, so as to gain technology and materials from the international nuclear market.[38]

Questions have been raised of the utility of India's no-first-use pledge in the wake of the Kargil offensive by Pakistan and in the post–September 11, 2001, fear of terrorist groups gaining access to chemical, biological, and nuclear weapons. The no-first-use pledge has been under severe criticism among some Indian strategists, who believe that the policy would leave the full initiative to Pakistan to undertake conventional offensives, given India's commitment against nuclear counterattack. This was evident in December 2003 when the National Security Advisory Board (NSAB), a government-appointed body consisting of the country's leading national security experts, recommended abandoning India's no-first-use pledge, "as the other nuclear weapon states have not accepted this policy," and lifting the self-imposed moratorium on nuclear testing.[39] The NSAB also proposed allowing nuclear use against non-nuclear allies of nuclear weapons states, somewhat similar to the policies of other nuclear states.[40] The Indian government, however, rejected these proposals, stating that "the policy could not be changed overnight unless there was an extraordinary situation."[41] Instead, India has chosen a "delayed but assured retaliation strategy," purely for deterrence purposes.[42]

It has also been argued that in order to maintain a no-first-use policy, "India must be prepared to absorb multiple strikes before launching its retaliatory forces." Indeed, the nuclear doctrine recognizes the likelihood of "repetitive attrition attempts" by its nuclear opponents. The survivability of India's command-and-control arrangements, especially between national command and storage facilities and predelegation of launch authority in the event of a decapitation strike, also pose a challenge to the no-first-use pledge.[43] The "widening of the core mission of nuclear weapons," to include deterrence against chemical and biological attacks, although consistent with the nuclear policies of all first-generation nuclear states except China, poses additional problems. Further, "given the volatile ground realities in South Asia, it is not clear how

India would react if attacked by chemical and biological weapons by a non-state actor."[44] It is also debatable if a large number of Indian nuclear missiles would survive an initial attack by Pakistan or China, and it may require multiple bombings of multiple targets of the opponents for retaliation to have a powerful impact.

A contingency that could severely test the Indian no-first-use policy would be a terrorist nuclear attack on Indian cities, troop formations, or nuclear facilities.[45] With the help of elements of the Pakistani nuclear establishment or rogue nuclear scientists, terrorist groups could acquire nuclear weapons or nuclear materials, then assemble a dirty bomb, and use it against Indian population centers, troop deployments, or civilian/military facilities. If this scenario develops, will India refrain from nuclear retaliation, especially if it has credible information that sections of the Pakistani military or scientific community have colluded with the terrorists? The terrorists need not come from Pakistan, but could be stationed in Afghanistan or another smaller neighboring state of India, like Nepal or Bangladesh. India is particularly vulnerable to nuclear terrorism given the presence of a number of terrorist outfits (some with the active support of the Pakistani intelligence agency, Inter-Services Intelligence [ISI]) in neighboring countries, including Bangladesh and Nepal. The Indian decision to keep the weapon disassembled may be useful in delaying a response, but it may have little or no relevance to terrorists using dirty bombs against Indian targets.

New Delhi's harsh reaction to the December 2001 attack on the Indian parliament suggests that in the event of a dirty bomb attack by terrorist groups trained in Pakistan, the Indian government will be forced to take drastic steps to bolster its deterrent and to regain domestic credibility. Its response to the 2001 crisis was to move toward a posture of massive mobilization of its troops all along the Pakistani border, initiating a limited war strategy with the assumption that Pakistan would not use nuclear weapons in response to India's conventional strikes against terrorist camps within Pakistani-controlled Kashmir, as those attacks would not challenge Pakistan's existence as a nation-state or its core strategic/security interests.

The mobilization crisis of 2002–03 ended inconclusively, leaving many questions about the Indian strategy. In response, in April 2004, India unveiled a new war doctrine called *Cold Start,* which changed the Indian defense posture from deterrence to compellence. As per *Cold Start,* India would station troops closer to the Pakistani border, cutting short the mobilization time for response and preventing international intervention. In response to Pakistani transgressions, India would strike back conventionally, with the assumption that Pakistan would be prevented from using nuclear weapons because of India's retaliatory capability. It adopted an offensive posture in response to any Pakistan-induced crisis similar to the 2001 terrorist attacks on the Indian Parliament. Taking a leaf from NATO's offensive doctrine during the Cold War, India now would mobilize its forces within a shorter span of time and engage in an integrated operation involving its Army, Navy, and Air Force. The blitzkrieg-style operation is meant to inflict multiple assaults on the Pakistani Army. For this purpose, India has constituted eight battle groups and deployed them nearer the border. The new doctrine and strategy are supposed to increase the political will of the Indian decision makers to use offensive power, prevent the United States and China from intervening in support of Pakistan, and put pressure on Islamabad to engage in peace negotiations.[46] According to some critics, this strategy is not all that credible and may cause nuclear war in the region.[47] The reason is that if Pakistan prepares for a nuclear launch, India may have to preempt the attack with its own nuclear strike, abrogating its no-first-use policy.

Although India's doctrinal commitment to non-use of nuclear weapons against nonnuclear states has some merits, critics point out that it is only a declaratory policy and that India could change it if and when a crisis emerges.[48] India has also been criticized for the exclusion of military allies of nuclear weapon states from the pledge of non-use. In India's favor it is argued that "a country's nuclear force structure, command and control system, alert status and its deployment posture are based on its nuclear doctrine. First use doctrines require hair trigger alerts, launch-on-warning and launch-through-attack strategies and elaborate surveillance, early warning and intelligence systems with nuclear warheads loaded on launchers and ready to fire."[49] In order to embellish its no-first-use policy, India has maintained its warheads in disassembled fashion and kept the delivery systems and nuclear core separately, and it takes several days to assemble them as usable weapons. The no-first-use policy also may be a factor in maintaining strategic stability in the region, given the short geographical distances between Indian and Pakistani cities and the danger associated with a policy of hair-trigger alert. Reputation considerations are also important here to the extent that India wants to project the image of a responsible nuclear weapon state and one that has kept nuclear capability for deterrence and status purposes only. It also wants to distinguish its policy from that of its archenemy, Pakistan.

Although there are indications of rethinking on the issue of nuclear use, India seems in general to be observing the tradition of non-use, and is partially influenced by it, as evident in its nuclear no-first-use policy, enshrined in the nuclear doctrine that it has adopted. India is treating nuclear weapons as different from war-fighting weapons and has been reluctant to engage in a massive arms buildup or the assembly of weapons which may change in the future if it gets into an arms race with China.[50] The low-key approach to nuclear arms as an operational weapon suggests that India, somewhat similar to China, perceives nuclear possession for deterrence and status purposes, and is unlikely to widen its use even in the face of security threats it is likely to confront in the short and medium terms.

PAKISTAN

Pakistan pursued a nuclear program largely in response to the Indian program and to offset its conventional inferiority vis-à-vis its longtime rival. Nuclear weapons have been perceived by the Pakistani elite as a great strategic equalizer in its relationship with India. In that sense, deterrence seems to be the main purpose of the Pakistani nuclear capability. However, the Pakistani military elite has found other uses for nuclear weapons, that is, as a means to obtain territorial gains in Kashmir in a limited war (with the nuclear threat shielding against India's escalation), as evident in the 1999 Kargil operations, and in its continued resort to asymmetric warfare to wrest the territory from Indian control.[51] Pakistan raised the nuclear threat in different crises involving India, in 1987, 1990, 1999, and 2002.[52] The nuclear-use threats came in the context of Pakistani fears that India might use its conventional superiority to escalate military conflict in response to Pakistan's asymmetric warfare in Kashmir.

How strongly ingrained is the tradition of non-use in the Pakistani case? There is no direct evidence of Pakistan's willingness to break the tradition of non-use. In fact, Pakistan rarely mentions its attitude regarding nuclear use in contingencies other than those involving its nuclear adversary, India. In 2001, when a U.S. official suggested the possibility of nuclear use against its non-nuclear neighbor Afghanistan, which was under the control of its former ally the Taliban, Pakistan countered that it could not entertain even the thought of using nuclear weapons in any fashion.[53] This might have been partly because any hint of use of nuclear weapons against the Taliban and al-Qaeda would have created considerable domestic problems for the Pervez Musharaff regime. The threat of nuclear use against Muslim brethren would cause strong opposition in the Islamic world.

Beyond the deliberate choices of national leaders, Pakistan poses another risk to the tradition of nuclear use, of an inadvertent variety. Pakistan's nuclear facilities may not be well-protected, despite American support in this regard, and the country is prone to large-scale internal conflicts. The danger is if a Pakistani nuclear capability falls into the hands of terrorist groups through sympathizers within the Pakistani nuclear establishment. Such a group might then develop dirty bombs. In such a scenario, Pakistan could become a source of the breaking of the tradition of non-use, through active or passive connivance of nuclear use by nonstate actors. In addition, Pakistan, like India, may be facing difficulties in the basing of delivery systems. Mobile launchers are vulnerable to accidents, theft, and counterforce attacks, and it may be difficult to maintain communication with the National Command Authority in times of crisis. Hardened silos are also susceptible to preemptive attack, thereby raising the prospects of nuclear use early in a crisis.[54]

It also appears that the Pakistani military and scientific elite have been the most careless among all the nuclear states in the spread of such weapons and materials to actors that might potentially use these weapons. In that sense, Pakistan has been challenging the tradition of non-use indirectly. This is evident in the network of nuclear supplies centering on Abdul Qadeer Khan, the father of the Pakistani bomb, who provided nuclear weapon materials and technology to Iran, Libya, North Korea, and Iraq under Saddam Hussein.[55]

A second source of concern is the sympathies that some members of the Pakistani elite, especially within the nuclear establishment and the military, hold for the al-Qaeda terrorist network. Concerns have been raised regarding the possibility of transfer of nuclear weapons or materials to the terrorist group for creating a dirty bomb. Paperwork on designs for dirty bombs was uncovered from al-Qaeda houses evacuated after the November 2001 American-led offensive in Afghanistan. These terrorist efforts benefited from the help of "two Pakistani nuclear scientists, Sultan Bashiruddin Mahmood and Chaudiri Abdul Majeed, who have admitted that they had had long discussions with al-Qaeda officials in August 2001 about nuclear, chemical, and biological weapons. Pakistani intelligence officials told The Washington Post that they believe that the scientists used a charity they had created as a cover to conduct secret talks with bin Laden."[56]

Domestic turmoil, violent regime changes in Pakistan, and the possibility of nuclear weapons falling into wrong hands are other related issues. Although

Pakistan may not resort to nuclear use against its enemy India due to fear of nuclear retaliation, the question arises as to what happens if a terrorist group based in Pakistan or Afghanistan acquires such weapons. Will such a group be bound by the tradition of non-use or no first use? Will it try to use the capability in Afghanistan against U.S. and allied troops or against India so as to draw the two nuclear enemies into a nuclear war? Pakistan thus could be dragged into a nuclear war due to the behavior of terrorist groups operating from its territory, although its leaders may not wish one. Pakistan may thus indirectly cause the breaking down of the tradition of non-use under certain circumstances, especially given the weaknesses of the Pakistani state and the security circumstances of the region involving substate actors.

The domestic support in Pakistan for nuclear use is again a cause of concern. Surveys conducted by the Kroc Institute at the University of Notre Dame prior to the 1998 nuclear tests showed that a large majority of the Pakistani elite and general public surveyed were willing to use nuclear weapons in response to an Indian conventional assault. To a question on when nuclear weapons could be used, 44 percent of all Indian respondents said "never," while only 1 percent of Pakistani respondents answered the same way. Among the Indian respondents, 30 percent believed that nuclear weapons could be used if Pakistan were about to take over Kashmir, 24 percent if China was about to overwhelm India militarily, while 99 percent of Pakistani respondents suggested that nuclear weapons could be used "if India were about to attack Pakistan across the international border," and "77 percent felt these weapons could be used if India were to intervene across Kashmir's Line of Control." According to the authors of this survey, "this difference in public opinion between the two countries may reflect both a greater sense of insecurity in Pakistan vis-à-vis the military superiority of its giant neighbor, as well as a lack of knowledge and informed debate about the actual consequences of using these weapons."[57] This lack of knowledge may mean that the tradition of non-use as well as deterrence based on caution and prudence may not have taken deep roots in Pakistan.

In the nuclear context, Pakistan's ambitious grand strategy and tumultuous domestic politics are part of the problem. A tendency on the part of the Pakistani elite to use any possible instrument to gain a tactical advantage in the zero-sum conflict with its larger neighbor, and also in its bargaining with the United States, suggests that nuclear weapons are yet to be perceived as very different instruments for conducting brinkmanship policies. According to one analyst, the Pakistani elite has viewed nuclear weapons as military "instruments that permit and facilitate low intensity conflict against India," " 'last resort' weapons to prevent the loss of Pakistan's territory or the military defeat of the Pakistan armed forces," and "deterrents to Indian conventional military attack." They are viewed politically as "instruments for nation-building," "tools for domestic political and civil-military competition," "symbols of defiance of Western influence and Pakistan's leadership within groups of regional and Islamic states," "devices to draw international attention to the Kashmir issue," and "materials and technology as potential goods to be sold or bartered for acquiring foreign exchange and/or promoting the causes of friendly states or non-state movements."[58] This is further compounded by deeply held Islamist notions among members of the elite, who may favor the spread of nuclear weapons to other Islamic countries in order to wage *jihad,* an acceptable form of warfare.[59]

An Italy-based arms control group, *Landau,* conducted extensive interviews with members of the Pakistani ruling elite which shed light on conceptions of nuclear use and the general utility of nuclear weapons. According to the report, General Musharaff has declared that the bomb is kept in a "disassembled state"—that is, "the fission core is kept separately from the non-nuclear (ignition) components" but can be assembled "very quickly." The authors of the report interviewed Lt. Gen. Khalid Kidwai of the Strategic Plan Division, which controls nuclear weapons. Kidwai stated that nuclear weapons "are aimed solely at India" and that Pakistan will use nuclear weapons "if the very existence of Pakistan as a state is at stake." However, he presented some thresholds or redlines under which the Pakistani military would consider nuclear use. These are: "a. India attacks Pakistan and conquers a large part of its territory; . . . b. India destroys a large part of either its land or air forces; . . . c. India proceeds to the economic strangling of Pakistan; . . . d. India pushes Pakistan into political destabilization or creates a large scale internal subversion in Pakistan." The authors of the report point out the problems with this approach, as it is an excessively diverse and broad set of motivations, and the use of "the nuclear threat to enforce a rational decision-making" by the opponent "is not reassuring."[60]

The Pakistani elite also suffers from a peculiar dysfunctional learning from one India-Pakistan crisis to the next. The primary lessons drawn from crises are that realpolitik approaches work, that failure in previous coercive bargaining was due to lack of serious effort, and that next time, coercion will be effective. This tendency on Pakistan's part to engage in multiple coercive bargaining crises has heightened the likelihood of nuclear use, as crisis begets

crisis.[61] Some suggest that the Pakistani elites also seem to hold benign assumptions about likely Indian responses to their conventional military offensives and asymmetric attacks. Evidence to this effect came from past behavior,
especially in 1999, when the elite believed that the "Indian response to the
Pakistani fait accompli would be passive and quiescent; and that the Kargil
war would have little effect on India-Pakistan relations."[62]

All this implies that Pakistan may be in the early stages of nuclear learning, and the tradition of non-use may have yet to take deep roots in Pakistani
calculations. The Pakistani elite has assigned a multitude of functions to
nuclear weapons beyond deterrence, which makes it difficult to maintain
a strong normative commitment against nuclear use or threat of use. Further, Pakistan's use of nuclear cover to continue an asymmetric war against
its stronger adversary also suggests a continuing revisionist streak in Pakistan's foreign policy, coupled with a high risk-taking propensity in pursuit
of that policy. Pakistan has attempted to make use of its nuclear capability
against India in a conflict characterized by a "stability-instability paradox"—
maintaining stability at the larger interstate level but instability at the substrategic level so as to force concessions by the stronger nuclear adversary. This
strategy has increased Indian resolve to confront Pakistan, and New Delhi
has now abandoned its earlier cautious approach to newly devised limited-
war strategies, and has conducted mobilization all across the border. Turning
stability into instability at all levels, the Indian proactive strategy may have
called Pakistan's strategic bluff, but it carries much higher risks that both an-
tagonists will allow nuclear brinkmanship beyond limits.[63]

CONCLUSION

The second-generation nuclear states—Israel, India, and Pakistan—exhibit
varying degrees of commitment to the tradition of non-use. Yet, how deeply
ingrained the tradition is in their national policies is yet to be determined.
Learning in these nuclear states may be taking place slowly. One problem for
all three is the possibility of terrorist strikes on their territories with WMD or
dirty bombs, and uncertainty about the possible responses they may resort to.

Although none of these three countries has used nuclear weapons, Israel
came closest in 1991, and has shown a willingness to employ the threat of use
of nuclear weapons for political bargaining with Washington. India is perhaps
the most committed to nuclear non-use and the tradition of non-use, as it has
been historically a major advocate of a nondiscriminatory NPT and nuclear

disarmament. Of the three states, Pakistan is the least normatively predisposed toward nuclear non-use, as its military elite has assigned a wide variety of goals to nuclear possession and has deliberately kept a low threshold for nuclear use, especially against its rival India. The willingness of its scientists and officials to spread nuclear materials and technology to regional challengers such as Iran and North Korea, as well as to terrorist groups who presumably do not hold any inhibitions against nuclear use, suggest that the tradition of non-use has yet to take deep roots in the Pakistani elite's calculations. However, as years pass by, Pakistan may recognize the need to observe more closely the norms against the spread of materials and realize the connection between such spread and the potential use of nuclear weapons or dirty bombs. Israel will still face challenges until a full-fledged peace develops with its Arab neighbors and subnational actors and a nuclear free zone is created in the Middle East, precluding nuclear acquisition by Arab states.

7 NONNUCLEAR STATES, THE TRADITION, AND LIMITED WARS

THE TRADITION OF NON-USE OF NUCLEAR WEAPONS has profound implications beyond the security policies of nuclear weapon states (NWS). Because the tradition chiefly refers to the non-use of nuclear weapons against nonnuclear weapon states (NNWS), it is imperative to see if it has influenced NNWS' foreign and security policy behaviors in a variety of regional and strategic contexts. How have NNWS perceived the operation of the tradition, and have they adjusted their policies in view of their understanding of it? Two areas can be identified in which the tradition seems to have been influential. The first area is the wars and crises involving NWS and NNWS and the role that nuclear weapons might have played in terms of both compellence and deterrence calculations. The second area relates to the bargaining between nuclear haves and have-nots in the nonproliferation realm, in particular the conclusion and extension of the unequal Nuclear Nonproliferation Treaty (NPT). This chapter focuses on the first subject, while Chapter 8 deals with the latter.[1]

THE TRADITION AND LIMITED WARS

Cases of limited wars involving NWS and NNWS constitute a major area to assess the role of nuclear weapons in the strategic calculations of belligerent states. In this regard, a major puzzle is why the possession of nuclear weapons did not prevent nonnuclear states from initiating wars and military crises against nuclear states. Some pertinent questions are: Why have nuclear weapons many times failed to produce the outcomes that are supposed to result from their possession? What role do they play in limited wars involving a nuclear-armed and a nonnuclear state? Are nuclear weapons irrelevant in strategic interactions between nuclear and nonnuclear states? More specifically, why would an NNWS initiate military action against an NWS adversary even when the possibility of a nuclear response exists?

It seems that the apparent boldness of nonnuclear states in initiating war against a nuclear adversary has been partially influenced by the tradition of non-use that all nuclear states have thus far observed. Nonnuclear initiators seem to believe that the nuclear defender is self-deterred through the operation of the tradition and other possible political and strategic constraints. The presence of the tradition in such contexts can be inferred from the fact that there exists no international law or treaty that explicitly bans the use of nuclear weapons, and yet nuclear states have refrained from making use of their advantages in armed confrontations vis-à-vis nonnuclear states, even when some such attacks would have made military sense. In addition, nonnuclear initiators did not possess nuclear capabilities so as to deter a potential nuclear retaliatory strike by their adversaries. If there existed neither an explicit legal ban nor a deterrent capability to prevent possible nuclear retaliation, what else could explain the belief among decision makers of nonnuclear states that nuclear weapons would not be used against them in their impending conflict?

A nonnuclear initiator could believe that its total obliteration by the nuclear state is unlikely to happen, especially in an asymmetric war in which combatants fight for limited stakes.[2] A nonnuclear state could calculate that the nuclear state would be reluctant to use nuclear weapons, as it would be breaking the global tradition against nuclear use. Infringing the tradition could involve high reputation costs, especially in terms of world public opinion. The key questions that decision makers of a nonnuclear initiator confront are: What would prevent the nuclear state from using its atomic weapons to obtain tactical and strategic objectives? Under what conditions could the war remain limited and nonnuclear?[3]

LIMITED WARS: CASES OF WAR INITIATION BY NONNUCLEAR STATES

Since the dawn of the nuclear age, a dozen significant wars have occurred between nuclear states and their nonnuclear adversaries. The cases of wars between nuclear and nonnuclear states are the Korean War (1950–53), the Suez Conflict (1956), the Algerian War of Independence (1954–62), the Vietnam War (1965–73), the June/Six-Day War (1967), the October/Yom Kippur

War (1973), the Sino-Vietnamese War (1979), the Afghan War (1979–89), the Falklands War (1982), the Lebanese War (1982), the Persian Gulf War (1990–91), Afghanistan (2001–), Gulf War II (2003–), and the Israel-Lebanon War (2006). Further, several wars and military assaults were initiated by the NNWS: the Chinese intervention in Korea against the United States/United Nations in 1950, the Vietnamese offensives against the United States in the 1960s and early 1970s, the Egyptian and Syrian offensives against Israel in 1973, the Argentine invasion of the British Falkland Islands in 1982, and the Iraqi attacks on Israel during the Persian Gulf War of 1991.[4] In addition, there are several instances of attacks by substate groups on NWS. The Lebanese and Palestinian militant groups' offensives against Israel since the 1970s, the attacks by Sri Lankan Tamil guerillas as well as Kashmiri militants against the forces of a presumably nuclear-armed India in the 1980s and since the 1990s, respectively, and the Chechen nationalist struggle against Russia since 1994 are major cases of subnational groups openly and continuously challenging nuclear states or undeclared nuclear states. The al-Qaeda strikes on the United States on September 11, 2001, were new major assaults on a nuclear state by a nonnuclear actor; the attacker in this instance was not a nation-state, but did have the active support of the Taliban regime of Afghanistan.

This section explores how the tradition may have affected limited wars in regional theaters. Specifically, I examine three cases of war initiation or other military assault by nonnuclear states against nuclear-armed adversaries.[5] These three cases are selected in order to examine how the tradition of non-use comes into play with regard to different types of deterrence, such as immediate and general. In one of the cases, the 1973 October/Yom Kippur War, the defender, Israel, had included nuclear retaliation in its deterrence strategy toward its Arab opponents. In the Falklands case, immediate deterrence was not the key element of British strategy vis-à-vis Argentina. But it is assumed that the superior nuclear and conventional capability that Britain possessed should have had a general deterrent effect, as there existed a possibility of the defender using such capabilities against the nonnuclear challenger in a worst-case contingency. In the third case, the Iraqi attack on Israel and Saudi Arabia (both directly and indirectly protected by U.S. alliance relationships), the nuclear factor is crucial as the defenders, Israel and the United States, on several occasions implicitly raised the possibility of nuclear retaliation, in particular against the use of chemical and biological attacks by the Iraqi leader. The strategic and political calculations of the decision makers of these states, especially with respect to their adversaries' possession and likely retaliatory use of nuclear weapons, form the main focus of the case studies.

CASE I: THE 1973 OCTOBER/YOM KIPPUR WAR

The October 1973 October/Yom Kippur War was initiated by two nonnuclear states—Egypt and Syria—against Israel, an undeclared nuclear state.[6] According to one account, Israel had begun nuclear arms production at the Dimona facility in the Negev desert in the second half of the 1960s, and by 1973 it possessed twenty to twenty-five nuclear weapons. In addition, Israel reportedly held three or more operational missile launchers at Hirbat Zachariah, several Jericho I mobile missile launchers that were capable of hitting all major Arab capitals, and a squadron of nuclear-capable F-4 fighter aircraft on full alert. Israel was also believed to have retained low-yield tactical nuclear weapons on artillery for battlefield purposes that were capable of striking targets at a twenty-five- to forty-five-mile distance.[7] The Israeli leadership had implicitly stated this capability as the ultimate deterrent against an Arab attack. Prior to the war, leaders such as Moshe Dayan had hinted at the Israeli nuclear deterrent and made ambiguous nuclear threats.[8]

The Israeli Calculations

By 1973, Israeli deterrence calculations were based on the possession of superior conventional and nuclear capability. The leadership believed that since Egypt did not hold sufficient conventional capability to launch a successful attack on Israeli airfields, nor could it match the Israeli preponderance in tanks and armored vehicles, it would be deterred from launching an offensive.[9] Defense Minister Dayan believed that the Arab states would not initiate a war before the early 1980s, and until then the Israeli nuclear capability was likely to act as a deterrent against a conventional attack. The Arabs would need at least ten years to produce their own bomb to neutralize the Israeli nuclear capability. Without explicit Soviet cooperation, Egypt would not be in a position to neutralize the Israeli nuclear capability. The Israeli leaders assumed that President Sadat's expulsion of Soviet advisers in 1972 would further reduce the credibility of any nuclear guarantee that the Soviets might have given to Egypt.[10] According to one account, Dayan believed that the Israeli capability to hit targets in the Soviet Union with nuclear weapons could also deter Moscow from supporting an Arab offensive, thereby removing a necessary precondition for military action.[11] While the threat of nuclear use is not the same as actual use, a threat implies a presumption and willingness to use, otherwise it is a meaningless bluff. Threats also "leave something to chance," and it is possible that the threatener will end up in a commitment trap. Accidental use is another possibility. A nonnuclear opponent has no guarantee that nuclear weapons will not be used for these reasons as well as in the more significant scenario that the defender loses the conventional battle. It may be politically suicidal for the defender to back off in defeat. However, a weaker initiator may be willing to take a chance when it initiates a war because of its belief that a tradition against nuclear use exists and that the nuclear state will not cross the threshold.

The Egyptian leaders, especially Gamal Abdel Nasser and Anwar Sadat, were well aware of the Israeli efforts to acquire nuclear weapons. In 1960, Nasser had threatened to go to war if Israel acquired nuclear weapons. He had warned that Egypt would invade Israel "to destroy the base of aggression before that base is used against us."[12] Some suggest that the 1967 Egyptian mobilization was partly motivated by a desire to engage in a preventive war against Israeli nuclear capability, although the Egyptian leader at the last minute had called off such an attack.[13] Nasser's initial response to the Israeli nuclear program was that "because of its destructive power, a nuclear weapon is not a real weapon that can be used to win regional wars. The Israeli atomic bomb, if such [a thing] existed, was therefore irrelevant to the Arab-Israeli conflict. Thus the Arabs ought not to be overly concerned about rumors of Israeli nuclear weapons, because Israel could not use them even if they had them."[14] Even with such a posture, from 1967 to 1973, Arab leaders and the media talked continuously of the Israeli nuclear capability and its implications.[15] The Egyptians were also presumed to have received intelligence information on the Israeli nuclear weapons and strategy from Soviet spies who had penetrated the Israeli defense and intelligence establishments.[16]

The Egyptian Assessment

The limited available accounts suggest that prior to launching the war in 1973, the Egyptian leadership's strategic assessment did take into account the Israeli nuclear capability, although outwardly they projected the impression that nuclear weapons did not matter in their war plans. To President Sadat and his advisors, a limited attack confined to the occupied Sinai would preclude the use of nuclear weapons by Israel. They believed that Israel would not use weapons of mass destruction (WMD) in order to protect the Sinai, a territory which was not included in the pre-1967 borders of Israel. Unless the population in Tel Aviv was attacked and the Israeli heartland was in grave danger, the Egyptian leadership calculated that there was little chance that Israel would unleash its nuclear weapons.[17]

Thus the Egyptian leadership calculated that possible Israeli nuclear use could be prevented if Egypt engaged in a limited war for limited military and political objectives, relying entirely on limited conventional capabilities. General Saad el-Shazly, the Egyptian chief of staff in 1973, points out that the military leadership adopted a limited-aims strategy as it realized that it was impossible for Egypt to "launch a large-scale offensive to destroy the enemy concentrations in Sinai or to force enemy withdrawal from Sinai and the Gaza strip. All that our capabilities would permit was a limited attack. We could aim to cross the Canal, destroy the Bar-Lev line and then take up a defensive posture."[18] The Egyptian leadership conceived war as a means to attract superpower attention to the stalemated dispute. Specifically, it was anticipated that a surprise attack, confined to an area of twenty miles on both sides of the Suez Canal, and a war fought for three weeks would attract U.S.-Soviet attention to the ongoing conflict. The superpower intervention, especially U.S. pressure, would force Israel to come to the negotiating table. The prior contacts by President Sadat with U.S. Secretary of State Henry Kissinger suggest that he wanted to convey to the United States, and through them to Israel, his limited war intentions and thereby restrain Israel from nuclear retaliation.[19]

In the early 1970s, the Egyptian leadership debated the issue of nuclear weapons and the need for Soviet nuclear arms to resist the Israeli threat. One group, consisting of Ali Sabri, Muhammed Heikal, General Mohammed Sadek, and Ismail Fahmi, demanded either the positioning of Soviet nuclear arms and delivery systems in Egypt or at least Soviet guarantees against possible future Israeli threats. Sadat feared political consequences in such a move. The Soviet rejection of the demand made it easier for Sadat to ignore the opposition to his policy on the Israeli nuclear capability.[20]

Although the Israeli nuclear capability figured in the Egyptian calculations, the strategy that the leadership adopted—limited aims/fait accompli—was expected to circumvent that capability. Nuclear weapons were not viewed as deterring a limited conventional war. The tradition of non-use resulting from reputational and instrumental considerations that prohibit the use of nuclear weapons for anything other than a mortal danger to the existence of a nuclear state, in this case Israel, seemed to have given sufficient assurance to Egyptian leaders that these weapons would not be used on the battlefield for the protection of the occupied Sinai, which Israel was ready to trade off for the correct diplomatic and political price. They also calculated that the anticipated intervention of the United States and the Soviet Union would act as an additional restraint on Israel from escalating the conflict to the nuclear level.

CASE II: THE 1982 FALKLANDS WAR

The invasion and occupation of the Falkland Islands by Argentina, a nonnuclear state, and its determination to wage a war against Britain, a nuclear state, in order to maintain its control over the islands, show the relevance and application of the tradition of non-use in regional conflicts. It can be argued that the British strategy toward Argentina prior to the war did not offer a credible immediate deterrent threat based on conventional or nuclear capability. The Argentine military junta was not given a convincing warning as to the seriousness of the British intent to protect the islands militarily. "No strongly worded warnings, even private ones, emanated from London until 31 March, when the invasion was all but a fait accompli."[21] Despite the lack of warning, the Argentine leadership should have pondered the British conventional and nuclear capability and its potential to inflict serious damage on Argentina's major population and industrial centers, as it was about to challenge a declared nuclear power and permanent member of the UN Security Council.

British Nuclear Presence

The British nuclear capability included two aircraft carriers—HMS *Invincible* and *Hermes*—with tactical nuclear weapons such as WE177 free-fall and depth bombs on board. The delivery systems comprised aircraft such as Buccaneer and Sea Harrier, and helicopters such as Sea King and Lynx. The Royal Air Force also possessed tactical aircraft such as Vulcan, Jaguar, Buccaneer, and Tornado that carried nuclear weapons. Forty of the British destroyers and frigates were capable of bearing depth bombs for helicopter delivery.[22] The nuclear force also included one hundred Polaris missiles, which could have been fired on Argentine targets from an appropriate distance in the Atlantic.[23]

The British apparently brought some of these nuclear arms to the theater during the war. Some reports suggested that HMS *Sheffield* carried nuclear weapons and that a few nuclear depth charges were available for use against Argentina if necessary. According to one report, the *Sheffield* brought down nuclear weapons when it sank.[24] The Sea King helicopters on the aircraft carriers reportedly possessed depth charges, while the Harrier jump jets carried free-fall bombs.[25] There were also reports of Britain sending a Polaris nuclear submarine to the South Atlantic following the sinking of *Sheffield*. The submarine was reportedly sent to the South Atlantic with the instruction "to be ready for action if need be."[26]

Partial revelations by the British Ministry of Defense (MOD) in December 2003 confirmed that British ships in the task force that recaptured the Falkland Islands in 1982 carried nuclear weapons. The MOD claimed, "there was never any intention to use the weapons during the war and that their presence did not break any disarmament treaties." Before the ships reached the combat zone, the weapons were transferred to returning ships and in the process, "seven containers were damaged 'in some way' when they were transporting the weapons on to other ships," although none of the weapons themselves was damaged. "The crippled ship [*Sheffield*] was towed for six days until it sank." According to the MOD, "the transfers of the WE177 depth charges took place at various times during April, May and June 1982, 'well away from other seagoing traffic, and the weapons were held in ships with the best protected magazines before being returned to Britain.' " However, it was "routine practice for British ships to carry nuclear weapons" as part of a policy of refusing "to confirm or deny the presence of nuclear weapons at any particular time or place." The MOD admission did not clear the allegation that "nuclear weapons were sunk along with the HMS *Sheffield* after the ship was hit by an Exocet a month into the War."[27] The MOD said a "decision not to use the weapons was made before the ships left port. But they were kept on board because to remove them would take 36 hours, delaying the Royal Navy deployment to the South Atlantic. In fact, the weapons did not reach the combat zone as they were removed on the journey and transferred to ships returning to the UK."[28] According to earlier estimates, "more than half of Britain's stock of naval nuclear weapons set off to the Falklands war aboard HMS *Hermes* and HMS *Invincible*."[29]

The MOD later declassified additional information on the nuclear question. Documents released in October 2005 revealed that 75 percent of the Royal Navy's nuclear depth charges were on board HMS *Hermes* and HMS *Invincible*. The papers revealed that British commanders were extremely concerned about the possibility that nuclear "weapons might fall into the hands of the Argentines, by salvage, if one of the [Royal Navy] ships had been sunk, stranded or captured," and that the acquisition of nuclear weapons by a nonnuclear state by this way would have "damaging consequences."[30] The British official history of the war contends that the Cabinet ministers wanted to remove the weapons from the task force, but the time it required and the publicity it would have received precluded such an action. The study also cites earlier internal papers discussing the nuclear option and its deletion from official considerations. However, the commander of the task force was willing to take nuclear weapons to the Falklands, just in case Russian submarines got involved on the Argentine side; the official history also declares that "while the main influences on decision-making were essentially logistical and political, an admittedly far-fetched operational possibility was also in play."[31] Two questions arise: What would have happened had the British suffered heavy losses including their warships? In the face of losing the battle, what would have been Prime Minister Margaret Thatcher's response? It still remains at the hypothetical realm whether Thatcher would have ordered a nuclear strike or threatened to use such weapons against Argentina. Having capabilities in the theater gave her options that she would not have had, had the task force unloaded its weapons prior to departure. The chance of a nuclear accident also looms large in this case, as the Argentine torpedoes could have destroyed one or more of the nuclear-carrying British vessels, posing the risk of radiation hazards to the region.

The Argentine Calculations

The Argentine calculations prior to the war rested on the premise that Britain would not use either conventional force or nuclear weapons to protect a faraway island group with little direct economic or strategic value. Moreover, the Argentine action did not directly challenge the survival of the British islands themselves in any sense.[32] The Argentine military and political assumptions were based on a limited-aims strategy under which the Argentine forces would occupy the islands and pursue negotiations thereafter to gain sovereignty over the disputed territories. The main objective of the April 2, 1982, invasion was to create a fait accompli which Britain would not be able to alter without incurring major political and economic costs. "Occupy to negotiate" was the key objective of the invasion.[33] Before the Argentine junta ordered the invasion, Foreign Minister Nicanor Costa Mendez sought opinion from the Argentine missions in London and New York regarding the likely response from Britain, and received the advice that the Thatcher government would most likely sever diplomatic relations and impose trade and economic sanctions, but would refrain from military counteractions.[34] The drastic reduction of the Royal Naval Fleet in the Atlantic—especially the decision to remove HMS *Endurance* from South Atlantic waters—and the previous decision to evacuate the British Antarctic mission from South Georgia confirmed the Junta's expectation that the British would not "deploy major forces to protect the islands."[35] Argentine strategists calculated that with surprise and a favorable local balance they could resist an unlikely British counterattack, and a force of five thousand men in defensive positions could protect the Islands against an attack by a British force three times larger.[36]

The crucial question for our purposes is the Argentine assessment of Britain's nuclear capability and the likelihood of nuclear use. The possibility existed because if Britain incurred major losses in the war and was still unable to dislodge the Argentines, the Thatcher government would have been under tremendous pressure to use all available capability to achieve Britain's strategic and battlefield objectives. The junta considered the chances of Britain using its nuclear forces in the event of its losing the conventional battle and discounted such a possibility. It was viewed as highly improbable, as Britain would incur the world's wrath by breaking the tradition of non-use. Additionally, the United States and the Soviet Union would have prevented the British from using nuclear weapons in a small conventional theater like the South Atlantic.[37] According to two Latin America scholars, "[w]hile Britain did possess nuclear weapons, normative inhibitions against the threat of their first use were no doubt severely constraining, and there is no evidence of the junta being intimidated by this extremely unlikely possibility."[38]

Although the initiator in this case did not directly attack the defender's home territory, the British nuclear capability was a factor that the military junta seems to have considered prior to their launching of the invasion of the Falkland Islands. The Argentine leadership believed that the British would not respond militarily, with either conventional or nuclear weapons. Even when the British task force, with reports of nuclear weapons aboard its ships, began to sail to liberate the islands, the Argentines were convinced that the formidable conventional and nuclear capability would not be used to liberate the islands or to attack the Argentine mainland. Nuclear retaliation by Britain was discounted and the tradition of non-use did play a major role in that calculation.

CASE III: THE 1991 PERSIAN GULF WAR

A third case under examination here is the 1991 Persian Gulf War, especially the Iraqi missile attacks on Israel, an undeclared NWS. The war is significant to the extent that Iraq, a nonnuclear state, was fighting a massive coalition led by the United States, in which other NWS such as Britain and France were participants. The U.S. efforts at compellence during the latter half of 1990 did not work, as the regime of Saddam Hussein chose to fight rather than withdraw from Kuwait. In addition to its resistance and missile attacks on Israel, Iraq also engaged in missile attacks on Saudi Arabia, arguably a state under U.S. security protection and an active member of the coalition.

U.S. Calculations

During several phases of the conflict, the allies threatened, implicitly and explicitly, the possibility of a nuclear strike in retaliation to a chemical or biological attack by the Iraqi forces. These threats included a letter that President George H. W. Bush wrote to Saddam Hussein, which was to be delivered to Iraqi Foreign Minister Tariq Aziz by U.S. Secretary of State James Baker at his meeting in Geneva on January 9, 1991, in which he warned against the use of chemical or biological weapons by Iraq.[39] Bush stated: "the American people will demand the strongest possible response. You and your country will pay a terrible price if you order unconscionable actions of this sort."[40] On August 14, 1990, Secretary of Defense Richard Cheney had warned that the United States had "a wide range of military capability that would let us respond with overwhelming force and extract a very high price should he be foolish enough to use chemical weapons on American forces."[41] In January Cheney stated:

> Were Saddam Hussein foolish enough to use weapons of mass destruction, the US response would be absolutely overwhelming and it would be devastating . . . I assume [Saddam] knows that if he were to resort to chemical weapons, that would be an escalation to weapons of mass destruction and that the possibility then would exist, certainly with respect to the Israelis, for example, that they might retaliate with unconventional weapons as well.[42]

In response to Iraq's biological weapons, American officials debated the best strategy to deal with the threat. Rick Atkinson states that to some U.S. officials, "detonating a small nuclear warhead may be a legitimate employment of one weapon of mass destruction to negate another. Temperatures reaching at least twenty thousand degrees Fahrenheit in three seconds were believed necessary to ensure that no spores survived an attack." Brigadier General Buster C. Glosson told Joint Chiefs of Staff (JCS) Chairman Colin Powell: "We both know there is one sure way to get the temperature hot enough," referring to thermonuclear weapons. " 'Yeah,' the Chairman replied, 'but we don't talk about that.' "[43] Powell also mentions in his memoirs that Cheney asked Powell about the nuclear option, to which he replied: "Let's not even think about nukes . . . you know we're not going to let that genie loose." Cheney said: "Of course not . . . But take a look to be thorough and just out of curiosity." Powell formed a small group to study the nuclear options and "the results unnerved" him. "To do serious damage to just one armored division dispersed in the desert would require a considerable number of small tactical nuclear weapons. I showed this analysis to Cheney and then had it destroyed. If I had had any doubts before about the practicality of nukes on the field of battle, this report clinched them."[44]

The Israeli Response

Although the Israeli government did not make an explicit threat of use of nuclear weapons in retaliation to chemical or biological weapons, statements they made suggested that the price could be very heavy for such an attack. Israeli Prime Minister Yizhak Shamir had warned in December 1990 that Iraq "will be harmed in [a] most serious way . . . whoever will dare to attack us will be attacked seven times more."[45] Given the Israeli population's sensitivity to gas attacks arising out of the Holocaust experience, it was highly likely that major casualties arising from an Iraqi chemical attack would have generated calls for a nuclear response. During the Iraqi missile attack, the Israelis reportedly activated their nuclear capability by bringing nuclear-capable Jericho missiles out of their storage facilities, although it was meant more as a warning to the United States to expedite its supply of Patriot missile batteries than as a signal to Hussein.[46] The possibility that nuclear weapons could be used in the war seems to have entered into the Iraqi leadership's calculations, but from actual behavior it appears that the Iraqis discounted such a use in response to a conventional attack.

Iraqi Calculations

From Saddam Hussein's behavior during the conflict, it can be inferred that the Iraqi calculations in 1991 were partially driven by the tradition of nonuse.[47] However, it also appears that deterrence was effective in preventing Iraqi use of WMD. In August 1995, UN Inspector Rolf Ekeus revealed, quoting Iraqi officials, that in December 1990, on the eve of the war, "they loaded three types of biological agents into roughly 200 missile warheads and aircraft bombs that were then distributed to airbases and a missile site." This decision was taken after the UN Security Council voted to liberate Kuwait "using all necessary means." Ekeus states that Iraq decided not to use these weapons following the ultimatum by Baker at the Geneva conference.[48] The decision by Saddam not to use chemical or biological weapons against Israel and the Allied forces suggests that he was deterred by the threat of overwhelming retaliation (including a possible nuclear attack). Tariq Aziz has acknowledged that the Iraqi leadership believed the prewar threat by Baker that an Iraqi WMD attack on coalition forces would be met with the "most terrible response," as equivalent to nuclear retaliation.[49]

In his memoirs, Baker acknowledges that he purposely left the impression to the Iraqis that the United States might retaliate with tactical nuclear weapons in response to their chemical or biological attack on coalition forces, even though President Bush had already decided not to resort to nuclear retaliation as he thought the best deterrent would be regime removal. To Baker, the calculated ambiguity regarding how the United States might act worked as a deterrent on Iraq against chemical use.[50] Hussein Kamal, cousin and son-in-law of Saddam Hussein and Iraq's minister of defense, who defected to Jordan, acknowledged: "Any mistake of using these unconventional weapons will make the major powers use nuclear weapons, which means Iraq will be exterminated."[51] The statements by Iraqi officials indicate that the fear of nuclear retaliation was part of the reason for Iraq's not using chemical and biological weapons in the war.

But his initial decision to assemble the chemical and biological weapons suggests that Saddam Hussein discounted nuclear retaliation by the allies. The question also remains as to why he continued the barrage of missile attacks on the Israeli civilian population in the heart of the country, Tel Aviv, for over a month and broke the psychological barrier that Israel had created since 1969 against an Arab state's direct attack on Israel proper. During this period, Iraq launched eighty-eight Scud missiles on targets in Israel and Saudi Arabia, killing about 32 people and wounding 250 or so. It was only under intense U.S. pressure and the transfer of U.S. Patriot antimissile batteries that Israel decided not to involve itself in the war.[52] Some have suggested that in addition to fear of retaliation, Hussein did not use nonconventional weapons because of their ineffectiveness.[53] It was reported that Iraq possessed thirty chemical warheads for its al-Husayn missiles, but the warheads were never tested and they were supposed to explode on impact and not in the air, suggesting that casualties from the attacks need not have been that high.[54]

However, these considerations would probably not have prevented Hussein from using such weapons if allied forces advanced to Baghdad and engaged in an offensive meant to topple him from power. Faced with the near certainty of death or life imprisonment Saddam Hussein could have unleashed his chemical or biological weapons against the advancing troops, a possible reason for President Bush to order a halt to the advance after the liberation of Kuwait, despite the recommendation by General H. Norman Schwarzkopf, commander of the operations, to continue the war. Indeed Hussein had reportedly dispersed chemical and biological weapons and predelegated to local commanders the authority to retaliate with chemical weapons in the event of a U.S. invasion of Baghdad.[55] Hussein also warned U.S. Senators at a meeting in February 1990 that he had given authority to commanders to use chemical and biological attacks on Israel if Israel used atomic weapons on Iraq. A former Egyptian army chief states that "If Israel strikes" Iraq with nuclear weapons, Baghdad was willing to "strike at it with the binary chemical weapon," and that Saddam Hussein had "given instructions to the commanders of the air bases and the missile formations that once they hear Israel has hit any place in Iraq with the atomic bomb, they will load the chemical weapon with as much as will reach Israel and direct it at its territory."[56] Here Saddam's threat appears to be deterrent, but the expectation was that chemical and biological weapons would act as a deterrent against nuclear attack.

The fact that Iraq engaged in several high-risk and high-profile missile attacks on the Israeli heartland and continued doing so for over a month suggests that Saddam Hussein was fairly confident that as long as he refrained from using nonconventional weapons, Israel would not retaliate with nuclear weapons. His calculation cannot be completely devoid of the tradition of nuclear non-use, as he was inferring that nuclear weapons were a special class apart and that the United States and Israel would not use these weapons even when the state of Israel was under missile attack, generating panic all over the country for a month. In his calculations, an Israeli retaliatory attack on Iraq could unravel the U.S.-led coalition, as its Arab members could withdraw their support for the U.S. war efforts. Saddam was willing to gamble here as he was discounting an Israeli nonconventional response in his risk assessment. In addition, Saddam burned oil fields in Kuwait, a redline which could have resulted in massive U.S. retaliation. The United States had warned of terrible consequences if he did burn the oil fields. President Bush had warned that three acts by Iraq, use of chemical or biological weapons, support of terrorist acts, and the burning of oil fields, were "unconscionable acts" that would "demand [the] strongest possible response."[57]

CONCLUSION

In the three asymmetric wars involving a nuclear and a nonnuclear state discussed here, the weaker initiator did not expect nuclear retaliation by its stronger opponents. The initiator's limited aims/fait accompli strategy particularly precluded the possibility of nuclear retaliation by the defender, and the tradition of non-use appears to have been a factor in their prewar assessments. The tradition enters the picture in such a way that it undermines the prospects of nuclear use and, therefore, deterrence at the substrategic level. The stronger nuclear power is often self-deterred from making explicit nuclear threats partially due to the tradition of non-use. Nuclear weapons are reserved for higher levels of conflict and if a state were to raise the nuclear threat, it would suffer reputation costs, as breaking the tradition is not easy in the face of limited challenges by a nonnuclear state.

It is arguable that the weaker challenger in at least one of the cases was deterred from using chemical and biological weapons against nuclear opponents, fearing nuclear retaliation. Saddam Hussein's unwillingness to use such weapons in both Gulf Wars might have been due to the fear of regime survival as well as possible nuclear retaliation. However, the weaker adversary in this case might have been self-deterred from using chemical and biological weapons because of fear of collateral damage to one's own population, fear of losing international support, fear of losing power, and fear of death if the stronger power occupied the state and destroyed the regime. Keeping war limited is a prerequisite for a weaker challenger to wage and win politically in an asymmetric war involving a larger nuclear power. The tradition appears to be part of the mix of reasons for nonnuclear states' direct military challenge to nuclear powers.

8 THE TRADITION AND THE NONPROLIFERATION REGIME

IN CHAPTER 7, I discussed the calculations of nonnuclear weapon states (NNWS) that confronted nuclear weapon states (NWS) in crises and wars. Beyond wars and crises, what role, if any, has the tradition of non-use of nuclear weapons played in the calculations of nonnuclear states in their bargaining with nuclear states on the conclusion and the renewal of the Nuclear Nonproliferation Treaty (NPT) and associated instruments of the nonproliferation regime? Although it is rarely stated explicitly, it seems the tradition has had an impact on the calculations of a large number of nonnuclear states with respect to their willingness to accede and continuously adhere to the nuclear nonproliferation regime. I argue that the presence of the quasi-norm inherent in the tradition of non-use has been one of the reasons for many of the technologically capable among the 187 states forswearing their nuclear weapons options and joining the NPT. Their choices in most instances arose from a belief that nuclear states are unlikely to attack them with their weapons unless their core security interests, including existence as nation-states, are threatened. In 2008, there were only four key non-NPT states (India, Israel, Pakistan, and North Korea) and one other, Iran, which is a signatory but is believed to be violating its NPT commitments. Although their choices for nuclear acquisition have several regional and domestic-level causes, one thing is common to them all: these states have good reason not to take for granted the implicit guarantee inherent in the NPT on non-use and other associated treaties such as nuclear free zones, and the partial negative security assurances made by the NWS.

While most states have conformed to the NPT, there are variations in national positions on the question of the significance of non-use guarantees implicit and explicit in the promises made by nuclear states. These variations in the approaches of different states have been partially a function of their particular strategic contexts—that is, are they in a hostile environment, do they have nuclear enemies, and are they adversarial to one or more of the nuclear powers, especially the United States? Thus, states that would characterize their security environment in the affirmative with respect to any one of the above questions have often been the most ardent advocates of explicit legal commitments by nuclear states in order to prevent the use of nuclear weapons against them. But the persistent demands on the part of some of the NNWS for legally binding security guarantees illustrate that even those states that do not face hostile security environments or adversarial relations with any of the nuclear powers are not fully convinced of the robustness of the tradition of non-use as a sufficient deterrent against nuclear use against them in all contingencies. Moreover, the efforts at creating nuclear-free zones in different regions of the world with additional protocols—meant for NWS to renounce the use or threat of use of nuclear weapons against contracting parties—suggest that NNWS are not fully convinced of the robustness of the tradition of non-use under all circumstances and that they would want to entrench the tradition in legally binding arrangements.

The efforts by the NNWS to convert the informal norm of the tradition of non-use into a codified and legally binding norm are evident in their positions at the negotiations that led to the conclusion of the NPT in 1968, and the several review conferences that followed the Treaty's commencement, especially the 1995 conference that resulted in the Treaty's extension in perpetuity; and, since then, the 2000 and 2005 review conferences. Further, NNWS were instrumental in the 1994 UN General Assembly referral to the International Court of Justice (ICJ) about the legality of nuclear weapons use. The fact that it was the UN General Assembly (where these states have equal voting rights with NWS), and not the Security Council, that decided to refer to the ICJ the question of the legality of nuclear use, attests to the concerns of the nonnuclear powers over the robustness of the quasi-norm. In addition, in four regions of the world, states have formed nuclear-free zones which include additional protocols to be signed by NWS promising no nuclear attack on the member states. These efforts also suggest the role of nonnuclear states as reputation intermediaries and norm entrepreneurs and as powerful advocates of the tradition of non-use in its creation and persistence.

Except for China, the five nuclear states that are also permanent members of the UN Security Council (P-5) have in general opposed offering a comprehensive and legally binding treaty or convention on nuclear non-use, largely due to their desire to maintain ambiguity surrounding nuclear use to deter war against them. Further, to them, much of the compellent value of nuclear weapons possession could evaporate if a legally binding non-use treaty exists. Moreover, the aura surrounding nuclear weapons and the special status the NWS enjoy in the international system as great powers and as P-5 member states could be depreciated if they formally gave up their right to use nuclear weapons forever.[1]

The chief venue where the nonnuclear states have tried to erect legal restraints on nuclear states regarding the non-use of nuclear weapons has been the United Nations.

THE UNITED NATIONS

At the United Nations, the nonnuclear states have made several attempts at nuclear disarmament in general and at obtaining a formal commitment on non-use of nuclear weapons in particular. These efforts were manifest in the debates at the annual First Committee meetings and General Assembly resolutions on nuclear weapons, in holding three special sessions on disarmament (1978, 1982, and 1988), and in commissioning studies on the effects of the use of nuclear weapons.[2] A significant effort by the nonnuclear states was to pass a resolution that referred the question of the legality of nuclear use to the ICJ in 1994. The history of their efforts needs to be traced back to the early years of the nuclear age.

During the 1950s and 1960s, the United Nations General Assembly and its disarmament forum—the Eighteen Nation Disarmament Committee (ENDC) and its successor, the Geneva Disarmament Conference—were the main venues for the NNWS campaign for nuclear non-use as well as for nonproliferation. The creation of the nascent tradition appears to have been helped by the activism of the nonnuclear states. In this sense, they played a key role of norm entrepreneurship along with scientists, strategists, and nongovernmental organizations such as peace movements. The efforts by nonnuclear states, especially those belonging to the nonaligned movement, for a legally binding non-use pledge, were most visible in the 1960s during the NPT negotiations at the United Nations. From the perspective of the nonaligned states, a ban on nuclear testing and eventual nuclear disarmament were very much part of the effort to make sure such weapons were never used. During the ENDC's deliberations, many nonaligned countries made attempts to obtain an agreement by nuclear states to end nuclear testing, which they viewed as the first step toward nuclear disarmament and eventual abolition of the weapon. These efforts were largely the result of the atmospheric nuclear tests conducted by the nuclear superpowers in the 1950s, which generated considerable anxiety internationally about the dangers of nuclear radiation and contamination.

As discussed in Chapter 3, beginning in 1946, the United States conducted several atmospheric tests over the Bikini Atoll in the Marshall Islands of Micronesia. The hydrogen bomb *Bravo* was tested in March 1954 by the United States at the Atoll, forcing the islanders to leave their homelands. The impact of the tests was felt in a large geographical area, and among the casualties were several Japanese fishermen in the area, one of whom was killed due to radiation poisoning. These tests also resulted in diseases such as thyroid cancer, eye cataracts, leukemia, birth defects, and miscarriages among the island populations for several years after the explosions.[3] This led to worldwide protests, including intellectuals such as Albert Schweitzer, Betrand Russell, and Albert Einstein. In April 1954, Prime Minister Jawaharlal Nehru of India proposed at the United Nations a standstill agreement on nuclear testing as a prelude to a ban on nuclear weapons production. In this regard, efforts by the Afro-Asian states at the United Nations had an impact, as the superpowers began to negotiate a test ban treaty. The Partial Test Ban Treaty (PTBT) was signed in 1963, banning nuclear tests in the atmosphere, in outer space, and underwater. Underground nuclear explosions were allowed to continue, but the eventual goal was stated as the permanent banning of all nuclear tests.[4]

But success in banning categories of tests was not matched by achievements in disarmament or legalizing non-use. Prior to the conclusion of the NPT, some limited declarations against first use were made both by UN bodies and nuclear states unilaterally; but the objective of a legally binding agreement was not met. In November 1961, the UN General Assembly passed, by a margin of fifty-five to twenty, a resolution that declared, "any use of nuclear weapons would be a violation of the UN charter and an international war crime."[5] The U.S. Secretary of State, Dean Rusk, while opposing the call for a conference to draft a treaty to ban nuclear first use, promised that "[t]he United States government can and does offer the fullest assurances that it will never use any weapon, large or small, with aggressive intent. But the United States, like other free nations, must be fully prepared to exercise effectively the inherent right of individual and collective self-defense as provided in the UN Charter."[6]

The issue of no first use would become a major topic as a result of China's nuclear tests in 1964 and the hue and cry it generated in neighboring countries, especially India. This did not produce any concrete results, however. The launching of the negotiations for the NPT provided the nonnuclear states a major opportunity to push for effective and verifiable negative an assurance by NWS. In 1966, eight nonaligned members of the Geneva Disarmament Conference (the successor to ENDC) proposed the "banning of the use of nuclear weapons and assurance of the security of non-nuclear weapon states," embodied in a treaty.[7] The nonaligned countries continued their efforts at the UN General Assembly in the fall of 1966 when forty-six members introduced a draft resolution asking the nuclear states "to give an assurance that they will not use, or threaten to use, nuclear weapons against non-nuclear weapon states."[8] The U.S. Arms Control and Disarmament Agency (ACDA) was in favor of the United States supporting a resolution that would declare its intention to refrain from making nuclear threats against a state that was party to the NPT that does not "engage in an act of aggression supported by a nuclear weapon state." The U.S. Joint Chiefs opposed such a move, arguing that it would create a "new norm limiting nuclear deterrence options."[9]

The efforts by the NNWS had some impact on the Soviet Union. In 1966, the Russian premier, Alexei Kosygin, made an offer to include a provision banning the use of nuclear weapons against nonnuclear treaty parties that had no nuclear weapons on their territory. The Western countries, led by the United States, opposed the proposal, arguing that it would discriminate against nonnuclear NATO allies that are participants in the alliance's defense plans and deployments (e.g., West Germany). Most nonaligned members supported the Kosygin plan, although they were in favor of a blanket undertaking by the nuclear powers never to use or threaten to use nuclear weapons against nonnuclear countries.[10] However, "the question of security assurances continued to be a major preoccupation of the nonnuclear powers throughout all the negotiations."[11]

THE NPT BARGAIN

The negotiating position of the NNWS on the non-use issue can be assessed by exploring their stated views and bargaining strategies at the diplomatic negotiations that led to the 1968 NPT, the several five-year review conferences, and the Prepcom meetings that preceded the review meetings, especially the 1995 review conference, which extended the NPT in perpetuity. During all these deliberations, a constant theme of many nonaligned NNWS has been the acceptance of legally binding negative security assurances, that is, a non-use pledge, by the NWS.[12] This suggests that the tradition of non-use has not been perceived by these states to be equal to a full legal commitment or as a sufficiently robust legal norm. The assumption here is that it would not be easy to break a legal norm, while a nonlegal norm like the tradition of non-use is breakable, especially if circumstances change and the NWS is under pressure to threaten nuclear coercion for compellence purposes or to obtain battlefield victory in a war involving a nonnuclear state. A legal norm is also breakable, but the threshold for infringement will be increased with legality as one more consideration for a nuclear state to take into account in its decision to use or not use nuclear weapons. It would also strengthen the political and moral claim of the target state vis-à-vis a nuclear aggressor.

During negotiations on the NPT in the 1960s, the nonnuclear states focused on three areas that were expected to improve their security in exchange for signing the treaty. First, they attempted to obtain positive reassurances from the nuclear powers in the form of credible guarantees "to protect and defend them if they are threatened or attacked with nuclear weapons." Second, they sought negative assurances "whereby the nuclear powers undertake not to attack or threaten them with nuclear weapons." Third, they sought to enhance their security indirectly by seeking to have the nuclear powers agree "to undertake to halt the nuclear arms race and to take concrete measures of nuclear disarmament leading eventually to the elimination of nuclear weapons, thus improving the security of the whole world."[13]

However, the nuclear states were not prepared to give either positive or negative assurances in the form of formal security commitments. All they would agree on was the inclusion of Article VI in the NPT, which called upon nuclear states to engage in disarmament negotiations in earnest, leading to eventual abolition of the bomb.[14] Credibility problems plagued the proposals for positive security assurances, while military establishments in the NWS objected to negative assurances, fearing a loosening of the credibility of their deterrence policies if such an assurance was given.[15] These establishments wanted to keep their options fully open with respect to nuclear weapons so that uncertainty could be maintained in the minds of potential aggressors when it came to war. Although initially in favor of offering nonnuclear states some form of positive security assurances, the NWS, especially the United

States, eventually balked, as Washington was worried about the impact such an undertaking would have on its nuclear commitment to allies.

Positive assurances were hampered by the fact that military action in response to a nuclear attack by a nuclear state on an NNWS carried the risk of nuclear retaliation against the intervening party, a situation it could not possibly sustain for both strategic and domestic public opinion reasons. It was difficult for an NWS to be willing to risk nuclear attack in order to defend a possibly nonallied NNWS. The guarantor of positive security assurances need not permanently hold such a policy, as attitudes toward a nonnuclear state are not immutable, and declarations without proper alliance commitments are not sufficiently reliable. However, positive assurances may have a political role, as they could constrain the options of the threatening nuclear power under some circumstances; for example, raising uncertainty as to how vital the NNWS is for the economic and security calculations of the guarantor in this instance.[16]

The Soviets, through the Kosygin Proposal, were willing to include negative security assurances in the NPT, which was opposed by the United States. Washington's chief concern was that given NATO's first-use policy, a negative security guarantee would have meant no attack on Warsaw Pact states that did not possess nuclear weapons.[17] States Epstein: "Thus the non-nuclear powers, despite their repeated insistence on the need for clear, adequate, and credible security guarantees, were left with only the flimsy formula of the Tripartite declarations [United States, Soviet Union, and Britain] and Security Council Resolution 255."[18] According to this resolution, the Security Council and "above all its nuclear-weapon state permanent members would have to act immediately to provide assistance, in accordance with their obligations under the United Nations Charter" to any NNWS party to the NPT that was a "victim of an act or object of a threat of aggression in which nuclear weapons are used."[19] This resolution had no real implementation mechanism, and nonnuclear states such as India rejected it as having little value to their security. The Conference of Non-Nuclear Weapon States in Geneva in September 1968 considered the security guarantee issue in detail. Of the ninety-two states present, eighty-one argued that a UN Security Council guarantee was not sufficient, as it was prone to veto by those P-5 states which were also nuclear powers. A proposal made by Latin American states on an international convention on security guarantees failed, by one vote, to receive a two-thirds majority. The conference ended with a declaration that called for undertaking further steps for an early solution of the security assurance problem.[20] Most nonnuclear states agreed to the treaty without formal security guarantees, as they thought an imperfect treaty then was better than none and that the NPT was the precursor to a larger disarmament treaty, a hope that was belied by later events.

The prospects of concluding bilateral security protection agreements were hampered as well by the difficulties in implementing them. Most nonaligned, nonnuclear states were reluctant to push for this option, which would have forced them to accept security protection equivalent to an alliance commitment from one or the other superpowers and the alliances they led, challenging their nonaligned credentials. They therefore focused on the United Nations for a multilateral security guarantee, but this was difficult to obtain given the intensity of the Cold War competition during that time.

Thus, efforts by the nonnuclear states to include a negative security assurance clause in the NPT did not succeed in 1968. It seems the politics behind the Treaty's conclusion precluded such an open commitment by the nuclear states. However, the nonnuclear states, under the banner of the nonaligned movement, continued their efforts at UN forums and NPT review conferences. Despite the absence of formal, legally binding negative or positive security guarantees, the NPT became acceptable to a large number of states, and it increased its membership to 190 by 2006, a near-universal figure.[21] Different classes of states accepted the NPT for different reasons, including national interests, benign strategic environments, and alliance relationships with one or the other superpower. Among the nonnuclear states, at least three types of states can be categorized in terms of their position on the NPT. Most of the supporters were from status quo-oriented middle powers and allied states such as Canada, Australia, Mexico, Sweden, and almost all small states that had no chance of obtaining nuclear weapons capability on their own. For them, the NPT and the nonproliferation regime offered benefits such as transparency, some amount of security, cost reduction, and other advantages that accrued from a multilateral regime that reduced the problems associated with collective action.[22]

However, a number of middle powers—India, Brazil (until 1996), South Africa (until 1991), and Argentina (until 1995)—opposed the NPT for some time:

> they perceived that adherence to this unequal treaty would foreclose their nuclear weapons options as well as make them more vulnerable to coercion by nuclear weapon states. In addition, it would threaten their potential for achieving a systemic leadership role. Some of these states had been engaged in

enduring conflicts and do not enjoy direct nuclear protection or other forms of security guarantees by the major powers.[23]

A key participant at the NPT deliberations, William Epstein, argues:

> The Treaty would be carried by an overwhelming majority because of the tacit alliance that had developed between the nuclear powers and those non-nuclear powers who had no hope whatsoever of going nuclear for the foreseeable future . . . Furthermore, it seemed that while many nations had serious reservations about the provisions of the treaty, very few, if any, would vote against it; most would confine themselves to abstaining.[24]

Some with potential capability decided against acquisition of the weapon, as they would become targets of nuclear weapon powers and could develop or intensify conflict relationships with their neighbors.[25] They, along with UN Secretary General U Thant, saw the NPT as an indispensable first step toward further progress on nuclear disarmament.[26] The implicit understanding among them has been that nuclear weapons are reserved for great-power-controlled high politics, as the major powers do not need nuclear weapons to attack, defeat, or conquer many of the smaller states. These states have more to worry about regarding security relationships with their neighbors than with the great powers, unless they challenge a great power frontally as Iraq did in the 1990s.

In the post–Cold War era, the issue of nuclear no first use has emerged as a major issue for the nonnuclear states. This is partly due to the changing nuclear postures of the United States, Russia, and Britain. These states have included deterrence against chemical and biological attacks as a raison d'être for their nuclear possession, and have announced plans to engage in preemptive and preventive attacks against so called "rogue states." The United States has also been making off-and-on efforts to develop usable "mini-nukes," and parallel efforts by Russia are probably underway. At the UN meeting to extend the NPT in 1995, security assurances became a make-or-break issue.

Despite their vociferous demands for binding non-use pledges, non-nuclear states agreed to the extension of the NPT in perpetuity in 1995, even when no legally binding pledges were forthcoming from the NWS.[27] However, in April 1995, prior to the extension, the Security Council adopted Resolution 984, which acknowledged the commitments made by nuclear states and recognized the "legitimate interest of the non-nuclear states party to the Treaty . . . to receive security assurance," and declared that in the event that a nonnuclear state became the "victim of an act of, or object of a threat of, aggression in which nuclear weapons are used . . . the Security Council and above all its nuclear-weapon-state permanent members [would] act immediately in accordance with the relevant provisions of the Charter of the United Nations." It also called upon the Security Council members to "bring the matter immediately to the attention of the Council and seek Council Action to provide, in accordance with the Charter, the necessary assistance to the State victim."[28] Negative security assurances from individual nuclear states (most of them promised no nuclear attacks on NPT parties in good standing and on those NNWS not in alliance with a nuclear power) were also part of the final document, titled "Principles and Objectives for Non-Proliferation and Disarmament," approved by the review meeting.[29] Since the extension conference, to the dismay of NNWS, these commitments have been progressively watered down by nuclear states, claiming they made "political" as opposed to "legal" commitments, and a binding no-first-use treaty has been as elusive as ever.[30]

At the 2000 NPT review conference, both nuclear and nonnuclear states accepted a Program of 13 Practical Steps for Nuclear Disarmament, proposed by the New Agenda Coalition consisting of Brazil, Egypt, Ireland, Mexico, New Zealand, South Africa, and Sweden and supported by the Middle Powers Initiative, a conglomerate of eight nongovernmental organization (NGO) groups that work for nuclear disarmament. These steps included agreement by NWS to "an unequivocal undertaking to accomplish the total elimination of their nuclear arsenals."[31] The conference agreed that "legally binding security assurances by the five NWS to the NNWS parties would strengthen the regime and called on the PrepCom to make recommendations to the 2005 Review Conference in this regard. At the 2002 PrepCom meeting, many NPT parties stressed that efforts to conclude a universal, unconditional, and legally binding instrument on security assurances to NNWS should be pursued as a matter of priority," preferably as an additional protocol to the NPT.[32] Since then the positions of the nuclear states, especially the United States under the George W. Bush administration, have become intransigent on the issue of nuclear disarmament.

The 2005 review conference failed to make any concluding statements, as the differences between nonnuclear and nuclear states, especially the United States, could not be bridged. The latter was unwilling to make any commitments on security guarantees or nuclear disarmament, but wanted the conference to focus exclusively on the nuclear proliferation issue, especially on the efforts by Iran and North Korea to acquire nuclear weapons and ways to prevent that from happening.[33] The United States also seemed to be backing off from previous commitments on negative assurances, arguing they were political assurances and not legal, and that new political circumstances required rethinking on such assurances. Since 1992, Washington has changed its policy to include nuclear first use against a nonnuclear state that is party to the NPT using chemical or biological weapons, in an effort to maintain "strategic ambiguity" for a potential attacker.[34] The U.S. position is that the negative security assurances "are not binding 'international agreements' because the assurances were not adopted domestically in accordance with the procedures mandated by the U.S. Constitution."[35] Even NATO, which contained sixteen nonnuclear states, adopted the U.S. approach in May 2000 that nuclear weapons could be used against states armed with biological or chemical weapons "even if they have signed the NPT."[36] In February 2002, State Department spokesperson Richard Boucher reaffirmed the U.S. commitment to no first use, but added a proviso: "the policy says that we will do whatever is necessary to deter the use of weapons of mass destruction against the United States, its allies and its interests. If a weapon of mass destruction is used against the United States or its allies, we will not rule out any specific type of military response."[37]

There thus exists a fundamental dissonance between nuclear and nonnuclear states, especially with respect to negative security assurances as well as to commitment to nuclear disarmament under Article VI of the NPT. Despite changes in the policies of nuclear states, especially the United States, it may well be argued that the NPT bargain, in particular the implicit and partial promise of non-use against NPT signatories, acts as a partial normative restraint on nuclear states from breaking the tradition of non-use. The tradition itself has been partially strengthened by these commitments and the persistent demands by the nonnuclear states to keep the torch alive in the global discourse on nuclear weapons and their potential use. But the future of these assurances looks bleak as nuclear states begin to look at their nuclear weapons as a usable weapon to prevent weapons of mass destruction (WMD) acquisition and to preempt WMD use by nonnuclear states and terrorist groups.

THE GENERAL ASSEMBLY REFERRAL
TO THE WORLD COURT

The NPT forum has been only one of the arenas where NNWS have made efforts to obtain security guarantees from nuclear powers. They have consistently made the UN General Assembly a venue for demanding negative security guarantees. The most significant efforts in this regard occurred in 1994, when the nonnuclear states succeeded in having the United Nations approach the ICJ at the Hague for its advisory opinion on nuclear use.[38] General Assembly Resolution 49/75K was adopted on December 15, 1994; it mentioned the several previous resolutions which had declared that "the use of nuclear weapons would be a violation of the Charter and a crime against humanity," and stated that the General Assembly was "convinced that the elimination of nuclear weapons is the only guarantee against the threat of nuclear war." The General Assembly resolved, "pursuant to Article 96, paragraph 1, of the Charter of the United Nations, to request the International Court of Justice urgently to render its advisory opinion on the following question: Is the threat or use of nuclear weapons in any circumstance permitted under international law?"[39]

During deliberations at the Court, many NNWS presented arguments on the illegality of nuclear use. Oral and written statements were made by many nuclear and nonnuclear states on the legal validity and utility of the General Assembly's seeking the ICJ's advisory opinion. Among the nonnuclear states giving written and oral statements were Egypt, India, Ireland, Iran, Italy, Japan, Malaysia, Mexico, New Zealand, and Sweden. The United States, Britain, and France objected to the referral itself. The U.S. statement to the ICJ summed up their positions:

> The question presented is vague and abstract, addressing complex issues which are the subject of consideration among interested states and within other bodies of the United Nations which have an express mandate to address these matters. An opinion by the Court in regard to the question presented would provide no practical assistance to the General Assembly in carrying out its functions under the Charter. Such an opinion has the potential of undermining progress already made or being made on this sensitive subject, and, therefore, is contrary to the interests of the United Nations organization.[40]

Some allies of the nuclear powers objected to the referral by contending that (a) "there exist[ed] no specific dispute on the subject-matter of the question"; (b) "the abstract nature of the question might lead the court to make hypothetical or speculative declarations outside the scope of its judicial functions"; (c) the General Assembly had not clarified the precise purposes in seeking the advisory; and (d) the Court would be going beyond its judicial role and "taking upon itself a law-making capacity." The ICJ judges rejected these arguments, declaring that they had "the authority to deliver an opinion on the question posed by the General Assembly, and that there exist[ed] no 'compelling reasons' which would lead the Court to exercise its discretion not to do so."[41]

In its judgment, delivered on July 8, 1996, although the Court did not unequivocally ban the use of nuclear weapons, it suggested that under most international humanitarian law, the use of nuclear weapons would be prohibited. It stated that there existed in either customary or conventional international law any "specific authorization" for the use or threat of use or any "comprehensive and universal prohibition" against the threat of use or use of nuclear weapons. By seven to seven votes (with the president casting his vote to break the tie), the court ruled:

> the threat [of use] or use of nuclear weapons would generally be contrary to the rules of international law applicable in armed conflict, and in particular the principles and rules of humanitarian law. However, in view of the current state of international law, and of the elements of fact at its disposal, the court cannot conclude definitively whether the threat [of use] or use of nuclear weapons would be lawful or unlawful in an extreme circumstance of self-defense, in which the very survival of the State would be at stake.[42]

The ICJ verdict thus did not conclusively end this debate and the nonnuclear states seem resigned to the next venue, NPT review conferences, as their best option to press for legally binding non-use pledges. As discussed before, these efforts have not met much success thus far. The ICJ ruling, however, did make it clear that nuclear use for anything other than survival would generally be inconsistent with the canons of international law.

THE NUCLEAR-WEAPON-FREE ZONES

Another major instrument for obtaining guarantees of nuclear non-use has been nuclear-weapon-free zones. The primary reason for the nonnuclear states to propose nuclear-free zones has been to stop the spread of nuclear weapons in their regions and to reinforce their nonproliferation credentials. A second crucial objective has been to prevent the deployment and use of such weapons by nuclear states against states parties to the zone. The zone idea is seen as strengthening the nonproliferation regime by erecting additional legal barriers on both nuclear proliferation and potential use or threat of use of nuclear weapons.

The key operational nuclear-free zones are the Latin American nuclear-free zone, created by the Tlatelolco Treaty of 1967; the South Pacific nuclear-free zone, under the Rarotonga Treaty of 1985; the Southeast Asia nuclear-free zone, under the Bangkok Treaty of 1995; and the Africa nuclear-free zone, under the Treaty of Pelindaba of 1996. There are some country-specific agreements as well. Prominent among these is the 1994 agreement between Ukraine and three nuclear states, Russia, the United States, and Britain. In return for Kiev's dismantling its nuclear arsenal, the three nuclear powers agreed to honor Ukraine's existing borders and not to use or threaten to use force, particularly with nuclear weapons, or to employ economic sanctions against Ukraine.[43] Other proposals for nuclear-free zones have been made for the Middle East, South Asia, Central Asia, and Central Europe, but none has produced an agreement.

Latin America

The Tlatelolco Treaty of 1967 created the first major nuclear-weapon-free zone in Latin America. The treaty was the result of the urgency felt by Latin American countries in the wake of the Cuban Missile Crisis in 1962. These states wanted to avoid getting embroiled in the superpower nuclear conflict by preventing a similar future occurrence. The crisis brought home the stark reality of a possible nuclear war in their backyard without their approval or involvement. A superpower nuclear conflict over Cuba, even if it remained limited, would have profoundly affected the region, especially the neighboring states. In view of this consideration, the initial proposal was made as a joint declaration in April 1963 by Latin American presidents from Bolivia, Brazil, Chile, and Ecuador. By 2002, all thirty-three countries of Latin America and the Caribbean had signed and ratified the treaty.[44]

For the purposes of this chapter, the crucial issue is the non-use provision of the Tlatelolco Treaty. By 1992, the Additional Protocols I and II had been signed and ratified by all nuclear states, although with some provisions. These protocols make it legally binding on the nuclear weapon powers not to use or threaten to use nuclear weapons against states that are parties to the treaty and to "undertake to apply the status of denuclearization in respect of warlike purposes."[45] In that sense, the Treaty of Tlatelolco has far-reaching implications for partially legalizing the tradition of non-use, as it is the first treaty in which all nuclear weapon powers have agreed to major limitations on their nuclear activities in a region. Disarmament expert William Epstein contends: "under the Treaty of Tlatelolco the nuclear powers are legally bound in the same way that the other parties to the Treaty are: not to test, manufacture, produce, deploy, station, use or threaten to use nuclear weapons against the parties to the Treaty. In this respect, Tlatelolco goes far beyond the promise that nuclear powers made in the NPT in July 1968."[46] However, the qualifications attached to the signatures of the nuclear weapons states make it a treaty applicable only in peacetime. For instance, the Soviet Union signed the protocols with the proviso that if a contracting party commits an "act of aggression in support of a nuclear-weapon State or jointly with that State," it . . . "reserves the right to review its obligations under Additional Protocol II."[47] Moreover, the Protocol States may denounce the Treaty under circumstances that "affect its supreme interests or the peace and security of one or more Contracting Parties."[48] Uniquely for a nuclear-weapon-free zone, all NWS have signed and ratified Tlatelolco's non-use protocols.[49]

South Pacific

The second major regional zone has been in the South Pacific; the treaty was concluded in August 1985 at Rarotonga in the Cook Islands. It entered into force in December 1986. Since the dawn of the nuclear age, the South Pacific has become a key area of nuclear activities by the nuclear powers, especially, the United States, Britain, and France. These activities include testing of nuclear and thermonuclear devices (in both underground and atmospheric tests), dumping of nuclear waste materials, transiting of warheads and delivery systems, stationing of nuclear communication facilities in Australia, and regular port calls of ships and submarines of the nuclear powers carrying nuclear weapons. The Treaty of Rarotonga was the result of the continuing concern of the regional states about French nuclear testing at the Mururoa Atoll in French Polynesia. From 1966 until 1992, France conducted more than one hundred explosions, of which forty-one were atmospheric tests. The regional states were also worried about the transit of nuclear weapons in the pristine waters of the South Pacific. Australia and New Zealand took the initiative at the South Pacific Forum for the conclusion of the treaty, in order to make sure that a modest zone was created so as not to upset their relations with the United States. Although the Treaty of Rarotonga has watered-down provisions with respect to the transit and stationing of nuclear weapons in view of Australia's ANZUS (Australia, New Zealand, and United States) Treaty commitments with the United States, it has utility as an instrument against nonproliferation and non-use by nuclear powers.

According to the provisions of the Treaty of Rarotonga, parties are forbidden from several activities. These include:

developing, manufacturing, or receiving from others any nuclear explosive devices in the South Pacific or on the territories of the participating countries. It stipulates that nuclear activities in the region, including the export of nuclear materials, should be conducted under strict safeguards to ensure non-explosive use. It allows South Pacific countries to retain their unqualified sovereign rights to decide [for] themselves such questions as access to their ports and airfields of vessels or aircraft of other countries and respects international law regarding the freedom of the seas and verification by international safeguards [of] the performance of obligations by the parties.[50]

However:

out of the 19 major categories of nuclear activity in the region, the Rarotonga Treaty bans only five. They are nuclear weapons acquisitions by signatories, nuclear weapon testing, permanent stationing of nuclear weapons on land, inland waters or the sea-bed within the territories of the zone member countries, the use or threat of use of nuclear weapons against the zone members by nuclear weapon powers and nuclear waste-dumping by the zone adherents themselves.[51]

In this sense, the treaty envisions the creation of a partial nuclear-free zone in the South Pacific.

The Treaty of Rarotonga has three additional protocols. Protocol I calls upon nuclear powers with territory in the zone—France, Britain, and the United States—to apply the basic provisions of the treaty to their respective territories. Protocols II and III would make NWS commit not to use or threaten to use nuclear explosive devices against any states that are party to the treaty or against the territories controlled by nuclear states in the zone. France and Britain had signed and ratified all the three protocols by September 1997, while China and the Soviet Union signed and ratified Protocols II and III in 1988. The United States signed Protocols I, II, and II in March 1996, but has yet to ratify them.[52] However, under customary international law, as reinforced by the Vienna Convention, the United States is bound to uphold the treaty provisions.[53] One major constraint with this zone is that Australia and New Zealand (with some limitations) are members of the U.S.–led alliance ANZUS, and, under the alliance terms, are obliged to come to the defense of each other during a conflict. The Treaty of Rarotonga, therefore, does not forbid the use of nuclear weapons in the zone by the United States against a nonzone member, nor does it place any restrictions on states from the zone participating in nuclear exercises along with NWS.[54] This has especially become an issue in the context of Australia's active participation in the U.S.-led "war on terror" and the close defense relationship between the two countries in the post–September 11, 2001, era.

Southeast Asia

The third nuclear-weapon-free zone was created in Southeast Asia under the Bangkok Treaty, which was signed on December 15, 1995, and which came into force in March 1997. This treaty was concluded thanks to efforts by the Association of Southeast Asian Nations (ASEAN) members to ensure that their region would not become a theater for nuclear weapons proliferation and great-power nuclear competition, especially involving China and the United States. The end of the Cold War greatly helped in the conclusion of this treaty.[55]

According to the Bangkok Treaty, the parties undertake not to develop, manufacture, acquire, possess, transport, or test nuclear weapons in the zone's territory. States also undertake not to allow another state to develop, manufacture, station, test, or use nuclear weapons on their territory. They are also forbidden from dumping or discharging radioactive materials on land and in their territories, except in accordance with International Atomic Energy Agency (IAEA) standards. However, it gives the right to each state to allow visits by nuclear-armed foreign ships and aircraft in territorial waters or airspace. The treaty has one additional protocol for NWS to sign. The articles of the protocol stipulate that each signatory undertakes "not to use or threaten to use nuclear weapons against any State Party to the treaty" or "within the Southeast Asia nuclear-free-zone." The protocol will be in force permanently, although a party can withdraw "if it decides that extraordinary events, related to the subject-matter of this Protocol, have jeopardized its supreme national interests."[56] The treaty came into force in March 1997 when seven ASEAN states had ratified it, and by 2001, all ten states of the zone area had signed and ratified the treaty.[57] The additional protocol has not been signed or ratified by the nuclear states because of their concerns about the "broad definition of the zone" and its potential impact on "freedom of navigation."[58] However, reportedly both China and India have committed to abide by the additional protocols.[59]

Africa

Africa has the fourth nuclear-free zone, created by the Pelindaba Treaty of April 1996. This treaty came into being as a result of the leading role played by South Africa at the end of the apartheid era and the dismantling of its

own nuclear weapons. The treaty's origins go back to 1960, when, in response
to the French nuclear tests in Algerian Sahara, eight African states proposed
to the United Nations a resolution for the creation of a nuclear-weapon-free
zone, which the General Assembly approved in November 1961 as Resolution
1652(16). In July 1964, the Organization of African Unity (OAU) adopted a
Declaration on Denuclearization of Africa, which the UN General Assembly
endorsed in December 1965. Despite these earlier efforts, the proposals stalled
as the U.S.-Soviet arms race and the South African nuclear program reached
high gear during the 1970s and 1980s. The big change occurred only in the
early 1990s, when the Cold War ended and South Africa agreed to dismantle
its nuclear program and join the NPT. Technical experts began to draft the
nuclear-free-zone treaty in May 1991, and after five years of considerations by
different bodies of the OAU, the treaty was adopted at the OAU heads-of-state
meeting in April 1996.[60]

The treaty parties undertake not to conduct research, develop, manufacture, acquire, or possess nuclear explosive devices, nor seek or offer assistance
from or to others, and to prevent the stationing and testing of nuclear weapons
on their territories, although it allows each state the right to decide whether to
allow foreign crafts carrying nuclear devices to enter their territories. It also
prohibits the dumping of radioactive waste anywhere in the zone, while allowing peaceful nuclear activities under IAEA safeguards. Treaty states have
to conclude a comprehensive safeguards agreement with the IAEA, undertake
to maintain the security and physical protection of nuclear facilities on their
territories, and prohibit armed attack on nuclear facilities within the zone.

The Pelindaba Treaty has three additional protocols. Protocol I calls upon
nuclear powers not to use or threaten to use nuclear explosive devices against
parties to the treaty or on any territory within the zone which a nuclear state is
responsible for administering. Under Protocol II, each NWS signatory undertakes "not to test or assist or encourage the testing of any nuclear explosive device anywhere within the African nuclear-free-zone." Protocol III enshrines
NWS commitments' application to territories for which they have de jure or
de facto international responsibility. However, it allows the NWS party to the
protocols to withdraw from them after giving twelve months' notice in the
event that "extra-ordinary events" have "jeopardized its supreme interests."[61]
As of May 2005, forty-nine of the fifty-three African countries had signed and
twenty had ratified it, although the treaty needs twenty-eight ratifications to
come into force.[62] As of March 2001, Protocols I and II had been signed and

ratified by China, France, and Britain, while the United States and Russia had signed but not ratified them. France had also signed and ratified Protocol III.[63]

Appraisal

Almost the entire Southern Hemisphere, with nearly 1.5 billion people, is covered under a nuclear-weapon-free zone. Although not all nuclear states have signed and ratified the protocols of non-use, a zone makes it harder to use or threaten to use nuclear weapons against member states in good standing. In that sense, nuclear-weapon-free zones offer a limited legal basis for the tradition of non-use, because in the specific regions, the nuclear states have to commit to non-use by signing the additional protocols. The zones thus contribute to a "global system of negative security guarantees," and "as long as negotiations about a multilateral treaty concerning security guarantees continue to be uncertain," the protocols offer a way to make progress in this matter.[64] However, the reluctance of some of the nuclear states to sign and ratify all the additional protocols, as in the cases of the Africa, South Pacific, and Southeast Asia nuclear-free zones, implies an unwillingness on the part of those states to give up their ultimate right to use nuclear weapons against states that are parties to nuclear-free-zone treaties. They also show the reluctance of nuclear states to accept legal restrictions on their freedom of action. In addition, the commitment to nuclear non-use is more or less a political commitment, and no effective verification mechanism has been created to guarantee that nuclear powers observe their pledges under the protocols, especially in the areas of storage and transit of weapons.

Another criticism is that the existing nuclear-free zones are in regions with low probability of nuclear attack by nuclear states. They are somewhat benign regions where almost all states had already become parties to the NPT or some other mechanisms, and this preexisting condition has been crucial for the conclusion of the treaties in the four zones. In those regions where the proliferation propensity is high and states are in conflict with nuclear powers, no nuclear-free zone has been created. Despite many proposals (as in the case of Middle East and South Asia), an agreement among the nuclear states for a non-use pledge through an additional protocol is not likely, even if the regional states created a nuclear-free zone. In fact the real test regions for a nuclear-free zone to emerge are where states are in conflict with nuclear powers.

Despite these limitations, the nuclear-free-zone concept has been promoted by nonnuclear states in some regions on the basis of the logic that it offers a "symbol to be used at the opportune moment." The nuclear powers, if they accede to the protocols, will be under legal and moral pressure to limit their nuclear activities in the region concerned. "Although the region cannot be completely decoupled from the dynamics of the central balance, even a partial decoupling is better than none."[65]

CONCLUSION

This chapter presented the various efforts by nonnuclear states to erect legal barriers against the use or threat of use of nuclear weapons by nuclear powers. These efforts have only met partial success, as nuclear powers have opposed a global regime to prevent the use of nuclear weapons or a legal convention that bans such use against nonnuclear states that are parties to the NPT and regional nuclear-free-zone arrangements. The discussion points to the powerful role nonnuclear states have played as norm entrepreneurs and reputation intermediaries in this area. The preceding discussion also shows that the tradition of non-use is only an informal intermediary norm, and until and unless it becomes a legal norm, it may generate questions about its vitality and strength in preventing the use of nuclear weapons by those states that possess them. A legal regime would raise the bar on nuclear use, although international law (or for that matter domestic law as well) offers no iron-clad guarantee against violation. The nonnuclear states are only partially convinced of the norm's robustness, and this is evident in their continuing efforts to obtain legal status for the tradition of non-use. For these states, the informal norm is not a stringent guarantee against nuclear use, but is dependent on the vagaries of world politics and technological changes. However, the fact almost all of them have signed onto the NPT even without stringent negative security guarantees suggests that they do see value in the informal norm inherent in the tradition of non-use. The nonnuclear states' concern about non-use assurances may be becoming louder with U.S., Russian, French, and British nuclear policies changing in response to the threats posed by transnational terrorism and new nuclear aspirants in regions of turmoil that are in conflict with the United States. Some of the previously nonnuclear states—for example, Iran and North Korea—have been pursuing independent nuclear programs, in response to these policy changes as well as in keeping with their own regional ambitions and domestic political calculations. More states are likely to follow their lead in years to come, although an overwhelming majority of nonnuclear states would abide by their commitment not to acquire such weapons.

9 CHANGING U.S. POLICIES AND THE TRADITION

THIS CHAPTER ADDRESSES the state of the tradition of non-use of nuclear weapons in the twenty-first century, especially in the context of the changing U.S. nuclear policy. The tradition has been under stress since the end of the Cold War, and particularly since the September 11, 2001, terrorist attacks on U.S. targets. Changes to U.S. nuclear policy have posed one of the major challenges to the tradition. Similar to the United States, other nuclear powers, in particular Russia, Britain, and France, have also expanded the role of nuclear weapons in their strategic doctrines to include the use of chemical and biological weapons by adversaries as a trigger for nuclear response.

At the global level, the stress that the tradition encounters in the early twenty-first century arises from the responses of nuclear states to two main challengers: regional powers and transnational terrorist networks such as al-Qaeda. The regional challengers are states in strategically pivotal regional theaters that hold revisionist ideologies or territorial ambitions. These states have been characterized by the United States as belonging to "the axis of evil" or as "rogue states," although a less pejorative characterization may be "new proliferators." Iran and North Korea are the two major challengers in this regard, but Syria is also considered part of this group, given its chemical weapons program and confrontational policies in the Middle East. North Korea is believed to have acquired a few rudimentary nuclear weapons and missiles, while Iran is presumed to be making efforts at developing nuclear weapons. During the 1980s and 1990s, two other states, Iraq and Libya, were also pursuing nuclear weapons. However, a decade of UN sanctions and the inspection regime that followed the 1991 Gulf War largely destroyed Iraq's nuclear infrastructure, which was further decimated during the 2003 Gulf War and the U.S.-led occupation since then. In December 2003, Libya agreed to disavow nuclear weapons in return for economic and diplomatic normalization with the West.[1]

Other states in the Middle East, such as Syria and Saudi Arabia, may have latent nuclear ambitions. They are also believed to be in possession of chemical and biological weapons that could be used as a "poor man's atomic weapon."[2] Regional states adversarial to the United States have been making sustained efforts to bury their weapons and command-and-control centers deep underground, to make it impossible for America to fully destroy their capabilities or remove their leaders. These problems have been compounded by the development of networks of nuclear transfers involving Pakistan, Iran, North Korea, and Libya. These networks have undermined the nonproliferation regime seriously as the transactions have been taking place even when some states involved are NPT members.[3]

The second source of challenge comes from transnational terrorist networks. Some such groups have reportedly been seeking chemical, biological, and nuclear weapons in order to engage in terrorist attacks that generate mass casualties and panic in urban centers. The potential for nuclear terrorism by groups against established states has gained greater attention since the September 11, 2001, strikes. Defense planners in nuclear states especially have become cognizant of this possibility. In response, nuclear states have begun to relax their no-first-use policies to include contingencies in which preventive and preemptive nuclear strikes have become a feasible option. Terrorist groups could acquire nuclear weapons or components on the black market, through theft, with the blackmailing of weapon storage and transportation facilities, or with the support of wayward scientists such as Pakistan's A. Q. Khan.[4] The problem of "dirty bombs" has also become a highly salient danger to international security. Such bombs can be assembled using nuclear materials in a cocktail fashion and then used to attack urban centers or places where large numbers of people assemble in order to cause maximum casualties through radiation effects.[5]

The most significant response to these twin challenges in terms of potential nuclear use has come from the United States.

THE U.S. RESPONSE

In the face of these security challenges, the United States has revised its nuclear use policy with the intention of preventing the acquisition of weapons of mass destruction (WMD) by regional challengers and terrorist groups and preempting their use. This policy potentially includes the use of nuclear weapons. Since taking office in January 2001, the Bush administration in particular has posed a direct challenge to the long-standing tradition against the use of nuclear weapons. This U.S. nuclear policy, which had been evolving for some time during the presidencies of both George H. W. Bush and Bill Clinton, contains two key elements that directly challenge the tradition. First, the new U.S. posture allows the use of nuclear weapons preemptively or preventively against "rogue states" or terrorist groups that hold any WMD, as well as the option of retaliating with nuclear arms if such actors use WMD. The preventive aspect of the posture is that the United States could use force, including nuclear weapons, in an effort to thwart the development of WMD by states that it perceives may use such capabilities once developed. These modifications are reflected in the changes to the negative security guarantees that the United States had offered to nonnuclear states. John Bolton, then undersecretary of state for Arms Control and International Security, argued in 2002 that these decisions were made in a different "geostrategic context," and that they needed to be reviewed in view of today's changed security environment.[6] And, second, the U.S. administration's off-and-on efforts at developing "usable" low-yield nuclear weapons in order to face the challenge of regional actors and terrorist groups and to be able to penetrate deeply buried bunkers or other underground facilities of regional foes also appear likely to adversely affect the tradition.

The Bush Changes
The United States has taken the lead in efforts to water down the tradition of non-use in response to pressures emanating from numerous sources: the asymmetric threats that Washington has been facing from both state and nonstate actors; new technological trends in warfare; and bureaucratic politics involving scientific laboratories that design and manufacture nuclear weapons. For a period of time after September 11, 2001, many of the changes in nuclear policy that the administration had initiated went unchallenged. Lately, however, a vocal group of Democratic and Republican senators and congressmen and nongovernmental organizations have emerged as strong opponents of radical changes to the U.S. nuclear policy in this regard. What are the manifestations of change in U.S. nuclear policy? What are the sources of these changes?

First, U.S. military planners have been considering the possibility of using nuclear weapons under certain circumstances against states possessing chemical, biological, and nuclear weapons, as these weapons are believed to have spread or are likely to spread to several states and possibly to terrorist groups. These modifications in policy come from changes in assessments of the security challenges facing the United States after the Cold War and from new assumptions about the behavior of regional states. As discussed in Chapter 4, the George H. W. Bush and Clinton administrations initiated a policy called "calculated ambiguity" as a way to deter the use of chemical and biological weapons by a regional adversary. These changes were accelerated by the 1991 Persian Gulf War and by the disclosures about Iraq's clandestine nuclear weapons program during and after the war. During that war, U.S. leaders made several implicit references to the possibility of nuclear use in the event of Iraq's using WMD against U.S. troops or allies. In January 1991, when U.S. forces were deployed to liberate Kuwait, Defense Secretary Dick Cheney issued the top secret Nuclear Weapons Employment Policy (NUWEP), which "formally tasked the military to plan for nuclear operations against nations capable of developing WMD. This guidance resulted in Single Integrated Operations Plan (SIOP) 93, the first overall nuclear war plan formally to incorporate Third World WMD targets."[7] The Clinton administration continued this trend toward widening the use of nuclear arms against states that would use chemical and biological weapons. Presidential Decision Directive (PDD) 60, signed by Clinton in November 1997, permitted U.S. nuclear strikes in retaliation to chemical or biological weapons use by enemy states.[8]

Since taking office in 2001, the George W. Bush administration has enlarged the potential role for nuclear weapons. Under the ambitious new policy guidelines issued by the administration, nuclear weapons have been assigned three purposes: to deter; to preempt the use of WMDs, including chemical and biological weapons; and to prevent their buildup by additional states. The preemptive dimension of the new doctrine implies that the United States can use nuclear weapons if it believes that a regional adversary is planning to use WMD in the battlefield or against U.S. troops stationed abroad. Unlike preemption, prevention implies that no imminent attack is likely, but the regional adversary is developing the WMD capability with the intention of using it against the United States at some future point. The United States perceives that it is in its interests to prevent this contingency by attacking WMD facilities early on, before they become a security menace. This idea is driven by the assumption that deterrence does not necessarily work against rogue states and terrorist organizations.[9] If the adversary is hiding WMD in deep bunkers or facilities that are not destroyable through conventional strikes, the

United States would keep open the option of using its capabilities, including nuclear weapons.

Thus the George W. Bush administration has ushered in the second nuclear age by transforming the utility of nuclear weapons and by widening the conditions under which they can be used—the conditions previously considered as "unworthy" and "unimaginable"—as well as by adding new missions for nuclear weapons. In the changed circumstances, the administration has refocused the nuclear threat from Russia to the regional states.[10] With this new policy, the United States has taken a major step toward the "conventionalization" of nuclear weapons and their potential use against foes that are not necessarily nuclear-armed states. The Bush administration made this policy more explicit through two documents: *The National Security Strategy of the United States of America* of September 2002, which stated that in order to "forestall or prevent . . . [attacks with WMD] by our adversaries, the United States will, if necessary, act preemptively," and the *National Strategy to Combat Weapons of Mass Destruction* (NSCWMD) of December 2002, which declared: "The United States will continue to make clear that it reserves the right to respond with overwhelming force—including through resort to all of our options—to the use of WMD against the United States, our forces abroad and friends and allies."[11]

In a classified document titled "Presidential Directive 17," signed on September 14, 2002, President George W. Bush authorized the United States to "continue to make clear that it reserves the right to respond with overwhelming force—including potentially nuclear weapons—to the use of [weapons of mass destruction] against the United States, our forces abroad, and friends and allies." However, the publicly released version of the NSCWMD document replaced the terms, "including potentially nuclear weapons" with "including through resort to all of our options." The document suggests that nuclear weapons are very much part of the overwhelming force that the United States could use in a regional conflict. There were indications that military planning included the use of nuclear weapons under certain circumstances if Iraq used chemical and biological weapons in the 2003 war.[12] Interestingly, such a use would have received strong public support in the United States.[13] The 2002 Nuclear Posture Review (NPR) added several functions to the U.S. nuclear capability in terms of regional security, especially in the Middle East and the Persian Gulf. They included the defense of Israel against states such as Iran and Syria, assurance to regional allies, dissuasion of potential adversaries from pursuing nuclear and other WMD capabilities, deterrence against the use of WMD against U.S. forces and allies, as well as the defeat of regional states bent on aggression.[14]

The Draft Doctrine for Joint Nuclear Operations prepared by the Pentagon in March 2005 incorporated preemption into the U.S. nuclear doctrine. It states that "integrating conventional and nuclear attacks will ensure the most efficient use of force and provide U.S. leaders with a broader range of strike options to address immediate contingencies."[15] The draft doctrine envisions "commanders requesting presidential approval to use them [nuclear weapons] to preempt an attack by a nation or a terrorist group using weapons of mass destruction." In addition, the draft talks about the option to use nuclear weapons to destroy existing stockpiles of nuclear, chemical, or biological weapons in regional states.[16] To arms control advocates, the draft doctrine envisages "nuclear pre-emption, which the new doctrine enshrines into official U.S. joint nuclear doctrine for the first time, where the objective no longer is deterrence through threatened retaliation but battlefield destruction of targets."[17] The underlying structural motivation seems to be attaining overwhelming nuclear and conventional superiority so that no regional challenger or peer great power state will challenge U.S. security interests for a long time to come.[18] Although the administration appears to have withdrawn the draft, its policy contents apparently were not changed.

One assumption running through the calculations of the U.S. administrations has been that the new regional challengers are not as deterrable with nuclear capability as the Soviet Union was, and that they may engage in behavior that contradicts the rationality assumptions of deterrence theory and policy. A former staff member of the George W. Bush administration, Keith Payne, captured the belief held by the administration officials that "potential U.S. enemies differ from the Cold War-era Soviet Union in that enemy leaders now may not value the welfare of their populations or their own survival, and may make decisions based on superstition or fanaticism." Officials also believe that "the United States might possibly face opponents driven by 'unquestioned adherence to a leader who has a bad dream' or relies on 'fortune-telling or astrology or all those things that underlie decision-making in many parts of the world." In his view, "interest in research on the new, low-yield nuclear weapons comes from a desire for a deterrent that is believable."[19] However, critics find problems in this approach toward deterrence. On the one hand, the administration believed that a nuclear-armed Iraq would not be bound by deterrence, but it also believed that America could be deterred by a nuclear-armed Iraq.[20]

During the military buildup prior to the attack on Iraq in March 2003, military planners were understood to have studied a list of potential targets for the use of tactical nuclear weapons to respond to or to preempt an Iraqi use of chemical or biological weapons, or to destroy deeply buried command and control facilities. The *Theater Nuclear Planning Document,* prepared by the U.S. Strategic Command, listed several potential targets for a nuclear strike.[21] Apparently referring to Iraq's use of chemical and biological weapons, Defense Secretary Donald Rumsfeld stated: "we will not foreclose the possible use of nuclear weapons if attacked," although "we can do what needs to be done using conventional capabilities."[22] Administration officials warned Saddam Hussein's regime against resorting to any WMD and threatened the use of any "means necessary," without ruling out nuclear retaliation.[23] The seriousness of the administration's nuclear planning was evident in the authority for such nuclear use given to the Omaha-based U.S. Strategic Command (STRATCOM), which was earlier focusing on strategic nuclear combat with Russia and China. STRATCOM became the single command for the planning and conduct of the full range of operations to combat terrorist states and organizations. The new U.S. policy has thus blurred the distinction between nuclear and conventional forces by mixing the two in the structure of military bureaucracy and practice.[24]

In the spring of 2006, a report emerged suggesting how seriously the Bush administration had been considering the use of nuclear weapons against regional proliferators. According to an article in the *New Yorker* magazine by veteran journalist Seymour Hersh, the administration had been actively considering a preventive attack on Iran's buried nuclear facilities with bunker-buster tactical nuclear weapons such as B61-11, as the facilities were beyond the reach of existing conventional bombs. Nuclear use, in addition to massive conventional bombing, to remove the Iranian regime had been proposed by the Defense Science Board, an advisory panel filled (by Defense Secretary Donald Rumsfeld) with members who were all known for their hawkishness on the question of nuclear use against regional proliferators. Although the Pentagon and the Joint Chiefs of Staff (JCS) opposed nuclear use, there is evidence that U.S. aircraft from the Arabian Sea had been flying simulated nuclear weapons delivery missions within Iranian radar reach. Reputational concerns are part of the reasons for the Pentagon's objection to an attack on Iran. Hersh quoted a Pentagon official as saying: "bombing of Iran could provoke 'a chain re-action' of attacks on American facilities and citizens throughout the world. 'What will 1.2 billion Muslims think the day we attack Iran?'"[25] The Pentagon initially suggested the nuclear option as the way to guarantee 100 percent re-moval of Iranian nuclear facilities. However, later the JCS wanted to withdraw the option, but the White House would not do so. The problem that is increas-ingly understood in the Pentagon is the impossibility of achieving a 100 per-cent removal without massive civilian casualties and radiation contamination with the existing bunker-buster nuclear bomb, B61-11. Moreover, the political implications of attacking a Muslim country "which is not armed with similar weapons and which says it has no intention of making" them, weigh heavily in the rethinking.[26] Hersh's implication is that the Pentagon wanted to foreclose the idea of attacking Iran at all, and saying nuclear use was the only way to guarantee success would remove the attack option from the table, as the mili-tary expected the administration not to be prepared to resort to nuclear use. To a great extent, this confirms the operation of the tradition of non-use. The military is confident that the administration will not initiate a war against Iran if it implies violating the tradition of non-use.

The plan for the development and potential use of low-yield mini-nukes and higher-yield bunker-buster bombs, debated by the administration and the Congress, is a second, related, manifestation of change in U.S. nuclear policy. Regional challengers are increasingly building sophisticated command-and-control and weapons storage facilities buried deep underground. There is a type of offense-defense arms race at work here. The building of deep bunkers by regional challengers is partially driven by improvements in U.S. interven-tion capabilities, especially precision-guided munitions technologies. More-over, U.S. conventional superiority is so overwhelmingly preponderant that some regional challengers assume that WMD possession is essential for de-terring the United States from military intervention or mounting coercive di-plomacy against them. They are especially worried about U.S. regime-change plans. This, in turn, encourages the United States to develop more accurate weapons to maintain its preponderance vis-à-vis regional actors. The U.S. determination to obtain overwhelming superiority there, in turn, compels smaller actors to develop capabilities that are necessary to deter and make war costly for the United States, if it occurs. The Robust Nuclear Earth Pen-etrator (RNEP) that the Pentagon proposed to the House and Senate Armed Services Committee in March 2003 has been touted as a "device designed to dig into the ground before it explodes and crush any facility buried beneath it. Already five times more powerful than the device detonated at Hiroshima, the bomb would have an even greater impact because a nuclear weapon's force is multiplied when its shock wave penetrates the rocky crust of the earth." The other weapon that was proposed was a low-yield mini-nuke of .01 kilotons. The latter proposal was meant to lift the 1993 Spratt-Furse amendment, which restricted development of low-yield warheads, below the 5 kiloton range.[27] Congress, however, after sanctioning research in 2003 and 2004, discontinued funding in November 2005.[28] This suggests that the majority of congressional members oppose diluting the tradition, as they fear the arrival of so-called "usable weapons" would adversely affect the tradition.

Supporters of the new weapons argue that the United States needs new nuclear weapons programs in order to keep its nuclear scientists and weapon designers on the job; these personnel will be able to pass on the technological skills to the next generation of weapon designers.[29] The weapons labs insist that research on low-yield weapons is essential to meet the new threats that the United States is facing. Los Alamos weapons analysts Thomas Dowler and Joseph Howard II argue that the United States has no proportionate response to a rogue dictator who uses chemical or biological weapons against U.S. troops. The smallest nuclear weapon in the U.S. arsenal is of Hiroshima-size yields, which would be so devastating that no U.S. president could use it, and, as a result, the United States would be self-deterred. To overcome this deficiency, Dowler and Howard argued that the United States should develop "mini-nukes" with yields equivalent to .01 kilotons. These low-yield weapons could provide an effective response for countering the new enemies in a crisis "while not violating the principle of proportionality."[30] It seems the two key makers of nuclear weapons, the Lawrence Livermore and the Los Alamos Laboratories, are keen to continue the research on these weapons with the hope of eventual development. Their interest in new weapons stem from their concern that most U.S. nuclear weapons were built during the Cold War period and that programs such as the Reliable Replacement Warhead (RRW) and Stockpile Stewardship Program will not be sufficient to develop nuclear weapons that can stay longer in U.S. arsenals and can meet the new security challenges.[31]

The rationale for low-yield weapons offered by Dowler and Howard in 1991 was given new impetus in American deliberations one decade later, in the new strategic environment that emerged after September 11, 2001. Proponents of mini-nukes and RNEP bunker-busters argue that the United States needs such weapons to deter the use of chemical, biological, and nuclear weapons buried underground. According to former Defense Secretary Donald Rumsfeld, the bunker busters are "needed to deter foes from trying to hide their arsenals in deep tunnels."[32] It is contended that the United States will not be "intentionally targeting civilians," but the "aim is to destroy command and control centers, leadership targets and key military-industrial assets." If thousands of "innocent civilians would be harmed in the process, this would be an unintentional by-product of the location of targets."[33] Some weapons makers and strategic planners argue that since the United States has signed onto the Chemical and Biological Weapons Conventions and has destroyed all its biological weapons agents, it has no meaningful reply to the threat posed by regional WMD.

The incentive also comes from the persistent dream of some weapon makers and their supporters to conventionalize nuclear arms and thereby remove the normative restraints attached to their use. To some analysts, the available bunker-buster, B61-11—a modified gravity bomb—cannot do the job, as it will not penetrate beyond 20 feet or so. Further, given the massive civilian casualties and environmental damage it would cause, a U.S. president would be self-deterred from using the weapon. An adversary, knowing these constraints, would not be deterred. By reducing the yield of a nuclear weapon to one hundredth of a kiloton, the gap between a nuclear and a conventional explosive could be bridged, and nuclear use would become more acceptable.[34] By developing new nuclear weapons, administration officials and some scientists in weapons labs hope to reduce the collateral damage, in the form of casualties and destruction of property, that characterizes the use of currently available nuclear weapons in the U.S. arsenal. The hope is that by removing some of the immense destructiveness of nuclear weapons, opposition to the use of nuclear weapons would be reduced, if not eliminated.[35] The tradition of non-use is thus a constraint on nuclear use, and the source of the tradition lies in the destructive power of the existing weapons, a confirmation of the model presented in Chapter 2.

Other arguments to justify the development of mini-nukes and RNEPs have to do with the bureaucratic politics of technological change. They include: (1) technological imperatives are difficult to arrest; (2) other states will develop them anyway; and (3) nuclear weapons cannot be disinvented, but if a useful purpose can be found for them, the billions of dollars that the United States spends on nuclear arms can be put to better use.[36]

CRITICISMS AGAINST THE U.S. POLICY

The changing U.S. nuclear policy that may allow the use of nuclear arms under certain circumstances has elicited several criticisms. The policy assumes that weaker regional challengers, especially hard-core opponents, will not be deterred without the United States presenting them with all retaliatory options, including the possible use of nuclear arms. Conversely, it assumes that a weaker challenger will be deterred if it realizes that U.S. nuclear retaliation is likely in the event of its using WMD. The assumption is that there are many weaker challengers out there who are undeterrable with conventional retaliatory threats alone.

Contrary to this assumption, however, in almost all cases, the weaker challenger may be deterred without the threat of nuclear retaliation, and nuclear use may be a highly disproportionate response to those few states or entities that would use chemical and biological weapons.[37] In the improbable event of the use of such weapons by a regional state challenger against the United States or its key allies (unlikely because of the near certainty of a powerful conventional retaliatory strike that would prove to be suicidal for the challenger), nuclear retaliation may be an unnecessary option as punishment can be achieved through other means. The U.S. conventional arsenal includes the BLU-82, a 6,800-kilogram Daisy Cutter bomb (used against Taliban caves in Afghanistan) and the more powerful GBU-43/B MOAB (Massive Ordnance Air Blast). In March 2003, the United States tested the latter, a 21,000-pound precision-guided munition, which is designed:

> to produce a tremendous explosion that would be effective against hard-target entrances, soft-to-medium surface targets, and for anti-personnel purposes. Because of the size of the explosion, it is also effective at [landing zone] clearance and mine and beach obstacle clearance . . . The massive weapon provides a capability to perform psychological operations, attack large area targets, or hold at-risk threats hidden within tunnels or caves.[38]

The pure conventional use of nuclear weapons for the demolition of hardened targets does not produce much utility for nuclear weapons, as this task can be accomplished with the help of new precision-guided munitions. Indeed, in March 2007, the head of STRATCOM, General James E. Cartwright, told a

Congressional committee that the United States has dominant conventional capabilities, replacing the need for nuclear use in almost all areas, except to "respond promptly to globally dispersed or fleeting threats." According to him, the U.S. Air Force was studying a conventional "precision global strike missile," using available intercontinental ballistic missiles (ICBMs).[39]

Some critics have argued that a low-yield mini-nuke will not accomplish the task of destroying all underground bunkers. Such weapons may not fully destroy biological and chemical agents buried deep underground or protected by water as radiation from nuclear attack would be absorbed by soil, moisture, and concrete.[40] Further, as a congressionally mandated study in April 2005 suggested, earth-penetrating nuclear weapons, even if they are able to destroy military targets buried deep underground, will inflict "massive casualties at ground level."[41] It is likely that regional challengers will make further efforts to dig deeper in order to circumvent a U.S. nuclear attack. "Even the most powerful weapons cannot destroy bunkers tunneled under just 400 meters of granite," and if a regional challenger finds that it is threatened with a mini-nuke or a bunker buster, it could deepen the underground facility beyond the reach of the weapon.[42] In addition, it can develop mobile facilities that are not always easy to detect.

U.S. conventional power is so overwhelmingly superior that in almost all conflict situations, it can, by itself, deter weaker regional adversaries from the use of chemical or biological weapons by it alone. The hard core challengers— for example, Iran and North Korea—are unlikely to cross the threshold, knowing well that the United States can retaliate with massive conventional capabilities. The failure to use chemical or biological weapons by Iraq during both the 1991 and 2003 Gulf Wars suggests that the threat of use of WMD by a hard-core regional challenger is not always as credible as it appears to be. Even in the North Korean case, Pyongyang's possession of nuclear weapons does not imply their use, as the country's leadership should know that a nuclear attack could invite a massive conventional counterstrike and possibly a nuclear counterattack. Moreover, the North Korean rhetoric about war cannot be construed as equivalent to an actual policy, because regional challengers may use language akin to compellence or deterrence in order to gain political concessions from stronger powers, but, when push comes to shove, it is not clear the North Korean elite would take excessive risks such as the use of WMD.

Proponents of nuclear use against "rogue states" argue that irrational actors cannot be deterred by conventional weapons—but this also suggests that they may not be easily deterred by nuclear weapons, either. Furthermore, the threat of nuclear use may not be credible to a regional challenger, as the tradition of non-use itself is a powerful consideration for a regional actor not to concede in a conflict with the United States. It is not easy to carry out a nuclear threat unless the use is in response to massive casualties inflicted by chemical and biological attacks. Similarly, as Scott Sagan argues, the new U.S. nuclear policy creates a "commitment trap," thus forcing the president to use nuclear weapons in an "inappropriate manner in a future conflict." To maintain the president's international and domestic reputation for honoring commitments, he would have to use nuclear weapons in response to a chemical or biological attack.[43]

Using nuclear weapons preemptively or preventively is easier said than done. The United States would be committing the same crime that it rightly accuses "rogue states" and terrorists of perpetrating—that is, the killing of innocent civilians—if it ever unleashes a nuclear attack on cities or states where terrorists have taken refuge or residence. Thus, the victims of rogue rulers—that is, the population of rogue states—will suffer for crimes that they never committed. This is tantamount to crimes against humanity. It would cause grave international condemnation. In opposing nuclear use against regional states, General Lee Butler, a former commander-in-chief of the U.S. Strategic Air Command (SAC) and now a powerful advocate of nuclear disarmament, put it succinctly: "there are no rogue nations, only rogue leaders."[44] His statement captures the fact that actions of leaders who usurp power through undemocratic means cannot be responded to by punishing their people, as the latter have little control over the selection of the leader or his or her subsequent policy choices. Nuclear retaliation for a chemical or biological attack will be highly disproportionate to the pain that chemical and biological attack would cause. While it may sound useful for deterrence purposes, a more credible strategy would be to build and improve defenses against such attacks. It is also argued that the U.S. aim should not be to wipe out the population of a "rogue" state that ordered chemical or biological use, but the defeat, reform, and transformation of that society as a normal member of the international system, which may not be achievable with a nuclear attack.[45] Regime change through a conventional offensive is a preferred option here to the mass destruction and killing of several thousand innocent citizens.

The use of nuclear weapons against terrorists is unlikely to succeed if the terrorist group in possession of WMD capabilities believes in cataclysmic attacks and does not mind martyrdom for its members and the societies that host them. In fact, it is perhaps in the interests of terrorist groups that hold millenarian ideologies that the United States use these weapons and thereby receive international condemnation and tarnish its image and reputation.

There may well be an argument in favor of the United States using nuclear weapons in certain conditions: a terrorist group holding nuclear weapons is about to launch an attack; U.S. intelligence has accurate information on this; and there is no other way to eliminate that capability quickly and effectively.[46] However, even in this case, nuclear use raises several problems. First, if the target is located in a heavily populated area, a nuclear attack could kill a massive number of civilians who have nothing to do with the terrorists or the rogue leaders. Even if it is an unpopulated area, the best weapon may still be conventional, as nuclear use need not result in the destruction of the nuclear device that the terrorist group holds. Using nuclear weapons against terrorists sounds appealing, but this is not all that simple a solution to the complex problem posed by transnational terrorism. In the most likely scenario, the terrorists would be smart enough to keep the weapon in a populated area, if they can, as the United States would find it difficult to attack with nuclear weapons; and if the United States did attack, the terrorists would obtain unparalleled publicity for their cause, especially if the intelligence report that formed the basis for attack proves to be wrong and the terrorist threat was a hoax.

A second problem with the U.S. strategy of preemptive or preventive nuclear use is the political constraint associated with such use and the physical occupation of the country afterwards. For instance, in 2003, had Saddam Hussein used WMD and the United States responded with nuclear weapons, such a retaliation would have killed a large number of innocent Iraqi civilians. The subsequent occupation and transformation of Iraq in accordance with U.S. goals would have become much more difficult as the popular support for any U.S.-installed regime would have been even less than it was in 2006. Further, the broad Arab public would have become even more inflamed against the United States as a result of such killings.

Third, opponents of mini-nukes argue that their development and deployment would make nuclear use more likely and thereby break the tradition of non-use. To them, nuclear weapons should be reserved as a class apart, a weapon that should be used only in response to a nuclear attack on the U.S. territory itself. This high threshold of nuclear use serves U.S. interests, especially since the United States holds such an overwhelming conventional superiority over regional challengers. The new U.S. nuclear policy "would put potential adversaries into a use-or-lose posture with their WMD if a U.S. attack appeared likely."[47]

Finally, intelligence failures regarding the capabilities and intentions of a regional challenger can have major consequences. It is unlikely that a regional power would stockpile its WMD in a single site far from population centers, and it is even more unlikely that the United States would receive accurate intelligence information in order to justify a preemptive nuclear strike. The grossly inaccurate intelligence warnings in 2002–03 on Iraq's WMD capabilities point to the problems in this area.[48] The consequences of nuclear use on Iraq in 2003 in response to dubious intelligence reports would have been highly negative.[49] The "Gulf War syndrome"—supposedly the result of chemical detonations or contaminated radioactive debris from the use of depleted uranium in conventional bombs during the 1991 war—caused enormous damage to the health and morale of exposed U.S. troops.[50] Operating in a nuclear-contaminated environment, the U.S. troops would have found it difficult to engage in postwar nation building and policing functions.

Political Risks

There are several risks in the United States developing usable mini-nukes and RNEP-type nuclear bunker busters, inducting them into its arsenal, and transforming its nuclear policy into one that calls for the early use of such weapons against nonnuclear states. The two key risks are emulation by other nuclear weapons states and the negative impact they will have on the nuclear nonproliferation regime.

Emulation Risk   States tend to emulate the defense policies of others, especially if they find that the leading actors are consistently pursuing a particular path. There is considerable fear that if the United States lowers the threshold of nuclear use, it may encourage other nuclear states, including the new ones, Israel, India, Pakistan, North Korea, and possibly Iran, to lower their threshold of use as well. "Until now the United States has reserved nuclear weapons for retaliation against nuclear attacks or immediate threats to national survival, a standard tacitly but widely accepted around the world."[51] If the United States engages in nuclear saber rattling, especially on the basis of dubious intelligence (as happened in the case on Iraq's WMD capabilities), it may have a hard time convincing other states to exercise nuclear restraint, especially if they perceive an immediate strategic advantage in not doing so. The U.S. strategic doctrine of deterrence was emulated by the Soviet Union, and, to a lesser extent, by the other NWS. The new U.S. policy of using nuclear weapons against chemical and biological weapons use has already been emulated by Russia, Britain, France, and India. A similar emulation could occur in the area of nuclear use as well.

Pressures on the Nonproliferation Regime and Increased Horizontal Proliferation   The use of nuclear weapons by the United States would be likely to adversely affect the nonproliferation regime which has been a facilitator of the current nuclear status quo. Nonnuclear states, especially those inimical to the United States, would learn a powerful lesson that nuclear attack against a state occurred because it lacked the capacity to retaliate, and hence it is wise to acquire such capabilities in order to deter potential U.S. nuclear attacks.[52] One study concludes:

> Targeting nuclear weapons at regional troublemakers will provide them with a justification to acquire nuclear weapons. By using nuclear weapons in this way, the United States is sending a message that nuclear weapons are important for achieving prestige in world affairs and for accomplishing military and political objectives. It also indicates that nuclear powers have no intention of eliminating their nuclear arsenals, as required by the NPT.[53]

Nonnuclear states have assiduously bargained for negative security assurances, and the 1995 extension of the NPT in perpetuity was largely due to the partial commitment made by the NWS, including the United States, of no first use against nonnuclear signatories to the treaty. Nonnuclear states have already expressed their opposition to the new nuclear policies of nuclear states by not agreeing to a final statement at the 2005 NPT review conference. Further, there is a disjunction between the nuclear policy of the George W. Bush administration and its declared "moral rejection of violence against civilians, and the categorical injunction against 'weapons of mass terror.'"[54] The hedged no-first-use policy has practically eroded much of the strength of such a commitment, to the detriment of nonproliferation goals.[55]

The policy of nuclear strikes for preventive and preemptive purposes can encourage potentially targeted states to vigorously pursue nuclear weapons. The U.S. policy of regime removal in those targeted countries has already put pressure on such states to pursue nuclear acquisition in the hopes of thwarting potential U.S. military intervention or diplomatic coercion. The incentives for nuclear acquisition for Iran and North Korea have increased since the two

Gulf Wars. North Korea already tested a nuclear device in October 2006, while Iran has accelerated its uranium enrichment program. If Iran acquires nuclear weapons, there will be pressure on some Gulf states to go nuclear. There are historical examples of U.S. pressure forcing states to acquire nuclear weapons. As discussed in Chapter 3, the Eisenhower administration's nuclear blackmail was one of the reasons for China's launching its nuclear program in 1955 in the middle of the Quemoy-Matsu crisis.

Although the technology for functional mini-nukes appears to be several years away, it is quite plausible that, if they are developed, the United States would deploy such weapons and a president would be tempted to use them under circumstances that are tactically driven. The potential test for the non-use norm would be if leaders use the new weapons despite having other options at their command, or rather desist from use even when other conventional options are not available. If mini-nukes are used, it would show that the non-use tradition is not a deeply embedded norm and that the distinctive characteristics of the weapons have had something to do with the observance of the norm thus far, as such weapons blur the boundaries between conventional and nuclear arms. The interaction of the material and the moral is thus crucial in this case. New ideas tend to arise from material sources, and the political elite is not driven purely by existing ideas (i.e., morally and ethically appropriate ones) devoid of consideration of the particular military and political consequences of the instrument of coercion of hand. Once the disproportionate destructive power of nuclear weapons is removed, the temptation to use them in battlefield situations could increase.

Reputation Costs   How would the reputational constraints inherent in the tradition of non-use of nuclear weapons affect a nuclear attacker? The tradition against the use of nuclear weapons arose partly because of a realization among nuclear states that a nuclear attack could not be contained and that the effects of such a use would severely harm their reputation and image nationally and internationally. The use of nuclear weapons by the United States could have tremendous consequences for America's international standing and alliance relationships. The reputation considerations that gave rise to the tradition will be so high that repairing the damage may not be easy.[56] It is very unlikely that even its closest allies would support nuclear use absent a clear and present danger of nuclear attack. Nuclear retaliation against chemical and biological attacks (most likely with limited impacts) is also unlikely to receive the support of allies.

The 2003 Gulf War offered an indication of the limited allied support and generally negative international reaction to a preventive or regime-changing war, especially one based on dubious intelligence. If the United States uses nuclear weapons, the leadership role of the United States could suffer irreparable damage, accentuating the legitimacy deficit for the United States that began since the 2003 Gulf War. Notes Quester: "A multinational instinct toward retreat would mean less support for Washington as an alliance leader, and it might even mean a total termination of some alliances or just an erosion of their effectiveness."[57] The use of nuclear weapons in the Middle East by the United States against a Muslim country could further embitter America's relationship with the states in the region, including its allies.[58] In October 2001, in the prelude to the Afghan War, U.S. Secretary of State Colin Powell stated that the United States would not rule out the use of nuclear weapons. This statement evoked the response from Washington's ally, Pakistan, that it "firmly and categorically rejects even the thought of using nuclear weapons tactically or otherwise."[59] Nuclear use in Afghanistan would have generated more terrorism as the images of the dead and injured would have propelled even moderate Muslims all over the world to turn against America and Americans.

CONCLUSION

As the twenty-first century dawned, the tradition of non-use came under increased pressure from established nuclear powers, especially the United States. Largely in response to asymmetric challenges posed by terrorist groups as well as regional states that hold WMD such as chemical and biological weapons and aspire to become nuclear states, the United States and other nuclear powers have restructured their nuclear doctrines and have tried to find new uses for their nuclear weapons. The effort to develop usable mini-nukes springs from a desire to redesign the material character of the weapon so as to undercut the reputational constraints inherent in the use of any of the currently available nuclear weapons. But the efforts of the domestic opposition, especially a majority in the U.S. Congress, have helped to curtail the development of such weapons. This opposition is indeed arising out of fear that if the weapons are developed, future leaders may break the tradition of non-use.

The challenge to the tradition is also coming from Russia, France, Britain, Israel, and India—the states that, along with the United States, have officially expanded nuclear deterrence to include retaliation against chemical and biological weapons. Meanwhile, China and Pakistan have engaged in activities such as nuclear transfers to aspiring states that violate the spirit of the nonpro-liferation regime and have thereby helped in the diffusion of capabilities that may be used by recalcitrant regional powers or disgruntled terrorist groups. There is also the question about how deeply ingrained the tradition is among the new nuclear states as well as the aspiring ones. Numerous sources, then, are presenting the tradition of non-use with some of the most difficult chal-lenges it has faced in its sixty-three-year history.

10 CONCLUSIONS

THE PRECEDING CHAPTERS discussed the tradition of non-use of nuclear weapons that has emerged during the sixty-three years since the first and last use of nuclear weapons against Hiroshima and Nagasaki in August 1945. A tradition in this respect is a time-honored practice of non-use generating expectations about the appropriate behavior of nuclear weapon states. I treat the normative prohibition inherent in the tradition as informal and intermediate, given that it has yet to become a legal or formal norm and that a majority of nuclear states retain their option of first use of nuclear arms against non-nuclear states. In Chapter 2, I argued that the tradition emerged largely due to material and reputational factors, that is, the immense destructive character of the weapon and the possible adverse reputational impact on nuclear states if they used their weapons against nonnuclear states. Moral and legal considerations are subsumed in the reputational variable. Tactical and strategic factors are important as well for the non-use of nuclear weapons, but country studies in various chapters show that they by themselves cannot fully account for the reluctance of nuclear states to resort to nuclear attacks. After 1945, but more prominently after the hydrogen bomb tests in the early 1950s, it began to dawn on decision makers that the use of nuclear weapons as a battlefield option is constrained: nuclear weapons are too destructive to obtain strategic and tactical objectives and political purposes without tarnishing the image and reputation of the user. The Hiroshima and Nagasaki experiences were pivotal in this regard. U.S. atomic scientists proposed international control of the atom as a way to prevent their use by aggressive governments. These scientists influenced the Truman administration's decision on this issue. They were indeed the first reputation intermediaries or norm entrepreneurs for the non-use norm; they would then be followed by strategic thinkers, peace movements, and nonaligned developing countries. President Truman also made the first formally enshrined distinction between atomic and conventional weapons by placing control of the former in the hands of the civilian leadership.

However, after the Soviets achieved nuclear weapons state (NWS) status in 1949 and the Cold War competition reached full steam, the issue of complete international control of the atom faded. Truman toyed with the idea of waging a preventive war against the Soviet Union before it acquired nuclear weapons. His refraining from such a preventive strike on the Soviet Union while the United States held an atomic monopoly gave birth to a nascent tradition of non-use. The next landmark event was the Korean War (1950–53), when the United States considered using nuclear arms to stop Chinese intervention and military advances against Allied forces, but Truman chose not to go that route and thereby strengthened the tradition. Truman's successor, Dwight Eisenhower, made serious efforts at nuclear brinkmanship with China on three major occasions during the 1950s. However, he eventually backed off due largely to reputational concerns, that is, fear of intense adverse international reaction, especially from Western allies. What is significant is that although tactical/strategic considerations were discussed by U.S. officials, in the end, reputational concerns appeared to be of higher salience in their calculations, as evident in the discussions at the National Security Council (NSC) meetings (as presented in Chapter 3) on the question of nuclear use.

The 1954 *Bravo* atmospheric tests of powerful hydrogen bombs by the United States at Bikini Atoll were perhaps the most pivotal events in the evolution of the tradition. These tests, and their radiation effects in the Pacific, prompted persistent demands by international protest movements and developing countries for a nuclear test ban treaty. The Soviet Union actively promoted and supported international peace movements, while projecting an image of a supporter of developing countries in the nuclear disarmament area. In 1963, the superpowers negotiated the Partial Test Ban Treaty (PTBT) as a way to forestall nuclear proliferation and quell international protests over nuclear testing; this treaty also helped to strengthen the tradition of non-use. The Cuban Missile Crisis, involving the two nuclear-armed superpowers, had a major spillover effect on the tradition, as the danger of a nuclear war became globally known. The superpowers stepped up their efforts at arms control and nonproliferation after the crisis. The fifth nuclear power, China, articulated its belief in nuclear non-use, and pledged a no-first-use policy against both nuclear and nonnuclear states following its nuclear tests in 1964. Both Presidents John F. Kennedy and Lyndon Johnson considered a preventive strike on China (see Chapter 4) to arrest the Communist regime's nuclear acquisition, but in the end refrained from doing so, partly due to reputation considerations.

The Nuclear Nonproliferation Treaty (NPT) of 1968 was critical in partially legitimizing the tradition of non-use. Although there were no specific negative security guarantees in the treaty, the bargaining between nuclear haves and have-nots included a tacit understanding that a state in good standing with the NPT would not be targeted with nuclear weapons. The negative security assurances that the nuclear states offered on various occasions in the context of the NPT review conferences and the treaty's renewal provide a limited legal basis to the tradition. Since these assurances lack the status of a full-fledged legal treaty or convention, and since the NWS declare that they are "political" as opposed to "legal" commitments, they have only partial value. However, they do add to the informal non-use norm inherent in the tradition. In Chapters 5 and 6, reasonable evidence was provided with respect to the calculations of the other four official NWS (Russia, Britain, France, and China) and the three second-generation nuclear powers (Israel, India, and Pakistan) on the question of nuclear non-use. These cases also show that differences in political systems played hardly any role in the tradition's emergence and persistence as it has been observed by all nuclear states, especially the Communist states. The persistent efforts by nonnuclear states to obtain legally binding negative security guarantees suggest that they do not yet view the tradition as a strong norm, but as an informal norm that needs to be reinforced by legal rules and agreements in order to make the barrier for use even higher. However, nuclear states do not want to trap themselves into legal commitments, as they fear that such pledges could further constrain them from resorting to nuclear threats for deterrence and compellence purposes. Although legal treaties can be violated just like an informal norm, the reluctance on the part of the nuclear states and eagerness among the nonnuclear states for such a treaty suggest that both view legal arrangements as placing a higher threshold on potential nuclear use.

By the late 1960s, the tradition of non-use had become part of the understanding of leaders in the United States and elsewhere. A concrete example was the statement by President Johnson in September 1964 to the effect that he was not willing to use nuclear weapons and break the nineteen-year-old tradition that his predecessors had been following. Successive developments suggest the deepening and broadening of the tradition in U.S. policy over time: the Carter administration's decision to scrap the development of the neutron bomb because of the fear of blurring the distinction between conventional and nuclear weapons; the decision by President George H. W. Bush, on the eve of the 1991 Persian Gulf War, not to use nuclear weapons even if Iraq resorted to chemical and biological weapons; the removal of the nuclear option from consideration by Joint Chiefs Chairman General Colin Powell during that war; the intense opposition (especially in Congress) to the George W. Bush administration's plans for the development of mini-nukes and high-yield bunker-buster weapons such as the Robust Nuclear Earth Penetrator (RNEP); and the 2006 Pentagon warning that nuclear use would be necessary to successfully wage a preventive war against Iran (in an effort to stop an attack, believing that U.S. leaders would be reluctant to use such weapons). At the global level, there seems to be a strong understanding of the dangers of nuclear war, although a handful of additional states have acquired or are in the process of acquiring such weapons as a "great equalizer" as a result of their rivalries with the United States and regional neighbors, as well as due to domestic considerations. While the tradition has become embedded globally, official discourses and postures since the end of the Cold War suggest that intermittent attempts are being made by nuclear states to alter the value of nuclear weapons in order to achieve certain tactical and strategic goals. The intense opposition among critics of such policies in the United States and elsewhere shows their apprehension that such changes will undermine the six-decade-long tradition of non-use.

Efforts to circumvent the tradition of non-use by developing "usable" low-yield weapons such as mini-nukes have come from the United States, because the tradition emerged from an appreciation of the material characteristics of the nuclear weapons available, particularly their massive destructiveness and collateral damage. Some proponents of low-yield nuclear arms believe that if one can limit the damage from a nuclear weapon, then it becomes yet another powerful bomb. The character of the weapon that produces the basic incentive for non-use is now being challenged, and the effort is to circumvent the tradition by developing a nuclear weapon that may not possess such intrinsic destructive characteristics. However, the scientific basis for a "usable" mini-nuclear weapon, producing minimal collateral damage, does not exist as of now. In addition, to many proponents of the tradition of non-use, a nuclear weapon is a WMD, whether it is large or small, and it is important not to distinguish between "usable" and "non-usable" weapons.

The tradition, although offering a partial normative restraint on nuclear use, is still not a full-fledged taboo, as the military and strategic doctrines of nuclear states envision weapons use under certain circumstances. In recent years, these circumstances have been broadened from existential threats to include lesser threats such as retaliation for chemical and biological weapons attacks on troops or territories of allied states; preventive attacks are now more widely considered as well. In that sense, the evolution of the tradition has been on a curvilinear path, and the possibility for its infraction has increased, especially in the twenty-first century.

In rhetoric and national planning, the tradition of non-use has been further challenged in the strategic environment that has emerged after September 11, 2001. The United States, the nuclear state which first helped to create the tradition by abstaining from nuclear use after 1945, has taken the lead in lowering the threshold of nuclear use. Russia, the other significant nuclear power that helped to shape the tradition, has followed suit. Other democratic nuclear powers—Britain, France, Israel, and India—have changed their doctrines to embrace nuclear weapons as a deterrent to counter lower-level threats, involving chemical and biological attacks. The established nuclear states thus have expanded the conditions under which nuclear weapons would be used, and in that process they have also created question marks about the vitality of the tradition. Efforts at blurring the distinction between nuclear and conventional weapons, by treating the former as just another weapon, are not new, as they have existed intermittently in U.S. strategic discourse from the beginning of the atomic age.[1] Regional powers such as Israel, Pakistan, and North Korea have also invoked nuclear use to deter or coerce their adversaries to accept their policies on issues other than existential challenge. None of this implies the imminent demise of the tradition, but it does suggest that the changing policies of nuclear states may damage its strength over the long haul.

What are the theoretical and policy implications of the tradition, especially for deterrence as it exists now?

IMPLICATIONS FOR DETERRENCE

The presence of the tradition has major implications for nuclear deterrence theory and policy. The key dimension in this regard is the notion of *self-deterrence*. While proponents of deterrence theory tend to ignore the tradition in their accounts, critics of the theory have rarely talked about the effect the tradition may have on the credibility of deterrent threats between nuclear and nonnuclear states. However, a tradition of non-use goes to the heart of deterrence. Deterrence theory rests on six elements: the presence of a severe conflict, the assumption that leaders of the opposing nations are rational, the presence of a strong retaliatory capability, the expectation of unacceptable damage in case of retaliation, the credibility of threats of retaliation, and finally, the existence of an adversarial but stable relationship between the parties.[2] Among these elements, as far as the relevance of the tradition of non-use is concerned, credibility of threat is the most significant one. The credibility of a deterrent threat relies on two necessary conditions: the political will to respond militarily and the possession of sufficient military capability to mount a retaliatory threat.[3] The rational expectation is that the retaliation would be so severe that the costs of attack would be immensely higher than the benefits that would result from military action. The costs are incredibly high if a particular hostile action prompts nuclear retaliation. As Morgan states, "credibility is the quality of being believed . . . it was not a state's capacity to do harm that enabled it to practice deterrence, it was others' belief that it had such a capacity. What deterred was not the threat but that it was believed."[4] It is precisely on the issue of belief where the tradition of non-use enters the realm of decision-makers' calculations.

Nuclear deterrence theory is purported to allow a state to prevent war as well as obtain its political objectives through the strategy of "leaving something to chance." This strategy attempts to solve any credibility problem involved in nuclear retaliation by assuming that states do not have complete collective control of events.[5] Both *deterrence by denial* and *deterrence by punishment* assume that capabilities are the significant component in preventing war initiations by challengers. Under the former, deterrence can be achieved if the defender has the "capability to deny the other party any gains deriving from the move which is to be deterred." In the latter, deterrence is achieved by "posing the prospect of war costs greater than the value of the gain."[6]

All of these strands of rational deterrence theory rest strongly on capability, to the detriment of a deep analysis of the component of will or resolve. The target state should believe that the deterrer has the will, intention, and resolve to retaliate. If the challenger is confident that the defender has weak resolve, the threat of retaliation will not be credible to the challenger. This is especially problematic if the defender has a poor reputation for carrying out previously announced threats.[7] The American notion of rational behavior may simply be inappropriate if an opponent is not acting irrationally but his behavior lacks reasonableness.[8] For example, a highly risk-taking leader such as Iraq's former President Saddam Hussein could believe in the weak resolve of his adversary and could engage in a brinkmanship crisis, even in the face of immense dangers to the survival of his country and regime. The tradition of non-use of nuclear weapons (i.e., the reputation problem inherent in it) could be one of the factors that encourage such leaders to engage in risk-taking behavior.

The tradition of non-use thus raises questions about the political commitment and credibility necessary for successful deterrence in a large number of strategic situations. The cases presented in Chapter 7 point to the difficulty in translating nuclear capability into credible deterrent threats and the constraints on committing one's capability for anything other than the supreme interests of a state such as national survival. But such existential threats are rare in the contemporary world. The credibility of declared or tacit commitment is questioned when a nonnuclear state initiates a war or limited probing action even when the adversary possesses weapons of mass destruction. Nuclear retaliation against a weaker challenger, for example against an ally's attacker, can be further constrained by the operation of the tradition of non-use.

More concretely, how does the tradition of non-use affect the credibility of deterrent threats?

The Problem of Self-Deterrence

In the nuclear context, both tactical constraints and normative prohibitions can act as sources of self-deterrence. The nuclear state can also be self-deterred by the fear of consequences, for reputation, image, prestige, power position, and general international standing. Similarly, if an actor is deterred from using nuclear weapons because of moral considerations, it is self-deterrence, given that there are no punishment mechanisms present other than reputation costs. In each of these scenarios, fear of other-imposed military costs is not the primary reason for the actor's desisting from executing a threat of retaliation.[9] For instance, Robert Jervis has argued that in the war on Iraq, the United States would have been self-deterred from using unlimited force including nuclear weapons, because of fear of adverse opinion, domestically and among allies; apprehensions of more states acquiring nuclear weapons; and the hatred that it would engender in the Arab world, leading to more terrorism. All these factors act as inhibitors on U.S. nuclear options in the Middle East.[10] These are indeed reputation calculations deriving from the tradition of non-use. Self-deterrence is also the reason why some U.S. policy makers and scientists have wanted to develop mini-nukes—and, prior to that, limited nuclear options and counterforce targeting—as these were seen as less likely to induce self-deterrence for the decision makers.

The presence of self-deterrence is not adequately addressed in the deterrence literature. This work points out that one of the conditions that affect the credibility of retaliatory threat is the informal norm of the tradition of non-use. Cost/benefit calculations based on military balance alone would not predict sufficiently a challenger's motives or incentives to launch an attack, especially of the limited-aims variety. Deterrence theorists should not only specify capability, commitment, and credibility in the abstract, but should also enumerate and investigate the key factors that could affect them in actual operational contexts.

Moreover, a nuclear-armed defender could face major hurdles in translating nuclear capability into an effective deterrent in limited war situations. These constraints are even larger if the conflict is of an insurgency variety. These constraints are not simply the result of tactical/military considerations but also of normative and reputational concerns, such as the fear of breaking the tradition against nuclear use, and the worry of generating adverse public opinion, nationally and internationally. Clearly, along with psychological and domestic variables, normative and reputational factors have a place in outcomes of deterrence failures as well as war initiations, a topic that needs further study. The tradition of non-use could generate incentives for rival states to engage in low-level military activities, assuming that there will be no punitive strikes on the part of the nuclear state. It could assure leaders that small-scale harassment or limited probes using asymmetric means would not result in any major retaliatory strikes, especially of a nuclear nature. The continued Pakistani activities in the Indian side of Kashmir and the raids by Palestinian and Islamist groups such as Hezbollah within Israel suggest this emerging phenomenon in regional conflict zones.

Similarly, the credibility of extended nuclear deterrence could be affected by the tradition of non-use, as a non-nuclear challenger's attack on an ally need not threaten the vital interests of the nuclear defender as much as would a direct attack on it. An attack on an ally is not equivalent to an attack on oneself, however close that ally is.

The case studies in Chapter 7 show that the mere possession of nuclear weapons need not deter a nonnuclear state from launching a conventional attack against the nuclear-armed state if the initiator believes that it can wage a limited war without provoking a nuclear response. Nuclear deterrence may be effective in circumstances when the nuclear weapon state's existence is at stake. But such challenges are rare in contemporary international politics, due largely to the legal and institutional norms against conquering and permanently occupying another state. Additionally, most of the declared nuclear states are superior to their actual and potential challengers in terms of aggregate conventional capability. It is therefore difficult to isolate the marginal utility added by nuclear weapons. This study reinforces the findings of aggregate studies that question the utility of nuclear weapons in conflicts involving nuclear and nonnuclear states.[11] Nuclear theorist George Quester acknowledges that the tradition has eroded the deterrent power of nuclear weapons, "as the world more and more [has come] to regard nuclear escalation, the backbone of 'extended nuclear deterrence,' as unthinkable. The erosion has been a source of concern for U.S. military strategists."[12]

However, exaggerated notions about the restraining power of the tradition of non-use could result in military catastrophes. A nuclear-armed state could be tempted or pressured to retaliate with nuclear weapons if it fears losing a war or its long-term credibility. The reported decisions by Israeli leaders to place their nuclear forces on alert during the 1973 October/Yom Kippur War and the 1991 Persian Gulf War suggest the dangers of conventional conflicts escalating to the nuclear level. A second danger would be pressures on the nuclear allies of regional powers to intervene in the protection of their client states. The superpower nuclear alert during the October/Yom Kippur War was a case in point. In these situations, a weapon of last resort could become a weapon of first resort. Even when the nuclear alerts are meant for deterrence or compellence efforts, they can result in "commitment traps" as well as cause accidents and inadvertent use.

The prospect of biological and chemical weapons use has increased the chances of a nuclear weapon state's breaking the tradition. Biological and chemical weapons are believed to be widely available and are supposed to be a "poor man's atomic weapons." A risk-taking leader can use them or threaten to use them to prevent intervention, as the Iraqi leader Saddam Hussein attempted in 1990–91 and 2002–03. Had Hussein used such capabilities against invading U.S. forces or American allies in the region such as Israel and Saudi Arabia, the deterrent credibility of the United States would have suffered a major setback if it had not used nuclear weapons in retaliation. The credibility of nuclear deterrence will be further damaged if policy makers pronounce that all and sundry threats are to be deterred with nuclear weapons. Non-nuclear states would disregard the threat of nuclear retaliation, thereby raising credibility questions.[13] The credibility problem is even higher for extended deterrence, especially for the protection of areas of secondary importance to the nuclear state. Thus, even if an ally is part of the U.S. umbrella, it may become extremely difficult to use nuclear weapons against a smaller adversary of that ally partially due to the normative inhibitions inherent in the tradition of non-use. As a result of a realization of this predicament, Washington probably would be under tremendous pressure to break the tradition and use nuclear weapons once a chemical or biological attack takes place against U.S. troops or allies in a theater like the Persian Gulf.

The chapters show the limitations of nuclear weapons as a usable source of power, largely because of the difficulty in converting the putative capability into actualized power except under rare circumstances such as those involving existential concerns. In the traditional sense, military power involves the ability of states to affect the will and behavior of other states by threatening or employing armed coercion. The tradition of non-use thus has ramifications for power in the international system. It shows the importance of soft-power variables in international politics. Analysts, especially realists, tend to denigrate soft-power elements such as reputation and image as insignificant or secondary in explaining national security choices of states. Based on the historical analysis provided in the chapters of this book, soft-power considerations—for example, reputation and image—have been dominant factors for the rise and observance of the tradition of non-use. Leaders want to look good in the eyes of the world and wish to receive favorable domestic opinion. These soft power considerations also act as self-deterrents when it comes to the use of nuclear weapons.

Compellence/Coercive Diplomacy

Nuclear weapons have been touted as instruments for coercive or compellent uses, in addition to deterrence. Unlike deterrence, which is aimed at preventing an aggressive act, compellence implies that the state has already undertaken such an action and the aim is to compel it to withdraw or surrender. The offensive use of military force is implied in a compellent threat. Coercive diplomacy is the simultaneous use of military threats and diplomacy to encourage a state to "comply with the demands" of the coercer or "work out an acceptable compromise."[14] The existence of the tradition raises a severe challenge to both compellence and coercive diplomacy. Similar to deterrence, compellence operates only when an opponent does something that the threatening state wants him to do on the basis of the threat to use force. Therefore, like deterrence, compellence relies upon credibility. Even in the conventional realm, compellence is more difficult to achieve than deterrence, as backing down under threat of an act already carried out can be politically very costly for the target state. With the tradition of non-use in mind, compellence may be even more costly, since the threat of nuclear weapons use for anything other than supreme national interests may not be credible to a weaker target of coercive diplomacy.

Compellence has been considered in the context of stopping nuclear proliferation efforts by regional challengers such as Iraq, Iran, and North Korea. In recent years, the United States has sought to change regimes in countries that it considers members of the "axis of evil." In Iraq, this generated a determination on the part of the target state to resist the compellent threats, leading to war. In Saddam Hussein's perceptions, his personal interests in the survival of the regime and the supreme national interests of Iraq coincided; hence his determination to resist the United States. A leader expecting defeat and inevitable death or life imprisonment by invading U.S. forces could opt to use chemical or biological weapons even when the United States has a policy of nuclear retaliation.[15] A leader who believes that the United States is bent on regime change and that in the postwar phase Washington would put his and his key supporters' lives in jeopardy may have little incentive not to use his capabilities while resisting this intervention. A dictatorial leader may also believe that the demand of the superior power is highly illegitimate and that that power has no broader world support for its actions.[16] This sense of illegitimacy could partially be based on expectations regarding the existence of the tradition of non-use.

Despite the presence of the tradition of non-use and its relevance for deterrence and compellence, in the future, nuclear states may break the tradition as changing strategic conditions place considerable stresses and strains on their security policies. But by placing nuclear weapons at the center of defense policy when security could be achieved by other, less damaging means, the chances for nuclear escalation could increase. This has happened before: the war in Vietnam was waged by the United States because of profound concerns about maintaining deterrent credibility.[17] Major powers such as the United States could ignore or underplay other policy options such as détente, accommodation, conciliation, integration, arms control, and confidence building to deal with regional challengers. By exaggerating the threat level, a nuclear state could create a condition of perpetual conflict, often harming the development of poorer societies that need democratic governance and economic investment. U.S. regional policies could help to generate nationalism in such countries, which would further strengthen ruthless and authoritarian regimes. During the post–September 11 era, U.S. policy toward Iran and North Korea, for instance, became belligerent and conflict-ridden, as alternative mechanisms of accommodation have been ignored while nuclear preemption, prevention, and deterrence have been given prominence. Similarly, trying to deter terrorism with nuclear weapons could simply exaggerate the power of terrorist groups, and ignore usable approaches such as active policing and intelligence operations. Moreover, efforts to place nuclear weapons in a deterrent and compellent mode against weaker regional challengers could put pressure on such states to obtain their own nuclear capability for mutual deterrence or to resort to asymmetric means such as terrorism and insurgency, for which the nuclear armed powers have very little answer.

POSSIBLE FUTURE INFRACTIONS

There is a risk in believing that the tradition of non-use is so well-ingrained or embedded in national policies that this norm itself would deter the use of nuclear weapons by states. In international politics, it is dangerous to leave everything to the operation of a normative force such as the tradition of non-use. The discussion so far points out that the tradition is anything but a deeply rooted taboo, and there is no guarantee that it will not be broken in the future. As noted, there may be strong incentives to break the tradition in order to maintain the credibility of nuclear weapons as a deterrent and to deal with emerging chemical and biological weapons attacks. Human action is needed to maintain the tradition, especially against the potential onslaught on it generated by technological innovations, the advent of new weapon systems, and the onset of complex political changes. It is also a mistake to assume that Western democracies are somehow going to abide by the norm all the time. In fact, the major challenge to the tradition today comes from Western powers such as the United States, Britain, and France, which have been making loose nuclear threats to confront a variety of asymmetric threats. Most Americans seem to want to maintain the tradition of non-use, but they also elect leaders who appoint unelected officials, in addition to scientists and military planners, who occupy pivotal positions and would be able to craft incremental changes, making infractions possible. The norm entrepreneurs and reputation intermediaries of yesteryear, including scientists, strategists, peace movements, and nonnuclear states have quieter voices, especially in the post–September 11 world.

Based on this study, two key factors could affect the probability of nuclear use and the breaking of the tradition. First, the character of the weapons could change; that is, technological breakthroughs could allow the creation of a weapon that will have minimum collateral damage and a general recognition that it is the only credible weapon that can destroy a target such as a deeply buried nuclear or command facility. Second, reputational costs could change, if the reputation for punishment becomes more important for nuclear states than the reputation for non-use. Successful chemical or biological attack by a weaker adversary could reduce the reputation costs involved in nuclear retaliation, at least in terms of domestic public support for nuclear retaliation. Opinion polls before the two Gulf Wars suggested that the majority of the American public did not oppose the United States using nuclear weapons if Saddam Hussein engaged in a chemical or biological attack against U.S. troops or U.S. allies in the region.

The conditions under which the tradition could be infringed are of special significance. If the nuclear state's vital interests are threatened, for example, with the loss of a large portion of territory, nuclear use is a possibility. Moreover, intrawar pressures tend to be high on decision makers, who might be tempted to make use of their nuclear capability as a war-terminating device before large-scale destruction of their forces or loss of their territory occurs. Additionally, a state or an armed force, not fully socialized into the tradition of non-use, could use its nuclear capability in the opening phase of a war, during a stalemated situation, or when facing military disaster. The further miniaturization of nuclear weapons with precision-guided applications could also provide temptation to break the tradition. Integration of low-yield nuclear weapons with conventional weapons could encourage the possessor to use them, especially if they became part of operational doctrines. Future research could identify (a) the larger implications of the tradition of non-use for deterrence theory and policy; (b) the conditions under which it could be broken; (c) the risks inherent in wars involving a nuclear and nonnuclear state; and (d) the importance of the tradition in preventing the proliferation of nuclear weapons to additional countries.

Explicit legal and normative international prohibitions, supported by global community threats of collective punishment for transgression, may strengthen the tradition and prolong the continued non-use of nuclear weapons. Conversion of the tradition of non-use to an explicit legal understanding is possible if it continues unbroken for a long time. Many laws of warfare that exist today have evolved through centuries of traditions and customs. For critics who would argue that international law does not matter because states can violate it at their will, the question is why the nuclear weapon states, led by the United States, are so hesitant to agree to a legal convention or agreement banning first use and also offering clear-cut negative security assurances. They know that by signing a treaty they are agreeing to raise the barrier for nuclear use. They are definitely concerned about harming their reputations even further by signing such a treaty and then resorting to nuclear use or threat of use. Similarly, if legal commitments do not matter, why is it that nonnuclear states have been adamantly pursuing legally binding negative security guarantees? These states want to place additional barriers in the way of the nuclear states in an effort to embed the norm of non-use.

Nonstate actors pose a major challenge to the preservation of the tradition. Groups that believe in suicidal terrorism or cataclysmic terrorism need not be bound by normative restraints. Nor would they be deterred by the threat of retaliation. This is because disproportionate retaliation by nuclear powers would punish the innocent and thereby make the cause of the terrorist groups even more popular. The United States, Russia, Britain, France, and India have included chemical and biological attacks by state or nonstate actors as reasons for nuclear retaliation. But a problem arises if the potential target is a terrorist group that does not mind taking high casualties or inflicting great pains upon the society where it is located.

This discussion also raises the issue of the socialization of new and aspiring nuclear states into the tradition of non-use. Is the sixty-three-year global history of non-use and global understanding sufficient to socialize new actors into the tradition of non-use and the informal norm inherent in it? Would a new nuclear state be tempted to make use of its nascent capabilities in order to pursue an ambitious regional or global agenda? The danger of revisionist states acquiring nuclear weapons lies in this problem; the initial period of learning and socialization could be one of turbulence, as the recent history of South Asia attests. This pattern may recur in the Middle East as well, if and when Iran acquires nuclear capability and pursues an active policy of support for forces of destabilization in the region, even short of war.

WHY THE TRADITION MUST BE PRESERVED

Scholars have argued that breaking the tradition need not be the end of it all. The taboo against chemical and biological weapons use and social taboos against cannibalism and incest are broken occasionally, but these infractions have not resulted in the disappearance of the taboos. Instead, scholars argue that an infraction may reinforce or strengthen the tradition and may intensify calls for a legally binding non-use convention. To George Quester, the extent of casualties, the target under attack, and the conditions under which the attack takes place, will determine the reactions of the world toward nuclear use. Cases of accidents will be perceived differently from instances of deliberate use of highly destructive escalation, with clear-cut responsibility assigned to governments.[18] Alternatively, the use of nuclear weapons could bring tremendous international pressure for legal sanctification of non-use. If the casualties are high and the long-term impact is immense, global disarmament movements could rejuvenate and demands for an international treaty banning nuclear use could become vociferous. The tradition need not die, but it could become the focal point of international efforts at both nuclear nonproliferation and disarmament. Similar to the impact that the Chernobyl nuclear accident in 1986 exerted on Soviet rethinking under Mikhail Gorbachev, nuclear use anywhere in the world may force nations to develop legally robust measures to prevent such use and even seek global nuclear disarmament.

However, despite these claims of limited repercussions of nuclear use, we simply cannot predict the possible consequences, which may be context dependent. Taking a chance with nuclear attack is very problematic, especially if it means the killing of thousands of innocent civilians and grave environmental disaster. Western democracies ought to have a greater interest in maintaining the tradition than in destroying it, and hence bear a major responsibility for its preservation. The use of nuclear weapons could be a precedent-setting event, affecting international security and international order negatively. If, for instance, the United States uses nuclear weapons in regional theaters, the precedent will be set for others, including new nuclear states and aspiring ones, that nuclear use is an acceptable response to less-than-existential military challenges. Setting a bad precedent would haunt the United States, as its condemnation of others' use would evoke little sympathy. In the worst-case scenario, many states that had given up their nuclear options could reconsider their policies, as national nuclear capabilities would become essential to deter possible future use of such weapons against them. Terrorist groups would justify their killings of innocents by claiming reprisals against the U.S. use of nuclear weapons.

The preservation of the tradition is in the national interest of the United States as the hegemonic power, as nuclear weapons can constitute a "great equalizer" in the hands of its weaker challengers, who may increasingly seek these weapons to thwart U.S. intervention. By propagating the virtues of the tradition to others, the United States can help legitimize its leadership role in the international system and exert considerable pressure on revisionist states that may plan to use WMD to advance their politico-military objectives. Global norms are important for status quo powers in order to legitimize the existing international order and reduce the likelihood that revisionist actors will seek to alter it forcefully. The use of WMD against U.S. troops in regional theaters does not constitute an existential threat, and so the use of nuclear weapons in response would not fall under the last-resort category. Creating ambiguity may have benefits in confusing the minds of rogue leaders, but what if one such leader calls the bluff? The credibility of the U.S. deterrent threat would be at stake, and the president would be compelled to use nuclear weapons and thereby break the tradition of non-use, which has served U.S. interests for well over half a century. The tradition of non-use is one norm that Washington would be well advised to preserve, for once it is broken, it may not be easy to resurrect it even if future leaders wished to do so.

These considerations should apply to the other nuclear weapon states as well. For instance, Russia's plans to develop mini-nukes and its expansion of threatened nuclear retaliation are not very credible against Chechen rebels. No regional state or former republic of the Soviet Union has the capability to attack Russia frontally, even with chemical weapons. The main threat to Russia comes from subnational groups and nontraditional sources. Similarly, for Britain and France, the likely direct threats are not clear. Terrorist groups such as the one which perpetrated the London subway attacks in July 2005 are not susceptible to deterrence by nuclear threat. France also has enemies who are mostly nonstate actors. Iran is perhaps several years away from developing nuclear weapons, and it is unlikely that mutual deterrence will not work against Teheran.[19] India has also expanded the possible use of nuclear weapons in response to chemical and biological weapons use by state and nonstate actors. A credibility problem abounds in this instance, because the terrorist groups associated with the Kashmiri insurgency are unlikely to be deterred by such threats. Even retaliation against Pakistan for its support of such an attack carries grave risks given Pakistan's possession of nuclear weapons.

The tradition of non-use serves several of the cherished goals of international community, such as preventing nuclear war, avoiding inadvertent escalations, helping to reduce the proliferation of nuclear weapons, and depreciating the value of nuclear weapons as a currency of power in the international system. In all these respects, the tradition and the normative prohibition inherent in it ought to be preserved and strengthened. Whatever limited value accrues from nuclear use could be nullified by the greater short- and long-term impact their use would generate for international order and global security.

REFERENCE MATTER

NOTES

Chapter 1: Introduction

1. For traditions and their legitimacy, see Max Weber, *Economy and Society: An Outline of Interpretative Sociology,* ed. Guenther Roth and Claus Wittich (New York: Bedminster Press, 1968), 216–31.

2. "Analytical eclecticism" means borrowing explanatory variables and causal logic from two or more distinct traditions or approaches in order to gain greater purchase on the cases or issue areas that scholars want to analyze. For this approach, see Peter J. Katzenstein and Rudra Sil, "Rethinking Asian Security: A Case for Analytical Eclecticism," in *Rethinking Security in East Asia,* ed. J. J. Suh, Peter J. Katzenstein, and Allen Carlson (Stanford: Stanford University Press, 2004), 1–33; John A. Hall and T. V. Paul, "Preconditions for Prudence: A Sociological Synthesis of Realism and Liberalism," in *International Order and the Future of World Politics,* ed. T. V. Paul and John A. Hall (Cambridge: Cambridge University Press, 1999), 67–77; and T. V. Paul, *Power versus Prudence: Why Nations Forgo Nuclear Weapons* (Montreal: McGill-Queen's University Press, 2000), ch. 2. Scholars in International Relations increasingly favor eclectic approaches. For instance, see Jeffrey W. Legro, *Rethinking the World: Great Power Strategies and International Order* (Ithaca, NY: Cornell University Press, 2005); and Norrin M. Ripsman, "Two Stages of Transition From a Region of War to a Region of Peace: Realist Transition and Liberal Endurance," *International Studies Quarterly* 49, no. 4 (December 2005): 669–93. On how moral norms and power considerations intersect, see Ward Thomas, *The Ethics of Destruction: Norms and Force in International Relations* (Ithaca, NY: Cornell University Press, 2001).

3. For the distinction and interaction between the logic of consequences and logic of appropriateness, see James G. March and Johan P. Olsen, "The Institutional Dynamics of International Political Orders," *International Organization* 52, no. 4 (Autumn 1998): 943–69.

4. Paradigms also allow continuity and transformation in research programs, measurement of variables deriving from a dominant theory, and criteria for their evaluation. On paradigms, see Thomas Kuhn, *The Structure of Scientific Revolutions* (Chicago: University of Chicago Press, 1962); Imre Lakatos, "Falsification and the Methodology of Scientific Research Programs," in *Criticism and the Growth of Knowledge,* ed. Imre Lakatos and Alan Musgrave (Cambridge: Cambridge University Press, 1970), 91–196.

5. On invented traditions, see Eric Hobsbawm and Terence Ranger, eds., *The Invention of Tradition* (Cambridge: Cambridge University Press, 1983).

6. They include both traditional rationalist scholars and Constructivist scholars of more recent vintage. For rational/materialist arguments, see Thomas C. Schelling, "The Role of Nuclear Weapons," in *Turning Point: The Gulf War and U.S. Military Strategy,* ed. Benjamin L. Ederington and Michael J. Mazarr (Boulder, CO: Westview Press, 1994), 110; Thomas C. Schelling, *The Strategy of Conflict,* 2nd ed. (Cambridge, MA: Harvard University Press, 1980), 260; Stanley Hoffmann, "Nuclear Proliferation and World Politics," in *A World of Nuclear Powers?* ed. Alastair Buchan (Englewood Cliffs, NJ: Prentice Hall, 1966), 99; and John Lewis Gaddis, "Nuclear Weapons, the End of the Cold War, and the Future of the International System," in *Nuclear Weapons in a Changing World,* ed. Patrick J. Garrity and Steven A. Maaranen (New York: Plenum Press, 1992), 21. For Constructivist views, see Nina Tannenwald, *The Nuclear Taboo* (Cambridge: Cambridge University Press, 2007); Nina Tannenwald, "Stigmatizing the Bomb: Origins of the Nuclear Taboo," *International Security* 29, no. 4 (Spring 2005): 5–49; Nina Tannenwald, "The Nuclear Taboo: The United States and the Normative Basis of Nuclear Non-use," *International Organization* 53, no. 3 (Summer 1999): 433–68; Richard Price and Nina Tannenwald, "Norms and Deterrence: The Nuclear and Chemical Weapons Taboos," in *The Culture of National Security,* ed. Peter J. Katzenstein (New York: Columbia University Press, 1996), 137; Peter Gizewski, "From Winning Weapon to Destroyer of the World: The Nuclear Taboo in International Politics," *International Journal* 51, no. 2 (Summer 1996): 397–419. I have also used the term *taboo* to describe the tradition of non-use, but in a figurative and less stringent manner than Constructivist scholars. See T. V. Paul, "Nuclear Taboo and War Initiation: Nuclear Weapons in Regional Conflicts," *Journal of Conflict Resolution* 39, no. 4 (December 1995): 696–717.

7. "Memorandum of Discussion at the 165th NSC Meeting, October 7, 1953," *Foreign Relations of the United States, 1952–54,* vol. 2 (Washington, DC: Department of State), 532–33. See also McGeorge Bundy, *Danger and Survival* (New York: Random House, 1988), 249.

8. George Ball, "The Cosmic Bluff," *New York Review of Books* (July 21, 1983): 37.

9. Schelling, *Strategy of Conflict,* 260. For the Brodie argument, see Bernard Brodie, ed., *The Absolute Weapon: Atomic Power and World Order* (New York: Harcourt, Brace, 1946), chs. 1–2.

10. Steven P. Lee, *Morality, Prudence and Nuclear Weapons* (Cambridge: Cambridge University Press, 1993), 320, 324.

11. Schelling, "The Role of Nuclear Weapons," 110.

12. A good example is the incendiary bombings of Tokyo during the waning days of World War II, which, during a very short period, killed more than the combined totals of the Hiroshima and Nagasaki attacks. Tom McGowen, *Air Raid! The Bombing Campaigns of World War II* (Brookfield, CT: Twenty-First Century Books, 2001), ch. 8.

13. Hutton Webster, *Taboo: A Sociological Study* (Stanford: Stanford University Press, 1942), 2, 13.

14. Ibid., 14, 17.

15. Sigmund Freud, *Totem and Taboo*, trans. James Strachey (London: Routledge & Kegan Paul, 1950), 22.

16. *Encyclopedia Britannica Online*, "Taboo," http://www.search.eb.com/eb/article-9070845.

17. For discussions of various social taboos, see James George Frazer, *Taboo and the Perils of Soul* (New York: Macmillan, 1935); Mary Douglas, *Purity and Danger: An Analysis of the Concepts of Pollution and Taboo* (New York: Routledge, 2002); Freud, *Totem and Taboo*; Franz Baermann Steiner, *Taboo, Truth, and Religion: Selected Writings*, vol. 1, ed. Jeremy Adler and Richard Fardon (New York: Berghahn Books, 1999).

18. States Freud: "Anyone who has violated a taboo becomes taboo himself because he possesses the dangerous quality of tempting others to follow his example . . . and for that reason he himself must be shunned." Freud, *Totem and Taboo*, 32.

19. On these taboos, see Arthur P. Wolf and William H. Durham, eds., *Inbreeding, Incest, and the Incest Taboo: The State of Knowledge at the Turn of the Century* (Stanford: Stanford University Press, 2004); Jonathan H. Turner and Alexandra Maryanski, *Incest: Origins of the Taboo* (Boulder, CO: Paradigm Publishers, 2005); Laurence R. Goldman, ed., *The Anthropology of Cannibalism* (Westport, CT: Bergin & Garvey, 1999); Eli Sagan, *Cannibalism: Human Aggression and Cultural Form* (New York: Harper & Row, 1974).

20. George Quester, "International Safeguards for Eliminating Weapons of Mass Destruction" (Occasional Paper no. 31, Henry L. Stimson Center, Washington, DC, December 1996): 7–8. To Quester, a taboo "is more than simply something we would want to avoid, something that we disapprove of, for we do not hear of a taboo on bank robberies or a taboo on murder. The word is distinctive in that it refers to something we are not willing even to think about doing. There is no weighing of benefits and costs; we simply reject the idea without further thought." George Quester, *Nuclear First Strike: Consequences of a Broken Taboo* (Baltimore: Johns Hopkins University Press, 2006), 12.

21. International Court of Justice, "Legality of the Threat or Use of Nuclear Weapons, Advisory Opinion," *I.C.J. Reports 1996* (8 July 1996), 44.

22. Richard Falk, "Nuclear Weapons, International Law and the World Court: A Historic Encounter," *American Journal of International Law* 91, no. 1 (January 1997): 64–75; see also Siddharth Mallavarapu, *Banning the Bomb: The Politics of Norm Creation* (New Delhi: Pearson, 2007).

23. A somewhat similar taboo exists in the area of chemical weapons. Many explanations of the non-use of chemical weapons by belligerents during World War II, despite their possessing huge chemical arsenals, give the taboo against their use a significant place. Richard Price, "A Genealogy of the Chemical Weapons Taboo," *International Organization* 49, no. 1 (Winter 1995): 73–103; Jeffrey Legro, *Cooperation under Fire* (Ithaca, NY: Cornell University Press, 1995). The difference, though, is that legal prohibitions against acquisition and use of chemical (and biological) weapons have developed over time; almost all nuclear states have signed on to these prohibitions.

24. Harald Mueller, "Constructing a Taboo against Weapons of Mass Destruction" (unpublished paper, Peace Research Institute, Frankfurt, 2003): 11.

25. Scott L. Feld, "On the Emergence of Social Norms," *Contemporary Sociology* 31, no. 6 (November 2002): 638.

26. Neil Duxbury, "Signaling and Social Norms," *Oxford Journal of Legal Studies* 21, no. 4 (Winter 2001): 719–36.

27. Martha Finnemore, *National Interests in International Society* (Ithaca, NY: Cornell University Press, 1996): 22.

28. Stephen J. Toope, "Formality and Informality," in *The Oxford Handbook of International Environmental Law,* ed. Daniel Bodansky, Jutta Brunnee, and Ellen Hey (Oxford: Oxford University Press, 2007), 108. See also Kenneth W. Abbott and Duncan Snidal, "Hard and Soft Law in International Governance," *International Organization* 53, no. 3 (August 2000): 421–56.

29. Toope, "Formality and Informality," 118, 121.

30. Ibid., 122.

31. Michael Hechter and Karl-Dieter Opp, "Introduction," in *Social Norms,* ed. Michael Hechter and Karl-Dieter Opp (New York: Russell Sage Foundation, 2001): xi.

32. Bruce Russett, "The Real Decline in Nuclear Hegemony," in *Global Changes and Theoretical Challenges,* ed. Ernst-Otto Czempiel and James N. Rosenau (Lexington, MA: Lexington Books, 1989): 185.

33. According to two strategic analysts, nuclear weapons, especially enhanced radiation weapons, might have been useful in Afghanistan destroying rural infrastructure or fixed Mujahideen strong points. Anthony H. Cordesman and Abraham R. Wagner, *The Lessons of Modern War,* vol. 3, *The Afghan and Falklands Conflicts* (Boulder, CO: Westview Press, 1990), 218–19.

34. Cathy Scott-Clark and Adrian Levy, "Spectre Orange," *The Guardian,* March 29, 2003; United States Department of State, "Case Study: Yellow Rain" (fact sheet, Bureau of Verification, Compliance, and Implementation, October 2005), http://www.state.gov/documents/organization/57428.pdf.

Chapter 2: Bases of the Tradition of Non-Use

1. Colin S. Gray, "To Confuse Ourselves: Nuclear Fallacies," in *Alternative Nuclear Futures,* ed. John Baylis and Robert O'Neill (Oxford: Oxford University Press, 2000), 27. Just before the Reagan era, Gray and Keith Payne advocated keeping the option of nuclear weapons use open, arguing that victory in nuclear war was possible. See Colin S. Gray and Keith B. Payne, "Victory is Possible," *Foreign Policy* no. 39 (Summer, 1980): 14–27.

2. Colin S. Gray, "Nuclear Weapons and the Revolution in Military Affairs," in *The Absolute Weapon Revisited: Nuclear Arms and the Emerging International Order,* ed. T. V. Paul, Richard J. Harknett, and James J. Wirtz (Ann Arbor: The University of Michigan Press, 1998), 119. See also Keith B. Payne, *Deterrence in the Second Nuclear Age* (Lexington: University Press of Kentucky, 1996).

3. For these moderate positions, see Scott D. Sagan, "Realist Perspectives on Ethical Norms and Weapons of Mass Destruction," in *Ethics and Weapons of Mass Destruction,* ed. Sohail H. Hashmi and Steven P. Lee (Cambridge: Cambridge University Press, 2004), 73–95; Susan B. Martin, "Realism and Weapons of Mass Destruction: A Consequentialist Analysis," in Hashmi and Lee, *Ethics and Weapons of Mass Destruction,* 76–110.

4. On Constructivist perspectives, see Martha Finnemore, *National Interests in International Society* (Ithaca, NY: Cornell University Press, 1996), 15; Vincent Pouliot, "The Essence of Constructivism," *Journal of International Relations and Development,* 7 no. 3 (September 2004): 319–36.

5. Richard Price and Nina Tannenwald, "Norms and Deterrence: The Nuclear and Chemical Weapons Taboos," in *The Culture of National Security,* ed. Peter J. Katzenstein (New York: Columbia University Press, 1996): 137. See also Richard Price, "A Genealogy of the Chemical Weapons Taboo," *International Organization* 49, no. 1 (Winter 1995): 73–103. For varieties of Constructivist schools, see Ted Hopf, *Social Construction of International Politics* (Ithaca, NY: Cornell University Press, 2002); Vendulka Kubalkova, Nicholas Onuf, and Paul Kowert, eds., *International Relations in a Constructed World* (Armonk, NY: M. E. Sharpe, 1998); Amitav Acharya, *Constructing a Security Community in Southeast Asia: ASEAN and the Problem of Regional Order* (New York: Routledge, 2000).

6. Nina Tannenwald, "Stigmatizing the Bomb: Origins of the Nuclear Taboo," *International Security* 29, no. 4 (Spring 2005): 5–49.

7. Nina Tannenwald, *The Nuclear Taboo* (Cambridge: Cambridge University Press, 2007), 3.

8. Ibid., 17.

9. United States Department of State, "Case Study: Yellow Rain" (fact sheet, Bureau of Verification, Compliance, and Implementation, October 2005), http://www.state.gov/documents/organization/57428.pdf. I acknowledge that the Soviet use of chemical weapons is still not completely verified for accuracy.

10. Further, critics themselves have not yet offered a powerful test for their contention of tactical/strategic unsuitability as the source of the continued non-use of nuclear weapons. Their "focus on extreme tests assumes in advance that nuclear weapons are extreme weapons that could only be used in the direst circumstances. Instead, the interesting question is the prior one of how and why this came to be," since the United States has, on many occasions "contemplated the use of nuclear weapons in cases of less than vital national interest." Tannenwald, *The Nuclear Taboo*, 368.

11. In recent years, some Constructivists have adopted a rationalist-constructivist or structuralist-constructivist approach. For instances, see Alexander Wendt, *Social Theory of International Politics* (Cambridge: Cambridge University Press, 1999); Emanuel Adler, "Seizing the Middle Ground: Constructivism in World Politics," *European Journal of International Relations* 3, no. 3 (September 1997): 319–63; James G. March and Johan P. Olsen, "The Institutional Dynamics of International Political Orders," *International Organization* 52, no. 4 (Autumn 1998): 943–69; James D. Fearon and Alexander Wendt, "Rationalism v. Constructivism: A Skeptical View," in *Handbook of International Relations,* ed. Walter Carlsnaes, Thomas Risse, and Beth A. Simmons (London: Sage, 2002), 52–72; Jeffrey T. Checkel, "International Norms and Domestic Politics: Bridging the Rationalist-Constructivist Divide," *European Journal of International Relations* 3, no. 4 (December 1997): 473–95; Thomas Risse, "Constructivism and International Institutions: Towards Conversions across Paradigms," in *Political Science: The State of the Discipline,* ed. Ira Katzenelson and Helen Milner (New York: W. W. Norton, 2002), 597–629.

12. Democracies are prone to fight high intensity wars with nondemocracies, as they tend to consider them as "unreasonable" and "potentially dangerous." John M. Owen, "How Liberalism Produces Democratic Peace," *International Security* 19, no. 2 (Autumn 1994): 87–125; see also Christian Reus-Smit, "Liberal Hierarchy and the License to Use Force," *Review of International Studies* 31, suppl. S1 (December 2005), 71–92; Bruce Russett and John Oneal, *Triangulating Peace* (New York: W. W. Norton, 2001), 115–16.

13. In my previous works I attempted to pursue a puzzle-based research agenda. See, for instance, T. V. Paul, *Asymmetric Conflicts: War Initiation by Weaker Powers* (Cambridge: Cambridge University Press, 1994); Paul, *Power versus Prudence: Why Nations Forgo Nuclear Weapons* (Montreal: McGill-Queen's University Press, 2000).

14. For the "uncontestable" nature of nuclear weapons, see Richard J. Harknett, "State Preferences, Systemic Constraints, and the Absolute Weapon," in Paul, Harknett, and Wirtz, *Absolute Weapon Revisited,* 53. See also Bernard Brodie, ed., *The Absolute Weapon: Atomic Power and World Order* (New York: Harcourt, Brace, 1946).

15. Thomas C. Schelling, "The Role of Nuclear Weapons," in *Turning Point: The Gulf War and U.S. Military Strategy,* ed. Benjamin L. Ederington and Michael J. Mazarr (Boulder, CO: Westview Press, 1994), 110.

16. Michael Mandelbaum, *The Nuclear Question: The United States and Nuclear Weapons, 1946–1976* (Cambridge: Cambridge University Press, 1979), 4.

17. George Quester, *Nuclear First Strike: Consequences of a Broken Taboo* (Baltimore: Johns Hopkins University Press, 2006), 102.

18. On these see Jeffrey W. Legro, "Which Norms Matter? Revisiting the 'Failure' of Internationalism," *International Organization* 51, no. 1 (Winter 1997): 31–61.

19. John Lewis Gaddis, "Nuclear Weapons, the End of the Cold War, and the Future of the International System," in *Nuclear Weapons in a Changing World,* ed. Patrick J. Garrity and Steven A. Maaranen (New York: Plenum Press, 1992), 21.

20. Robert Jervis, *The Illogic of American Nuclear Strategy* (Ithaca, NY: Cornell University Press, 1984), 23.

21. Steven P. Lee, *Morality, Prudence and Nuclear Weapons* (Cambridge: Cambridge University Press, 1993), 18.

22. Ronald L. Jepperson, Alexander Wendt, and Peter J. Katzenstein, "Norms, Identity, and Culture in National Security," in *Culture of National Security,* ed. Peter J. Katzenstein (New York: Columbia University Press, 1996), 54.

23. On the self-interest dimension of norms, see Gary Goertz and Paul F. Diehl, "International Norms and Power Politics," in *Reconstructing Realpolitik,* ed. Frank W. Wayman and Paul F. Diehl (Ann Arbor: University of Michigan Press, 1994), 102.

24. In the context of international politics, image is the idealized conception of a state or its leader held by other members of the international community. Scholars of soft power give considerable importance to reputation and image, as these intangible factors are important for states, especially major powers seeking to retain primacy. On this, see Joseph S. Nye, *Soft Power: The Means to Success in World Politics* (New York: Public Affairs, 2004). Image is very much based on what inferences a state makes about the likely behavior of another in a given area. On this, see Robert Jervis, *The Logic of Images in International Relations,* 2nd ed. (New York: Columbia University Press, 1989). To Schelling, in the deterrence context, image relates to a country's reputation for action. Thomas Schelling, *Arms and Influence* (New Haven, CT: Yale University Press, 1966), 124.

25. Thomas Schelling, *The Strategy of Conflict* (Cambridge, MA: Harvard University Press, 1980), 260.

26. George W. Downs and Michael A. Jones, "Reputation, Compliance, and International Law," *Journal of Legal Studies* 31, no. 1 (January 2002): S96.

27. On different approaches to compliance, see Beth A. Simmons, "Compliance with International Agreements," *Annual Review of Political Science* 1 (1998): 75–93; Abram Chayes and Antonia Handler Chayes, *The New Sovereignty: Compliance with International Regulatory Agreements* (Cambridge, MA: Harvard University Press, 1995).

28. Downs and Jones, "Reputation, Compliance and International Law," S96 and S101.

29. Beth A. Simmons, "International Law and State Behavior: Commitment and Compliance in International Monetary Affairs," *American Political Science Review* 94, no. 4 (December 2000): 820. An interesting case of the relationship between norms and reputation is presented in Audie Klotz, *Norms in International Relations: The Struggle against Apartheid* (Ithaca, NY: Cornell University Press, 1995). See also Charles Lipson, *Reliable Partners: How Democracies Have Made a Separate Peace* (Princeton: Princeton University Press, 2003).

30. Reputation is widely considered as "a mechanism concerning attitude toward reciprocity," especially among firms, and as a "deterrent factor, acting through threatened punishment, or as an incentive entering the agents' (often the sellers) decision-making and possibly compensating for any incentive to violate contracts." Rosaria Conte and Mario Paolucci, *Reputation in Artificial Societies: Social Beliefs for Social Order* (Boston: Kluwer Academic Publishers, 2002), 32.

31. I owe Jeff Knopf for clarifying these dimensions.

32. Eric Herring, "Double Standards and the Myth of the Third World Nuclear Fanatic," paper presented at the Annual Convention of the American Political Science Association, Chicago (September 3–6, 1992): 8.

33. Moral concerns could augment reputation considerations. For instance, Cohen and Lee argue that nuclear weapons fail to fit either "other-imposed" (e.g., constraints caused by limited capabilities and lack of public support) or "self-imposed" (prudential and moral) limits on war. Avner Cohen and Steven Lee, "The Nuclear Predicament," in *Nuclear Weapons and the Future of Humanity,* ed. Avner Cohen and Steven Lee (Totowa, NJ: Rowman and Allanheld, 1986), 1–37.

34. Harold Hongju Koh, "Why do Nations Obey International Law?" *The Yale Law Journal* 106, no. 8 (June 1997): 2609.

35. On definitions of legitimacy, see Christopher Gelpi, *The Power of Legitimacy: Assessing the Role of Norms in Crisis Bargaining* (Princeton: Princeton University Press, 2003), 14. See also Maire A. Dugan, "Legitimacy," *Beyond Intractability,* January 2004, http://www.beyondintractability.org/essay/legitimacy/.

36. On exchange power, see Peter M. Blau, *Exchange and Power in Social Life* (New York: John Wiley & Sons, 1964); David A. Baldwin, "Exchange Theory and International Relations," *International Negotiation* 3, no. 2 (1998): 139–49.

37. On public diplomacy, see Christopher Ross, "Public Diplomacy Comes of Age", *Washington Quarterly* 25, no. 2 (2002): 75–83; Charles Wolf Jr. and Brian Rosen, "Public Diplomacy: How to Think About and Improve It" (Occasional Paper, RAND Corporation, Santa Monica, CA, 2004).

38. Jonathan Mercer defines reputation as "a judgment of someone else's character (or disposition) that is then used to predict or explain future behavior." See his *Reputation and International Politics* (Ithaca, NY: Cornell University Press, 1996), 6.

Thomas C. Schelling points out the critical role of reputation in deterrence. See Schelling's *Arms and Influence*.

39. Mercer, *Reputation and International Politics*. On the role of costly signals for deterrence reputation, see James D. Fearon, "Domestic Political Audiences and the Escalation of International Disputes," *American Political Science Review* 88, no. 3 (September 1994): 577–92. For a review, see Paul K. Huth, "Reputations and Deterrence: A Theoretical and Empirical Assessment," *Security Studies* 7, no. 1 (Autumn 1997): 72–99. For an opposite view that argues that there exists no relationship between past decisions to back down and credibility in future crises, see Daryl G. Press, *Calculating Credibility: How Leaders Assess Military Threats* (Ithaca, NY: Cornell University Press, 2005).

40. Jervis, *Logic of Images*, 82.

41. Credibility is defined as the "perceived likelihood that the threat will be carried out if the conditions that are supposed to trigger it are met." Press, *Calculating Credibility*, 10.

42. Kenneth E. Boulding, *The Meaning of the Twentieth Century: The Great Transition* (New York: Harper & Row, 1964), 81.

43. Downs and Jones, "Reputation, Compliance and International Law," S96.

44. Robert Axelrod, *The Evolution of Cooperation* (New York: Basic Books, 1984).

45. Robert O. Keohane, *After Hegemony: Cooperation and Discord in the World Political Economy* (Princeton: Princeton University Press, 1984), 105–6.

46. Similar processes seem to work in other areas such as human rights. According to one study, "[t]he effectiveness of international and nongovernmental organizations in promoting human rights is largely based on political and economic elites' sensitivity to the delegitimizing effects of a damaged international image, and the belief that a bad reputation may somehow result in sanctioning by other states and in a weakened position at home." Susan Burgerman, *Moral Victories: How Activists Provoke Multilateral Action* (Ithaca, NY: Cornell University Press, 2001), 15.

47. Werner Raub and Jeroen Weesie, "Reputation and Efficiency in Social Interactions: An Example of Network Effects," *The American Journal of Sociology* 96, no. 3 (November 1990): 626.

48. Martha Finnemore and Kathryn Sikkink, "International Norm Dynamics and Political Change," *International Organization* 52, no. 4 (Autumn 1998): 897.

49. The literature on norm entrepreneurs includes: Finnemore, *National Interests in International Society*; Margaret Keck and Kathryn Sikkink, *Activists Beyond Borders: Advocacy Networks in International Politics* (Ithaca, NY: Cornell University Press, 1998): Matthew Evangelista, *Unarmed Forces: The Transnational Movement to End the Cold War* (Ithaca, NY: Cornell University Press, 1999); Burgerman, *Moral Victories;* and Ann Marie Clark, *Diplomacy of Conscience: Amnesty International and*

Changing Human Rights Norms (Princeton: Princeton University Press, 2001). For a review of these works, see Richard Price, "Transnational Civil Society and Advocacy in World Politics," *World Politics* 55, no. 4 (July 2003): 579–606.

50. Mandelbaum, *The Nuclear Question*, 19. Oppenheimer and many other scientists involved in the Manhattan Project did not initially have any doubts about their work, but began to feel a considerable ethical dilemma in the immediate post-Hiroshima era. They even wanted to share the technology with the Soviets to avoid conflict, but Truman was not willing to do so without the development of proper mechanisms for cooperation. Gerard J. DeGroot, *The Bomb: A Life* (Cambridge, MA: Harvard University Press, 2005), 113–14.

51. On the role of the scientists in the antinuclear movement, see Alice Kimball Smith, *A Peril and a Hope: The Scientists' Movement in America, 1945–47* (Chicago: University of Chicago Press, 1965); Mandelbaum, *The Nuclear Question*, 24.

52. Mandelbaum, *The Nuclear Question*, 25.

53. Lawrence S. Wittner, *The Struggle Against the Bomb*, vol. 1, *One World or None* (Stanford: Stanford University Press, 1993), 60.

54. DeGroot, *The Bomb*, 124.

55. For their influence in the American context, see Jeffrey W. Knopf, *Domestic Society and International Cooperation: The Impact of Protest on U.S. Arms Control Policy* (Cambridge: Cambridge University Press, 1998).

56. Lawrence S. Wittner, *The Struggle Against the Bomb*, vol. 2, *Resisting the Bomb* (Stanford: Stanford University Press, 1997), 5, 30, 33. See all three volumes of Wittner's *Struggle Against the Bomb* (Stanford: Stanford University Press, 1993–2003) for a comprehensive history of the role that different nuclear disarmament groups played worldwide. See also Gunter Wernicke, "The Communist-led World Peace Council and the Western Peace Movements," *Peace & Change* 23, no. 3 (July 1998): 265–311; Leonard E. Schwartz, "Perspectives on Pugwash," *International Affairs* 43, no. 3 (July 1967): 498–515.

57. Brodie, "War in the Atomic Age," in Brodie, *The Absolute Weapon*, 52, 28. See also Paul, Harknett, and Wirtz, *The Absolute Weapon Revisited*.

58. Bernard Brodie, "Implications for Military Policy," in Brodie, *The Absolute Weapon*, 76. There is evidence that Brodie's writings influenced General Eisenhower, who in 1946, as the U.S. Army Chief of Staff, distributed copies of the volume to his staff members. Alfred D. Chandler Jr., and Louis Galambos Jr., eds., *The Papers of Dwight D. Eisenhower*, vol. 7, *The Chief of Staff* (Baltimore: Johns Hopkins University Press, 1970), 1196–97.

59. On the role of this group of strategists and scholars, see Fred Kaplan, *The Wizards of Armageddon* (New York: Simon & Schuster, 1983), ch 2. Many strategists also focused on how to obtain deterrence through manipulation of extreme risks and preparing to wage a nuclear war. Among the second wave of theorists were Thomas

Schelling, Herman Kahn, Glenn Snyder, and Albert Wohlstetter, who laid the foundations of a threat-based deterrence strategy. Schelling, however, also talked about the tradition of non-use in his writings very early on. The third wave of deterrence theorists pointed out the many problems associated with deterrence theory and policy. They include Robert Jervis, Alexander George, Janice Stein, Richard Ned Lebow, and Patrick Morgan. See Robert Jervis, "Deterrence Theory Revisited," *World Politics* 31, no. 2 (January 1979): 289–324.

60. Some of these include Albert Wohlstetter, "The Delicate Balance of Terror," *Foreign Affairs,* 37, no. 2 (January 1959): 211–34; Herman Kahn, *On Thermonuclear War,* 2nd ed. (Princeton: Princeton University Press, 1961); Kahn, *On Escalation: Metaphors and Scenarios* (Baltimore: Penguin Books, 1968); Glenn H. Snyder, *Deterrence and Defense: Toward a Theory of National Security* (Princeton: Princeton University Press, 1961); Schelling, *Strategy of Conflict;* Schelling, *Arms and Influence.*

61. Quoted in Wittner, *Resisting the Bomb,* 99.

62. On the role of the non-aligned states in nuclear disarmament campaigns, see Alva Myrdal, *The Game of Disarmament* (New York: Pantheon Books, 1982), 84–89; William Epstein, *The Last Chance: Nuclear Proliferation and Arms Control* (New York: The Free Press, 1976); M. A. Husain, "Third World and Disarmament: Shadow and Substance," *Third World Quarterly* 2, no. 1 (January 1980): 76–99; T. T. Poulose, *United Nations and Nuclear Proliferation* (New Delhi: B. R. Publishing, 1988).

63. Paul S. Boyer, *By the Bomb's Early Light: American Thought and Culture at the Dawn of the Atomic Age* (New York: Pantheon, 1985), 353. On the impact of peace movements on U.S. nuclear policy under Eisenhower, see Knopf, *Domestic Society and International Cooperation,* chs. 4 and 5.

64. Jervis, "Deterrence Theory Revisited."

65. Boyer, *By the Bomb's Early Light,* 353.

66. On this, see Knopf, *Domestic Society and International Cooperation.*

67. Boyer, *By the Bomb's Early Light,* 352–67.

Chapter 3: The United States and the Tradition I:
The Truman and Eisenhower Years (1945–1961)

1. I acknowledge that only when other nuclear states release their records will we know if this assertion is fully accurate or not.

2. Ronald Takaki, *Hiroshima: Why America Dropped the Bomb* (Boston: Little, Brown, 1995), 47. The impact of the attacks is powerfully attested in the novel by Masuji Ibuse, *Black Rain,* trans. John Bester (Tokyo: Kodansha International, 1969). The most influential article on the attack was John Hersey, "Hiroshima," *The New Yorker,* August 31, 1946. See also John Hersey, *Hiroshima* (New York: Alfred A. Knopf, 1972); Kai Bird and Lawrence Lifschultz, eds., *Hiroshima's Shadow* (Stony Creek, CT: The Pamphleteer's Press), 1998.

3. Harry S. Truman, *Memoirs*, vol. 1: *Year of Decisions, 1945* (Garden City, NY: Doubleday, 1955), 417. Truman states that he "regarded the bomb as a military weapon and never had any doubt that it should be used." Ibid., 419.

4. New evidence also suggests that it was Russia's intervention two days after the Hiroshima bombing that convinced the Japanese to surrender. For this, see Tsuyoshi Hasegawa, *Racing the Enemy: Stalin, Truman, and the Surrender of Japan* (Cambridge, MA: Belknap Press, 2005); Ward Wilson, "The Winning Weapon? Rethinking Nuclear Weapons in Light of Hiroshima," *International Security* 31, no. 4 (Spring 2007): 162–179.

5. On this, see Gar Alperovitz, *The Decision to Use the Atomic Bomb and the Architecture of an American Myth* (New York: Alfred A. Knopf, 1995); Dennis D. Wainstock, *The Decision to Drop the Atomic Bomb* (Wesport, CT: Praeger, 1996); Barton J. Bernstein, "Truman and the A-Bomb: Targeting Noncombatants, Using the Bomb, and His Defending the Decision," *The Journal of Military History* 62, no. 3 (July 1998): 547–70; Robert James Maddox, *Weapons for Victory: The Hiroshima Decision* (Columbia: University of Missouri Press, 1995).

6. Takaki, *Hiroshima*, ch. 3.

7. Peter R. Beckman et al., *The Nuclear Predicament*, 2nd ed. (Englewood Cliffs, NJ: Prentice Hall, 1992), 12; Arnold A. Offner, *Another Such Victory: President Truman and the Cold War, 1945–1953* (Stanford: Stanford University Press, 2002), 96–99.

8. This does not mean that U.S. public opinion opposed the use of atomic weapons on Japan. A Gallup poll two weeks after the bombings found 85 percent of Americans approved the bombing, and it took some years for the human toll that resulted from the nuclear attack to come to popular attention. Greg Herken, *The Winning Weapon: The Atomic Bomb in the Cold War, 1945–1950* (New York: Alfred A. Knopf, 1980), 311.

9. Truman, *Year of Decisions*, 524. Truman might have been influenced by the publications that were released after the attacks, especially John Hersey's *New Yorker* article "Hiroshima," that created considerable publicity and knowledge on the ill effects of the atomic attacks on Japan. The article, based on interviews with the survivors of Hiroshima, covered the entire issue of the August 31, 1946 *New Yorker* magazine. It sold out quickly, was read out by radio stations around the world, and was subsequently published as a book which is in print even today. On this, see Steve Rothman, "The Publication of 'Hiroshima' in *The New Yorker*" (unpublished paper, Harvard University, 1997), http://www.herseyhiroshima.com/hiro.php.

10. McGeorge Bundy, *Danger and Survival* (New York: Random House, 1988), 138–39. A few months after the nuclear bombings of the Japanese cities, Truman met with two of his wartime allies, Prime Ministers Clement Attlee of Britain and William Lyon Mackenzie King of Canada, to set up a commission under the United Nations to make specific proposals to extend the exchange of scientific information for peaceful purposes, to eliminate nuclear weapons from national control, and to establish

safeguards and inspections to achieve compliance. On this, see "Declaration on Atomic Bomb by President Truman and Prime Ministers Attlee and King," Washington, DC, November 15, 1945, www.nuclearfiles.org/menu/key-issues/nuclear-energy/history/dec_truman-attlee-king_1945_11-15.htm. See also Barton J. Bernstein, "The Quest for Security: American Foreign Policy and International Control of Atomic Energy, 1942–1946," *The Journal of American History* 60, no. 4 (March 1974): 1003–44.

11. Even before the Hiroshima attack, leading scientists warned of the need to develop an international mechanism for control, as they feared the U.S. monopoly would not last long and that secrecy could not be maintained indefinitely. Vannevar Bush and James B. Conant, "Memorandum to the Secretary of War, on Salient Points Concerning Future International Handling of Subject of Atomic Bombs," September 30, 1944, www.gwu.edu/~nsarchiv/NSAEBB/NSAEBB162/1.pdf. The Franck Committee, headed by physicist James Franck and actively influenced by Leo Szilard, had recommended the above proposals, but they did not seem to receive much attention in official policy. Glenn T. Seaborg and Benjamin S. Loeb, *Stemming the Tide: Arms Control in the Johnson Years* (Lexingon, MA: Lexington Books, 1987): 60.

12. Michael Mandelbaum, *The Nuclear Question: The United States and Nuclear Weapons, 1946–1976* (Cambridge: Cambridge University Press, 1979), 25. If the proposals had been accepted, it would have been an "unprecedentedly radical step toward a limited world government." Hans J. Morgenthau, *The Purpose of American Politics* (New York: Alfred A. Knopf, 1960): 172–73.

13. "A Report on the International Control of Atomic Energy," Washington, DC, March 16, 1946, www.learnworld.com/ZNW/LWText.Acheson-Lilienthal.html. The plan was heavily influenced by the ideas of Oppenheimer, especially on the proposed Atomic Development Authority. Bundy, *Danger and Survival,* 159.

14. S. David Broscious, "Longing for International Control, Banking on American Superiority: Harry S. Truman's Approach to Nuclear Weapons," in *Cold War Statesmen Confront the Bomb: Nuclear Diplomacy Since 1945,* ed. John Lewis Gaddis et al. (Oxford: Oxford University Press, 1999), 27.

15. For the Plan, see *New York Times,* June 15, 1946:1. See also Herken, *The Winning Weapon,* ch. 9.

16. "Statement by the Soviet Representative on the Security Council (Gromyko) Concerning the Report of the Atomic Energy Commission, March 5, 1947," reprinted in *International Organization* 1, no. 2 (June 1947): 395–409; *New York Times,* June 20, 1946:1; Offner, *Another Such Victory,* 149; Herken, *The Winning Weapon,* 174.

17. On this duality in Truman's approach, see Broscious, "Longing for International Control," 15–38.

18. On these, see Gian P. Gentile, "Planning for Preventive War, 1945–1950," *Joint Forces Quarterly,* no. 24 (Spring 2000): 68–74; Herken, *The Winning Weapon,* ch. 11.

19. Truman had assured the Pentagon that "as much as he would hate to do it, he would approve the use of atomic weapons if circumstances warranted it. Soon

thereafter, the NSC concluded that military planning should proceed on the assumption that atomic weapons would be employed in wartime. Although Truman neither approved nor rejected this recommendation, his subordinates thereafter began to institutionalize the air/atomic strategy into their war plans." Melvin P. Leffler, *A Preponderance of Power: National Security, The Truman Administration, and the Cold War* (Stanford: Stanford University Press, 1992), 226. For the war plans, see Steven T. Ross and David Alan Rosenberg, eds., *America's Plan for War against the Soviet Union 1945–1950*, 15 vols. (New York: Garland Publishing, 1990).

20. JCS 1844/4, Brief of War Plan "Halfmoon," May 6, 1948, and Decision on JCS 1844/4, May 19, 1948, CCS 381 U.S.S.R. 13-2-46, section 12, Papers of the United States Joint Chiefs of Staff, cited in David Alan Rosenberg, "American Atomic Strategy and the Hydrogen Bomb Decision," *Journal of American History* 66, no. 1 (June 1979): 68.

21. Steven L. Rearden, *The Formative Years 1947–1950* (Washington, DC: Historical Office, Office of the Secretary of Defense, 1984), 434. See also, Richard K. Betts, *Nuclear Blackmail and Nuclear Balance* (Washington, DC: The Brookings Institution, 1987): 27.

22. Quoted in David Lilienthal, *The Journals of David E. Lilienthal*, vol 2., *The Atomic Energy Years, 1945–1950* (New York: Harper and Row, 1964), 391.

23. David Alan Rosenberg, "The Origins of Overkill: Nuclear Weapons and American Strategy, 1945–1960," *International Security* 7, no. 4 (Spring 1983): 13.

24. Walter Millis, ed., *The Forrestal Diaries* (New York: Viking, 1951), 488.

25. Ibid., 458. However, months later, at a meeting at the White House of key military and civilian officials on September 13, 1948, the issue of nuclear use in an emergency came up. The president answered that he "prayed that he would never have to make such a decision, but that if it became necessary, no one need to have a misgiving but that he would do so." Ibid., 487.

26. Harry S. Truman, *Memoirs,* vol. 2, *Years of Trial and Hope* (Garden City, NY: Doubleday, 1956), 383. See also David Holloway, *Stalin and the Bomb* (New Haven, CT: Yale University Press, 1994), 228.

27. *Time,* "Pax Americana," April 5, 1948, http://www.time.com/time/magazine/article/0,9171,798280,00.html. See also Karl P. Mueller et. al., *Striking First* (Santa Monica, CA: RAND Corporation, 2006), 121–49.

28. Betts, *Nuclear Blackmail,* 28.

29. "Evaluation of Effect on Soviet War Effort Resulting from the Strategic Air Offensive, 12 May 1949," JCS 1953/1, reprinted in *Containment: Documents on American Policy and Strategy,* ed. Thomas Etzold and John Lewis Gaddis (New York: Columbia University Press, 1978), 360–64.

30. Rosenberg, "Origins of Overkill," 16.

31. Gerard J. DeGroot, *The Bomb: A Life* (Cambridge, MA: Harvard University Press, 2005), 124–25.

32. Holloway, *Stalin and the Bomb*, 229.

33. On this, see Herbert York, *The Advisors: Oppenheimer, Teller, and the Super-bomb* (San Francisco: W. H. Freeman, 1976). Oppenheimer would emerge as a vocal opponent of the nuclear bomb and pronuclear culture, leading the AEC to declare him a security risk. McCarthy-era anti-Communist witch hunts would silence him further. On this, see Kai Bird and Martin J. Sherwin, *American Prometheus: The Triumph and Tragedy of J. Robert Oppenheimer* (New York: Vintage Books, 2006).

34. Campbell Craig, *Destroying the Village: Eisenhower and Thermonuclear War* (New York: Columbia University Press, 1998), 27. On the story of the development of the hydrogen bomb, see Richard Rhodes, *Dark Sun: The Making of the Hydrogen Bomb* (New York: Touchstone, 1995); Rosenberg, "American Atomic Strategy."

35. Quoted in John Lewis Gaddis, *The Long Peace: Inquiries into the History of the Cold War* (Oxford: Oxford University Press, 1987): 114.

36. "NSC-68: United States Objectives and Programs for National Security," April 14, 1950, reprinted in Etzold and Gaddis, *Containment*, 385–442.

37. "Annex No. 7 to NSC-68," reprinted in *SAIS Review* 19, no. 1 (Winter/Spring 1999), 21, quoted in Scott A. Silverstone, *Preventive War and American Democracy* (New York: Routledge, 2007), 70.

38. The basis of Eisenhower's massive retaliation is in NSC-100. On this, see Herken, *The Winning Weapon*, 334–36. For the text of NSC-100, see United States Department of State, *Foreign Relations of the United States* (hereafter *FRUS*), *1951*, vol. 1 (Washington, DC: United States Government Printing Office, 1979), 7–18.

39. Leffler, *Preponderance of Power*, 323.

40. Harry S. Truman, "Farewell Address," January 15, 1953, reprinted in Louis W. Koening, *The Truman Administration: Its Principles and Practice* (New York: New York University Press, 1956), 287–88.

41. "Memorandum of Conversation, by the Ambassador at Large (Jessup)," Washington, June 25, 1950, *FRUS, 1950*, vol. 7, *Korea*, 159–60, quoted in Lawrence S. Wittner, *The Struggle against the Bomb*, vol. 1, *One World or None* (Stanford: Stanford University Press, 1993), 260.

42. Bruce Cumings, "On the Strategy and Morality of American Nuclear Policy in Korea, 1950 to the Present," *Social Science Japan Journal* 1, no. 1 (1998): 58. See also Cumings, *The Origins of the Korean War*, vol. 2, *The Roaring of the Cataract, 1947–1950* (Princeton: Princeton University Press, 1990), 749–50. Despite this, in July 1950, the administration dispatched ten nuclear-configured B-29 aircraft to the Pacific in order to show resolve. See Roger Dingman, "Atomic Diplomacy During the Korean War," *International Security* 13, no. 3 (Winter 1988–1989): 63–64.

43. General Maxwell D. Taylor, from his experience as Assistant Chief of Staff for Operations and Training, and Deputy Chief of Staff for Operations and Administration, argues that there were "cogent military reasons" for refraining from atomic use: a

small number of weapons, in a time when the key theatre of conflict was Europe; limitations imposed by Korea's mountainous terrain; and fears that an atomic attack would reveal unforeseen shortcomings, reducing the credibility of "deterrent effect elsewhere." Taylor, *Swords and Plowshares* (New York: W. W. Norton, 1972), 134.

44. Quoted in Betts, *Nuclear Blackmail,* 37.

45. *New York Times,* December 1, 1950:1, 3.

46. Quoted in Cumings, *Origins of the Korean War,* 749. Attlee and Truman held six rounds of meetings in December 1950 and the communiqué issued at the end of the meetings expressed the hope that world conditions would never call for the use of the atomic bomb. "Communiqué Issued at the Conclusion of the Truman-Attlee Discussions," Washington, December 8, 1950, *FRUS 1950,* vol. 7, *Korea,* 1479.

47. *New York Times,* December 1, 1950:4.

48. Cumings, "Strategy and Morality," 59; Cumings, *Origins of the Korean War,* 750. See also Rosemary J. Foot, *The Wrong War: American Policy and the Dimensions of the Korean Conflict, 1950–53* (Ithaca, NY: Cornell University Press, 1985), 114–15, 126–27. However, it is argued that Truman was simply responding to the JCS request on possible targets and was not planning to use the weapons. Gaddis, *Long Peace,* 116.

49. Quoted in Seaborg and Loeb, *Stemming the Tide,* 29.

50. Offner, *Another Such Victory,* 403; Cumings, "Strategy and Morality," 750–51.

51. Cumings, "Strategy and Morality," 59.

52. Offner, *Another Such Victory,* 421. Offner contends that by 1952, Truman "was ready to go 'all out' against the PRC if it undertook major escalation in Korea, and it is not inconceivable that political and military circumstances in an election year—in which MacArthur sought the Republican nomination—might have driven or tempted a president to an atomic strike." Ibid., 422.

53. Dingman, "Atomic Diplomacy," 74.

54. Foot, *The Wrong War,* 105.

55. "Memorandum of the Planning Adviser, Bureau of Far Eastern Affairs (Emmerson) to the Assistant Secretary of State for Far Eastern Affairs (Rusk)", Washington, November 8, 1950, *FRUS 1950,* vol. 7, *Korea,* 1098–1100, cited in Gaddis, *Long Peace,* 118.

56. Quoted in Gaddis, *Long Peace,* 119–20.

57. Truman, *Years of Trial and Hope,* 395.

58. John Lewis Gaddis, *The Cold War: A New History* (New York: The Penguin Press, 2005), 55.

59. Harry S. Truman, "Address in Milwaukee, Wisconsin," October 14, 1948, http://www.trumanlibrary.org/publicpapers/index.php?pid=1989&st=&st1=.

60. Gaddis, *Long Peace,* 108.

61. For these statistics, see "Korean War Casualty Statistics," 1999, http://www.centurychina.com/history/krwarcost.html.

62. Andrew P. N. Erdmann, "War No Longer has Any Logic Whatever: Dwight D. Eisenhower and the Thermonuclear Revolution," in Gaddis et al., *Cold War Statesmen,* 96.

63. Dwight D. Eisenhower, *The White House Years,* vol. 1, *Mandate for Change, 1953–1956* (Garden City, NY: Doubleday, 1963), 180.

64. Ibid.

65. Cited in Seymour M. Hersh, *The Price of Power: Kissinger in the Nixon White House* (New York: Summit Books, 1983), 51.

66. When asked by Adams what brought the truce in Korea, Eisenhower replied: "Danger of an atomic war . . . We told them we could not hold it to a limited war any longer if the Communists welched on a treaty of truce. They didn't want a full-scale war or an atomic attack. That kept them under some control." Sherman Adams, *Firsthand Report: The Inside Story of the Eisenhower Administration* (London: Hutchinson, 1962), 55.

67. Ibid.

68. Quoted in Edward C. Keefer, "President Dwight D. Eisenhower and the End of the Korean War," *Diplomatic History* 10, no. 3 (Summer 1986): 280.

69. On this, see Rosemary J. Foot, "Nuclear Coercion and the Ending of the Korean Conflict," *International Security* 13, no. 3 (Winter 1988–1989): 111.

70. Richard H. Immerman, *John Foster Dulles: Piety, Pragmatism, and Power in U.S. Foreign Policy* (Washington, DC: Scholarly Resources, 1999), 72.

71. On this, see Robert R. Bowie and Richard H. Immerman, *Waging Peace: How Eisenhower Shaped an Enduring Cold War Strategy* (New York: Oxford University Press, 1998), 123–38.

72. "Memorandum of Discussion at the 165th Meeting of the National Security Council," October 7, 1953, *FRUS, 1952–54,* vol. 2, 532–33. See also H. W. Brands, Jr., "The Age of Vulnerability: Eisenhower and the National Security State," *The American Historical Review* 94, no. 4 (October 1989): 971.

73. "Statement of Policy by the National Security Council," Washington, n.d. (NSC 162/2). *FRUS 1952–54* volume 2 part 1, 593. This appears to be an effort by the Eisenhower administration to bolster Western deterrence against the Soviet Union.

74. Ronald H. Spector, *Advice and Support: The Early Years, 1941–1960* (Washington, DC: U.S. Army Center for Military History, 1983), 201.

75. Cited in Gaddis, *Long Peace,* 130. See also Bundy, *Danger and Survival,* 260–70.

76. "Douglas MacArthur II to Dulles," Washington, April 7, 1954, *FRUS 1952–54,* vol. 13, 1270–1272, cited in Gaddis, *Long Peace,* 130.

77. Stephen E. Ambrose, *Eisenhower,* vol. 2 (New York: Simon & Schuster, 1983), 184.

78. Gordon H. Chang, "To the Nuclear Brink: Eisenhower, Dulles, and the Quemoy-Matsu Crisis," *International Security* 12, no. 4 (Spring 1988): 98.

79. For both, see Eisenhower, *White House Years,* 476–77.

80. "Memorandum Prepared by the Secretary of State," Washington, September 12, 1954. *FRUS 1952–54,* volume 14, 611, quoted in Gaddis, *Long Peace,* 134.

81. Joint State Department/US Information Agency Message, 25 February 1955, in folder, "Re Atomic Energy, Atomic Weapons and Disarmament," Box 89, John

Foster Dulles Papers, Seeley G. Mudd Library, cited in Neal Rosendorf, "John Foster Dulles' Nuclear Schizophrenia," in Gaddis et al., *Cold War Statesmen*, 76.

82. Quoted in Townsend Hoopes, *The Devil and John Foster Dulles* (Boston: Little, Brown, 1973), 277–78.

83. Quoted in Ambrose, *Eisenhower*, 239.

84. Quoted in Hoopes, *Devil and John Foster Dulles*, 278.

85. Quoted in Ambrose, *Eisenhower*, 239.

86. "Dulles Memorandum of Conversation with Eisenhower," March 6, 1955, *FRUS, 1955–57*, vol. 2, 336–37, cited in Gaddis, *Long Peace*, 136.

87. National Intelligence Estimate 100-4-55, "Communist Capabilities and Intentions with Respect to the Offshore Islands and Taiwan through 1955," 379, cited in Gaddis, *The Long Peace*, 137.

88. Cited in Gaddis, *Long Peace*, 138.

89. H. W. Brands, Jr., "Testing Massive Retaliation: Credibility and Crisis Management in the Taiwan Strait," *International Security* 12, no. 4 (Spring 1988): 124–51.

90. On this crisis, see Bundy, *Danger and Survival*, 279–86.

91. "Memorandum of Discussion at the 277th Meeting of the National Security Council," Washington, February 27, 1956, *FRUS, 1955–1957*, vol. 19, 204.

92. Cited in Wittner, *Resisting the Bomb*, 173.

93. "Memorandum of Conversation Between the President and the Secretary of State," Washington, April 11, 1955, *FRUS, 1955–1957*, vol. 2, 471.

94. "Memorandum of Discussion at the 285th Meeting of the National Security Council," Washington, May 17, 1956, *FRUS, 1955–1957*, vol. 19, 307.

95. "Memorandum of Discussion at the 325th Meeting of the National Security Council," Washington, May 27, 1957, *FRUS 1955–1957*, vol. 19, 501.

96. On this, see Rosendorf, "John Foster Dulles' Nuclear Schizophrenia."

97. For a thesis of this nature, see Craig, *Destroying the Village*, 68–69.

98. In an April 1957 meeting of the NSC, Dulles stated that "[w]hat worried him most in this problem area was the probability that unless the United States, the United Kingdom and the USSR found some safe way to stop the building up of nuclear weapon stockpiles, other countries would presently begin to fabricate nuclear weapons. Such a development would certainly decrease the security of the United States. The President stated his thorough agreement with Secretary Dulles' position." "Memorandum of Discussion at the 320th Meeting of the National Security Council," Washington, April 17, 1957, *FRUS 1955–57*, vol. 19, 482.

99. "Address by President Dwight D. Eisenhower to the United Nations General Assembly, 470th Plenary Meeting," December 8, 1953, reprinted in *IAEA Bulletin* 45, no. 2 (December 2003): 66–67.

100. On the Eisenhower efforts at nonproliferation, see Shane Maddock, "The Fourth Country Problem: Eisenhower's Nuclear Nonproliferation Policy," *Presidential Studies Quarterly* 28, no. 3 (Summer 1998): 553–72.

101. Mitchell Reiss, *Without the Bomb: The Politics of Nuclear Nonproliferation* (New York: Columbia University Press, 1988), 11.

102. Lawrence Scheinman, "Shadow & Substance: Securing the Future of Atoms for Peace," *IAEA Bulletin* 45, no. 2 (December 2003): 7–9.

103. Glenn T. Seaborg and Benjamin S. Loeb, *Kennedy, Khrushchev and the Test Ban* (Berkeley: University of California Press, 1981), 3–4.

104. Gaddis, *Cold War,* 64.

105. Ibid., 65.

106. William Burr and Hector L. Montford, "The Making of the Limited Test Ban Treaty, 1958–1963" (National Security Archive, Electronic Briefing Book no. 94, August 8, 2003): 2.

107. On this, see Lawrence S. Wittner, *The Struggle Against the Bomb,* vol. 2, *Resisting the Bomb* (Stanford: Stanford University Press, 1997), chs. 1–5.

108. Burr and Montford, "The Making of the Limited Test Ban Treaty," 2.

109. On this, see Maddock, "The Fourth Country Problem," 555.

110. "Memorandum of Discussion of the 195th Meeting of the National Security Council," Washington, May 6, 1954, *FRUS, 1952–1954,* vol. 2, 1426.

111. "Memorandum of Telephone Conversation Between the Secretary of State and the Chairman of the United States Atomic Energy Commission (Strauss)," Washington, March 29, 1954, *FRUS, 1952–54,* vol. 2, 1380.

112. "Memorandum of Discussion at the 195th Meeting of the National Security Council," Thursday, May 6, 1954, *FRUS, 1952–1954,* vol. 2, 1425, 1427–28.

113. "Memorandum of Conversation, Meeting with Disarmament Advisors," April 26, 1958: 1, http://www.gwu.edu/~nsarchiv/NSAEBB/NSAEBB94/tb04.pdf.

114. Seaborg and Loeb, *Kennedy, Khrushchev and the Test Ban,* 1–26.

115. In addition, it states: "Where the consent of an ally is required for the use of these weapons from the U.S. bases on the territory of such ally, the United States should promptly obtain the advance consent of such ally for such use. The United States should also seek, as and when feasible, the understanding and approval of this policy by free nations." "Statement of Policy by the National Security Council on Basic National Security Policy," 30 October 1953, sec. 39B(1), http://mtholyoke.edu/acad/intrel/pentagon/doc18.htm.

116. Morton H. Halperin and Madalene O'Donnell, "The Nuclear Fallacy," *Bulletin of the Atomic Scientists* 44, no. 1. (January/February 1988):8.

117. National Security Archive, "First Documented Evidence the U.S. Presidents Predelegated Nuclear Weapons Release Authority to the Military," March 20, 1998, http://www.gwu.edu/~nsarchiv/news/19980319.htm. Eisenhower himself was actively involved in the drafting of the authority "in order to avoid imprecisely worded instructions that could permit the reckless or accidental use of nuclear weapons." William Burr, ed., "First Declassification of Eisenhower's Instructions to Commanders Predelegating

Nuclear Weapon Use, 1959–1960" (National Security Archive Electronic Briefing Book no. 45, May 18, 2001), para. 4, http://www.gwu.edu/~nsarchiv/NSAEBB/NSAEBB45/.

118. William Burr, ed., "The Creation of SIOP-62: More Evidence on the Origin of Overkill" (National Security Archive Electronic Briefing Book No. 130, July 13, 2004), http://www.gwu.edu/~nsarchiv?NSAEBB/NSAEBB130/index.htm.

119. He stated: "In the councils of Government we must guard against the acquisition of unwarranted influence, whether sought or unsought, by the military-industrial complex. The potential for the disastrous rise of misplaced power exists and will persist." For the text of the speech, see http://www.eisenhower.archives.gov/speeches/farewell_address.html. See also Ralph Lapp, *The Weapons Culture* (Baltimore: Penguin Books, 1969), 17.

120. Mandelbaum, *The Nuclear Question,* 54.

121. Lawrence Freedman, *The Evolution of Nuclear Strategy* (New York: St. Martin's Press, 1983), 76.

122. Mandelbaum, *The Nuclear Question,* 59.

123. Maddock, "The Fourth Country Problem," 553–72.

124. Although Eisenhower initially did not see much difference between nuclear and conventional weapons, by 1956 he had begun to realize that a thermonuclear war with the Soviets would be catastrophic, diminishing his belief that he could control crisis escalation and the actual use of nuclear weapons. Erdmann, "War No Longer Has Any Logic," 118. It is also reported that Eisenhower, as a young officer in Panama, had read Clausewitz's *On War* and was convinced by his argument that "war was politics by other means" and the "means must be proportional to the end." To Eisenhower, the "nuclear revolution made this proportional relationship impossible." Bowie and Immerman, *Waging Peace,* 48.

125. For instance, see Michael Gordon Jackson, "Beyond Brinkmanship: Eisenhower, Nuclear Warfighting, and Korea, 1953–1968," *Presidential Studies Quarterly* 35, no. 1 (March 2005): 52–75. See also Craig, *Destroying the Village.*

126. John Lewis Gaddis, *We Now Know: Rethinking Cold War History* (Oxford: Oxford University Press, 1997), 233.

127. Gaddis, *Long Peace,* 142–43.

128. "Goodpaster Memorandum, Eisenhower Conversation with John McCone and Edward Teller," August 14, 1958, *Eisenhower Papers,* Whitman files, Eisenhower diary, box 22, Aug 58 staff notes, cited in Gaddis, *Long Peace,* 144.

Chapter 4: The United States and the Tradition II: Kennedy to Clinton (1961–2001)

1. Morton H. Halperin and Madalene O'Donnell, "The Nuclear Fallacy," *Bulletin of the Atomic Scientists* 44, no. 1 (January/February 1988): 8.

2. Fred Kaplan, "JFK's First-Strike Plan," *Atlantic Monthly,* October 2001: 81.

3. William Burr, ed., "First Strike Options and the Berlin Crisis, September 1961" (National Security Archive Electronic Briefing Book no. 56, September 25, 2001), http://www.gwu.edu/~nsarchiv/NSAEBB/NSAEBB56/.

4. Sheldon M. Stern, *Averting "the Final Failure": John F. Kennedy and the Secret Cuban Missile Crisis Meetings* (Stanford: Stanford University Press, 2003), 32; Graham Allison and Philip Zelikow, *Essence of Decision: Explaining the Cuban Missile Crisis*, 2nd ed. (New York: Addison Wesley Longman, 1999), 357; James G. Blight and David A. Welch, eds., *Intelligence and the Cuban Missile Crisis* (London: Frank Cass, 1998).

5. McGeorge Bundy, *Danger and Survival* (New York: Random House, 1988), 461. The crisis "enabled them to begin exploring ways of reducing superpower tension, improving their ability to communicate, and lowering the risks of future crisis." Don Munton and David A. Welch, *The Cuban Missile Crisis: A Concise History* (Oxford: Oxford University Press, 2007), 99.

6. Joseph M. Siracusa and David G. Coleman, "Scaling the Nuclear Ladder: Deterrence from Truman to Clinton," *Australian Journal of International Affairs* 54, no. 3 (November 2000): 287–88.

7. Munton and Welch, *Cuban Missile Crisis*, 94.

8. Francis J. Gavin, "Blasts from the Past: Proliferation Lessons from the 1960s," *International Security* 29, no. 3 (Winter 2004–05): 100–35.

9. *Public Papers of the Presidents of the United States: John F. Kennedy, 1963* (Washington, DC: United States Government Printing Office, 1964), 280.

10. On negotiations that led to the Treaty, see Glenn T. Seaborg and Benjamin S. Loeb, *Kennedy, Khrushchev and the Test Ban* (Berkeley: University of California Press, 1981). The Kennedy era also saw major developments in the arms control area such as the creation of the Arms Control and Disarmament Agency (ACDA) and the establishment of a hotline between Washington and Moscow. On these, see Michael O. Wheeler, "A History of Arms Control," in *Arms Control: Cooperative Security in a Changing Environment*, ed. Jeffrey A. Larsen (Boulder, CO: Lynne Rienner, 2002), 27.

11. For an extensive analysis on this on the basis of declassified documents, see William Burr and Jeffrey T. Richelson, "Whether to 'Strangle the Baby in the Cradle': The United States and the Chinese Nuclear Program, 1960–64," *International Security* 25, no. 3 (Winter 2000–01): 54–99. See also Gordon H. Chang, "JFK, China, and the Bomb," *The Journal of American History* 74, no. 4 (March 1988): 1287–1310. At a meeting of senior advisors of the National Security Council on September 15, 1964, unilateral military action was rejected for the time being, but in any future conflict, military action against Chinese nuclear facilities would receive appropriate attention. It was agreed that there were possibilities for joint preventive action with the Soviet government, and that the secretary of state would explore with Ambassador Dobrynin such options as soon as possible. McGeorge Bundy, "Memorandum for the Record," September 15, 1964, http://www.gwu.edu/NSAEBB/NSAEBB38/China-document16.pdf.

12. "New Tapes: JFK Questioned Value of Nuclear Build-up," John F. Kennedy Presidential Library and Museum, Boston, February 6, 2002.

13. "Newly Released Tape Shows Nuclear Weapons Considered as Alternative to Ground War in Combating Chinese Aggression," John F. Kennedy Presidential Library

and Museum, Boston, August 25, 2005. See also Anand Giridharadas, "JFK's Nuclear Dilemma over China and India," *International Herald Tribune,* August 26, 2005.

14. Quoted in Bundy, *Danger and Survival,* 537.

15. George W. Ball, "Top Secret: The Prophecy the President Rejected: How Valid are the Assumptions Underlying Our Vietnam Policies?" (memorandum, October 5, 1965), reprinted in *The Atlantic Monthly* 230, no. 1 (July 1972): 41–42.

16. Nina Tannenwald, *The Nuclear Taboo* (Cambridge: Cambridge University Press, 2007), 210.

17. Bundy, *Danger and Survival,* 536–37.

18. Lawrence S. Wittner, *The Struggle Against the Bomb,* vol. 2, *Resisting the Bomb* (Stanford: Stanford University Press, 1997), 439.

19. On this group, see Ann Finkbeiner, *The Jasons: The Secret History of Science's Postwar Elite* (New York: Penguin, 2007).

20. F. J. Dyson, R. Gomer, S. Weinberg, and S. C. Wright, "Tactical Weapons in Southeast Asia" (Washington, DC: Jasons Division, Institute for Defense Analyses, March 1967): 7–8, http://nautilus.org/archives/VietnamFOIA/report/dyson67.pdf. See also Peter Hayes and Nina Tannenwald, "Nixing Nukes in Vietnam," *Bulletin of the Atomic Scientists* 59, no. 3 (May–June 2003): 52–59.

21. A senior member of the Pentagon-funded Institute for Defense Analysis (IDA) at that time, Seymour Deitchman, suggests that the talk of using nuclear weapons stopped after the JASON study was presented to the Secretary of Defense. Deitchman, "'Essentially Annihilated': An Insider's Account," The Nautilus Institute, San Francisco. February 25, 2003, http://www.nautilus.org/archives/VietnamFOIA/report/insider.html.

22. The Johnson administration explored preventive and preemptive attacks against Chinese nuclear facilities in various studies. See "The United States, China and the Bomb" (National Security Archive Electronic Briefing Book no. 1, n.d.), http://www.gwu.edu/~nsarchiv/NSAEBB/NSAEBB1/nsaebb1.htm.

23. Burr and Richelson, "Whether to Strangle the Baby," 82.

24. Robert H. Johnson, "The Chinese Communist Nuclear Capability and some Unorthodox Approaches to the Problem of Nuclear Proliferation," Washington, Department of State, Policy Planning Council, June 1, 1964, http://www.gwu.edu/NSAEBB/NSAEBB38/document13.pdf.

25. Burr and Richelson, "Whether to Strangle the Baby," 99.

26. In a letter to Russian leader Khrushchev on January 18, 1964, Johnson presented his arms control agenda in which preventing the spread of nuclear weapons appeared as the lead item. Other related objectives included ending production of fissionable materials, banning all nuclear testing, placing limitations on nuclear weapon systems, and reducing the risk of nuclear war by accident or by design. Glenn T. Seaborg and Benjamin S. Loeb, *Stemming the Tide: Arms Control in the Johnson Years* (Lexington, MA: Lexington Books, 1987), 7.

27. "The United States, China, and the Bomb," 9; Committee on Nuclear Proliferation, "Report to the President," Washington, DC, January 21, 1965, www.gwu.edu/~nsarchiv/NSAEBB/NSAEBB1/nhch7_1.htm.

28. Other developments during the Johnson era included the signing of the Outer Space Treaty with Moscow (preventing weapons deployment in outer space) and the deployment of a limited ballistic missile system, called *Sentinel*. Wheeler, "A History of Arms Control," 28.

29. Melvin R. Laird, "Memorandum from Secretary Laird Enclosing Preliminary Draft of Potential Military Actions re Vietnam," March 2, 1969 (declassified document, National Security Archives, Washington, DC, National Security Council Files, Box 1007, *Haig Vietnam Files,* vol. 1, *January–March 1969*).

30. William Burr and Jeffrey Kimball, "Nixon's Nuclear Ploy," *Bulletin of the Atomic Scientists* 59, no. 1 (January/February 2003): 28.

31. Scott D. Sagan and Seremi Suri, "The Madman Nuclear Alert: Secrecy, Signaling, and Safety in October 1969," *International Security* 27, no. 4 (Spring 2003): 150–83.

32. Quoted in Seymour M. Hersh, *The Price of Power: Kissinger in the Nixon White House* (New York: Summit Books, 1983), 52.

33. Quoted in ibid., 53. On the Nixon strategy and its limitations, see Edward Rhodes, *Power and Madness: The Logic of Nuclear Coercion* (New York: Columbia University Press, 1989), 167.

34. Hersh, *The Price of Power,* 120.

35. Ibid., 126

36. "Nixon Had Notion to Use Nuclear Bomb in Vietnam," *USA Today,* February 28, 2002, http://www.usatoday.com/news/washington/2002/02/28/nixon-tapes.htm.

37. *Time,* "What the President Saw," July 29, 1985: 53.

38. Bundy, *Danger and Survival,* 538–41.

39. Henry Kissinger, *The White House Years* (Boston: Little, Brown, 1979): 66–67.

40. Richard M. Nixon, *No More Vietnams* (New York: Arbor House, 1985), 102.

41. White House Tapes, May 5, 1972, quoted in Tannenwald, *The Nuclear Taboo,* 237.

42. Because only 7 percent of the U.S. public supported sending additional troops and stepped up fighting, "small wonder that Nixon had shelved Duck Hook." Robert Dallek, *Nixon and Kissinger: Partners in Power* (New York: HarperCollins, 2007), 183.

43. On this, see Henry A. Kissinger, *Nuclear Weapons and Foreign Policy* (New York: Harper & Brothers, 1957).

44. William Burr, "The Nixon Administration, the 'Horror Strategy,' and the Search for Limited Nuclear Options, 1969–1972," *Journal of Cold War Studies* 7, no. 3 (2005): 50.

45. Terry Terriff, *The Nixon Administration and the Making of U.S. Nuclear Strategy* (Ithaca, NY: Cornell University Press, 1995), 3–4.

46. William Burr, "The Nixon Administration, the SIOP, and the Search for Limited Nuclear Options, 1969–1974," (National Security Archive Electronic Briefing Book no. 173, November 23, 2005), 4, www.gwu.edu/~nsarchiv/NSAEBB/NSAEBB173/index .htm.

47. William Burr, "Looking Back: The Limits of Limited Nuclear War," *Arms Control Today* 36, no. 1 (January/February 2006), http://www.armscontrol.org/act/2006 _01-02/JANFEB-Lookingback.

48. Burr, "The Nixon Administration," 77. Despite his bellicose policy in Vietnam, the Nixon years saw his signing of several arms control agreements. They included the interim Strategic Arms Limitation Talks (SALT I), which set limits on the number of ballistic missile launchers; the Anti-Ballistic Missile (ABM) Treaty, which prevented both sides from deploying such missiles for the defense of their territories; the 1971 Accidents Measures Agreement; the 1972 Seabed Treaty; and the 1973 Prevention of Nuclear War Agreement. Talks also began on the Threshold Test Ban Treaty (TTBT). Wheeler, "A History of Arms Control," 29.

49. Terriff, *Nixon Administration*, 82. See also Jack Anderson, *The Anderson Papers* (New York: Random House, 1973), 264.

50. "The Chinese were climbing the walls. We were concerned that the Chinese might intervene to stop India. We didn't learn till later that they didn't have that kind of conventional capability. But if they did step in, and the Soviets reacted, what would we do? There was *no question* what we would have done." *Time,* "What the President Saw," 53.

51. David K. Hall, "The Laotian War of 1962 and the Indo-Pakistani War of 1971," in *Force without War: U.S. Armed Forces as a Political Instrument,* ed. Barry M. Blechman and Stephen S. Kaplan (Washington DC: Brookings Institution, 1978), 178. According to Hall, the United States aimed primarily to compel India to stop the war and deter it from invading Pakistan, although a secondary motive was to send a message to the Soviet Union and China. Ibid., 189.

52. Michael Karpin, *The Bomb in the Basement* (New York: Simon & Schuster, 2006), 334. See also Michael Brecher with Benjamin Geist, *Decisions in Crisis: Israel, 1967 and 1973* (Berkeley: University of California Press, 1980), 224–25; Barry M. Blechman and Douglas M. Hart, "The Political Utility of Nuclear Weapons: The 1973 Middle East Crisis," *International Security* 7, no. 1 (Summer 1982): 132–56.

53. *Time,* "What the President Saw," 53.

54. Germany especially opposed the weapon, arguing that its introduction in the country, purportedly to stop East German tanks from entering, would make battlefield use of nuclear weapons more likely, while undermining the political nature of deterrence based on mutual retaliation. Alton Frye, "Opinion: Slow Fuse on the Neutron Bomb," *Foreign Policy* no. 31 (Summer 1978): 100; McGeorge Bundy et al., "Nuclear Weapons and the Atlantic Alliance," *Foreign Affairs* 60, no. 4 (Spring 1982): 756.

55. Carter Presidency Project, "Interview with Dr. James Schlesinger" (Miller Center of Public Affairs, University of Virginia, 2005): 58.

56. *BBC News Online*, "1978: Carter Delays N-bomb Production," n.d., http://news .bbc.co.uk/onthisday/hi/dates/stories/april/7/newsid_2523000/2523051.stm.

57. On the campaign, see Maynard W. Glitman, *The Last Battle of the Cold War* (New York: Palgrave-Macmillan, 2006), 24–25.

58. Lawrence S. Wittner, *The Struggle against the Bomb*, vol. 3, *Toward Nuclear Abolition* (Stanford, CA: Stanford University Press, 2003), 48–49.

59. Thomas C. Schelling, "The Legacy of Hiroshima: A Half Century without Nuclear War," *Institute for Philosophy and Public Policy Report* 20, no. 2/3 (Summer 2000), http://www.puaf.umd.edu/IPPP/Summeroo/legacy_of_hiroshima.htm. Some of these same arguments seem relevant to the debate over mini-nukes in recent years. Earlier, the defense secretary under the Johnson administration, Robert McNamara, had rejected the development of small nuclear weapons and neutron bombs, arguing, "while we may find very low yield weapons and enhanced radiation warheads *to be of military utility, we should not acquire them simply for the purpose of breaking down the distinction between non-nuclear and nuclear warfare.*" Robert McNamara, Draft Presidential Memorandum, "The Role of Tactical Nuclear Forces in NATO Strategy," January 15, 1965, 35–37, cited in Tannenwald, *Nuclear Taboo,* 277.

60. Tannenwald, *Nuclear Taboo,* 280.

61. Jimmy Carter, "Presidential Directive/NSC-59," Washington, July 25, 1980, www.jimmycarterlibrary.org/documents/pddirectives/pd59.pdf.

62. Jimmy Carter, "State of the Union Address 1980," Washington, January 23, 1980.

63. There is evidence that Carter administration officials considered using tactical nuclear weapons in the event of a Soviet assault on Iran, and the reconnaissance flights of B-52s into the Arabian Sea caused the Soviets to take notice of the potential for nuclear war. Richard K. Betts, *Nuclear Blackmail and Nuclear Balance* (Washington, DC: The Brookings Institution, 1987), 130–31. Although this episode was an effort at extended deterrence, it still raises some interesting questions about Carter's willingness to raise the nuclear card to obtain political and strategic goals in a theater which was not traditionally considered as important as Europe or East Asia.

64. Lawrence Freedman, *The Evolution of Nuclear Strategy* (New York: St. Martin's Press, 1983), 393; Carter, "Presidential Directive/NSC-59."

65. Fred Kaplan, *The Wizards of Armageddon* (New York: Simon & Schuster, 1983), 382.

66. "Statement of Secretary of State Vance: U.S. Assurance on Non-Use of Nuclear Weapons, June 12, 1978," *Department of State Bulletin,* August 1978: 52.

67. John Prados, "Team B: The Trillion Dollar Experiment," *Bulletin of the Atomic Scientists* 49, no. 3 (April 1993): 23. Even before his election as President, Reagan had argued his opposition to MAD and advocated a massive military buildup by the United

States which the Soviets would not be able match. Paul Lettow, *Ronald Reagan and His Quest to Abolish Nuclear Weapons* (New York: Random House, 2005), 28–29.

68. Daryl G. Kimball, "The Mixed Arms Control Legacy of Ronald Reagan," *Arms Control Today* 34, no. 6 (July/August 2004): 45.

69. William Arkin, "The Buildup That Wasn't," *Bulletin of the Atomic Scientists* 45, no. 1 (January/February 1989): 6.

70. On the Reagan strategy, see Barry R. Posen and Stephen Van Evera, "Defense Policy and the Reagan Administration: Departure from Containment," *International Security* 8, no. 1 (Summer 1983): 3–45; Fareed Zakaria, "The Reagan Strategy of Containment," *Political Science Quarterly* 105, no. 3 (Autumn 1990): 373–95.

71. Jeffrey W. Knopf, *Domestic Society and International Cooperation: The Impact of Protest on U.S. Arms Control Policy* (Cambridge: Cambridge University Press, 1998), ch. 7.

72. *Public Papers of the Presidents of the United States, Ronald Reagan, 1983*, bk. 1 (Washington, DC: United States Government Printing Office, 1984), 443.

73. Peter R. Beckman et al., *The Nuclear Predicament*, 2nd ed. (Englewood Cliffs, NJ: Prentice Hall, 1992), 108.

74. See Leon V. Sigal, "Warming to the Freeze," *Foreign Policy* no. 48 (Autumn 1982): 54–65.

75. Arkin, "The Buildup That Wasn't," 7.

76. According to one study, Reagan became conciliatory to the Soviets in late 1983, in part because of the Able Archer crisis (a crisis resulting from a ten-day nuclear exercise by NATO in November 1983 which provoked the Soviets to go on nuclear alert) and the resulting increased fear of nuclear war. See Beth A. Fischer, *The Reagan Reversal: Foreign Policy and the End of the Cold War* (Columbia: University of Missouri Press, 2002), 122–43.

77. The President told Gorbachev that he "would like to see a world without nuclear missiles," to which Gorbachev responded that he was "in favor of proposals which were aimed at total elimination of nuclear arms, and on the way to this goal there should be equality and equal security." Quoted in Lettow, *Ronald Reagan and His Quest,* 218.

78. In one of his personal letters to long-term friend Laurence Beilenson, Reagan stated: "We will not allow SDI to become a bargaining chip. My own view is that we may be able to develop a defensive shield so effective that we can use it to rid the world once and for all of nuclear missiles. Then—since we all know how to make them we preserve SDI as we did our gas masks in the event a madman comes along some day and secretly puts some together." "Reagan letter to Lawrence Beilenson," August 1, 1986, in Kiron K. Skinner, Annelise Anderson, and Martin Anderson eds., *Reagan: A Life in Letters* (New York: Free Press, 2003), 428. See also Douglas J. Hoekstra, "Presidential Beliefs and the Reagan Paradox," *Presidential Studies Quarterly* 27, no.3 (Summer 1997): 429–50.

79. David B. Cohen, "From START to START II: Dynamism and Pragmatism in the Bush Administration's Nuclear Weapons Policies," *Presidential Studies Quarterly* 27, no. 3 (Summer 1997): 416.

80. *Los Angeles Times*, "Text of Bush's Letter to Saddam Hussein," January 13, 1991:A21.

81. James A. Baker III, *The Politics of Diplomacy* (New York: G. P. Putnam's Sons, 1995), 359.

82. See George Bush, "The President's News Conference," February 5, 1991, www .presidency.ucsb.edu/ws/print.php?pid=19278; "Excerpts from Talk by Bush on Gulf War," *New York Times*, February 6, 1991:A10.

83. Stephen I. Schwartz, "Miscalculated Ambiguity: U.S. Policy on the Use and Threat of Use of Nuclear Weapons," *Disarmament Diplomacy* no. 23 (February 1998): 3, http://www.bu.edu/globalbeat/nuclear/schwartz0298.html.

84. Baker, *Politics of Diplomacy*, 359.

85. William M. Arkin, "Calculated Ambiguity: Nuclear Weapons and the Gulf War," *The Washington Quarterly* 19, no. 4 (Autumn 1996): 4, citing "Desert Storm Weapons," *Air Force News Service*, March 25, 1996; *Frontline*, "Oral History: Norman Schwarzkopf," January 9, 1996, www.pbs.org/wgbh/pages/frontline/gulf/oral/schwarzkopf/ 1.html; Norman Schwarzkopf with Peter Petre, *It Doesn't Take a Hero* (New York: Bantam Books, 1992), 313; Colin L. Powell with Joseph E. Persico, *My American Journey* (New York: Random House, 1995), 485–86.

86. "A Gulf War Exclusive: President Bush Talking with David Frost," transcript No. 51, 16 January 1996, 5, cited in Keith B. Payne, *Deterrence in the Second Nuclear Age* (Lexington: The University Press of Kentucky, 1996), 139.

87. Catherine Thomasson, "Health Effects of War: Seeking SMART Security" (report, Physicians for Social Responsibility, n.d.), 5, www.oregonpsr.org/Documents/ HEWHandoutSMART.doc. "This guidance resulted in SIOP-93, the first overall nuclear war plan formally to incorporate Third World WMD Targets." USSTRATCOM, "Strategic Planning Study" Final Report, 1 October 1993, 3–35, cited in Hans M. Kristensen, "Nuclear Futures: Proliferation of Weapons of Mass Destruction and US Nuclear Strategy" (BASIC Research Report 98.2, March 1998): 10.

88. McGeorge Bundy, "Nuclear Weapons and the Gulf," *Foreign Affairs* 70, no. 4 (Fall 1991): 83.

89. Ibid., 85.

90. At the peak of the war, nearly 60 percent of public opinion also favored nuclear use in response to Iraqi use of chemical and biological weapons. Tannenwald, *Nuclear Taboo*, chs. 9, 11. This shows a change in the perceptions of the public due largely to official propaganda on the possibility of chemical and biological attack by Saddam Hussein. It also suggests that the American public was willing to loosen the

upper threshold reserved for nuclear response and thereby break the tradition under conditions in which supreme national interests were not under threat.

91. Quoted in Bundy, "Nuclear Weapons and the Gulf," 83.

92. Les Aspin, "Counterproliferation Initiative" (remarks to the National Academy of Science, December 7, 1993), www.fas.org/irp/offdocs/pdd18.htm; Ashton B. Carter, "Counterproliferation Initiative: Managing Three Crises" (remarks prepared for the Conference on Nuclear, Biological and Chemical Weapons Proliferation, Washington, DC, May 23, 1996), http://www.defenselink.mil/speeches/speech.aspx?speechid=1005.

93. Hans Kristensen, "Targets of Opportunity," *Bulletin of the Atomic Scientists,* 53, no. 5 (September/October 1997), 26.

94. For the Doctrine, see http://www.fas.org/nuke/guide/usa/doctrine/dod/jp3_12_1.pdf. In the January 2002 Nuclear Posture Review Report, the administration called for developing a broad array of capabilities in order to credibly deter "potential adversaries who have access to modern military technology including NBC weapons and the means to deliver them over long distances . . . US nuclear forces still require the capability to hold at risk a wide range of target types." "Nuclear Posture Review Report," Excerpts, January 8, 2002, 2, 3, http://www.globalsecurity.org/wmd/library/policy/dod/npr.htm.

95. *Federal News Service,* "Hearing of the Senate Foreign Relations Committee," March 28, 1996:121.

96. Quoted in http://www.armscontrol.org/factsheets/negsec; see also Amy F. Woolf, "U.S. Nuclear Weapons: Changes in Policy and Force Structure," Library of Congress, Congressional News Service Report for Congress, January 13, 2005. Harold Smith, an assistant to Perry, clarified to reporters that as the United States lacked the conventional capability to destroy Libya's buried facilities, the B61-11 bunker-buster nuclear bomb would be the "weapon of choice" should the United States decide to strike at Libya. Art Pine, "Only A-Bomb Could Destroy Libya Plant, Scientist Says," *Los Angeles Times,* April 24, 1996:A7.

97. William M. Arkin, "Those Lovable Little Bombs," *Bulletin of the Atomic Scientists* 49, no. 6 (July 1993): 23.

98. Craig Cerniello, "Clinton Issues New guidelines on Nuclear Weapons Doctrine," *Arms Control Today* 27, no. 8 (November/December 1997): 23, http://www.armscontrol.org/ act/1997_11-12/pdd.asp?print.

99. R. Jeffrey Smith, "Clinton Directive Changes Strategy on Nuclear Arms," *Washington Post,* December 7, 1997:A1; see also Kristensen, "Nuclear Futures," 7.

100. Quoted in Wade Boese, "Germany Raises No-First Use Issue at NATO Meeting," *Arms Control Today* 28, no. 8 (November/December 1998): 24.

101. Scott A. Silverstone, "The Preventive War Taboo vs. the Anti-Proliferation Imperative: Contested Norms and Strategic Responses to Nuclear Proliferation" (paper presented at the Annual Convention of the International Studies Association, San Diego, March 22, 2006): 4.

102. Leon V. Sigal, *Disarming Strangers: Nuclear Diplomacy with North Korea* (Princeton: Princeton University Press, 1998), 75–77.

103. Silverstone, "Preventive War Taboo," 34.

104. NBC News, *Meet the Press,* 3 April 1994, transcript, 7–8, cited in Payne, *Deterrence,* 139.

105. "Statement of Secretary of State Christopher Regarding a Declaration by the President of the United States on Security Assurances for Non-nuclear Weapon States Parties to the Treaty on the Non-Proliferation of Nuclear Weapons," United Nations Security Council A/50/153, 5/1995/263, April 5, 1995.

106. Arms Control Association, "U.S. Nuclear Policy: Negative Security Assurances," March 2002, www.armscontrol.org/factsheets/negsec.asp.

Chapter 5: Russia, Britain, France, China, and the Tradition

1. This does not mean that the Soviet Union was entirely passive in its nuclear behavior vis-à-vis nuclear powers. Soviet attempts at compellence are visible at the Suez Crisis in 1956, the Berlin Blockade in 1961, the Cuban Missile Crisis in 1962, and the Ussuri River border conflict with China in 1969. In addition, in the Middle East, the Soviets raised the nuclear threat to a higher level after a similar move by the United States in 1973.

2. See "Statement by the Soviet Representative on the Security Council (Gromyko) Concerning the Report of the Atomic Energy Commission, March 5, 1947," reprinted in *International Organization* 1, no. 2 (June 1947): 395–409.

3. On the Plan, see Adam Rapacki, "The Polish Plan for a Nuclear-Free Zone Today," *International Affairs* 39, no. 1 (January 1963): 1–12.

4. George Quester, *The Politics of Nuclear Proliferation* (Baltimore: Johns Hopkins University Press, 1973), 33–55.

5. Lawrence S. Wittner, *The Struggle Against the Bomb,* vol. 2, *Resisting the Bomb* (Stanford: Stanford University Press, 1997), 345; Günter Wernicke, "The Communist-Led World Peace Council and the Western Peace Movements: The Fetters of Bipolarity and Some Attempts to Break Them in the Fifties and Early Sixties," *Peace & Change* 23, no. 3 (1998): 265–311.

6. Cited in David Holloway, *Stalin and the Bomb* (New Haven, CT: Yale University Press, 1994), 161–62. For the proposal, see *USSR Proposes Disarmament* (Moscow: Progress Publishers, 1986), 106–107.

7. For these, see *USSR Proposes Disarmament,* 113–45.

8. Peter R. Beckman, Larry Campbell, and Paul W. Crumlish, *The Nuclear Predicament,* 2nd ed. (Englewood Cliffs, NJ: Prentice Hall, 1992); Holloway, *Stalin and the Bomb,* 271–72.

9. Holloway, *Stalin and the Bomb,* 271–72. See also Vladislav M. Zubok, "Stalin and the Nuclear Age," in John Lewis Gaddis et al., eds., *Cold War Statesmen Confront the Bomb: Nuclear Diplomacy Since 1945* (Oxford: Oxford University Press, 1999), 39–61.

10. Gerard J. DeGroot, *The Bomb: A Life* (Cambridge, MA: Harvard University Press, 2005), 133.

11. *Pravda,* October 6, 1951, cited in Nikolai Sokov, "Russia's Approach to Nuclear Weapons," *Washington Quarterly* 20, no. 3 (Summer 1997): 112.

12. Fritz W. Ermarth, "Contrast in American and Soviet Strategic Thought," in *Soviet Military Thinking,* ed. Derek Leebaert (London: George Allen & Unwin, 1981), 57. Some scholars believe that Soviet statements on war winning were meant to sustain the morale of the troops and that Moscow had accepted mutual deterrence by early 1970s. Raymond Garthoff, "Mutual Deterrence and Strategic Arms Limitation in Soviet Policy," *International Security* 3, no. 1 (Summer 1978): 112–47. For an opposite view see Richard Pipes, "Why the Soviet Union Thinks it Could Fight and Win a Nuclear War," *Commentary* 64, no. 1 (July 1977): 21–34.

13. Sokov, "Russia's Approach," 107.

14. Beckman, Campbell, and Crumlish, *Nuclear Predicament;* Robbin F. Laird and Dale R. Herspring, *The Soviet Union and Strategic Arms* (Boulder, CO: Westview Press, 1984), 13.

15. Beckman, Campbell, and Crumlish, *Nuclear Predicament,* 131.

16. Ibid., 132; See also Andrei A. Kokoshin, *Soviet Strategic Thought, 1917–91* (Cambridge, MA: MIT Press, 1998), ch. 2; Vladislav M. Zubok and Hope M. Harrison, "The Nuclear Education of Nikita Khrushchev," in Gaddis et al., *Cold War Statesmen,* 141–68.

17. Zubok and Harrison, "Nuclear Education," 148.

18. Quoted in Mohammed Heikal, *The Sphinx and the Commissar: The Rise and Fall of Soviet Influence in the Arab World* (London: Collins, 1978), 129.

19. Beckman, Campbell, and Crumish, *Nuclear Predicament,* 131.

20. Nikita Khrushchev, *Khrushchev Remembers,* trans. and ed. Strobe Talbott (Boston: Little, Brown, 1970), 518.

21. Cited in Wittner, *Resisting the Bomb,* 171.

22. Ibid.

23. Christer Jonsson, *Soviet Bargaining Behavior: The Nuclear Test Ban Case* (New York: Columbia University Press, 1979), 126.

24. Benjamin S. Lambeth, "Nuclear Proliferation and Soviet Arms Control Policy," *Orbis* 14, no. 2 (Summer 1970): 309–11. See also Lorenz M. Luthi, *The Sino-Soviet Split* (Princeton: Princeton University Press, 2008).

25. Raymond L. Garthoff, "Berlin 1961: The Record Corrected," *Foreign Policy* no. 84 (Autumn 1991): 142–56; Hannes Adomeit, *Soviet Risk Taking and Crisis Behaviour: A Theoretical and Empirical Analysis* (London: George Allen and Unwin, 1982), 240–41.

26. Don Munton and David A. Welch, *The Cuban Missile Crisis: A Concise History* (New York: Oxford University Press, 2007), 30.

27. Zubok and Harrison, "Nuclear Education," 158–60.

28. Beckman, Campbell, and Crumlish, *Nuclear Predicament,* 135–36.

29. Vojtech Mastny and Malcolm Byrne, eds., *A Cardboard Castle? An Inside History of the Warsaw Pact, 1955–1991* (Budapest: Central European University Press, 2005).

30. On the Kosygin Plan, see Mohamed I. Shaker, *The Nuclear Nonproliferation Treaty: Origins and Implementation 1959–1979*, vol. 2 (London: Oceana Publications, 1980): ch. 8.

31. *USSR Proposes Disarmament*, 229. Although the Soviet policy toward the nonnuclear states was one of no first use, on two occasions it raised the nuclear alert vis-à-vis nuclear states. The first one was in 1969 during the Ussuri River crisis involving China and the second was in 1973 during the Middle East war, in support of Egypt. For these, see Elizabeth Wishnick, *Mending Fences: The Evolution of Moscow's China Policy from Brezhnev to Yeltsin* (Seattle: University of Washington Press, 2001); Barry M. Blechman and Douglas M. Hart, "The Political Utility of Nuclear Weapons: The 1973 Middle East Crisis," *International Security* 7, no. 1 (Summer 1982): 132–56.

32. *USSR Proposes Disarmament*, 247.

33. Matthew Evangelista, "Sources of Moderation in Soviet Policy," in Philip E. Tetlock et al., eds., *Behavior, Society and Nuclear War*, vol. 2 (Oxford: Oxford University Press, 1991), 307–08. For contradictions in the no-first-use policy, see John Van Oudenaren, "Deterrence, War-fighting and Soviet Military Doctrine" (Adelphi Paper no. 210, London, International Institute for Strategic Studies, Summer 1986), 11.

34. Evangelista, "Sources of Moderation," 306–07.

35. William Maley, *The Afghanistan Wars* (New York: Palgrave-Macmillan, 2002), 61; on the Soviet intervention, see Anthony Arnold, *Afghanistan: The Soviet Invasion in Perspective* (Stanford: Hoover Institution Press, 1981).

36. Cited in Maley, *Afghanistan Wars*, 61.

37. Henry S. Bradsher, *Afghanistan and the Soviet Union* (Durham, NC: Duke University Press, 1985), 284. See also Anthony H. Cordesman and Abraham R. Wagner, *The Lessons of Modern War*, vol. 3, *The Afghanistan and Falklands Conflicts* (Boulder, CO: Westview Press, 1990).

38. On this, see Bradsher, *Afghanistan and the Soviet Union*, ch. 7.

39. Gorbachev told the French Parliament in October 1985 that there would be "no victors in a nuclear war," and that during the twenty-first century the world should achieve "life without fear of universal death." Quoted in Lawrence S. Wittner, "Gorbachev Wages the Good Fight against WMDs" (Nuclear Age Peace Foundation, October 1, 2004), http://www.wagingpeace.org/articles/2004/10/01_wittner_gorbachev -wages-good-fight.htm.

40. Beckman, Campbell, and Crumlish, *Nuclear Predicament*, 145.

41. Vladislav M. Zubok, "Gorbachev's Nuclear Learning," *Boston Review*, April– May 2000, http://bostonreview.net/BR25.2/zubok.html. Gorbachev told the Politburo on July 3, 1986: "For thirty years you scientists, specialists and ministers have been telling us that everything was safe. And you think that we will look on you as gods.

But now we have ended up with a fiasco . . . Chernobyl made me and my colleagues rethink a great many things." He became convinced that "we had to move perestroika forward." Mikhail Gorbachev, *Memoirs* (New York: Doubleday, 1995), 191, 193. For Gorbachev and Foreign Minister Shevardnadze, the cover-up convinced the leadership of the need for more reforms, "the opposite of what the hardliners had hoped for." Robert D. English, "The Road(s) Not Taken: Causality and Contingency in Analysis of the Cold War's End," in *Cold War Endgame,* ed. William C. Wohlforth (University Park: Pennsylvania State University Press, 2003), 261. See also Robert D. English, *Russia and the Idea of the West* (New York: Columbia University Press, 2000).

42. On how Gorbachev approached nuclear weapons, see Zubok, "Gorbachev's Nuclear Learning." Gorbachev is said to have developed a moral revulsion to nuclear weapons after he realized that detonation of one tenth of the existing nuclear weapons could result in a nuclear winter and that he would have to sign the decision to use nuclear weapons in a crisis situation. Ibid., 2. Those who influenced Gorbachev's thinking included Western arms control organizations such as the Federation of American Scientists, International Physicians for the Prevention of Nuclear War, and the National Resources Defense Council. English, "The Road(s) Not Taken," 259. See also Anatoly S. Chernyaev, *My Six Years with Gorbachev,* trans. and ed. Robert D. English and Elizabeth Tucker (University Park: The Pennsylvania University Press, 2000), 45–47.

43. On these, see Matthew Evangelista, "Turning Points in Arms Control," in *Ending the Cold War,* ed. Richard K. Hermann and Richard Ned Lebow (New York: Palgrave-Macmillan, 2004), 83–105.

44. *Izvestia,* November 18, 1993, quoted in Nikolai Sokov, "Russia's Approach," 113–14. See also Serge Schmemann, "Russia Drops Pledge of No First Use of Atom Arms," *New York Times,* November 4, 1993:A8.

45. See George Bunn and Roland M. Timerbaev, "Security Assurances to Non-Nuclear Weapon States," *The Nonproliferation Review* 1, no. 1 (Fall 1993): 15.

46. "Appendix A: Russian Federation Military Doctrine," in Alexei Arbatov, "The Transformation of Russian Military Doctrine: Lessons Learned from Kosovo and Chechnya" (The Marshall Center Papers no. 2, July 2000), http://www.marshallcenter.org/site-graphic/lang-en/page-pubs-index-1/static/xdocs/coll/static/mcpapers/mc-paper_2-en.pdf.

47. Rose Gottemoeller, "Nuclear Necessity in Putin's Russia," *Arms Control Today* 34, no. 3 (April 2004), http://www.armscontrol.org/act/2004_04/Gottemoeller.asp.

48. Nikolai Sokov, "An Assessment of the Draft Russian Military Doctrine" (Nuclear Threat Initiative, revised ed., July 2004), http://www.nti.org/db/nisprofs/over/doctrine.htm.

49. On this, see Arbatov, "Transformation of Russian Military Doctrine."

50. Cited in Dimitri Trenin, "Russia's Nuclear Policy in the 21st Century Environment," (Paris, Institut français des relations internationales, Autumn 2005): 13.

51. Yuri Fedorov, "Russia's Doctrine on the Use of Nuclear Weapons," (working paper, Columbia International Affairs Online, November 2002), http://www.ciaonet .org/wps/fey02.

52. Alexei Arbatov, "Russian Military Doctrine and Strategic Nuclear Forces to the Year 2000 and Beyond" (paper prepared for the conference "Russian Defense Policy Towards the Year 2000," Naval Postgraduate School, Monterey, CA, March 26–27, 1997), http://fas.org/nuke/guide/russia/doctrine/arbatov.htm.

53. Trenin, "Russia's Nuclear Policy," 13.

54. Vladimir Isachenkov, "U.S. Decision to Develop Nuclear Bunker-buster Irks Moscow," *The Gazette* (Montreal), November 27, 2003:A22.

55. Quoted in *Gulf News,* February 12, 2004.

56. David S. Yost, "Russia's Non-strategic Nuclear Forces," *International Affairs* 77, no. 3 (2001): 531–51. Russia is believed to hold about twenty thousand nonstrategic or substrategic tactical weapons, while the United States has about fifteen hundred and several thousand in storage, including one hundred fifty B61 warheads stored in five NATO countries. These "sub-strategic nuclear weapons traditionally have been deemed the most dangerous and most destabilizing due to their portability, proximity to zones of conflict, lack of strong permissive action links, dangers of pre-delegation, and the risk of early, preemptive or accidental use." Tariq Rauf, "Towards Nuclear Disarmament: What Next for the NPT?" *Disarmament Forum* no. 1 (2000): 44.

57. Russia, however, fears that new member states would become eligible for NATO's nuclear protection despite NATO's declarations to the effect that it has no intention to deploy nuclear weapons in the new member states closer to Russia. The lack of a legally binding commitment has been part of the Russian concern in this regard. Martin Butcher, Otfried Nassauer, and Stephen Young, "Nuclear Futures: Western European Options for Nuclear Risk Reduction," (BASIC Research Report 98.6, December 1998), ch. 5, http://www.basicint.org/pubs/Research/1998nuclearfutures6.htm.

58. DeGroot, *The Bomb,* 217–18.

59. Margaret Gowing, *Independence and Deterrence: Britain and Atomic Energy, 1945–1952* (London: Macmillan, 1974), 240–72.

60. "Memorandum from Richard C. Breithut (special assistant to the Secretary of State) to British Representative Robert Murphy," Washington, Department of State, May 8, 1958.

61. "Record of a Meeting of the Prime Minister and Foreign Secretary with the French Prime Minister and Minister for Foreign Affairs" London, December 2, 1950, *Documents on British Policy Overseas,* ser. 2 vol. 4, *Korea June 1950–April 1951,* 232.

62. Bruce Cumings, *The Origins of the Korean War,* vol. 2, *The Roaring of the Cataract, 1947–1950* (Princeton: Princeton University Press, 1990), 749.

63. Rebecca Johnson, "British Perspectives on the Future of Nuclear Weapons" (Washington, DC: Henry L. Stimson Center Occasional Paper no. 37, January 1998): 7.

64. Cited in Susanna Schrafstetter and Stephen Twigge, *Avoiding Armageddon: Europe, the United States and the Struggle for Nuclear Non-Proliferation, 1945–1970* (Westport, CT: Praeger, 2004), 24.

65. Jonathan Rosenberg, "Before the Bomb and After: Winston Churchill and the Use of Force," in Gaddis et al., *Cold War Statesmen*, 171–93.

66. In the aftermath of the Bravo test, Churchill reversed his position, arguing that just a few hydrogen bomb explosions could make the British Islands uninhabitable. John Lewis Gaddis, *The Cold War: A New History* (New York: The Penguin Press, 2005), 65.

67. Wittner, *Resisting the Bomb*, 162–63.

68. Schrafstetter and Twigge, *Avoiding Armageddon*, 196.

69. Alistair Horne, *Macmillan*, vol. 2, *1957–1986* (New York: Viking USA), 325, cited in Scrafstetter and Twigge, *Avoiding Armageddon*, 204.

70. Douglas Holdstock and Frank Barnaby, *The British Nuclear Weapons Programme, 1952–2002* (London: Frank Cass, 2003), 15.

71. John Baylis and Kristan Stoddart, "Britain and the Chevaline Project: The Hidden Nuclear Programme, 1967–82," *Journal of Strategic Studies* 26, no.4 (2003): 124–55.

72. For a discussion of the nuclear dimension, see Lawrence Freedman, *The Official History of the Falklands Campaign*, vol. 2: *War and Diplomacy* (London: Routledge, 2005), 57–62.

73. The revelations were published by Magoudi in his book, *Rendez-vous: The Psychoanalysis of Mitterrand*, excerpts of which were published in the *Sunday Times*. Mitterrand adds: "You can't win a struggle against the insular syndrome of an unbridled Englishwoman. To provoke a nuclear war for small islands inhabited by three sheep who are as hairy as they are frozen! Fortunately I yielded to her. Otherwise, I assure you, the metallic index finger of the lady would press the button." Quoted in John Follain, "The Sphinx and the Curious Case of the Iron Lady's H-bomb," *The Sunday Times* (London), November 20, 2005, http://www.margaretthatcher.org/commentary/displaydocument.asp?docid=110663.

74. "London Declaration on a Transformed North Atlantic Alliance," reprinted in *Survival* 32, no. 5 (September/October 1990): 469–70.

75. Johnson, "British Perspectives," 23.

76. Peter M. Jones and Gordon Reece, *British Public Attitudes to Nuclear Defence* (Houndsmills, UK: Macmillan, 1990), 1.

77. Sheila Gunn, "Hurd Sets Rule for Tactical Weapons," *The Times*, London, January 17, 1991.

78. Malcolm Chalmers, "Bombs Away? Britain and Nuclear Weapons under New Labour," *Security Dialogue* 30, no. 1 (1999): 61–74.

79. Ministry of Defence (United Kingdom), "The Strategic Defence Review" (Cm3999, The Stationery Office, July 1998): para. 63.

80. Michael Clarke, "How Strategic Was the Review?" *Disarmament Diplomacy* no. 28 (July 1998): 3.

81. BBC News Online, "UK 'Prepared to Use Nuclear Weapons,'" March 20, 2002, http://news.bbc.co.uk/2/hi/uk_news/politics/1883258.stm; Michael Evans and David Brown, "Britain's Nuclear Warning to Saddam," *The Times* (London), March 21, 2002.

82. *BBC News Online*, "UK Restates Nuclear Threat," February 2, 2003, http://news.bbc.co.uk/2/hi/uk_news/politics/2717939.stm.

83. In December 2006, the Blair government announced plans to replace current Vanguard (Trident) submarines and cut warheads by 20 percent to around one hundred sixty in twenty years. *Nuclear Threat Initiative Global Security Newswire*, December 4, 2006.

84. Ironically, the British possession of nuclear weapons had no effect on its performance in the Suez War where it fought along with France and Israel against Egypt. Alfred Grosser, *French Foreign Policy under De Gaulle* (Boston: Little Brown, 1965), 100, 103. On the history of the French nuclear program, see Philip Gordon, *A Certain Idea of France: French Security Policy and the Gaullist Legacy* (Princeton: Princeton University Press, 1993).

85. Pierre Gallois, *The Balance of Terror: Strategy for the Nuclear Age* (Boston: Houghton Mifflin, 1961), ch. 3.

86. Camille Grand, "A French Nuclear Exception?" (Washington DC: Henry L. Stimson Center Occasional Paper no. 38, January 1998): 9. See also Carey Sublette, "France's Nuclear Weapons: Origin of the Force de Frappe" (Nuclear Weapon Archive, May 2001), nuclearweaponarchive.org/France/FranceOrigin.html.

87. Anand Menon, "Explaining Defence Policy: The Mitterrand Years," *Review of International Studies* 21, no. 3 (July 1995): 285.

88. Rebecca Grant, "Dien Bien Phu," *Air Force Magazine Online* 87, no. 8 (August 2004): 14–15. See also Chapter 3 for more details of this incident.

89. George C. Herring and Richard H. Immerman, "Eisenhower, Dulles and Dienbienphu: 'The Day We Didn't Go to War' Revisited," *The Journal of American History* 71, no. 2 (September 1984): 343–63.

90. Sublette, "France's Nuclear Weapons."

91. On the Algerian war of independence and the army insurrection, see Matthew Connelly, *A Diplomatic Revolution* (New York: Oxford University Press, 2002), 237–41.

92. David S. Yost, "Nuclear Weapons Issues in France." In *Strategic Views from the Second Tier: The Nuclear Weapons Policies of France, Britain and China,* ed. John C. Hopkins and Weixing Hu (New Brunswick, NJ: Transaction Publishers, 1995), 48–49.

93. Grand, "French Nuclear Exception," 11, 15.

94. Cited in Bruno Tertrais, "Nuclear Policy: France Stands Alone," *Bulletin of the Atomic Scientists* 60, no. 4 (July/August 2004): 51.

95. Letter dated April 6, 1995, to the UN Secretary General, cited in Grand, "French Nuclear Exception," 28.

96. David S. Yost, "France's Nuclear Dilemmas," *Foreign Affairs* 75, no. 1 (January/February 1996): 115.

97. Cited in Ibid.

98. Yost, "France's Nuclear Dilemmas," 115.

99. Grand, "French Nuclear Exception," 29.

100. Adam Sage, "Chirac Sets New Terms for Nuclear Weapon Use," *The Times* (London), October 28, 2003: 13.

101. John Lichfield, "Chirac Threatens Nuclear Attack on States Sponsoring Terrorism," *The Independent,* online ed., January 20, 2006, http://news.independent.co.uk/europe/article339823.ece. Chirac's successor, Nicolas Sarkozy, announced in March 2008 that France would reduce its nuclear forces to three hundred warheads from double that size during the Cold War era, calling its deterrence a "life insurance policy" and declaring that the weapons are not "targeted at anybody." *BBC News Online,* "France to Reduce Nuclear Warheads," March 21, 2008, http://news.bbc.co.uk/2/hi/europe/7308563.stm.

102. "Chirac's Atomic Bombshell," editorial, *The Guardian,* January 21, 2006:32. France has about three hundred fifty nuclear warheads, and their maintenance costs 3.5 million Euros, or nearly 10 percent of the defense budget per year. Kim Rahir, "France Has Nuclear Retaliation Option," *Der Spiegel,* January 19, 2006.

103. Pascal Boniface, "The Future of the French Nuclear Posture," *Strategic Analysis* 23, no. 8 (November 1999), http://www.ciaonet.org/olj/sa/sa_99bop01.html. See also Pascal Boniface, "France and the Dubious Charms of a Post-Nuclear World," in *Pondering NATO's Nuclear Options,* ed. David G. Haglund (Kingston, ON: Queen's Quarterly, 1999), 151–62.

104. Admiral Marcel Duval, "De la non-proliferation à la contre-proliferation?" *Défense Nationale* (August–September 1995): 37, 39, quoted in David S. Yost, "New Approaches to Deterrence in Britain, France, and the United States," *International Affairs* 81, no. 1 (January 2005): 106.

105. "Statement of the Government of the People's Republic of China, October 16, 1964," *People's Daily,* October 17, 1964, cited in Pan Zhenqiang, "On China's No First Use of Nuclear Weapons" (paper presented at Pugwash Meeting 279, London, November 15–17, 2002), http://www.pugwash.org/reports/nw/zhenqiang.htm.

106. Zhenqiang, "China's No First Use."

107. Ibid.

108. *People's Daily,* November 25, 1971, cited in Zhenqiang, "China's No First Use."

109. "China and the World (2)," *Beijing Review Foreign Affairs Series,* 1982, 20, cited in Zhenqiang, "China's No First Use."

110. *China's National Defense in 2002* (Beijing, December 2002), http://www.china
.org.cn/e-white/20021209/VII.htm.

111. Cited in Allen S. Whiting, *China Crosses the Yalu: The Decision to Enter the
Korean War* (New York: Macmillan, 1960), 135.

112. On the Maoist approach, see Shu Guang Zhang, "Between 'Paper' and 'Real
Tigers': Mao's View of Nuclear Weapons," in Gaddis et al., *Cold War Statesmen*,
194–215.

113. Mark A. Ryan, *Chinese Attitudes toward Nuclear Weapons* (Armonk: M. E.
Sharpe, 1989), 40.

114. On this, see John Wilson Lewis and Xue Litai, *China Builds the Bomb* (Stanford: Stanford University Press, 1988), 24–34. At an April 1956 meeting, Mao argued
that China would develop nuclear weapons and missiles to avoid being bullied by others. Zhang, "Between 'Paper' and 'Real Tigers,'" 205.

115. See Gordon H. Chang, "To the Nuclear Brink: Eisenhower, Dulles, and the
Quemoy-Matsu Crisis," *International Security* 12, no. 4 (Spring 1988): 96–123.

116. Alastair Iain Johnston, "Prospects for Chinese Nuclear Force Modernization: Limited Deterrence Versus Multilateral Arms Control," *The China Quarterly*
no. 146 (June 1996): 552.

117. Savita Pande, "Chinese Nuclear Doctrine," *Strategic Analysis* 23, no. 12
(March 2000): 4.

118. Cited in Alastair Iain Johnston, "China's New 'Old Thinking': The Concept
of Limited Deterrence," *International Security* 20, no. 3 (Winter 1995–96): 18.

119. "China's Nuclear Doctrine," (Center for Nonproliferation Studies, Monterey,
December 1998), cns.miis.edu/research/china/coxrep/doctrine.htm. See also Litai
Xue, "Evolution of China's Nuclear Strategy," in John C. Hopkins and Weixing Hu,
*Strategic Views from the Second Tier: The Nuclear Weapons Policies of France, Britain
and China* (New Brunswick, NJ: Transaction Publishers, 1995), 167–89.

120. Johnston, "China's New 'Old Thinking,'" 18.

121. Cited in Ibid., 19.

122. Zhen Huang, "Whither China's Strategic Nuclear Posture? An Assessment of
Existing Constraints and Prospects," *Political Science* 53, no. 2 (December 2001): 42;
Johnston, "China's New 'Old Thinking.'"

123. Brad Roberts, Robert A. Manning, and Ronald N. Montaperto, "China: The
Forgotten Nuclear Power," *Foreign Affairs*, 79, no. 4 (July/August 2000): 55.

124. Joanne Tompkins, "How U.S. Strategic Policy is Changing China's Nuclear
Plans," *Arms Control Today* 33, no. 1 (January/February 2003), http://www.armscontrol
.org/act/2003_01-02/tompkins_janfeb03.asp.

125. Allen S. Whiting, "China's Use of Force, 1950–96, and Taiwan," *International
Security* 26, no. 2 (Fall 2001): 120.

126. Chris Buckley, "Beijing Leaders Speak of Force to Keep Taiwan 'Chinese,'" *New York Times*, March 8, 2005.

127. Tai Ming Cheung, "New Bomb Makers," *Far Eastern Economic Review* (March 16, 1989): 27. See also Swaran Singh, "China's Nuclear Weapons and Doctrine," in *Nuclear India*, ed. Jasjit Singh (New Delhi: Knowledge World, July 1998), 152.

128. Joseph Kahn, "Chinese General Threatens Use of A-bombs if U.S. Intrudes," *New York Times*, July 15, 2005.

129. Some Chinese strategists believe that China should abandon its no-first-use pledge in the face of major conventional attacks on its key cities such as Beijing and Shanghai and against major command and control centers. However, these arguments are yet to become dominant in the military's thinking. Joanne Tompkins, "Influences on Chinese Nuclear Planning" (Washington, DC: Henry L. Stimson Center Fellowship in PRC Report, Summer 2002), 18.

130. There is dispute as to whether these missiles—numbering between one hundred sixty and two hundred deployed by the mid-1990s—have conventional or nuclear warheads. Roberts, Manning, and Montaperto, "China: The Forgotten Nuclear Power," 56.

131. "China Says It Will Not Use Nuclear Weapons against Taiwan," *New York Times*, September 3, 1999:A3.

132. On this, see T. V. Paul, "Chinese/Pakistani Nuclear/Missile Ties and Balance of Power Politics," *The Nonproliferation Review* 10, no. 2 (Summer 2003): 1–9.

133. See Jeffrey Lewis, "The Ambiguous Arsenal," *Bulletin of the Atomic Scientists* 61, no. 3 (May/June 2005): 52–59.

134. On these, see Zhang Ming, *China's Changing Nuclear Posture* (Washington, DC: Brookings Institution Press, 1999), 4.

135. On the suspected missile bases and targets, see Robert S. Norris and Hans M. Kristensen, "Chinese Nuclear Forces, 2003," *Bulletin of the Atomic Scientists* 59, no. 6 (November/December 2003): 77–80.

136. Ibid; Ming, *China's Changing Nuclear Posture*, 45. See also Praveen Swami, "A Hawkish Line on China," *Frontline*, May 23, 1998.

137. For this, see "Statement by Qian Qichen, Vice Premier and Foreign Minister, at the 49th Session of the UN General Assembly," September 28, 1994, reprinted in *Beijing Review* 37, no. 41 (October 10–16, 1994).

138. For a restatement of Chinese commitment, see Zhang 'Van, "Statement by Zhang 'Van, Head of the Chinese Delegation in the General Debate at the 2005 NPT Review Conference" (New York, May 3, 2005), www.un.org/events/npt2005/statements/npto3china.pdf

139. Abandoning no first use "would require an immense buildup of Chinese nuclear forces in order to reach parity with the US, something China could not afford to do." Tompkins, "Influences on Chinese Nuclear Planning," 7.

Chapter 6: The Second-Generation Nuclear States

1. "North Korea—Denuclearization Action Plan" (U.S. Department of State, February 13, 2007), http://www.state.gov/r/pa/prs/ps/2007/february/80479.htm.

2. The most recent figures are from *The Military Balance 2007* (London: International Institute for Strategic Studies, 2007), 228; for a comparison with the size of other nuclear forces, see ibid., 111, 148, 195, 346, 315. See also *BBC News Online*, "Israel May Have 200 Nuclear Weapons," June 2, 2003, http://news.bbc.co.uk/1/Li/World/middle_east/892941.stm; Joseph Cirincioni, Jon. B. Wolfstal, and Miriam Rajkumar, *Deadly Arsenals* (Washington, DC: Carnegie Endowment for International Peace, 2002), 221.

3. The Israeli nuclear ambiguity is characterized by the absence of a nuclear doctrine and operational military doctrine, and ambiguity regarding the size and uses of actual nuclear capability. On this policy, see Yair Evron, "Opaque Proliferation: The Israeli Case," in *Opaque Nuclear Proliferation*, ed. Benjamin Frankel (London: Frank Cass, 1991), 52.

4. On this, see Shai Feldman, *Nuclear Weapons and Arms Control in the Middle East* (Cambridge, MA: MIT Press, 1997), 98–99.

5. Avner Cohen, "The Last Taboo: Israel's Bomb Revisited," *Current History*, April 2005: 169–75.

6. Greg Myre, "In a Slip, Israel's Leader Appears to Confirm its Nuclear Arsenal," *New York Times*, December 12, 2006.

7. In the same breath, they also say Israel will not be the second to introduce nuclear weapons either. Yigal Allon, *Jewish Observer*, December 24, 1964, quoted in Ernest W. Lefever, *Nuclear Arms in the Third World* (Washington, DC: The Brookings Institution, 1979), 67.

8. In July 2000, Israel reportedly began developing a sea-based deterrent based on the Dolphin class submarines it has purchased from Germany. "Today it is believed that Israel is on its way toward restructuring its nuclear forces into a triad form—with potential delivery by aircraft, missile or submarine—assuring the capability to retaliate if hit first with WMDs." Cohen, "The Last Taboo," 173.

9. For the history of the Israeli nuclear program, see Michael Karpin, *The Bomb in the Basement: How Israel Went Nuclear and What that Means for the World* (New York: Simon & Schuster, 2006).

10. Cohen, "The Last Taboo," 171.

11. Avner Cohen, "Crossing the Threshold: The Untold Nuclear Dimension of the 1967 Arab-Israeli War and its Contemporary Lessons," *Arms Control Today* 37, no. 5 (June 2007): 15.

12. Avner Cohen, "Nuclear Arms in Crisis under Secrecy: Israel and the Lessons of the 1967 and 1973 Wars," in *Planning the Unthinkable*, ed. Peter R. Lavoy, Scott D. Sagan, and James J. Wirtz (Ithaca, NY: Cornell University Press, 2000), 109, 113.

13. Karpin, *Bomb in the Basement,* 268.

14. Avner Cohen, *Israel and the Bomb* (New York: Columbia University Press, 1998), 237.

15. Ibid., 275–76.

16. Seymour M. Hersh, *The Samson Option: Israel's Nuclear Arsenal and American Foreign Policy* (New York: Random House, 1991), 225–26.

17. Ibid., 227. Hersh's account has been challenged by Shimon Peres, who confirmed that Dayan conducted an operational test of Jericho missiles, but they were not made ready or armed. Quoted in Cohen, "Nuclear Arms in Crisis Under Secrecy," 117.

18. Richard Sale, "Yom Kippur: Israel's 1973 Nuclear Alert," *Washington Times,* September 16, 2002.

19. Avner Cohen, "The Last Nuclear Moment," *New York Times,* October 6, 2003: A17.

20. Karpin, *Bomb in the Basement,* 324.

21. The reference is to the destruction of the first two temples in Jerusalem by occupying forces—the Babylonians in the sixth century BC and the Romans in the first century AD.

22. David A. Welch, "The Politics and Psychology of Restraint: Israeli Decisionmaking in the Gulf, in *Choosing to Cooperate: How States Avoid Loss,* ed. Janice Gross Stein and Louis W. Pauly (Baltimore: Johns Hopkins University Press, 1993), 149.

23. Me'ir Stiglitz, "Not to Violate the Nuclear Taboo," Commentary, *Yedi'ot Aharonot,* August 25, 2002:5.

24. Asher Arian, "Israeli Public Opinion on National Security, 1998" (Memorandum no. 49, Tel Aviv, Jaffee Center for Strategic Studies, July 1998), http://www.tau.ac.il/jcss/memoranda/memo49chp5.html.

25. Cited in Warner D. Farr, "The Third Temple's Holy of Holies: Israel's Nuclear Weapons" (The Counter Proliferation Papers, Future Warfare Series No. 2, Maxwell Air Force Base, Alabama, September 1999): 18–19.

26. Scott D. Sagan, "The Commitment Trap: Why the United States Should Not Use Nuclear Threats to Deter Biological and Chemical Weapons Attacks," *International Security* 24, no. 4 (Spring 2000): 85–115.

27. On the development of India's nuclear program, see George Perkovich, *India's Nuclear Bomb: The Impact on Global Proliferation* (Berkeley: University of California Press, 1990); Itty Abraham, *The Making of the Indian Atomic Bomb* (London: Zed Books, 1998). For the view of a participant in the long march toward nuclear acquisition, see K. Subrahmanyam, "Indian Nuclear Policy, 1964–98: A Personal Recollection," in *Nuclear India,* ed. Jasjit Singh (New Delhi: Knowledge World, July 1998), 26–53. See also T. V. Paul, "The Systemic Bases of India's Challenge to the Global Nuclear Order," *The Nonproliferation Review* 6, no. 1 (Fall 1998): 1–11.

28. On the ambivalence of Nehru's approach, see Perkovich, *India's Nuclear Bomb,* 34–37.

29. Ibid., 134.

30. Subrahmanyam, "Indian Nuclear Policy," 31.

31. Embassy of India, Washington, DC, "Evolution of India's Nuclear Policy," May 27, 1998, http://www.indianembassy.org/pic/nuclearpolicy.htm.

32. "Suo Motu Statement by Prime Minister Atal Bihari Vajpayee in the Indian Parliament," New Delhi, May 27, 1998:2.

33. Ashley J. Tellis, *India's Emerging Nuclear Posture* (Santa Monica, CA: RAND Corporation, 2001), 267.

34. "Cabinet Committee on Security Reviews Progress in Operationalizing India's Nuclear Doctrine" (Press Information Bureau, Government of India, January 4, 2003), http://pib.nic.in/archive/Ireleng/lyr2003/rjan2003/04012003/r040120033.html.

35. C. Raja Mohan, "No First Use and India's Nuclear Transition" (paper presented at Pugwash Meeting 279, London, November 15–17, 2002): 5, http://www.pugwash.org/reports/nw/rajamohan.htm.

36. Cited in Ibid, 4.

37. Ibid.

38. On this, see T. V. Paul, "The U.S.-India Nuclear Accord: Implications for the Non-Proliferation Regime," *International Journal* 62, no. 4 (Autumn, 2007): 845–61.

39. Vishal Thaper, "Scrap Nuclear No-first-use Policy, Advises Security Panel," *Hindustan Times,* January 10, 2003.

40. Tellis, *India's Emerging Nuclear Posture,* 304.

41. *Organization of Asia-Pacific News Agencies,* "No Change in 'No First Use of Nuclear Weapons,'—Fernandes," February 7, 2003.

42. Tellis, *India's Emerging Nuclear Posture,* 321.

43. P.R. Chari, "India's Nuclear Doctrine: Confused Ambitions," *The Nonproliferation Review* 7, no. 3 (Fall/Winter 2000): 132.

44. Harsh V. Pant, "India's Nuclear Doctrine and Command Structure: Implications for India and the World," *Comparative Strategy* 24, no.3 (July 2005): 282.

45. On the dangers of nuclear terrorism in South Asia, see Rajesh M. Basrur, *Minimum Deterrence and India's Nuclear Security* (Stanford: Stanford University Press, 2006), ch. 6.

46. On this, see Subhash Kapila, "India's New 'Cold Start' War Doctrine Strategically Reviewed" (Paper no. 991, South Asia Analysis Group, May 4, 2004).

47. Critics point out that the complex regional order could create an escalation to nuclear conflict, while if war remains limited it would be a stalemate, not solving any of the security problems of the two states. On these and other constraints of the limited war option, see Arzan Tarapore, "Holocaust or Hollow Victory: Limited War

in Nuclear South Asia" (Research Paper no. 6, Institute of Peace and Conflict Studies, New Delhi, February 2005).

48. Rajesh M. Basrur, "International Relations Theory and Minimum Deterrence," *India Review* 4, no. 2 (April 2005): 137.

49. Gurmeet Kanwal, "India's Nuclear Doctrine and Policy," *Strategic Analysis* 26, no. 11 (February 2001): 5.

50. A study contends that the nuclear danger in South Asia is not as frightening as presented in many Western analyses, largely because India and Pakistan, despite the latter's first-use policy, treat nuclear weapons as instruments of existential deterrence; hence, the probability of nuclear use is extremely limited. See Rajesh Rajagopalan, *Second Strike: Arguments about Nuclear War in South Asia* (New Delhi: Penguin-Viking, 2005).

51. During the Kargil conflict, Pakistan raised the nuclear threat several times, in order to make sure India would not escalate the limited war in Kargil to Pakistani-controlled Kashmir or other parts of its territory. The conflict showed the high risk-taking propensity of the Pakistani elite, and it disproved a cardinal basis of deterrence theory that states with nuclear weapons will not fight each other. Peter R. Lavoy, ed., *Asymmetric Warfare in South Asia: The Causes and Consequences of the Kargil Conflict* (Cambridge: Cambridge University Press, forthcoming); see also General V.P. Malik, *Kargil: From Surprise to Victory* (New Delhi: HarperCollins, 2006).

52. On the nuclear dimensions of these crises, see Waheguru Pal Singh Sidhu, "India's Nuclear Use Doctrine," in Peter R. Lavoy, Scott D. Sagan, and James J. Wirtz, eds., *Planning the Unthinkable* (Ithaca, NY: Cornell University Press, 2000), 132–145.

53. Sridhar Krishnaswamy, "N-weapons Not Ruled Out?" *The Hindu,* October 30, 2001, http://www.hinduonnet.com/2001/10/30/stories/01300004.htm.

54. On these problems, see Feroz Hassan Khan, "Command-and-Control Challenges in New Nuclear States" (paper presented at the Annual Convention of the International Studies Association, San Diego, March 23–25, 2006).

55. On this, see Chaim Braun and Christopher F. Chyba, "Proliferation Rings: New Challenges to the Nonproliferation Regime," *International Security* 29, no. 2 (Fall 2004): 5–49.

56. David Albright, "Al Qaeda's Nuclear Program: Through the Window of Seized Documents" (The Nautilus Institute Policy Forum Online, Special Forum 47, November 6, 2002), http://www.nautilus.org/archives/fora/Special-Policy-Forum/47_Albright .html#sect2. See also Kamran Khan and Molly Moore, "2 Nuclear Experts Briefed Bin Laden, Pakistanis Say," *Washington Post,* December 12, 2001; David Albright and Corey Hinderstein, "Unraveling the A. Q. Khan and Future Proliferation Networks," *The Washington Quarterly* 28, no. 2 (Spring 2005): 111–28.

57. Samina Ahmed, David Cortright, and Amitabh Mattoo, "Public Opinion and Nuclear Options for South Asia," *Asian Survey* 38, no. 8 (1998): 737.

58. Peter R. Lavoy, "Pakistan's Nuclear Doctrine," in *Prospects for Peace in South Asia,* ed. Rafiq Dossani and Henry S. Rowen (Stanford: Stanford University Press, 2005), ch. 11. See also Zafar Iqbal Cheema, "Pakistan's Nuclear Use Doctrine and Command and Control," in Lavoy, Sagan, and Wirtz, *Planning the Unthinkable,* 158–81.

59. Sohail Hashmi has identified three viewpoints in the Islamic world on WMD which have direct relevance to the Pakistani case. They are Jihadists who believe in the acquisition and use of WMD under the right circumstances; WMD terrorists who are prepared to use WMD as a first resort; and WMD pacifists who "renounce the acquisition and possible use of WMD as contrary to Islamic ethics." He states, "of these three positions, the WMD Jihadists comprise by far the majority of Muslim scholars who deal with this issue." Hashmi, "Islamic Ethics and Weapons of Mass Destruction," in *Ethics and Weapons of Mass Destruction,* ed. Sohail Hashmi and Steven P. Lee (Cambridge: Cambridge University Press, 2004), 322–23.

60. Paolo Cotta-Ramusino and Maurizio Martellini, "Nuclear Safety, Nuclear Stability and Nuclear Strategy in Pakistan" (report, Landau Network-Centro Volta, January 21, 2002): 3, 5–6, http://lxmi.mi.infn.it/~landnet/Doc/pakistan.pdf.

61. Russell Leng, "Realpolitik and Learning in the India-Pakistan Rivalry," in *The India-Pakistan Conflict: An Enduring Rivalry,* ed. T. V. Paul (Cambridge: Cambridge University Press, 2005), 103–30.

62. Ahmad Faruqui, "Failure in Command: Lessons from Pakistan's India Wars," *Defense Analysis* 17, no. 1 (2001): 31–40, cited in Ashley Tellis, C. Christine Fair, and Jamison J. Medby, *Limited Conflicts and the Nuclear Umbrella: Indian and Pakistani Lessons for the Kargil Crisis* (Santa Monica, CA: RAND Corporation, 2002), 81. This pattern of decision making was also evident in war decisions in 1965. See T. V. Paul, *Asymmetric Conflicts: War Initiation by Weaker Powers* (Cambridge: Cambridge University Press, 1994), ch. 6.

63. On this, see Rajesh Basrur, "Kargil, Terrorism and India's Strategic Shift," *India Review* 1, no. 4 (October 2002): 39–56.

Chapter 7: Nonnuclear States, the Tradition, and Limited Wars

1. This chapter draws from my article "Nuclear Taboo and War Initiation: Nuclear Weapons in Regional Conflicts," *Journal of Conflict Resolution* 39, no. 4 (December 1995): 696–717.

2. T. V. Paul, *Asymmetric Conflicts: War Initiation by Weaker Powers* (Cambridge: Cambridge University Press, 1994), 28.

3. For these considerations, see Paul, "Nuclear Taboo and War Initiation."

4. For some of these cases, see Paul, *Asymmetric Conflicts.*

5. I discussed the Chinese calculations in Korea as well as U.S. nuclear threats in various crises in Chapters 3 and 5.

6. The Israeli calculations are discussed in Chapter 6.

7. Seymour M. Hersh, *The Samson Option: Israel's Nuclear Arsenal and American Foreign Policy* (New York: Random House, 1991), 215–16.

8. Yair Evron, "Opaque Proliferation: The Israeli Case," *Journal of Strategic Studies* 13, no. 3 (September 1990): 44–63; Shai Feldman, *Israeli Nuclear Deterrence* (New York: Columbia University Press, 1982); Lawrence Freedman, "Israel's Nuclear Policy," *Survival* 17, no. 3 (May–June 1975): 114–20.

9. Michael Handel, "Perception, Deception and Surprise: The Case of the Yom Kippur War," *Jerusalem Papers on Peace Problems* 19 (1976): 49–50; Michael Brecher with Benjamin Geist, *Decisions in Crisis: Israel, 1967 and 1973* (Berkeley: University of California Press, 1980), 53–54.

10. Shlomo Aronson, *Conflict and Bargaining in the Middle East* (Baltimore: Johns Hopkins University Press, 1978), 164–65; Aronson, "The Nuclear Dimension of the Arab-Israeli Conflict: The Case of the Yom Kippur War," *Jerusalem Journal of International Relations* 7, nos. 1–2 (1984): 107–42.

11. Hersh, *Samson Option*, 220–21.

12. "Nasser Threatens Israel on A-Bomb," *New York Times,* December 24, 1960: A1, A2.

13. On the calculations and miscalculations of both sides, see Michael B. Oren, *Six Days of War: June 1967 and the Making of the Modern Middle East* (New York: Presidio Press, 2003).

14. Ariel E. Levite and Emily B. Landau, *Israel's Nuclear Image: Arab Perceptions of Israel's Nuclear Posture* (in Hebrew) (Tel Aviv: Papyrus, 1994), 41–42. See also Avner Cohen, "Cairo, Dimona, and the June 1967 War," *Middle East Journal* 50, no. 2 (Spring 1996): 192. Despite these pronouncements, Dimona was a major target of Egyptian military planners, showing the importance they paid to Israeli nuclear capability during that time.

15. Martin Van Creveld, *Nuclear Proliferation and the Future of Conflict* (New York: The Free Press, 1993), 108–10; Yair Evron, "The Arab Position in the Nuclear Field: A Study of Policies up to 1967," *Cooperation and Conflict* 8, no. 1 (1973): 19–31.

16. Hersh, *Samson Option*, 219.

17. Abdul Ghani al-Gamasi (former Egyptian Army Chief of Staff), personal communication, Cairo, December 14, 1990; Tahseen Basheer (Egyptian government spokesman in 1973), personal interview, Cairo, September 19, 1990.

18. Gen. Saad el-Shazly, *The Crossing of the Suez* (San Francisco: American Mideast Research, 1980), 24–25.

19. Shlomo Aronson, *The Politics and Strategy of Nuclear Weapons in the Middle East* (Albany: State University of New York Press, 1992), 145. To one scholar, the Egyptian posture toward Israeli nuclear capability was to ignore it, similar to the nonnuclear USSR's confrontation of the United States during the late 1940s. It could also be based on a "genuine belief that nuclear weapons are less important in the strategic balance." Yair Evron, *Israel's Nuclear Dilemma* (Ithaca, NY: Cornell University Press, 1994), 75.

20. Uri Bar-Joseph, "The Hidden Debate: The Formation of Nuclear Doctrines in the Middle East," *Journal of Strategic Studies* 5, no. 2 (June 1982): 207.

21. Richard N. Lebow, "Miscalculation in the South Atlantic: The Origins of the Falklands War," in *Psychology and Deterrence*, ed. Robert Jervis, Richard N. Lebow, and Janice Gross Stein (Baltimore: Johns Hopkins University Press, 1985), 110.

22. Paul Rogers, "Tactical Trident in Historical Context" (paper presented at the Annual Meeting of the British International Studies Association, University of York, UK, December 1994).

23. R. S. Norris, A. S. Burrows, and R. W. Fieldhouse, *Nuclear Weapons Databook*, vol. 5, *British, French and Chinese Nuclear Weapons* (Boulder: Westview Press, 1994), 64–65.

24. *Latin American Weekly Report* (London), November 12, 1982. This was confirmed by the International Atomic Energy Agency in a report in September 1991 that on May 10, 1982, a nuclear weapon was lost in the South Atlantic when HMS *Sheffield* sank. Rob Edwards, "Nuclear Weapons Lost in Falklands Conflict," *The Guardian*, September 23, 1991.

25. *The Times* (London), November 3, 1982:3a.

26. According to papers obtained by *New Statesman*, the Polaris submarine was sent to the South Atlantic as far as the South Ascension Island. The Belgrano Papers, leaked to parliament member Tam Dalyell and obtained by the newspaper, said that "the likely target for a threatened or demonstration nuclear attack was said to be Cordoba, northern Argentina. The nuclear threat might have been used if any of the task force's capital ships—one of the carriers, or the troop ship *Canberra*—had been destroyed in a missile attack. The Polaris deployment was said to have been ordered in the wake of the sinking of HMS *Sheffield*, after ministers had to confront the possibility that Argentine air superiority and Exocet missiles could mean the military defeat of the British task force, and the rapid political extinction of the Thatcher government." *The New Statesman*, "Falklands: All Out War," August 24, 1984:8–9. However, the official history of the Falklands War rejects this "as a mischievous test of the latter's gullibility." Lawrence Freedman, *The Official History of the Falklands Campaign*, vol. 2, *War and Diplomacy* (London: Routledge, 2005), 59.

27. All from Rob Evans and David Leigh, "Falklands Warships Carried Nuclear Weapons, MOD Admits," *The Guardian*, December 6, 2003.

28. *BBC News Online*, "Argentina Seeks Nuclear Apology," December 7, 2003, http://news.bbc.co.uk/2/hi/americas/3297805.stm.

29. Paul Brown, "UK 'Cannot Fully Arm Trident Subs,'" *The Guardian*, November 28, 1985.

30. Rob Evans and Richard Norton-Taylor, "MoD Papers Reveal Falklands Nuclear Fear," *The Guardian*, October 10, 2005, http://www.guardian.co.uk/uk/2005/oct/10/military.falklands.

31. Freedman, *Official History*, 59.

32. Jonathan Alford, "Conventional Conflicts in a Nuclear Age, Falkland Islands: The Limited Use of Limited Power," *Jerusalem Journal of International Relations* 7, nos. 1–2 (1984): 79–91.

33. *Infrome Rattenbach* (Buenos Aires: Ediciones Espartaco, Serie Documentos Historicos, 1988), 190. Military action was also conceived of as a means to "maintain the international credibility" of Argentina's claims over the Islands, and to avoid a "definitive freezing" of decade-long negotiations. N. Costa Mendez, "Beyond Deterrence: The Malvinas-Falklands Case," *Journal of Social Issues* 43, no. 4 (Winter 1987): 119–22.

34. Arthur Gavshon and Desmond Rice, *The Sinking of the Belgrano* (London: Secker & Warburg, 1984), 21.

35. Costa Mendez, "Beyond Deterrence."

36. Peter Calvert, *The Falklands Crisis: The Rights and Wrongs* (London: Frances Pinter, 1982), 86.

37. Admiral Carlos Busser (Malvinas Naval Expedition Commander) and General Garcia Enciso (Brigadier General in the Army), personal interviews, Buenos Aires, May 26, 1990.

38. John Arquilla and Maria Moyano Rasmussen, "The Origins of the South Atlantic War," *Journal of Latin American Studies* 33, no. 4 (November 2001): 754.

39. In his memoirs, Baker states that he "purposely" left the impression to Tariq Aziz that if Iraq used chemical and biological weapons it "could invite tactical nuclear retaliation." James A. Baker III, *The Politics of Diplomacy* (New York: G. P. Putnam's Sons, 1995), 359.

40. *Los Angeles Times,* "Text of Bush's Letter to Saddam Hussein," January 13, 1991:A21.

41. Lee May, "Troops Quiz Cheney on Saudi Assignment," *Los Angeles Times,* August 15, 1990:A7.

42. Robert C. Toth, "American Support Grows for Use of Nuclear Arms," *Los Angeles Times,* February 3, 1991:A1, cited in Martin Navias, "Non-Conventional Weaponry and Ballistic Missiles during the 1991 Gulf War," in *Non-Conventional Weapons Proliferation in the Middle East,* ed. Efraim Karsh, Martin S. Navias, and Philip Sabin (Oxford: Clarendon Press, 1993), 62.

43. Rick Atkinson, *Crusade: The Untold Story of the Persian Gulf War* (Boston: Houghton Mifflin, 1993), 89. See also George C. Wilson, "Worst Case: Iraqi War Goes Nuclear," *National Journal* 34, no. 41 (October 12, 2002): 2992–3.

44. Colin L. Powell, *My American Journey,* (New York: Random House, 1995), 738. However, it is argued that the commander-in-chief of the U.S.-led coalition forces, General H. Norman Schwarzkopf, had asked at the outset of the campaign for the use of nuclear weapons to jam Iraqi communication and radar facilities, and that the Pentagon had hired consultants to study the option. *Newsweek,* January 14, 1991, cited in Barry R. Posen, "U.S. Security Policy in a Nuclear-Armed World," *Security Studies* 6, no. 3 (Spring 1997): 20.

45. Philip Shenon, "Standoff in the Gulf: Pentagon Calls Israel Likely Iraqi Target," *New York Times,* December 27, 1990:A12, cited in Navias, "Non-Conventional Weaponry," 62.

46. David Welch, "The Politics and Psychology of Restraint: Israeli Decision-Making in the Gulf War," *International Journal* 47, no. 2 (1992): 328–69.

47. Other calculations could have been the inability to overcome U.S. military power and effectively apply chemical weapons, especially after the crippling of the Iraqi command, control, and intelligence networks after they were destroyed by the coalition attacks. William J. Perry, "Desert Storm and Deterrence in the Future," in *After the Storm: Lessons from the Gulf War,* ed. Joseph S. Nye and Roger K. Smith (Colorado Springs, CO: The Aspen Institute, 1992), 261.

48. R. Jeffrey Smith, "U.N. Says Iraqis Prepared Germ Weapons in Gulf War; Baghdad Balked, Fearing U.S. Nuclear Retaliation," *Washington Post,* August 26, 1995:A1.

49. Richard Butler, *The Greatest Threat: Iraq, Weapons of Mass Destruction, and the Crisis of Global Security* (New York: Public Affairs, 2000), 37. It is argued that although the Iraqis did not state it in so many words, they "considered the Coalition's greatest technological advantage to be the American nuclear capability." Ibrahim al-Marashi, "Saddam's Iraq and Weapons of Mass Destruction: Iraq as a Case Study of a Middle Eastern Proliferant," *Middle East Review of International Affairs* 8, no. 3 (September 2004): 88.

50. Baker, *Politics of Diplomacy,* 359.

51. Dean Fischer, "Inside Saddam's Brutal Regime," *Time,* September 18, 1995:82. In an interview after the war, Tariq Aziz, on a question why Iraq did not use WMD, replied, "it was not wise to use such kind of weapons in such kind of war, with such an enemy." Asked whether he meant an enemy with nuclear weapons, Aziz said: "You can . . . make your own conclusions." *Frontline,* "Oral History: Norman Schwarzkopf," January 9, 1996, http://www.pbs.org/wgbh/pages/frontline/gulf/oral/aziz/2.html. According to General Waffic al-Sammarai, former head of Iraq's military intelligence, Baghdad did not use chemical or biological weapons because "the warning was quite severe, and quite effective. The allied troops were certain to use nuclear arms and the price will be too dear and too high." Quoted in Keith B. Payne, "Why We Must Sustain Nuclear Deterrence" (National Institute for Public Policy, April 1998), http://www.nipp.org/Adobe/Op%20Ed%203_20_98.pdf.

52. Lt. Col. Jeffrey McCausland, "The Gulf Conflict: A Military Analysis," (Adelphi Paper no. 282, International Institute for Strategic Studies, London, November 1993): 34. It was reported that on January 19, 1991, Israel was about to launch a 100-plane counterstrike followed by helicopter and "commando raids through Saudi Arabian airspace." Ibid., 33.

53. According to McCausland, the "Iraqi leadership was deterred from escalating the war by fear of retaliation . . . If he had truly wished to involve Israel in the war there can be little doubt that the delivery of chemical weapons on Israeli territory by

a Scud (or any other system for that matter) would have ensured Israeli intervention whether or not any casualties resulted." Ibid, 36.

54. Amatzia Baram, "Israeli Deterrence, Iraqi Responses," *Orbis* 36, no. 3 (Summer 1992): 400. After the war, UN inspectors found that the missile modifications were unbalanced, explaining the breakup of Scuds before they hit the targets, and that chemical weapons would have burned up before impact, thereby depriving them of effectiveness. Anthony H. Cordesman, *Iran and Iraq: The Threat from the Northern Gulf* (Boulder, CO: Westview Press, 1994), 243.

55. Charles A. Duelfer, "Testimony before the Subcommittee on Emerging Threats & Capabilities, Armed Services Committee of the United States Senate" (Washington, DC, February 27, 2002), http://bioterrorism.slu.edu/bt/official/congress/duelfer022702 .pdf. See also Derek D. Smith, *Deterring America: Rogue States and the Proliferation of Weapons of Mass Destruction* (Cambridge: Cambridge University Press, 2006), 50–51.

56. Quoted in Timothy V. McCarthy and Jonathan B. Tucker, "Saddam's Toxic Arsenal: Chemical and Biological Weapons in the Gulf War," in *Planning the Unthinkable,* ed. Peter R. Lavoy, Scott D. Sagan, and James J. Wirtz (Ithaca, NY: Cornell University Press, 2000), 58; see also Mohamed Heikal, *Illusions of Triumph* (London: HarperCollins, 1992), 131.

57. Robert M. Norris and Hans M. Kristensen, "U.S. Nuclear Threats: Then and Now," *Bulletin of the Atomic Scientists* 62, no. 5 (September/October 2006): 69–71.

Chapter 8: The Tradition and the Nonproliferation Regime

1. On the limitations of nuclear weapons, see T. V. Paul, "Power, Influence and Nuclear Weapons: A Reassessment," in *The Absolute Weapon Revisited: Nuclear Arms and the Emerging International Order,* ed. T. V. Paul, Richard J. Harknett, and James J. Wirtz (Ann Arbor: University of Michigan Press, 1998), 19–46.

2. International Court of Justice (hereafter ICJ), "Legality of the Threat or Use of Nuclear Weapons, Advisory Opinion," *I.C.J. Reports 1996* (8 July 1996), 11. On the question of disarmament in general, the developing countries were active, as evident in their supporting or sponsoring over two hundred resolutions on the issue at the United Nations as of the late 1970s. See M. A. Husain, "Third World and Disarmament: Shadow and Substance," *Third World Quarterly* 2, no. 1 (January 1980): 76.

3. Jonathan M. Weisgall, *Operation Crossroads: The Atomic Tests at Bikini Atoll* (Annapolis, MD: Naval Institute Press, 1994); Jack Niedenthal, "A Short History of the People of Bikini Atoll," n.d., http://www.bikiniatoll.com/history.html.

4. On these, see Alva Myrdal, *The Game of Disarmament* (New York: Pantheon Books, 1982), 84–89; William Epstein, *The Last Chance: Nuclear Proliferation and Arms Control* (New York: The Free Press, 1976), 52–53.

5. UN General Assembly, "Resolution 1653 (XVI)," November 28, 1961, reprinted in U.S. Arms Control and Disarmament Agency (hereafter ACDA), *Documents on*

Disarmament, 1961, 648, cited in George Bunn, "The Legal Status of U.S. Negative Security Assurances to Non-Nuclear Weapon States," *The Nonproliferation Review* 4, no. 3 (Summer 1997): 2.

6. "Letter of Secretary Rusk to Acting UN Secretary General U Thant," June 30 1962, UN Doc A/5174, annex II, 78–80, reprinted in ACDA, *Documents on Disarmament, 1962,* 629, 630, cited in Bunn, "Legal Status," 2.

7. "Eight Nation Joint Memorandum submitted to the Eighteen Nation Disarmament Committee," August 19, 1966, UN Doc. ENDC/178, reprinted in ACDA, *Documents on Disarmament, 1966,* 576, 578, cited in Bunn, "Legal Status," 3.

8. ACDA, *International Negotiations on the Treaty on the Nonproliferation of Nuclear Weapons* (Washington, DC: U.S. Government Printing Office, 1969), 59, cited in Bunn, "Legal Status," 3.

9. Bunn, "Legal Status," 4.

10. Epstein, *Last Chance,* 69.

11. Ibid.

12. On the several efforts by nonnuclear states in this area, see Programme for Promoting Nuclear Non-proliferation, *Briefing Book,* vol. 1, *The Evolution of the Nuclear Non-Proliferation Regime,* 6th ed. (Southampton, UK: The Mountbatten Center for International Studies, 2000), ch. 6.

13. Epstein, *Last Chance,* 105.

14. The Article reads: "Each of the parties to the Treaty undertakes to pursue negotiations in good faith on effective measures relating to cessation of the nuclear arms race at an early date and to nuclear disarmament, and on a treaty on general and complete disarmament under strict and effective international control." *The Treaty on the Non-Proliferation of Nuclear Weapons,* 1968, www.un.org/events/npt2005/npttreaty.html. The nuclear states have, since then, continuously proclaimed their adherence to Article VI even when they were engaging in an unbridled arms race during the Cold War and, since then, attempting to widen the uses of nuclear weapons. The NPT conferences would produce contentious debates about the character and meaning of the article, and whether nuclear states have fulfilled their obligations under it or not. The NWS perceive the Article as "ancillary" and "subordinate" to the main purpose of the NPT, that is, preventing the spread of nuclear weapons to new states. On this, see Steven E. Miller, "The Haves and Have Nots: Proliferation, Disarmament, and the Future of the NPT System" (paper presented at the Norwegian Institute for International Affairs Conference, "Halting Nuclear Proliferation in the 21st Century," Oslo, October 2005). The hypocrisy involved in this is well-captured in Michael Lipson, "Organized Hypocrisy and the NPT" (paper presented at the Annual Meeting of the American Political Science Association Washington, DC, September 1–4, 2005).

15. One major hurdle that nonnuclear states faced has been that all the nuclear states parties to the NPT (except China until 1972) have held veto power in the Security Council. United Nations approval, let alone sponsorship, of an action against

nuclear weapons states thus became a highly improbable event. Myrdal, *The Game of Disarmament,* 172.

16. On the complexities of positive assurances, see Bruce D. Larkin, *Nuclear Designs* (New Brunswick, NJ: Transaction Publishers, 1996), 16–17.

17. E.L.M. Burns, "The Nonproliferation Treaty: Its Negotiations and Prospects," *International Organization* 23, no. 4 (Autumn 1969): 788–807.

18. Epstein, *Last Chance,* 106.

19. UN Security Council, "Resolution 255," 1968, cited in Joseph F. Pilat, "Reassessing Security Assurances in a Unipolar World," *The Washington Quarterly* 28, no. 2 (Spring 2005): 160.

20. Glenn T. Seaborg and Benjamin S. Loeb, *Stemming the Tide: Arms Control in the Johnson Years* (Lexington, MA: Lexington Books, 1987), 382.

21. The list of signatories is available at the UN Office for Disarmament Affairs, "Status of Multilateral Arms Regulation and Disarmament Agreements—NPT (in alphabetical order)," n.d., http://disarmament.un.org/TreatyStatus.nsf/NPT%20(in% 20alphabetical%20order)?OpenView.

22. T. V. Paul, "Systemic Conditions and Security Cooperation: Explaining the Persistence of the Nuclear Nonproliferation Regime," *Cambridge Review of International Affairs* 16, no. 1 (2003): 135–54. See also Christopher Way and Karthika Sasikumar, "Leaders and Laggards: When and Why do Countries Sign the NPT?" (Working Paper no. 16, McGill-University of Montreal Research Group in International Security, November 2004).

23. Paul, "Systemic Conditions," 147.

24. Epstein, *Last Chance,* 118–19.

25. On this, see T. V. Paul, *Power versus Prudence: Why Nations Forgo Nuclear Weapons* (Montreal: McGill-Queen's University Press, 2000), ch. 2.

26. Epstein, *Last Chance,* 124.

27. Tariq Rauf and Rebecca Johnson, "After the NPT's Indefinite Extension: The Future of the Global Nonproliferation Regime," *Non-Proliferation Review* 3, no. 1 (Fall 1995): 28–41; Paul, "Systemic Conditions," 148–50; Randy Rydell, "The 1995 Nuclear Non-Proliferation Treaty Review and Extension Conference," *Arms Control Today* 35, no. 3 (April 2005): 47–48.

28. UN Security Council, "Resolution 984," 11 April 1995.

29. Ibid.

30. The proposals in this regard include a protocol to the NPT, a treaty under the auspices of the Conference on Disarmament (CD), strengthened additional protocols under the existing nuclear-free-zone treaties, and unilateral security assurances similar to those offered by nuclear states to Ukraine. On these, see Jean du Preez, "The 2005 NPT Review Conference: Can it Meet the Nuclear Challenge?" *Arms Control Today* 35, no. 3 (April 2005): 6–12.

31. Douglas Roche, "Deadly Deadlock" (Middle Powers Initiative Briefing Paper, San Francisco, June 2005), 4.

32. Jean du Preez, "Security Assurances against the Use or Threat of Use of Nuclear Weapons: Is Progress Possible at the NPT PrepCom?" (Center for Nonproliferation Studies Reports, Monterey Institute of International Studies, April 24, 2003), http://www.cns.miis.edu/research/npt/nptsec.htm.

33. For an analysis of the 2005 review conference, see Roche, "Deadly Deadlock"; David E. Sanger, "Month of Talks Fails to Bolster Nuclear Treaty," *New York Times,* May 28, 2005.

34. Arms Control Association, "U.S. 'Negative Security Assurances' At a Glance" (Arms Control Association Fact Sheet, Washington, DC, January 2008), http://www.armscontrol.org/factsheets/negsec.asp.

35. Leonard Spector and Aubrie Ohlde, "Negative Security Assurances: Revisiting the Nuclear-Weapon-Free Zone Option," *Arms Control Today* 35, no. 3 (April 2005): 13–17.

36. The NATO military committee agreed to such a doctrinal change in February 2000. Karel Koster, "An Uneasy Alliance: NATO Nuclear Doctrine & NPT," *Disarmament Diplomacy,* 49, August 2000:10.

37. U.S. Department of State, "Daily Press Briefing," February 22, 2002, http://www.state.gov/r/pa/prs/dpb/2002/8421.htm.

38. The World Court Project was actively promoted by a coalition of nongovernmental organizations such as The International Association of Lawyers against Nuclear Arms (IALANA), the International Peace Bureau (IPB), and the International Physicians for the Prevention of Nuclear War (IPPNW). Siddharth Mallavarapu, *Banning the Bomb: The Politics of Norm Creation* (New Delhi: Pearson, 2007), 43.

39. ICJ, "Legality of the Threat," 6.

40. United States of America, Written Statement, cited in ICJ, "Legality of the Threat," 14.

41. ICJ, "Legality of the Threat," 15–16.

42. Ibid., 44.

43. Sherman W. Garnett, "Ukraine's Decision to Join the NPT," *Arms Control Today* 25, no. 1 (January-February 1995): 7–12.

44. On the genesis of the treaty, see Alfonso Garcia Robles, "Latin American Nuclear Weapon Free Zone," (The Stanley Foundation Occasional Paper no. 19, Muscatine, IA, 1979); Monica Serrano, "Latin America—The Treaty of Tlatelolco," in *Nuclear Weapons-Free Zones,* ed. Ramesh Thakur (New York: St. Martin's Press, 1998), 35–58. For the signatory list, see UN Office for Disarmament Affairs, "Status of Multilateral Arms Regulation and Disarmament Agreements—Treaty of Tlatelolco (in alphabetical order)," n.d., http://disarmament2.un.org/Treatystatus.nsf/Treaty%20of%20Tlatelolco %20(in%20alphabetical%20order)?OpenView.

45. *Treaty for the Prohibition of Nuclear Weapons in Latin America,* Additional Protocols I and II, 1967, http://www.iaea.org/Publications/Documents/Treaties/tlatelolco.html.

46. William Epstein, "Tlatelolco and a Nuclear-Weapon-Free World," in *Nuclear Weapon-free Zones in the 21st Century,* ed. Pericles Gasparani Alves and Daiana Belinde Cipollone (New York: United Nations, 1997), 25.

47. For the Soviet statement see http://disarmament.un.org/treatystatus.nsf/faf74ecab0618ca185256cf400806a63/e48b23572ce844198525688f006d2895?OpenDocument.

48. Cited in Arlene Idol Broadhurst, "Nuclear Weapon-Free Zones: A Comparative Analysis of Theory and Practice" (Aurora Paper no. 5, The Canadian Center for Arms Control and Disarmament, Ottawa, 1985): 25.

49. Spector and Ohlde, "Negative Security Assurances," 15.

50. T. V. Paul, "Nuclear Free-zone in the South Pacific: Rhetoric or Reality?" *The Round Table* no. 299 (July 1986): 252–62. For the provisions of the Treaty, see *The Australian,* August 8, 1985.

51. Michael Hamel-Green, "South Pacific: A Not So Nuclear-Free zone," *Peace Studies,* November–December 1985: 6–8.

52. Makurita Baaro, "The South Pacific Nuclear-Free-Zone Treaty (The Treaty of Rarotonga)" in Gasparini Alves and Cipollone, *Nuclear Weapon-Free Zones,* 49–54. For the status of the signatory list, see the UN Office for Disarmament Affairs, "Status of Multilateral Arms Regulation and Disarmament Agreements—Treaty of Rarotonga (in alphabetical order)" http://disarmament.un.org/TreatyStatus.nsf/Treaty%20of%20Rarotonga%20(in%20alphabetical%20order)?OpenView.

53. Spector and Ohlde, "Negative Security Assurances," 15.

54. Michael Hamel-Green, "The South Pacific—The Treaty of Rarotonga," in Thakur, *Nuclear Weapons-Free Zones,* 63–64.

55. On the history of the Treaty's rise, see Carolina G. Hernandez, "Southeast Asia—The Treaty of Bangkok," in Thakur, *Nuclear Weapons-Free Zones,* 81–92.

56. For these provisions of the Treaty, see its text, *Treaty of Bangkok,* 1995, http://www.opanal.org/NWFZ/Bangkok/Bangkok_iT.htm.

57. See the UN Office for Disarmament Affairs, "Status of Multilateral Arms Regulation and Disarmament Agreements—Bangkok Treaty (in alphabetical order)," http://disarmament.un.org/TreatyStatus.nsf/Bangkok%20Treaty%20(in%20alphabetical%20order)?OpenView.

58. Spector and Ohlde, "Negative Security Assurances," 15.

59. "Southeast Asia Nuclear-Weapon-Free Zone Treaty (Treaty of Bangkok)." (Center for Nonproliferation Studies, Monterey, 2006), 3, cns.miis.edu/pubs/inven/pdfs/seanwfz.pdf.

60. On the origins of the Treaty, see Ruchita Beri, "African Nuclear Weapon-Free Zone Treaty," *Strategic Analysis* 19, no. 4 (July 1996): 615–624; Oluyemi Adeniji, *The*

Treaty of Pelindaba: On the African Nuclear-Weapon-Free-Zone (Geneva: UNIDIR, 2002). On the position of the ANC, see Stephen F. Burgess, "Nuclear Rollback in Africa: The Role of the African National Congress and the 'Nuclear Taboo'" (paper presented at the Annual Meeting of the American Political Science Association, Washington, DC, September 2005).

61. For these provisions of the Treaty, see *African Nuclear Weapon-Free Zone Treaty (Pelindaba Treaty),* 1995, http://www.iaea.org/Publications/Documents/Treaties/pelindaba.html. See also Julius O. Ihonvbere, "Africa—The Treaty of Pelindaba," in Thakur, *Nuclear Weapons-Free Zones,* 93–119.

62. African Union, "List of Countries which have Signed, Ratified/Acceded To the African Union Convention on African Nuclear-Weapon-Free Zone Treaty (The Treaty of Pelindaba)," Addis Ababa, June 12, 2007, http://www.africa-union.org/root/au/Documents/Treaties/List/Pelindaba%20Treaty.pdf.

63. UN Office for Disarmament Affairs, "Status of Multilateral Arms Regulation and Disarmament Agreements—Pelindaba Treaty (Protocols)," http://disarmament.un.org/TreatyStatus.nsf/Pelindaba%20Treaty%20(Protocols)?OpenView. Despite signing the protocols, the United States made a conditional statement, that "it will not limit options available to the United States in response to an attack by [a treaty] party using weapons of mass destruction," implying that the United States could rely on the doctrine of "belligerent reprisals" in order to respond with a nuclear attack to a chemical or biological attack by a zone member. *Federal News Service,* "White House Briefing," April 11, 1996, quoted in Mark McDonough, *Tracking Nuclear Proliferation* (Washington, DC: Carnegie Endowment for International Peace), Appendix E, 303.

64. Joelle Bourgois, "The Role Carried out by the Zones Exempt from Nuclear Arms," in Gasparini Alves and Cipollone, *Nuclear Weapon Free-Zones,* 126.

65. This logic is provided in the context of the ASEAN Region. See Muthiah Alagappa, "Towards a Nuclear-Weapons-Free Zone in Southeast Asia" (Research Note, Institute of Strategic and International Studies, Kuala Lumpur, 1987): 7.

Chapter 9: Changing U.S. Policies and the Tradition

1. The Libyan decision to abandon nuclear weapons is credited to a deft policy of coercive diplomacy that the United States has engaged in with the aid of European partners since the days of the George H. W. Bush administration. On this, see Bruce W. Jentleson and Christopher A. Whytcock, "Who 'Won' Libya: The Force-Diplomacy Debate and Its Implications for Theory and Policy," *International Security* 30, no. 3 (Winter 2005–06): 47–86.

2. To these states, a strong chemical weapons capability is necessary as a deterrent against Israel's nuclear capability. See Eitan Barak, "Where Do We Go from Here? Implementation of the Chemical Weapons Convention in the Middle East in the Post-Saddam Era," *Security Studies* 13, no. 1 (Autumn 2003): 106–55.

3. Chaim Braun and Christopher F. Chyba, "Proliferation Rings: New Challenge to the Nuclear Nonproliferation Regime," *International Security* 29, no. 2 (Fall 2004): 5–49.

4. On the activities of the Khan Network, see "A. Q. Khan Nuclear Chronology" (Carnegie Endowment for International Peace Issue Brief 8, no. 8, Washington, DC, September 7, 2005); David Albright and Corey Hinderstein, "Unraveling the A. Q. Khan and Future Proliferation Networks," *Washington Quarterly* 28, no. 2 (Spring 2005): 111–28.

5. Graham Allison, *Nuclear Terrorism* (New York: Times Books, 2004); Charles D. Ferguson and William C. Potter, *The Four Faces of Nuclear Proliferation* (New York: Routledge, 2005), 259–317.

6. "Expounding Bush's Approach to U.S. Nuclear Security: An Interview with John Bolton," *Arms Control Today* 32, no. 2 (March 2002): 3–8. See also Joseph F. Pilat, "Reassessing Security Assurances in a Unipolar World," *The Washington Quarterly* 28, no. 2 (Spring 2005): 159–70.

7. Cited in Hans M. Kristensen, "Nuclear Futures: Proliferation of Weapons of Mass Destruction and US Nuclear Strategy" (British American Security Information Council BASIC Research Report 98.2, March 1998): 10.

8. R. Jeffrey Smith, "Clinton Directive Changes Strategy on Nuclear Arms," *Washington Post,* December 7, 1997:A1.

9. James J. Wirtz and James A. Russell, "U.S. Policy on Preventive War and Preemption," *The Nonproliferation Review* 10, no. 1 (Spring 2003): 113–23; Charles L. Glaser and Steve Fetter, "Counterforce Revisited: Assessing the Nuclear Posture Review's New Missions," *International Security* 30, no. 2 (Fall 2005): 84–126.

10. The administration has signed an arms control agreement with Russia that would reduce approximately 6,000 U.S. warheads to 2,200 in a decade, although the warheads will not be destroyed but will be placed in storage in case a future contingency arises. See *Treaty between the United States of America and the Russian Federation on Strategic Offensive Reductions,* May 24, 2002, http://www.armscontrol.org/documents/sort.asp?print.

11. U.S. president, "The National Security Strategy of the United States of America" (Washington, DC, September 17, 2002): 15; U.S. White House, "National Strategy to Combat Weapons of Mass Destruction" (Washington, DC, December 2002): 3.

12. Nicholas Kralev, "Bush Approves Nuclear Response," *Washington Times,* January 31, 2003.

13. In a *Washington Post*-ABC News Poll during the run-up to the War, six in ten Americans surveyed found a U.S. nuclear response acceptable "if Hussein orders use of chemical or biological weapons on U.S. troops." Richard Morin, "Most Favor Nuclear Option against Iraq," *Washington Post,* December 18, 2002:A18.

14. For these objectives and the problems associated with them, see James A. Russell, "Nuclear Strategy and the Modern Middle East," *Middle East Policy* 11, no. 3 (Fall 2004): 98–117.

15. U.S. Department of Defense, "Doctrine For Joint Nuclear Operations (Draft)" (Joint Publication 3–12, Washington, DC, 15 March 2005): xi.

16. Walter Pincus, "Pentagon Revises Nuclear Strike Plan," *Washington Post,* September 11, 2005:A1.

17. Hans M. Kristensen, "The Role of U.S. Nuclear Weapons: New Doctrine Falls Short of Bush Pledge," *Arms Control Today* 35, no. 7 (September 2005): 13–19.

18. Keir A. Lieber and Daryl G. Press, "The Rise of U.S. Nuclear Primacy," *Foreign Affairs* 85, no. 2 (March/April 2006): 42–54.

19. David Ruppe, "United States I: Former Bush Official Advocates Low-Yield Weapon Research," *NTI Global Security Newswire,* June 11, 2003, http://www.nti.org/d_newswire/issues/2003/6/11/6p.html.

20. See Robert L. Jervis, "The Confrontation between Iraq and the U.S.: Implications for the Theory and Practice of Deterrence," *European Journal of International Relations* 9, no. 2 (June 2003): 315–37.

21. William M. Arkin, "The Nuclear Option in Iraq," *Los Angeles Times,* January 26, 2003, http://www.latimes.com/news/printededition/opinion/la_op_arkin26jan26001512.story.

22. Nicholas D. Kristof, "Flirting with Disaster," *New York Times,* February 14, 2003:A31.

23. Paul Ritcher, U.S. Weighs Tactical Nuclear Strike on Iraq," *Los Angeles Times,* January 26, 2003:A1; *Reuters,* "U.S. Warns Iraq over Using Mass Destruction Arms," January 26, 2003.

24. William M. Arkin, "The Nuclear Option in Iraq," *Los Angeles Times,* January 26, 2003:M1.

25. Seymour M. Hersh, "The Iran Plans," *The New Yorker,* April 17, 2006, http://www.newyorker.com/printables/fact/060417fa_fact. Hersh identified the proponents of nuclear option as members of the Defense Science Board, chairman William Schneider, Stephen Hadley, Stephen Cambone, Robert Joseph, and other neoconservative members of the Bush administration.

26. Paul Reynolds, "Iran Attack Debate Raises Nuclear Prospect," *BBC News Online,* April 10, 2006, http://news.bbc.co.uk/1/hi/world/middle_east/4895212.stm.

27. Walter Pincus, "Pentagon Pursues Nuclear Earth Penetrator," *Washington Post,* March 7, 2003:A25.

28. James Sterngold, "U.S. Alters Nuclear Weapons Policy," *San Francisco Chronicle,* November 28, 2005:A1.

29. Bruce Blair, "We Keep Building Nukes for all the Wrong Reasons," *Washington Post,* May 25, 2003:B1.

30. Thomas W. Dowler and Joseph S. Howard II, "Countering the Threat of the Well-Armed Tyrant: A Modest Proposal for Small Nuclear Weapons," *Strategic Review* 19, no. 4 (Fall 1991): 34–40. See also Robert W. Nelson, "Low-Yield Earth Penetrating Nuclear Weapons," *FAS Public Interest Report* 54, no. 1 (January/February

2001): www.fas.org/faspir/2001/v54n1/weapons.htm; C. Paul Robinson, "Pursuing a New Weapons Policy for the 21st Century" (Sandia National Laboratories White Paper, Albuquerque, NM, March 22, 2001), http://www.sandia.gov/media/whitepaper/2001-04-Robinson.htm.

31. *ABC News Online* (Australia), "Scientists Back New US Nuclear Weapons," June 29, 2005, http://www.abc.net.au/news/newsitems/200506/s1402870.htm.

32. Quoted in James Sterngold, "Fallout Seen from White House Nuclear Policy," *San Francisco Chronicle,* March 1, 2003.

33. George Perkovich, "Bush Doctrine Makes Nuclear Weapons Morally Obsolete" (unpublished paper, Carnegie Endowment for International Peace, Washington, DC, June 2003): 1–2.

34. "Mini-Nukes, Bunker-Busters, and Deterrence: Framing Debate," (Center for Defense Information, Washington, DC, April 26, 2002), http://www.cdi.org/terrorism/mininukes-pr.cfm. The B61-11 was developed by the weapon labs in 1997 "by putting the nuclear explosive from an earlier bomb design into a hardened steel casing with a new nose cone to provide ground penetration capability." Nelson, "Low-Yield Earth-Penetrating Nuclear Weapons."

35. Roger Speed and Michael May, "Dangerous Doctrine," *Bulletin of the Atomic Scientists* 61, no. 2 (March/April 2005): 38–49.

36. Blair, "We Keep Building Nukes," B1.

37. Computer simulations suggest that chemical and biological attacks under most scenarios may cause only a limited number of casualties compared to nuclear attack on a city or heavily populated area. For instance, see Natural Resources Defense Council, "Consequences of Using Weapons of Mass Destruction in a U.S.-Iraqi War" (press backgrounder, March 13, 2003), http://www.nrdc.org/media/pressreleases/030313.asp.

38. *GlobalSecurity.org,* "GBU-43/B 'Mother of All Bombs,'" n.d., http://www.globalsecurity.org/military/systems/munitions/moab.htm.

39. Walter Pincus, "Nuclear Weapons Rarely Needed, General Says," *Washington Post,* March 10, 2007:A8.

40. Ian Hoffman, "Mini Nukes are too Risky, Experts Say," *Oakland Tribune,* March 5, 2003.

41. Ann Scott Tyson, "Bunker Buster Casualty Risk Cited," *Washington Post,* April 28, 2005:A7; See also Christopher E. Paine, "Countering Proliferation, or Compounding It?" (Natural Resources Defense Council, Washington, DC, May 2003).

42. Michael A. Levi, "Fire in the Whole: Nuclear and Non-Nuclear Options for Counter-Proliferation" (Carnegie Endowment for International Peace Working Paper no. 31, Washington, DC, November 2002): 29.

43. Scott D. Sagan, "The Commitment Trap: Why the United States should Not Use Nuclear Threats to Deter Biological and Chemical Weapons Attacks," *International Security* 24, no. 4 (Spring 2000): 87.

44. R. Jeffrey Smith, "The Dissenter," *Washington Post,* December 7, 1997.

45. Victor A. Utgoff, "Nuclear Weapons and Deterrence of Biological and Chemical Warfare" (Henry L. Stimson Center Occasional Paper no. 36, Henry L. Stimson Center, Washington, DC, October 1997).

46. I owe Tariq Rauf of the International Atomic Energy Agency for this point.

47. Jonathan Medalia, "Nuclear Earth Penetrator Weapons" (Congressional Research Service Report for Congress, Washington, DC, January 27, 2003): 5.

48. John Holum, "Don't Make Mini-Nukes," *International Herald Tribune,* June 9, 2003. It has been argued that the overall performance of the CIA in gauging potential WMD threats for over a decade has been "dismal." See Richard L. Russell, "A Weak Pillar for American National Security: The CIA's Dismal Performance against WMD Threats," *Intelligence and National Security* 20, no. 3 (September 2005): 466–85.

49. In March 2005, a Presidential Commission appointed by the Bush administration reported that the intelligence community was "dead wrong on Iraq's weapons arsenal" and that the "erroneous assumption by intelligence agencies that Saddam Hussein possessed deadly chemical and biological weapons had damaged American credibility before a world audience, and that the damage would take years to undo." David Stout, "Panel Says 'Dead Wrong' Data on Prewar Iraq Demands Overhaul," *New York Times,* March 31, 2005.

50. There are those who argue that the syndrome was not caused by the depleted uranium, but by sporadic chemical weapons use by Saddam's forces or as a result of coalition attacks on Iraq's chemical weapons dispersed in the theater. The debate on the syndrome remains inconclusive. On the issue, see Steve Fetter and Frank N. von Hippel, "The Hazard Posed by Depleted Uranium Munitions," *Science & Global Security* 8, no. 2 (1999): 125–61. See also Jonathan B. Tucker, "Evidence Iraq Used Chemical Weapons During the 1991 Persian Gulf War," *The Nonproliferation Review* 4, no. 3 (Spring/Summer 1997): 114–22.

51. Arkin, "Nuclear Option."

52. George Quester, *Nuclear First Strike: Consequences of a Broken Taboo* (Baltimore, MD: Johns Hopkins University Press, 2006), 68.

53. Kristensen, "Nuclear Futures," 21.

54. Perkovich, "Bush Doctrine," 4.

55. Harold A. Feiveson and Ernst Jan Hogendoorn, "No First Use of Nuclear Weapons," *The Nonproliferation Review* 10, no. 2 (Summer 2003): 1–9.

56. Former Secretary of State General Colin Powell captured the essence of the reputation problem. In an interview during the India-Pakistan standoff of 2002, he stated: "The thought of a nuclear conflict in the year 2002—with what that would mean with respect to the loss of life, what that would mean with respect to the condemnation, the worldwide condemnation, that would come down on whatever nation chose to take that course of action, would be such that I can see very little military, political,

or any other kind of justification for the use of nuclear weapons." *Online Newshour,* "Newsmaker: Colin Powell," May 30, 2002, http://www.pbs.org/newshour/bb/asia/jan-june02/powell_5-30.html.

57. Quester, *Nuclear First Strike,* 61. On the political problems of nuclear strategy, see James A. Russell, "Nuclear Strategy and the Modern Middle East," *Middle East Policy* 11, no. 3 (Fall 2004): 98–117.

58. Edward Kennedy, a vehement critic of the Bush administration's nuclear policy, told a Senate Arms Services Committee meeting on the eve of the Gulf War II, "I am concerned that the use of nuclear weapons in Iraq in the absence of an imminent, overwhelming threat to our national security would bring a near-total breakdown in our relations between the United States and the rest of the world, particularly with regard to the Arab world." He was referring to Defense Secretary Rumsfeld not ruling out nuclear use in Iraq under certain circumstances. Will Dunham, "Update I—Rumsfeld Won't Rule Out Nuclear Bomb against Iraq," *Reuters,* February 13, 2003.

59. Sridhar Krishnaswamy, "N-weapons Not Ruled Out?" *The Hindu,* October 30, 2001, http://www.hinduonnet.com/2001/10/30/stories/01300004.htm.

Chapter 10: Conclusions

1. Thomas Schelling criticized the efforts to blur the distinction in the 1960s: "It is difficult to imagine that the tacit agreement that nuclear weapons are different would be as powerfully present on the occasion of the *next* limited war after they had already been used in one. We can probably not, therefore, ignore the distinction and use nuclears in a particular war where their use might be of advantage to us and *subsequently* rely on the distinction in the hope that we and the enemy might both abstain. One potential limitation of war will be substantially discredited for all time if we shatter the tradition and create a contrary precedent," *The Strategy of Conflict,* 2nd ed. (Cambridge, MA: Harvard University Press, 1980), 265.

2. On these components, see Patrick M. Morgan, *Deterrence Now* (Cambridge: Cambridge University Press, 2003), 8.

3. Richard J. Harknett, "The Logic of Conventional Deterrence and the End of the Cold War," *Security Studies* 4, no. 1 (Autumn 1994): 89.

4. Morgan, *Deterrence Now,* 15.

5. Robert Powell, *Nuclear Deterrence Theory: The Search for Credibility* (Cambridge: Cambridge University Press, 1990), 110; Schelling, *Strategy of Conflict,* 187–203.

6. Glenn H. Snyder, "Deterrence and Power," *Journal of Conflict Resolution* 4 (1960): 163; see also Snyder, *Deterrence and Defense: Toward a Theory of National Security* (Princeton: Princeton University Press, 1961), 15–16.

7. Dean Wilkening and Kenneth Watman, *Nuclear Deterrence in a Regional Context* (Santa Monica, CA: RAND Corporation, 1995), 14.

8. Colin S. Gray, *Maintaining Effective Deterrence* (Carlisle, PA: U.S. Army War College, Strategic Studies Institute, August 2003), vii.

9. The term *self-deterrence* is used prominently in John Lewis Gaddis, *The Long Peace: Inquiries into the History of the Cold War* (New York: Oxford University Press, 1987), ch. 5.

10. Robert L. Jervis, "The Confrontation between Iraq and the U.S.: Implications for the Theory and Practice of Deterrence," *European Journal of International Relations* 9, no. 2 (June 2003): 329.

11. Paul K. Huth and Bruce Russett, "General Deterrence Between Enduring Rivals: Testing Three Competing Models," *American Political Science Review* 87, no. 1 (March 1993): 61–73; Dan S. Geller, "Nuclear Weapons, Deterrence, and Crisis Escalation," *Journal of Conflict Resolution* 34, no. 2 (1990): 291–310.

12. George Quester, *Nuclear First Strike: Consequences of a Broken Taboo* (Baltimore: Johns Hopkins University Press, 2006), 32. A 1993 exercise of selected policy makers by the Rand Corporation concluded that "American expressions of reliance on nuclear weapons to defend allies, to redress disparities in conventional forces, or even to deter nuclear attacks contradict the thrust of our non-proliferation polices." Marc Dean Millot, Roger Molander, and Peter A. Wilson, *"The Day After . . ." Study: Nuclear Proliferation in the Post-Cold War World,* vol. 2 (Santa Monica, CA: RAND Corporation, 1993), 69.

13. This problem is becoming more acute with U.S. nuclear policy as the George W. Bush administration, despite the use of ideas like "tailored deterrence," has widened the scope of nuclear retaliation against chemical and biological attacks in both preventive and preemptive modes. Thus there exists a tension in U.S. policy between two strands of reputation, one for resolve and the other for appropriate behavior. The character of the weapon concerned is a key factor in the creation of this tension.

14. For these concepts see, Alexander L. George, "Coercive Diplomacy: Definition and Characteristics," in *The Limits of Coercive Diplomacy,* ed. Alexander L. George and William E. Simons, 2nd ed. (Boulder, CO: Westview Press, 1994), 7.

15. On this, see Wilkening and Watman, *Nuclear Deterrence,* 18–19.

16. Ibid., 19.

17. Morgan, *Deterrence Now,* 40.

18. Quester, *Nuclear First Strike.*

19. Barry Posen, "A Nuclear-Armed Iran: A Difficult but Not Impossible Policy Problem" (Century Foundation Report, New York, December 6, 2006).

SELECT BIBLIOGRAPHY

Abraham, Itty. *The Making of the Indian Atomic Bomb*. London: Zed Books, 1998.

Acharya, Amitav. *Constructing a Security Community in Southeast Asia: ASEAN and the Problem of Regional Order*. New York: Routledge, 2001.

Adams, Sherman. *Firsthand Report: The Inside Story of the Eisenhower Administration*. London: Hutchinson, 1962.

Adeniji, Oluyemi. *The Treaty of Pelindaba: On the African Nuclear-Weapon-Free-Zone*. Geneva: UNIDIR, 2002.

Adler, Emanuel. "Seizing the Middle Ground: Constructivism in World Politics," *European Journal of International Relations* 3(3) (September 1997): 319–63.

Adomeit, Hannes. *Soviet Risk Taking and Crisis Behaviour: A Theoretical and Empirical Analysis*. London: George Allen and Unwin, 1982.

Ahmed, Samina, David Cortright, and Amitabh Mattoo. "Public Opinion and Nuclear Options for South Asia." *Asian Survey* 38(8) (August 1998): 727–44.

Alagappa, Muthiah. "Towards a Nuclear-Weapons-Free Zone in Southeast Asia." ISIS Research Note. Kuala Lumpur: Institute of Strategic and International Studies, 1987.

Albright, David. "Al Qaeda's Nuclear Program: Through the Window of Seized Documents." *The Nautilus Institute Policy Forum Online* Special Forum 47 (6 November 2002).

Albright, David, and Corey Hinderstein. "Unraveling the A. Q. Khan and Future Proliferation Networks." *The Washington Quarterly* 28(2) (Spring 2005):111–28.

Alford, Jonathan. "Conventional Conflicts in a Nuclear Age, Falkland Islands: The Limited Use of Limited Power." *The Jerusalem Journal of International Relations* 7(1/2) (1984): 79–91.

Allison, Graham. *Nuclear Terrorism*. New York: Times Books, 2004.

Allison, Graham, and Philip Zelikow. *Essence of Decision: Explaining the Cuban Missile Crisis.* Second Edition. New York: Addison Wesley Longman, 1999.

al-Marashi, Ibrahim. "Saddam's Iraq and Weapons of Mass Destruction: Iraq as a Case Study of a Middle Eastern Proliferant." *Middle East Review of International Affairs* 7(3) (September 2004): 81–90.

Alperovitz, Gar. *The Decision to Use the Atomic Bomb and the Architecture of an American Myth.* New York: Alfred A. Knopf, 1995.

Ambrose, Stephen E. *Eisenhower.* Vol. 2. New York: Simon & Schuster, 1983.

Anderson, Jack. *The Anderson Papers.* New York: Random House, 1973.

Arbatov, Alexei. "Russian Military Doctrine and Strategic Nuclear Forces to the Year 2000 and Beyond" (Paper Prepared for the Conference "Russian Defense Policy Towards the Year 2000," Naval Postgraduate School, Monterey, CA, March 26–27, 1997),

———. "The Transformation of Russian Military Doctrine: Lessons Learned from Kosovo and Chechnya." (The Marshall Center Papers no. 2, July 2000).

Arian, Asher. "Israeli Public Opinion on National Security, 1998." Memorandum 49. Tel Aviv: Jaffee Center for Strategic Studies, July 1998.

Arkin, William M. "The Buildup That Wasn't." *Bulletin of the Atomic Scientists* 45(1) (January/February 1989): 6–10.

———. "Those Lovable Little Bombs." *Bulletin of the Atomic Scientists* 49(6) (July 1993): 22–27.

———. "Calculated Ambiguity: Nuclear Weapons and the Gulf War." *The Washington Quarterly* 19(4) (Autumn 1996): 3–18.

Arnold, Anthony. *Afghanistan: The Soviet Invasion in Perspective.* Stanford, CA: Hoover Institution Press, 1981.

Aronson, Shlomo. *Conflict and Bargaining in the Middle East.* Baltimore, MD: Johns Hopkins University Press, 1978.

———. "The Nuclear Dimension of the Arab-Israeli Conflict: The Case of the Yom Kippur War." *The Jerusalem Journal of International Relations* 7(1/2) (1984): 107–42.

———. *The Politics and Strategy of Nuclear Weapons in the Middle East.* Albany: State University of New York Press, 1992.

Arquilla, John, and Maria Moyano Rasmussen. "The Origins of the South Atlantic War." *Journal of Latin American Studies* 33(4) (November 2001): 739–75.

Atkinson, Rick. *Crusade: The Untold Story of the Persian Gulf War.* Boston: Houghton Mifflin, 1993.

Axelrod, Robert. *The Evolution of Cooperation.* New York: Basic Books, 1984.

Baaro, Makurita. "The South Pacific Nuclear-Free-Zone Treaty (The Treaty of Rarotonga)." In *Nuclear Weapon-free Zones in the 21st Century,* edited by Pericles Gasparani Alves and Daiana Belinde Cipollone, 49–54. New York: United Nations, 1997.

Baker, James A., III. *The Politics of Diplomacy.* New York: G. P. Putnam's Sons, 1995.

Baldwin, David A. "Exchange Theory and International Relations." *International Negotiation* 3(2) (1998): 139–49.

Ball, George. "The Cosmic Bluff." *New York Review of Books,* 21 July, 1983.

Barak, Eitan. "Where do We Go from Here? Implementation of the Chemical Weapons Convention in the Middle East in the Post-Saddam Era." *Security Studies* 13(1) (Autumn 2003): 106–55.

Baram, Amatzia. "Israeli Deterrence, Iraqi Responses." *Orbis* 36(3) (Summer 1992): 397–409.

Bar-Joseph, Uri. "The Hidden Debate: The Formation of Nuclear Doctrines in the Middle East." *Journal of Strategic Studies* 5(2) (June 1982): 205–27.

Basrur, Rajesh. "Kargil, Terrorism and India's Strategic Shift." *India Review* 1(4) (October 2002): 39–56.

———. "International Relations Theory and Minimum Deterrence." *India Review* 4(2) (April 2005): 125–43.

———. *Minimum Deterrence and India's Nuclear Security.* Stanford, CA: Stanford University Press, 2006.

Baylis, John, and Kristan Stoddart. "Britain and the Chevaline Project: The Hidden Nuclear Programme, 1967–82." *Journal of Strategic Studies* 26(4) (2003): 124–55.

Beckman, Peter R., Larry Campbell, and Paul W. Crumlish. *The Nuclear Predicament.* Englewood Cliffs, NJ: Prentice Hall, 1992.

Beri, Ruchita. "African Nuclear Weapon-Free Zone Treaty." *Strategic Analysis* 19(4) (July 1996): 615–24.

Bernstein, Barton J. "The Quest for Security: American Foreign Policy and International Control of Atomic Energy, 1942–1946," *The Journal of American History* 60(4) (March 1974): 1003–44.

———. "Truman and the A-Bomb: Targeting Noncombatants, Using the Bomb, and His Defending the Decision." *The Journal of Military History* 62(3) (July 1998): 547–70.

Betts, Richard K. *Nuclear Blackmail and Nuclear Balance.* Washington, DC: The Brookings Institution, 1987.

Bird, Kai, and Lawrence Lifschultz, eds. *Hiroshima's Shadow.* Stony Creek, CT: The Pamphleteer's Press, 1998.

Bird, Kai, and Martin J. Sherwin. *American Prometheus: The Triumph and Tragedy of J. Robert Oppenheimer.* New York: Vintage Books, 2006.

Blau, Peter M. *Exchange and Power in Social Life.* New York: John Wiley & Sons, 1964.

Blechman, Barry M., and Douglas M. Hart. "The Political Utility of Nuclear Weapons: The 1973 Middle East Crisis." *International Security* 7(1) (Summer 1982):132–56.

Blight, James G., and David A. Welch, eds. *Intelligence and the Cuban Missile Crisis.* London: Frank Cass, 1998.

Bodansky, Daniel, Jutta Brunnee, and Ellen Hey, eds. *The Oxford Handbook of International Environmental Law.* Oxford: Oxford University Press, 2007.

Boese, Wade. "Germany Raises No-first Use Issue at NATO Meeting." *Arms Control Today* 28(8) (November/December 1998): 24.

Boniface, Pascal. "The Future of the French Nuclear Posture." *Strategic Analysis* 23(8) (November 1999): 1319–32.

———. "France and the Dubious Charms of a Post-Nuclear World." In *Pondering NATO's Nuclear* Options, edited by David G. Haglund, 151–62. Kingston, ON: Queen's Quarterly, 1999.

Boulding, Kenneth E. *The Meaning of the Twentieth Century: The Great Transition.* New York: Harper & Row, 1964.

Bourgois, Joelle. "The Role Carried out by the Zones Exempt from Nuclear Arms." In *Nuclear Weapon Free-Zones in the 21st Century,* edited by Pericles Gasparini Alves and Daiana Belinda Cipollone, 123–33. New York: United Nations, 1997.

Boyer, Paul S. *By the Bomb's Early Light: American Thought and Culture at the Dawn of the Atomic Age.* New York: Pantheon, 1985.

Bowie, Robert R., and Richard H. Immerman. *Waging Peace: How Eisenhower Shaped an Enduring Cold War Strategy.* New York: Oxford University Press, 1998.

Bradsher, Henry S. *Afghanistan and the Soviet Union.* Durham, NC: Duke University Press, 1985.

Brands, H. W. Jr. "Testing Massive Retaliation: Credibility and Crisis Management in the Taiwan Strait." *International Security* 12(4) (Spring 1988): 124–51.

———. "The Age of Vulnerability: Eisenhower and the National Security State." *The American Historical Review* 94(4) (October 1989): 963–89.

Braun, Chaim, and Christopher F. Chyba. "Proliferation Rings: New Challenges to the Nonproliferation Regime." *International Security* 29(2) (Fall 2004): 5–49.

Brecher, Michael, with Benjamin Geist. *Decisions in Crisis: Israel, 1967 and 1973.* Berkeley: University of California Press, 1980.

Broadhurst, Arlene Idol. *Nuclear Weapon-Free Zones: A Comparative Analysis of Theory and Practice.* Aurora Paper No. 5. Ottawa, ON: The Canadian Center for Arms Control and Disarmament, 1985.

Brodie, Bernard. "War in the Atomic Age." In *The Absolute Weapon: Atomic Power and World Order,* edited by Bernard Brodie, 21–69. New York: Harcourt Brace, 1946.

Broscious, S. David. "Longing for International Control, Banking on American Superiority: Harry S. Truman's Approach to Nuclear Weapons." In *Cold War Statesmen Confront the Bomb: Nuclear Diplomacy Since 1945,* edited by John Lewis Gaddis, Philip H. Gordon, Ernest R. May, and Jonathan Rosenberg, 15–38. Oxford: Oxford University Press, 1999.

Bundy, McGeorge. *Danger and Survival.* New York: Random House, 1988.

———. "Nuclear Weapons and the Gulf." *Foreign Affairs* 70(4) (Fall 1991): 83–94.

Bundy, McGeorge, George F. Kennan, Robert S. McNamara, and Gerard C. Smith. "Nuclear Weapons and the Atlantic Alliance." *Foreign Affairs* 60(4) (Spring 1982): 752–68.

Bunn, George. "The Legal Status of U.S. Negative Security Assurances to Non-Nuclear Weapon States." *The Nonproliferation Review* 4(3) (Spring/Summer 1997): 1–17.

Bunn, George, and Roland M. Timerbaev. "Security Assurances to Non-Nuclear Weapon States," *The Nonproliferation Review* 1(1) (Fall 1993): 11–20.

Burgerman, Susan. *Moral Victories: How Activists Provoke Multilateral Action.* Ithaca, NY: Cornell University Press, 2001.

Burgess, Stephen F. "Nuclear Rollback in Africa: The Role of the African National Congress and the 'Nuclear Taboo.'" Paper presented at the APSA Convention, Washington, DC, September 2005.

Burns, E. L. M. "The Nonproliferation Treaty: Its Negotiations and Prospects." *International Organization* 23(4) (Autumn 1969): 788–807.

Burr, William. "The Nixon Administration, the 'Horror Strategy,' and the Search for Limited Nuclear Options, 1969–1972." *Journal of Cold War Studies* 7(3) (Summer 2005): 34–78.

———. "Looking Back: The Limits of Limited Nuclear War." *Arms Control Today* 36(1) (January/February 2006): 45–48.

Burr, William, and Jeffrey T. Richelson. "Whether to Strangle the Baby in the Cradle: The United States and the Chinese Nuclear Program, 1960–64." *International Security* 25(3) (Winter 2000–2001): 54–99.

Burr, William, and Jeffrey Kimball. "Nixon's Nuclear Ploy." *Bulletin of the Atomic Scientists* 59(1) (January/February 2003): 28–39.

Butcher, Martin, Otfried Nassauer, and Stephen Young. "Nuclear Futures: Western European Options for Nuclear Risk Reduction" (BASIC Research Report (98.6, December 1998).

Butler, Richard. *The Greatest Threat: Iraq, Weapons of Mass Destruction, and the Crisis of Global Security.* New York: Public Affairs, 2000.

Calvert, Peter. *The Falklands Crisis: The Rights and Wrongs.* London: Frances Pinter, 1982.

Cerniello, Craig. "Clinton Issues New Guidelines on U.S. Nuclear Weapons Doctrine." *Arms Control Today* 27(8) (November/December 1997): 23.

Chalmers, Malcolm. "Bombs Away? Britain and Nuclear Weapons under New Labour." *Security Dialogue* 30(1) (March 1999): 61–74.

Chandler, Alfred D., Jr., and Louis Galambos Jr., eds. *The Papers of Dwight D. Eisenhower* Vol. 7: *The Chief of Staff.* Baltimore, MD: Johns Hopkins University Press, 1970.

Chang, Gordon H. "JFK, China, and the Bomb." *The Journal of American History* 74(4) (March 1988): 1287–1310.

———. "To the Nuclear Brink: Eisenhower, Dulles, and the Quemoy-Matsu Crisis." *International Security* 12(4) (Spring 1988): 96–123.

Chari, P. R. "India's Nuclear Doctrine: Confused Ambitions." *The Nonproliferation Review* 7(3) (Fall/Winter 2000): 123–35.

Chayes, Abram, and Antonia Handler Chayes. *The New Sovereignty: Compliance with International Regulatory Agreements.* Cambridge, MA: Harvard University Press, 1995.

Checkel, Jeffrey T. "International Norms and Domestic Politics: Bridging the Rationalist-Constructivist Divide." *European Journal of International Relations* 3(4) (December 1997): 473–95.

Cheema, Zafar Iqbal. "Pakistan's Nuclear Use Doctrine and Command and Control." In *Planning the Unthinkable,* edited by Peter R. Lavoy, Scott D. Sagan, and James J. Wirtz, 158–81. Ithaca, NY: Cornell University Press, 2000.

Chernyaev, Anatoly S. *My Six Years with Gorbachev.* Translated and edited by Robert D. English and Elizabeth Tucker. University Park: The Pennsylvania University Press, 2000.

Cheung, Tai Ming. "New Bomb Makers." *Far Eastern Economic Review,* March 16, 1989.

Cirincioni, Joseph, Jon B. Wolfstal, and Miriam Rajkumar. *Deadly Arsenals.* Washington, DC: Carnegie Endowment for International Peace, 2002.

Clark, Ann Marie. *Diplomacy of Conscience: Amnesty International and Changing Human Rights Norms.* Princeton, NJ: Princeton University Press, 2001.

Clarke, Michael. "How Strategic Was the Review?" *Disarmament Diplomacy* 28 (July 1998): 3–5.

Cohen, Avner. "Cairo, Dimona, and the June 1967 War." *Middle East Journal* 50(2) (Spring 1996): 190–210.

———. *Israel and the Bomb.* New York: Columbia University Press, 1998.

———. "Nuclear Arms in Crisis under Secrecy: Israel and the Lessons of the 1967 and 1973 Wars." In *Planning the Unthinkable,* edited by Peter R. Lavoy, Scott D. Sagan, and James J. Wirtz, 104–24. Ithaca, NY: Cornell University Press, 2000.

———. "The Last Taboo: Israel's Bomb Revisited." *Current History* (April 2005): 169–75.

———. "Crossing the Threshold: The Untold Nuclear Dimension of the 1967 Arab-Israeli War and its Contemporary Lessons," *Arms Control Today* 37, no. 5 (June 2007).

Cohen, Avner, and Steven Lee. "The Nuclear Predicament." In *Nuclear Weapons and the Future of Humanity,* edited by Avner Cohen and Steven Lee, 1–45. Totowa, NJ: Rowman and Allanheld, 1986.

Cohen, David B. "From START to START II: Dynamism and Pragmatism in the Bush Administration's Nuclear Weapons Policies." *Presidential Studies Quarterly* 27(3) (Summer 1997): 412–28.

Connelly, Matthew. *A Diplomatic Revolution*. New York: Oxford University Press, 2002.

Conte, Rosaria, and Mario Paolucci. *Reputation in Artificial Societies: Social Beliefs for Social Order*. Boston: Kluwer Academic Publishers, 2002.

Cordesman, Anthony H. *Iran and Iraq: The Threat from the Northern Gulf*. Boulder, CO: Westview Press, 1994.

Cordesman, Anthony H., and Abraham R. Wagner. *The Lessons of Modern War* Vol. 3: *The Afghan and Falklands Conflicts*. Boulder, CO: Westview Press, 1990.

Costa Mendez, N. "Beyond Deterrence: The Malvinas-Falklands Case." *Journal of Social Issues* 43(4) (Winter 1987): 119–22.

Cotta-Ramusino, Paolo, and Maurizio Martellini. "Nuclear Safety, Nuclear Stability and Nuclear Strategy in Pakistan." Concise Report of a Visit by Landau Network-Centro Volta, January 21, 2002.

Craig, Campell. *Destroying the Village: Eisenhower and Thermonuclear War*. New York: Columbia University Press, 1998.

Cumings, Bruce. *The Origins of the Korean War* Vol. 2: *The Roaring of the Cataract, 1947–1950*. Princeton, NJ: Princeton University Press, 1990.

———. "On the Strategy and Morality of American Nuclear Policy in Korea, 1950 to the Present." *Social Science Japan Journal* 1(1) (April 1998): 57–70.

Dallek, Robert. *Nixon and Kissinger: Partners in Power*. New York: HarperCollins, 2007.

DeGroot, Gerard J. *The Bomb: A Life*. Cambridge, MA: Harvard University Press, 2005.

Dingman, Roger. "Atomic Diplomacy During the Korean War." *International Security* 13(3) (Winter 1988/89): 50–89.

Douglas, Mary. *Purity and Danger: An Analysis of the Concepts of Pollution and Taboo*. New York: Routledge, 2002.

Dowler, Thomas W., and Joseph S. Howard, II. "Countering the Threat of the Well-Armed Tyrant: A Modest Proposal for Small Nuclear Weapons." *Strategic Review* 19(4) (Fall 1991): 34–40.

Downs, George W., and Michael A. Jones. "Reputation, Compliance and International Law." *Journal of Legal Studies* 31(1) (January 2002): S95–114.

du Preez, Jean. "Security Assurances against the Use or Threat of Use of Nuclear Weapons: Is Progress Possible at the NPT PrepCom?" (Center for Nonproliferation Studies Reports, Monterey Institute of International Studies, April 24, 2003).

———. "The 2005 NPT Review Conference: Can It Meet the Nuclear Challenge?" *Arms Control Today* 35(3) (April 2005): 6.

Duxbury, Neil. "Signaling and Social Norms." *Oxford Journal of Legal Studies* 21(4) (Winter 2001): 719–36.

Dyson, F. J., R. Gomer, S. Weinberg, and S. C. Wright. "Tactical Nuclear Weapons in Southeast Asia." Jason's Division Institute for Defense Analysis, Washington, DC, March 1967.

Eisenhower, Dwight D. *The White House Years* Vol. 1: *Mandate for Change, 1953–1956.* Garden City, NY: Doubleday, 1963.

el-Shazly, Saad. General. *The Crossing of the Suez.* San Francisco, CA: American Mideast Research, 1980.

English, Robert D. *Russia and the Idea of the West.* New York: Columbia University Press, 2000.

———. "The Road(s) Not Taken: Causality and Contingency in Analysis of the Cold War's End." In *Cold War Endgame,* edited by William C. Wohlforth, 243–72. University Park: The Pennsylvania State University Press, 2003.

Epstein, William. *The Last Chance: Nuclear Proliferation and Arms Control.* New York: The Free Press, 1976.

———. "Tlatelolco and a Nuclear-Weapon-Free World." In *Nuclear Weapon-Free Zones in the 21st Century,* edited by Pericles Gasparani Alves and Daiana Belinde Cipollone, 23–27. New York: United Nations, 1997.

Erdmann, Andrew P. N. "War No Longer Has Any Logic Whatever: Dwight D. Eisenhower and the Thermonuclear Revolution." In *Cold War Statesmen Confront the Bomb: Nuclear Diplomacy Since 1945,* edited by John Lewis Gaddis, Philip H. Gordon., Ernest R. May, and Jonathan Rosenberg, 87–119. Oxford: Oxford University Press, 1999.

Ermarth, Fritz W. "Contrasts in American and Soviet Strategic Thought." In *Soviet Military Thinking,* edited by Derek Leebaert, 50–72. London: George Allen & Unwin, 1981.

Etzold, Thomas, and John Lewis Gaddis, eds. *Containment: Documents on American Policy and Strategy.* New York: Columbia University Press, 1978.

Evangelista, Matthew. "Sources of Moderation in Soviet Security Policy." In *Behavior, Society and Nuclear War,* edited by Philip E. Tetlock, Jo L. Husbands, Robert Jervis, Paul C. Stern, and Charles Tilly, 254–354. Oxford: Oxford University Press, 1991.

———. *Unarmed Forces: The Transnational Movement to End the Cold War.* Ithaca, NY: Cornell University Press, 1999.

———. "Turning Points in Arms Control." In *Ending the Cold War: Interpretations, Causation, and the Study of International Relations,* edited by Richard K. Hermann and Richard Ned Lebow, 83–107. New York: Palgrave-Macmillan, 2004.

Evron, Yair. "The Arab Position in the Nuclear Field: A Study of Policies up to 1967." *Cooperation and Conflict* 8(1) (1973): 19–31.

———. "Opaque Proliferation: The Israeli Case." In *Opaque Nuclear Proliferation: Methodological and Policy Implications,* edited by Benjamin Frankel, 45–64. London: Frank Cass, 1991.

———. *Israel's Nuclear Dilemma.* Ithaca, NY: Cornell University Press, 1994.

Falk, Richard. "Nuclear Weapons, International Law and the World Court: A Historic Encounter." *American Journal of International Law* 91(1) (January 1997): 64–75.

Farr, Warner D. "The Third Temple's Holy of Holies: Israel's Nuclear Weapons," Future Warfare Series No. 2. Maxwell Air Force Base, AL, September 1999.

Faruqui, Ahmad. "Failure in Command: Lessons from Pakistan's India Wars." *Defense Analysis* 17(1) (2001): 31–40

Fearon, James D. "Domestic Political Audiences and the Escalation of International Disputes." *American Political Science Review* 88(3) (September 1994): 577–92.

Fearon, James D., and Alexander Wendt. "Rationalism v. Constructivism: A Skeptical View," In *Handbook of International Relations,* edited by Walter Carlsnaes, Thomas Risse, and Beth A. Simmons, 52–72. London: Sage, 2002.

Fedorov, Yuri. "Russia's Doctrine on the Use of Nuclear Weapons" (Working Paper, Columbia International Affairs Online, November 2002).

Feiveson, Harold A., and Ernst Jan Hogendoorn. "No First Use of Nuclear Weapons." *The Nonproliferation Review* 10(2) (Summer 2003): 1–9.

Feld, Scott L. "On the Emergence of Social Norms." *Contemporary Sociology* 31(6) (November 2002): 638–40.

Feldman, Shai. *Israeli Nuclear Deterrence.* New York: Columbia University Press, 1982.

———. *Nuclear Weapons and Arms Control in the Middle East.* Cambridge, MA: MIT Press, 1997.

Ferguson, Charles D., and William C. Potter. *The Four Faces of Nuclear Proliferation.* New York: Routledge, 2005.

Fetter, Steve, and Frank N. von Hippel. "The Hazard Posed by Depleted Uranium Munitions." *Science and Global Security* 8(2) (1999): 125–61.

Finkbeiner, Ann. *The Jasons: The Secret History of Science's Postwar Elite.* New York: Penguin, 2007.

Finnemore, Martha. *National Interests in International Society.* Ithaca, NY: Cornell University Press, 1996.

Finnemore, Martha, and Kathryn Sikkink. "International Norm Dynamics and Political Change." *International Organization* 52(4) (Autumn 1998): 887–917.

Fischer, Beth A. *The Reagan Reversal: Foreign Policy and the End of the Cold War.* Columbia, MO: University of Missouri Press, 2002.

Fischer, Dean. "Inside Saddam's Brutal Regime." *Time,* September 18, 1995.

Foot, Rosemary J. *The Wrong War: American Policy and the Dimensions of the Korean Conflict, 1950–53.* Ithaca, NY: Cornell University Press, 1985.

———. "Nuclear Coercion and the Ending of the Korean Conflict." *International Security* 13(3) (Winter 1988/89): 92–112.

Frazer, James George. *Taboo and the Perils of Soul.* New York: Macmillan, 1935.

Freedman, Lawrence. "Israel's Nuclear Policy." *Survival* 17(3) (May–June 1975): 114–20.

———. *The Evolution of Nuclear Strategy.* New York: St. Martin's Press, 1983.

———. *The Official History of the Falklands Campaign* Vol. 2: *War and Diplomacy.* London: Routledge, 2005.

Freud, Sigmund. *Totem and Taboo.* Translated by James Strachey. London: Routledge & Kegan Paul, 1950.

Frye, Alton. "Opinion: Slow Fuse on the Neutron Bomb." *Foreign Policy* 31 (Summer 1978): 95–103.

Gaddis, John Lewis. *The Long Peace: Inquiries into the History of the Cold War.* Oxford: Oxford University Press, 1987.

———. "Nuclear Weapons, the End of the Cold War, and the Future of the International System." In *Nuclear Weapons in a Changing World,* edited by Patrick J. Garrity and Steven A. Maaranen, 15–31. New York: Plenum Press, 1992.

———. *We Now Know: Rethinking Cold War History.* Oxford: Oxford University Press, 1997.

———. *The Cold War: A New History.* New York: The Penguin Press, 2005.

Gallois, Pierre. *The Balance of Terror: Strategy for the Nuclear Age.* Boston, MA: Houghton Mifflin, 1961.

Garnett, Sherman W. "Ukraine's Decision to Join the NPT." *Arms Control Today* 25(1) (January/February 1995): 7–12.

Garthoff, Raymond. "Mutual Deterrence and Strategic Arms Limitation in Soviet Policy." *International Security* 3(1) (Summer 1978): 112–47.

———. "Berlin 1961: The Record Corrected." *Foreign Policy* 84 (Autumn 1991): 142–56.

Gavin, Francis J. "Blasts from the Past: Proliferation Lessons from the 1960s." *International Security* 29(3) (Winter 2004–05): 100–35.

Gavshon, Arthur, and Desmond Rice. *The Sinking of the Belgrano.* London: Secker & Warburg, 1984.

Geller, Dan S. "Nuclear Weapons, Deterrence, and Crisis Escalation." *Journal of Conflict Resolution* 34 (2) (1990): 291–310.

Gelpi, Christopher. *The Power of Legitimacy: Assessing the Role of Norms in Crisis Bargaining.* Princeton, NJ: Princeton University Press, 2003.

Gentile, Gian P. "Planning for Preventive War, 1945–1950." *Joint Forces Quarterly* 24 (Spring 2000): 68–74.

George, Alexander L. "Coercive Diplomacy: Definition and Characteristics." In *The Limits of Coercive Diplomacy,* edited by Alexander L. George and William E. Simons, 7–11. Boulder: CO: Westview Press, 1994.

Giridharadas, Anand. "JFK's Nuclear Dilemma over China and India." *International Herald Tribune,* August 26, 2005.

Gizewski, Peter. "From Winning Weapon to Destroyer of the World: The Nuclear Taboo in International Politics." *International Journal* 51(2) (Summer 1996): 397–419.

Glaser, Charles L., and Steve Fetter. "Counterforce Revisited: Assessing the Nuclear Posture Review's New Missions." *International Security* 30(2) (Fall 2005): 84–126.

Glitman, Maynard W. *The Last Battle of the Cold War*. New York: Palgrave-Macmillan, 2006.

Goertz, Gary, and Paul F. Diehl. "International Norms and Power Politics." In *Reconstructing Realpolitik,* edited by Frank W. Wayman and Paul F. Diehl, 101–22. Ann Arbor, MI: University of Michigan Press, 1994.

Goldman, Laurence R., ed. *The Anthropology of Cannibalism*. Westport, CT: Bergin & Garvey, 1999.

Gorbachev, Mikhail. *Memoirs*. New York: Doubleday, 1995.

Gordon, Philip. *A Certain Idea of France: French Security Policy and the Gaullist Legacy*. Princeton, NJ: Princeton University Press, 1993.

Gottemoeller, Rose. "Nuclear Necessity in Putin's Russia." *Arms Control Today* 34(3) (April 2004): p. 14.

Gowing, Margaret. *Independence and Deterrence: Britain and Atomic Energy, 1945–52* Vol. 1 and Vol. II. London: Palgrave-Macmillan, 1974.

Grand, Camille. "A French Nuclear Exception?" Henry L. Stimson Center Occasional Paper No. 38. Washington, DC: Henry L. Stimson Center, January 1998.

Grant, Rebecca. "Dien Bien Phu." *Air Force Magazine Online* 87(8) (August 2004): 78–84.

Gray, Colin S. "Nuclear Weapons and the Revolution in Military Affairs." In *The Absolute Weapon Revisited: Nuclear Arms and the Emerging International Order,* edited by T. V. Paul, Richard J. Harknett, and James J. Wirtz, 99–134. Ann Arbor: The University of Michigan Press, 1998.

———. "To Confuse Ourselves: Nuclear Fallacies." In *Alternative Nuclear Futures,* edited by John Baylis and Robert O'Neill, 4–30. Oxford: Oxford University Press, 2000.

———. *Maintaining Effective Deterrence*. Carlisle, PA: U.S. Army War College, 2003.

Gray, Colin S., and Keith B. Payne, "Victory is Possible." *Foreign Policy* no. 39 (Summer, 1980): 14–27.

Grosser, Alfred. *French Foreign Policy under De Gaulle*. Boston: Little, Brown, 1965.

Haglund, David G. "Pondering NATO's Nuclear Options." *Queen's Quarterly* (1999): 151–62.

Hall, David K. "The Laotian War of 1962 and the Indo-Pakistani War of 1971." In *Force Without War: U.S. Armed Forces as a Political Instrument,* edited by Barry M. Blechman and Stephen S. Kaplan, 135–221. Washington, DC: Brookings Institution, 1978.

Hall, John A., and T. V. Paul. "Preconditions for Prudence: A Sociological Synthesis of Realism and Liberalism." In *International Order and the Future of World Politics,* edited by T. V. Paul and John A. Hall, 67–77. Cambridge: Cambridge University Press, 1999.

Halperin, Morton H., and O'Donnell, Madalene, "The Nuclear Fallacy." *Bulletin of the Atomic Scientists* 44(1) (January/February 1988): 6–11.

Hamel-Green, Michael. "South Pacific: A Not So Nuclear-Free Zone." *Peace Studies* (November–December 1985): 6–8.

———. "The South Pacific—The Treaty of Rarotonga." In *Nuclear Weapons-Free Zones,* edited by Ramesh Thakur, 59–80. New York: St. Martin's Press, 1998.

Handel, Michael I. "Perception, Deception and Surprise: The Case of the Yom Kippur War," *Jerusalem Papers on Peace Problems* no. 19. Hebrew University of Jerusalem, 1976.

Harknett, Richard J. "The Logic of Conventional Deterrence and the End of the Cold War." *Security Studies* 4(1) (Autumn 1994): 86–114.

———. "State Preferences, Systemic Constraints, and the Absolute Weapon." In *The Absolute Weapon Revisited: Nuclear Arms and the Emerging International Order,* edited by T. V. Paul, Richard J. Harknett, and James J. Wirtz, 47–72. Ann Arbor, MI: The University of Michigan Press, 1998.

Harrison, Hope M. "The Nuclear Education of Nikita Khrushchev." In *Cold War Statesmen Confront the Bomb: Nuclear Diplomacy Since 1945,* edited by John Lewis Gaddis, Philip H. Gordon, Ernest R. May, and Jonathan Rosenberg, 141–68. Oxford: Oxford University Press, 1999.

Hasegawa, Tsuyoshi. *Racing the Enemy: Stalin, Truman, and the Surrender of Japan.* Cambridge, MA: Belknap Press, 2005.

Hashmi, Sohail H. "Islamic Ethics and Weapons of Mass Destruction." In *Ethics and Weapons of Mass Destruction,* edited by Sohail H. Hashmi and Steven P. Lee, 321–52. Cambridge: Cambridge University Press, 2004.

Hayes, Peter, and Nina Tannenwald. "Nixing Nukes in Vietnam." *Bulletin of the Atomic Scientists* 59(3) (May–June 2003): 52–59.

Hechter, Michael, and Karl-Dieter Opp, eds. *Social Norms.* New York: Russell Sage Foundation, 2001.

Heikal, Mohammed. *Illusions of Triumph.* London: HarperCollins, 1992.

———. *The Sphinx and the Commissar: The Rise and Fall of Soviet Influence in the Arab World.* London: Collins, 1978.

Herken, Greg. *The Winning Weapon: The Atomic Bomb in the Cold War, 1945–1950.* New York: Alfred A. Knopf, 1980.

Hernandez, Carolina G. "Southeast Asia—The Treaty of Bangkok." In *Nuclear Weapons-Free Zones,* edited by Ramesh Thakur, 81–92. New York: St. Martin's Press, 1998.

Herring, Eric. "Double Standards and the Myth of the Third World Nuclear Fanatic." Paper Presented at the American Political Science Association Convention, Chicago, September 3–6, 1992.

Herring, George C., and Richard H. Immerman. "Eisenhower, Dulles and Dienbienphu: 'The Day We Didn't Go to War' Revisited." *The Journal of American History* 71(2) (September 1984): 343–63.

Hersey, John. *Hiroshima*. New York: Alfred A. Knopf, 1972.

Hersh, Seymour M. *The Price of Power: Kissinger in the Nixon White House*. New York: Summit Books, 1983.

———. *The Samson Option: Israel's Nuclear Arsenal and American Foreign Policy*. New York: Random House, 1991.

———. "The Iran Plans." *The New Yorker,* April 17, 2006.

Hobsbawm, Eric, and Terence Ranger, eds. *The Invention of Tradition*. Cambridge: Cambridge University Press, 1983.

Hoekstra, Douglas J. "Presidential Beliefs and the Reagan Paradox." *Presidential Studies Quarterly* 27(3) (Summer 1997): 429–50.

Hoffmann, Stanley. "Nuclear Proliferation and World Politics." In *A World of Nuclear Powers?,* edited by Alastair Buchan, 89–122. Englewood Cliffs, NJ: Prentice Hall, 1966.

Holdstock, Douglas, and Frank Barnaby. *The British Nuclear Weapons Programme 1952–2002*. London: Frank Cass, 2003.

Holloway, David. *Stalin and the Bomb*. New Haven, CT: Yale University Press, 1994.

Hoopes, Townsend. *The Devil and John Foster Dulles*. Boston: Little, Brown, 1973.

Hopf, Ted. *Social Construction of International Politics*. Ithaca, NY: Cornell University Press, 2002.

Hopkins, John C., and Weixing Hu, eds. *Strategic Views from the Second Tier: The Nuclear Weapons Policies of France, Britain and China*. New Brunswick, NJ: Transaction Publishers, 1995.

Huang, Zhen, "Whither China's Strategic Nuclear Posture? An Assessment of Existing Constraints and Prospects," *Political Science* 53(2) (December 2001): 39–54.

Husain, M. A. "Third World and Disarmament: Shadow and Substance." *Third World Quarterly* 2(1) (January 1980): 76–99.

Huth, Paul. "Reputations and Deterrence: A Theoretical and Empirical Assessment." *Security Studies* 7(1) (Autumn 1997): 72–99.

Huth, Paul, and Bruce Russett. "General Deterrence between Enduring Rivals: Testing Three Competing Models." *American Political Science Review* 87(1) (March 1993): 61–73.

Ibuse, Masuji. *Black Rain*. Trans. John Bester. Tokyo: Kodansha International, 1969.

Ihonvbere, Julius O. "Africa—The Treaty of Pelindaba." In *Nuclear Weapons-Free Zones,* edited by Ramesh Thakur, 93–120. New York: St. Martin's Press, 1998.

Immerman, Richard H. *John Foster Dulles: Piety, Pragmatism, and Power in U.S. Foreign Policy*. Washington, DC: Scholarly Resources, 1999.

Jackson, Michael Gordon. "Beyond Brinkmanship: Eisenhower, Nuclear Warfighting, and Korea, 1953–1968." *Presidential Studies Quarterly* 35(1) (March 2005): 52–75.

Jentleson, Bruce W., and Christopher A. Whytcock "Who 'Won' Libya: The Force-Diplomacy Debate and Its Implications for Theory and Policy." *International Security* 30(3) (Winter 2005–06): 47–86.

Jepperson, Ronald L., Alexander Wendt, and Peter J. Katzenstein. "Norms, Identity, and Culture in National Security." In *The Culture of National Security,* edited by Peter J. Katzenstein, 33–75. New York: Columbia University Press, 1996.

Jervis, Robert. "Deterrence Theory Revisited." *World Politics* 31(2) (January 1979): 289–24.

———. *The Illogic of American Nuclear Strategy.* Ithaca, NY: Cornell University Press, 1984.

———. *The Logic of Images in International Relations.* New York: Columbia University Press, 2nd edition, 1989.

———. "The Confrontation between Iraq and the U.S.: Implications for the Theory and Practice of Deterrence." *European Journal of International Relations* 9(2) (June 2003): 315–37.

Johnson, Rebecca. "British Perspectives on the Future of Nuclear Weapons." *Occasional Paper No. 37.* Washington DC: The Henry L. Stimson Center, January 1998.

Johnston, Alastair Iain. "China's New 'Old Thinking': The Concept of Limited Deterrence." *International Security* 20(3) (Winter 1995–96): 5–42.

———. "Prospects for Chinese Nuclear Force Modernization: Limited Deterrence Versus Multilateral Arms Control." *The China Quarterly* 146 (June 1996): 548–76.

Jones, Peter M., and Gordon Reece. *British Public Attitudes to Nuclear Defence.* Houndmills, UK: Macmillan, 1990.

Jonsson, Christer. *Soviet Bargaining Behavior: The Nuclear Test Ban Case.* New York: Columbia University Press, 1979.

Kahn, Herman. *On Thermonuclear War,* 2nd edition. Princeton, NJ: Princeton University Press, 1961

———. *On Escalation: Metaphors and Scenarios.* Baltimore, MD: Penguin Books, 1968.

Kanwal, Gurmeet. "India's Nuclear Doctrine and Policy." *Strategic Analysis* 26(11) (February 2001): 247–64.

Kapila, Subhash. "India's New 'Cold Start' War Doctrine Strategically Reviewed." South Asia Analysis Group Paper (no. 991) May 4, 2004.

Kaplan, Fred. "JFK's First-Strike Plan." *Atlantic Monthly* 288(3) (October 2001): 81–86.

———. *The Wizards of Armageddon.* New York: Simon & Schuster, 1983.

Karpin, Michael. *The Bomb in the Basement: How Israel Went Nuclear and What that Means for the World.* New York: Simon & Schuster, 2006.

Katzenstein, Peter J., ed. *The Culture of National Security.* New York: Columbia University Press, 1996.

Katzenstein, Peter J., and Rudra Sil. "Rethinking Asian Security: A Case for Analytical Eclecticism." In *Rethinking Security in East Asia,* edited by J. J. Suh, Peter J. Katzenstein, and Allen Carlson, 1–33. Stanford, CA: Stanford University Press, 2004.

Keck, Margaret, and Kathryn Sikkink. *Activists Beyond Borders: Advocacy Networks in International Politics.* Ithaca, NY: Cornell University Press, 1998.

Keefer, Edward C. "President Dwight D. Eisenhower and the End of the Korean War." *Diplomatic History* 10(3) (Summer 1986): 267–89.

Keohane, Robert O. *After Hegemony: Cooperation and Discord in the World Political Economy.* Princeton, NJ: Princeton University Press, 1984.

Khan, Feroz Hassan. "Command-and-Control Challenges in New Nuclear States." (Paper presented at the Annual Convention of the International Studies Association, San Diego, CA, March 23–25, 2006).

Khrushchev, Nikita. *Khrushchev Remembers.* Translated and edited by Strobe Talbott. Boston: Little, Brown, 1970.

Kimball, Daryl G. "The Mixed Arms Control Legacy of Ronald Reagan." *Arms Control Today* 34(6) (July/August 2004): 44–47.

Kissinger, Henry A. *Nuclear Weapons and Foreign Policy.* New York: Harper & Brothers, 1957.

———. *The White House Years.* Boston: Little, Brown, 1979.

Klotz, Audie. *Norms in International Relations: The Struggle against Apartheid.* Ithaca, NY: Cornell University Press, 1995.

Knopf, Jeffrey W. *Domestic Society and International Cooperation: The Impact of Protest on U.S. Arms Control Policy.* Cambridge: Cambridge University Press, 1998.

Koening, Louis W. *The Truman Administration: Its Principles and Practice.* New York: New York University Press, 1956.

Koh, Harold Hongju. "Why do Nations Obey International Law?" *The Yale Law Journal* 106(8) (June 1997): 2599-2659.

Kokoshin, Andrei A. *Soviet Strategic Thought, 1917–91.* Cambridge, MA: MIT Press, 1998.

Koster, Karel. "An Uneasy Alliance: NATO Nuclear Doctrine & NPT." *Disarmament Diplomacy* 49 (August 2000): 10.

Kristensen, Hans M. "Targets of Opportunity." *Bulletin of the Atomic Scientists* 53(5) (September/October 1997): 22–28.

———. "Nuclear Futures: Proliferation of Weapons of Mass Destruction and U.S. Nuclear Strategy." *BASIC Research Report* 98(2) (March 1998).

———. "The Role of U.S. Nuclear Weapons: New Doctrine Falls Short of Bush Pledge." *Arms Control Today* 35(7) (September 2005): 13.

Kubalkova, Vendulka, Nicholas Onuf, and Paul Kowert, eds. *International Relations in a Constructed World.* Armonk, NY: M. E. Sharpe, 1998.

Kuhn, Thomas. *The Structure of Scientific Revolutions*. Chicago: University of Chicago Press, 1962.

Laird, Robbin F., and Dale R. Herspring. *The Soviet Union and Strategic Arms*. Boulder, CO: Westview Press, 1984.

Lakatos, Imre. "Falsification and the Methodology of Scientific Research Programs." In *Criticism and the Growth of Knowledge,* edited by Imre Lakatos and Alan Musgrave, 91–196. Cambridge: Cambridge University Press, 1970.

Lambeth, Benjamin S. "Nuclear Proliferation and Soviet Arms Control Policy." *Orbis* 14(2) (Summer 1970): 298–323.

Lapp, Ralph. *The Weapons Culture*. Baltimore, MD: Penguin Books, 1969.

Larkin, Bruce D. *Nuclear Designs*. New Brunswick, NJ: Transaction Publishers, 1996.

Larsen, Jeffrey A., ed. *Arms Control: Cooperative Security in a Changing Environment*. Boulder, CO: Lynne Rienner, 2002.

Lavoy, Peter R., ed. *Asymmetric Warfare in South Asia: The Causes and Consequences of the Kargil Conflict*. Cambridge: Cambridge University Press, forthcoming.

———. "Pakistan's Nuclear Doctrine." In *Prospects for Peace in South Asia,* eds. Rafiq Dossani and Henry S. Rowen, 280–300. Stanford, CA: Stanford University Press, 2005.

Lebow, Richard Ned. "Miscalculation in the South Atlantic: The Origins of the Falklands War." In *Psychology and Deterrence,* edited by Robert Jervis, Richard N. Lebow, and Janice Gross Stein, 89–124. Baltimore, MD: Johns Hopkins University Press, 1985.

Lee, Steven P. *Morality, Prudence and Nuclear Weapons*. Cambridge: Cambridge University Press, 1993.

Lefever, Ernest W. *Nuclear Arms in the Third World*. Washington, DC: The Brookings Institution, 1979.

Leffler, Melvin P. *A Preponderance of Power: National Security, the Truman Administration, and the Cold War*. Stanford, CA: Stanford University Press, 1992.

Legro, Jeffrey W. *Cooperation Under Fire*. Ithaca, NY: Cornell University Press, 1995.

———. "Which Norms Matter? Revisiting the 'Failure' of Internationalism." *International Organization* 51(1) (Winter 1997): 31–61.

———. *Rethinking the World: Great Power Strategies and International Order*. Ithaca, NY: Cornell University Press, 2005.

Leng, Russell. "Realpolitik and Learning in the India-Pakistan Rivalry." In *The India-Pakistan Conflict: An Enduring Rivalry,* edited by T. V. Paul, 103–30. Cambridge: Cambridge University Press, 2005.

Lettow, Paul. *Ronald Reagan and His Quest to Abolish Nuclear Weapons*. New York: Random House, 2005.

Levi, Michael A. "Fire in the Whole: Nuclear and Non-Nuclear Options for Counter-Proliferation." Carnegie Endowment Working Paper no. 31. Washington, DC: Carnegie Endowment for International Peace, November 2002.

Levite, Ariel E., and Emily B. Landau. *Israel's Nuclear Image: Arab Perceptions of Israel's Nuclear Posture.* In Hebrew. Tel Aviv: Papyrus, 1994.

Lewis, Jeffrey. "The Ambiguous Arsenal." *Bulletin of the Atomic Scientists* 61(3) (May/June 2005): 52–59.

Lewis, John Wilson, and Xue Litai. *China Builds the Bomb.* Stanford, CA: Stanford University Press, 1988.

Lieber, Keir A., and Daryl G. Press. "The Rise of U.S. Nuclear Primacy." *Foreign Affairs* 85(2) (March/April 2006): 42–54.

Lilienthal, David. *The Journals of David E. Lilienthal Vol 2: The Atomic Energy Years, 1945–1950.* New York: Harper and Row, 1964.

Lipson, Charles. *Reliable Partners: How Democracies Have Made a Separate Peace.* Princeton, NJ: Princeton University Press, 2003.

Lipson, Michael. "Organized Hypocrisy and the NPT." Paper presented at the annual meeting of the American Political Science Association, Washington, DC, September 1–4, 2005.

Luthi, Lorenz M. *The Sino-Soviet Split.* Princeton, NJ: Princeton University Press, 2008.

Maddock, Shane. "The Fourth Country Problem; Eisenhower's Nuclear Nonproliferation Policy." *Presidential Studies Quarterly* 28(3) (Summer 1998): 553–72.

Maddox, Robert James. *Weapons for Victory: The Hiroshima Decision.* Columbia: University of Missouri Press, 1995.

Maley, William. *The Afghanistan Wars.* New York: Palgrave-Macmillan, 2002.

Malik, General V. P. *Kargil: From Surprise to Victory.* New Delhi: Harper Collins, 2006.

Mallavarapu, Siddharth. *Banning the Bomb: The Politics of Norm Creation.* New Delhi: Pearson, 2007.

Mandelbaum, Michael. *The Nuclear Question: The United States and Nuclear Weapons, 1946–1976.* Cambridge: Cambridge University Press, 1979.

March, James G., and Johan P. Olsen. "The Institutional Dynamics of International Political Orders." *International Organization* 52(4) (Autumn 1998): 943–69.

Martin, Susan B. "Realism and Weapons of Mass Destruction: A Consequentialist Analysis." In *Ethics and Weapons of Mass Destruction,* edited by Sohail H. Hashmi and Steven P. Lee, 96–110. Cambridge: Cambridge University Press, 2004.

Mastny, Vojtech, and Malcolm Byrne, eds. *A Cardboard Castle? An Inside History of the Warsaw Pact, 1955–1991.* Budapest: Central European University Press, 2005.

McCarthy, Timothy V., and Jonathan B. Tucker. "Saddam's Toxic Arsenal: Chemical and Biological Weapons in the Gulf War." In *Planning the Unthinkable,* edited by Peter R. Lavoy, Scott D. Sagan, and James J. Wirtz, 47–78. Ithaca, NY: Cornell University Press, 2000.

McCausland, Lt. Col. Jeffrey. "The Gulf Conflict: A Military Analysis." *Adelphi Papers* no. 282. London: International Institute for Strategic Studies, November 1993.

McDonough, Mark. *Tracking Nuclear Proliferation.* Washington, DC: Carnegie Endowment for International Peace, 1998.

McGowen, Tom. *Air Raid! The Bombing Campaigns of World War II.* Brookfield, CT: Twenty-First Century Books, 2001.

Medalia, Jonathan. "Nuclear Earth Penetrator Weapons." Congressional Research Service Report, Washington, DC, January 27, 2003.

Menon, Anand. "Explaining Defence Policy: The Mitterrand Years." *Review of International Studies* 21(3) (July 1995): 279–99.

Mercer, Jonathan. *Reputation and International Politics.* Ithaca, NY: Cornell University Press, 1996.

Miller, Steven E. "The Haves and Have Nots: Proliferation, Disarmament, and the Future of the NPT System." Paper presented at the Norwegian Institute for International Affairs Conference on "Halting Nuclear Proliferation in the 21st Century," Oslo, October 2005.

Millis, Walter, ed. *The Forrestal Diaries.* New York: Viking, 1951.

Millot, Marc Dean, Roger Molander, and Peter A. Wilson. *"The Day After . . ." Study: Nuclear Proliferation in the Post-Cold War World.* Santa Monica, CA: RAND Corporation, 1993.

Ming, Zhang. *China's Changing Nuclear Posture.* Washington, DC: Brookings Institution Press, 1999.

Morgan, Patrick M. *Deterrence: A Conceptual Analysis.* Beverly Hills: Sage Publications, 1983.

———. *Deterrence Now.* Cambridge: Cambridge University Press, 2003.

Morgenthau, Hans J. *The Purpose of American Politics.* New York: Alfred A. Knopf, 1960.

Mueller, Harald. "Constructing a Taboo against Weapons of Mass Destruction" (Unpublished Paper, Peace Research Institute, Frankfurt, 2003).

Mueller, John, and Karl P. Mueller. "The Methodology of Mass Destruction: Assessing Threats in the New World Order." *Journal of Strategic Studies* 23(1) (March 2000): 163–87.

Mueller, Karl P. et al. *Striking First* (Santa Monica, CA: RAND Corporation, 2006).

Munton, Don, and David A. Welch. *The Cuban Missile Crisis: A Concise History.* New York: Oxford University Press, 2007.

Myrdal, Alva. *The Game of Disarmament.* New York: Pantheon Books, 1982.

Navias, Martin. "Non-Conventional Weaponry and Ballistic Missiles during the 1991 Gulf War." In *Non-Conventional Weapons Proliferation in the Middle East,* edited by Efraim Karsh, Martin S. Navias, and Philip Sabin, 49–66. Oxford: Clarendon Press, 1993.

Nelson, Robert W. "Low-Yield Earth Penetrating Nuclear Weapons." *FAS Public Interest Report* 54(1) (January/February 2001): 1–5.

Nixon, Richard M. *No More Vietnams*. New York: Arbor House, 1985.

Norris, Robert S., and Hans M. Kristensen, "Chinese Nuclear Forces, 2003," *Bulletin of the Atomic Scientists* 59(6) (November/December 2003): 77–80.

———. "U.S. Nuclear Threats: Then and Now," *Bulletin of the Atomic Scientists* 62(5) (September/October 2006): 69–71.

Norris, R. S., A. S. Burrows, and R. W. Fieldhouse. *Nuclear Weapons Databook* Vol. V: *British, French and Chinese Nuclear Weapons*. Boulder, CO: Westview Press, 1994.

Nye, Joseph S. *Soft Power: The Means to Success in World Politics*. New York: Public Affairs, 2004.

Offner, Arnold A. *Another Such Victory: President Truman and the Cold War, 1945–1953*. Stanford, CA: Stanford University Press, 2002.

Oren, Michael B. *Six Days of War: June 1967 and the Making of the Modern Middle East*. New York: Presidio Press, 2003.

Owen, John M. "How Liberalism Produces Democratic Peace," *International Security* 19(2) (Autumn 1994): 87–125.

Paine, Christopher E. "Countering Proliferation, or Compounding It?" Washington, DC: Natural Resources Defense Council, May 2003.

Pande, Savita. "Chinese Nuclear Doctrine." *Strategic Analysis* 23(12) (March 2000): 2011–35.

Pant, Harsh V. "India's Nuclear Doctrine and Command Structure: Implications for India and the World." *Comparative Strategy* 24(3) (July 2005): 277–93.

Paul, T. V. "Nuclear Free-zone in the South Pacific: Rhetoric or Reality?" *The Round Table* 299 (July 1986): 252–62.

———. *Asymmetric Conflicts: War Initiation by Weaker Powers*. Cambridge: Cambridge University Press, 1994.

———. "Nuclear Taboo and War Initiation: Nuclear Weapons in Regional Conflicts." *Journal of Conflict Resolution* 39(4) (December 1995): 696–717.

———. "Power, Influence and Nuclear Weapons: A Reassessment." In *The Absolute Weapon Revisited: Nuclear Arms and the Emerging International Order*, edited by T. V. Paul, Richard J. Harknett, and James J. Wirtz, 19–46. Ann Arbor: University of Michigan Press, 1998.

———. "The Systemic Bases of India's Challenge to the Global Nuclear Order," *The Nonproliferation Review* 6(1) (Fall 1998): 1–11.

———. *Power versus Prudence: Why Nations Forgo Nuclear Weapons*. Montreal, QC: McGill-Queen's University Press, 2000.

———. "Systemic Conditions and Security Cooperation: Explaining the Persistence of the Nuclear Nonproliferation Regime." *Cambridge Review of International Affairs* 16(1) (April 2003): 135–54.

———. "Chinese/Pakistani Nuclear/Missile Ties and Balance of Power Politics." *The Nonproliferation Review* 10(2) (Summer 2003): 1–9.

———, ed. *The India-Pakistan Conflict: An Enduring Rivalry.* Cambridge: Cambridge University Press, 2005.

———. "The US.-India Nuclear Accord: Implications for the Non-Proliferation Regime." *International Journal* 62(4) (Autumn 2007): 845–61.

Paul, T. V., and John A. Hall, eds. *International Order and the Future of World Politics.* Cambridge: Cambridge University Press, 1999.

Payne, Keith B. *Deterrence in the Second Nuclear Age.* Lexington: University Press of Kentucky, 1996.

———. "Why We Must Sustain Nuclear Deterrence." (National Institute for Public Policy, April 1998).

Perkovich, George. *India's Nuclear Bomb: The Impact on Global Proliferation.* Berkeley: University of California Press, 1990.

———. "Bush Doctrine Makes Nuclear Weapons Morally Obsolete." Unpublished paper, Carnegie Endowment for International Peace (Washington, DC, June 2003).

Perry, William J. "Desert Storm and Deterrence in the Future." In *After the Storm: Lessons from the Gulf War,* edited by Joseph S. Nye and Roger K. Smith, 241–64. Colorado Springs, CO: The Aspen Institute, 1992.

Pilat, Joseph F. "Reassessing Security Assurances in a Unipolar World." *The Washington Quarterly* 28(2) (Spring 2005): 159–170.

Pipes, Richard. "Why the Soviet Union Thinks it Could Fight and Win a Nuclear War." *Commentary* 64(1) (July 1977): 21–34.

Posen, Barry R. "A Nuclear-Armed Iran: A Difficult but Not Impossible Policy Problem." New York: The Century Foundation, December 6, 2006.

———. "U.S. Security Policy in a Nuclear-Armed World," *Security Studies* 6, no. 3 (Spring 1997): 1–31.

Posen, Barry R., and Stephen Van Evera. "Defense Policy and the Reagan Administration: Departure from Containment." *International Security* 8(1) (Summer 1983): 3–45.

Pouliot, Vincent. "The Essence of Constructivism." *Journal of International Relations and Development* 7(3) (September 2004): 319–36.

Poulose, T. T. *United Nations and Nuclear Proliferation.* New Delhi: B. R. Publishing, 1988.

Powell, Colin L., with Joseph E. Persico. *My American Journey.* New York: Random House, 1995.

Powell, Robert. *Nuclear Deterrence Theory: The Search for Credibility.* Cambridge: Cambridge University Press, 1990.

Prados, John. "Team B: The Trillion Dollar Experiment." *Bulletin of the Atomic Scientists* 49(3) (April 1993): 22–31.

Press, Daryl G. *Calculating Credibility: How Leaders Assess Military Threats.* Ithaca, NY: Cornell University Press, 2005.

Price, Richard. "A Genealogy of the Chemical Weapons Taboo." *International Organization* 49(1) (Winter 1995): 73–103.

———. "Transnational Civil Society and Advocacy in World Politics." *World Politics* 55(4) (July 2003): 579–606.

Price, Richard, and Nina Tannenwald. "Norms and Deterrence: The Nuclear and Chemical Weapons Taboos." In *The Culture of National Security,* edited by Peter J. Katzenstein, 114–52. New York: Columbia University Press, 1996.

Quester, George. *The Politics of Nuclear Proliferation.* Baltimore, MD: Johns Hopkins University Press, 1973

———. "International Safeguards for Eliminating Weapons of Mass Destruction." Occasional Paper No. 31. Washington, DC: The Henry L. Stimson Center, December 1996.

———. *Nuclear First Strike: Consequences of a Broken Taboo.* Baltimore, MD: Johns Hopkins University Press, 2006.

Raja Mohan, C. "No First Use and India's Nuclear Transition." Paper Presented at the Pugwash Conference on No First Use of Nuclear Weapons, London, November 15–17, 2002.

Rajagopalan, Rajesh. *Second Strike: Arguments about Nuclear War in South Asia.* New Delhi: Penguin-Viking, 2005.

Rapacki, Adam. "The Polish Plan for a Nuclear-Free Zone Today." *International Affairs* 39(1) (January 1963): 1–12.

Raub, Werner, and Jeroen Weesie. "Reputation and Efficiency in Social Interactions: An Example of Network Effects." *The American Journal of Sociology* 96(3) (November 1990): 626–54.

Rauf, Tariq. "Towards Nuclear Disarmament: What Next for NPT?" *Disarmament Forum 2000*(1) (2000): 39–50.

Rauf, Tariq, and Rebecca Johnson. "After the NPT's Indefinite Extension: The Future of the Global Nonproliferation Regime." *Nonproliferation Review* 3(1) (Fall 1995): 28–41.

Rearden, Steven L. *The Formative Years 1947–1950.* Washington DC: Historical Office, Office of the Secretary of Defense, 1984.

Reiss, Mitchell. *Without the Bomb: The Politics of Nuclear Nonproliferation.* New York: Columbia University Press, 1988.

Reus-Smit, Christian. "Liberal Hierarchy and the License to Use Force." *Review of International Studies* 31 (December 2005): 71–92.

Rhodes, Edward. *Power and Madness: The Logic of Nuclear Coercion.* New York: Columbia University Press, 1989.

Rhodes, Richard. *Dark Sun: The Making of the Hydrogen Bomb.* New York: Touchstone, 1995.

Ripsman, Norrin M. "Two Stages of Transition From a Region of War to a Region of Peace: Realist Transition and Liberal Endurance." *International Studies Quarterly* 49(4) (December 2005): 669–93.

Risse-Kappen, Thomas. "Constructivism and International Institutions: Towards Conversions Across Paradigms." In *Political Science: The State of the Discipline,* edited by Ira Katznelson and Helen Milner, 597–629. New York: W. W. Norton, 2002.

Roberts, Brad, Robert A. Manning, and Ronald N. Montaperto. "China: The Forgotten Nuclear Power." *Foreign Affairs* 79(4) (July–August 2000): 53–63.

Robinson, C. Paul. "Pursuing a New Weapons Policy for the 21st Century" (Sandia National Laboratories White Paper, Albuquerque, NM, March 22, 2001).

Robles, Alfonso Garcia. "Latin American Nuclear Weapon Free Zone." Stanley Foundation Occasional Paper no. 19. Muscatine, IA: The Stanley Foundation, 1979.

Roche, Douglas. "Deadly Deadlock." Middle Powers Initiative Briefing Paper. San Francisco: Middle Powers Initiative, June 2005.

Rogers, Paul. "Tactical Trident in Historical Context." Paper presented at the annual meeting of the British International Studies Association, University of York, UK, December 1994.

Rosenberg, David Alan. "American Atomic Strategy and the Hydrogen Bomb Decision." *Journal of American History* 66(1) (June 1979): 62–87.

———. "The Origins of Overkill: Nuclear Weapons and American Strategy, 1945–1960." *International Security* 7(4) (Spring 1983): 3–71.

Rosenberg, Jonathan. "Before the Bomb and After: Winston Churchill and the Use of Force." In *Cold War Statesmen Confront the Bomb: Nuclear Diplomacy Since 1945,* edited by John Lewis Gaddis, Philip H. Gordon, Ernest R. May, and Jonathan Rosenberg, 171–93. Oxford: Oxford University Press, 1999.

Rosendorf, Neal. "John Foster Dulles' Nuclear Schizophrenia." In *Cold War Statesmen Confront the Bomb: Nuclear Diplomacy Since 1945,* edited by John Lewis Gaddis, Gordon, Philip H. Gordon, Ernest R. May, and Jonathan Rosenberg, 62–86. Oxford: Oxford University Press, 1999.

Ross, Christopher. "Public Diplomacy Comes of Age." *Washington Quarterly* 25(2) (2002): 75–83.

Ross, Steven T., and David Alan Rosenberg, eds. *America's Plans for War against the Soviet Union 1945–1950.* New York: Garland Publishing, 1990.

Rothman, Steve, "The Publication of 'Hiroshima' in *The New Yorker*" (Unpublished Paper, Harvard University, 1997), http://www.herseyhiroshima.com/hiro.php.

Russell, James A. "Nuclear Strategy and the Modern Middle East." *Middle East Policy* 11(3) (Fall 2004): 98–117.

Russell, Richard L. "A Weak Pillar for American National Security: The CIA's Dismal Performance against WMD Threats." *Intelligence and National Security* 20(3) (September 2005): 466–85.

Russett, Bruce. "The Real Decline in Nuclear Hegemony." In *Global Changes and Theoretical Challenges,* edited by Ernst-Otto Czempiel and James N. Rosenau, 177–93. Lexington, MA: Lexington Books, 1989.

Russett, Bruce, and John Oneal. *Triangulating Peace.* New York: W. W. Norton, 2001.

Ryan, Mark A. *Chinese Attitudes Toward Nuclear Weapons.* Armonk, NY: M. E. Sharpe, 1989.

Rydell, Randy. "The 1995 Nuclear Non-Proliferation Treaty Review and Extension Conference." *Arms Control Today* 35(3) (April 2005): 47–48.

Sagan, Eli. *Cannibalism: Human Aggression and Cultural Form.* New York: Harper & Row, 1974.

Sagan, Scott D. "The Commitment Trap: Why the United States Should Not Use Nuclear Threats to Deter Biological and Chemical Weapons Attacks." *International Security* 24(4) (Spring 2000): 85–115.

———. "Realist Perspectives on Ethical Norms and Weapons of Mass Destruction." In *Ethics and Weapons of Mass Destruction,* edited by Sohail H. Hashmi and Steven P. Lee, 73–95. Cambridge: Cambridge University Press, 2004.

Sagan, Scott D., and Seremi Suri. "The Madman Nuclear Alert: Secrecy, Signaling, and Safety in October 1969." International Security 27(4) (Spring 2003): 150–83.

Scheinman, Lawrence. "Shadow & Substance: Securing the Future of Atoms for Peace." *IAEA Bulletin* 45(2) (December 2003): 7–9.

Schelling, Thomas C. *Arms and Influence.* New Haven, CT: Yale University Press, 1966.

———. *The Strategy of Conflict,* 2nd edition. Cambridge, MA: Harvard University Press, 1980.

———. "The Role of Nuclear Weapons." In *Turning Point: The Gulf War and U.S.* Military *Strategy,* edited by Benjamin L. Ederington and Michael J. Mazarr, 105–16. Boulder, CO: Westview Press, 1994.

———. "The Legacy of Hiroshima: A Half Century Without Nuclear War." Institute for *Philosophy and Public Policy* 20(2/3) (Summer 2000).

Schrafstetter, Susanna, and Stephen Twigge. *Avoiding Armageddon: Europe, the United States and the Struggle for Nuclear Non-Proliferation, 1945–1970.* Westport, CT: Praeger, 2004.

Schwartz, Leonard E. "Perspectives on Pugwash." *International Affairs* 43(3) (July 1967): 498–515.

Schwartz, Stephen I. "Miscalculated Ambiguity: U.S. Policy on the Use and Threat of Use of Nuclear Weapons." *Disarmament Diplomacy* 23 (February 1998).

Schwarzkopf, Norman, with Peter Petre. *It Doesn't Take a Hero.* New York: Bantam Books, 1992.

Seaborg, Glenn T., and Benjamin S. Loeb. *Kennedy, Khrushchev and the Test Ban.* Berkeley: University of California Press, 1981.

——. *Stemming the Tide: Arms Control in the Johnson Years.* Lexingon, MA: Lexington Books, 1987.

Serrano, Monica. "Latin America—The Treaty of Tlateloco." In *Nuclear Weapons-Free Zones,* edited by Ramesh Thakur, 35–58. New York: St. Martin's Press, 1998.

Shaker, Mohamed I. *The Nuclear Nonproliferation Treaty: Origins and Implementation 1959–1979.* Vol. 2. London: Oceana Publications, 1980.

Sidhu, Waheguru Pal Singh. "India's Nuclear Use Doctrine." In *Planning the Unthinkable,* edited by Peter R. Lavoy, Scott D. Sagan, and James J. Wirtz, 125–57. Ithaca, NY: Cornell University Press, 2000.

Sigal, Leon V. "Warming to the Freeze." *Foreign Policy* 48 (Autumn 1982): 54–65.

——. *Disarming Strangers: Nuclear Diplomacy With North Korea.* Princeton, NJ: Princeton University Press, 1998.

Silverstone, Scott A. *Preventive War and American Democracy.* New York: Routledge, 2007.

Simmons, Beth A. "Compliance with International Agreements." *Annual Review of Political Science* 1 (1998): 75–93.

——. "International Law and State Behavior: Commitment and Compliance in International Monetary Affairs." *American Political Science Review* 94(4) (December 2000): 819–35.

Singh, Swaran. "China's Nuclear Weapons and Doctrine." In *Nuclear India,* edited by Jasjit Singh, 140–56. New Delhi: Knowledge World, 1998.

Siracusa, Joseph M., and David G. Coleman. "Scaling the Nuclear Ladder: Deterrence from Truman to Clinton." *Australian Journal of International Affairs* 54(3) (November 2000): 277–96.

Skinner, Kiron K., Annelise Anderson, and Martin Anderson, eds. *Reagan: A Life in Letters.* New York: Free Press, 2003.

Smith, Alice Kimball. *A Peril and a Hope: The Scientists' Movement in America, 1945–47.* Chicago: University of Chicago Press, 1965.

Smith, Derek D. *Deterring America: Rogue States and the Proliferation of Weapons of Mass Destruction.* Cambridge: Cambridge University Press, 2006.

Snyder, Glenn H. "Deterrence and Power." *Journal of Conflict Resolution* 4 (1960): 163–78.

——. *Deterrence and Defense: Toward a Theory of National Security.* Princeton, NJ: Princeton University Press, 1961.

Sokov, Nikolai. "Russia's Approach to Nuclear Weapons." *The Washington Quarterly.* 20(3) (Summer 1997): 107–14.

——. "An Assessment of the Draft Russian Military Doctrine." (Nuclear Threat Initiative, Revised ed., July 2004), http://www.nti.org/db/nisprofs/over/doctrine.htm.

Spector, Leonard, and Aubrie Ohlde. "Negative Security Assurances: Revisiting the Nuclear-Weapon-Free Zone Option." *Arms Control Today* 35(3) (April 2005): 13–17.

Spector, Ronald H. *Advice and Support: The Early Years, 1941–1960.* Washington, DC: U.S. Army Center for Military History, 1983.

Speed, Roger, and Michael May. "Dangerous Doctrine." *Bulletin of the Atomic Scientists* 61(2) (March/April 2005): 38–49.

Steiner, Franz Baermann. *Taboo, Truth, and Religion: Selected Writings* Vol. 1, edited by Jeremy Adler and Richard Fardon. New York: Berghahn Books, 1999.

Stern, Sheldon M. *Averting "the Final Failure": John F. Kennedy and the Secret Cuban Missile Crisis Meetings.* Stanford, CA: Stanford University Press, 2003.

Subrahmanyam, K. "Indian Nuclear Policy—1964–98: A Personal Recollection," In *Nuclear India,* edited by Jasjit Singh, 26–53. New Delhi: Knowledge World, 1998.

Swami, Praveen. "A Hawkish Line on China." *Frontline,* May 23, 1998.

Takaki, Ronald. *Hiroshima: Why America Dropped the Bomb.* Boston: Little, Brown, 1995.

Tannenwald, Nina. "The Nuclear Taboo: The United States and the Normative Basis of the Nuclear Non-use." *International Organization* 53(3) (Summer 1999): 433–68.

———. "Stigmatizing the Bomb: Origins of the Nuclear Taboo." *International Security,* 29(4) (Spring 2005): 5–49.

———. *The Nuclear Taboo.* Cambridge: Cambridge University Press, 2007.

Tarapore, Arzan. "Holocaust or Hollow Victory: Limited War in Nuclear South Asia." IPCS Research Paper no. 6. New Delhi: Institute of Peace and Conflict Studies, 2005.

Taylor, Maxwell D. *Swords and Plowshares.* New York: W. W. Norton, 1972.

Tellis, Ashley J. *India's Emerging Nuclear Posture.* RAND Monograph Report. Santa Monica, CA: RAND Corporation, 2001.

Tellis, Ashley, C., Christine Fair, and Jamison J. Medby. *Limited Conflicts Under the Nuclear Umbrella: Indian and Pakistani Lessons for the Kargil Crisis.* Santa Monica, CA: RAND Corporation, 2002.

Terriff, Terry. *The Nixon Administration and the Making of U.S. Nuclear Strategy.* Ithaca, NY: Cornell University Press, 1995.

Tertrais, Bruno. "Nuclear Policy: France Stands Alone." *Bulletin of the Atomic Scientists* 60(4) (July/August 2004): 48–55.

Thomas, Ward. *The Ethics of Destruction: Norms and Force in International Relations.* Ithaca, NY: Cornell University Press, 2001.

Tompkins, Joanne. "Influences on Chinese Nuclear Planning." Washington DC: Henry L. Stimson Center, 2002.

———. "How U.S. Strategic Policy is Changing Chain's Nuclear Plans." *Arms Control Today* 33(1) (January–February 2003): 11.

Toope, Stephen J. "Formality and Informality." In *The Oxford Handbook of International Environmental Law,* edited by Daniel Bodansky, Jutta Brunnee, and Ellen Hey, 107–24. Oxford: Oxford University Press, 2007.

Trenin, Dimitri. "Russia's Nuclear Policy in the 21st Century Environment" (Paris, Institut français des relations internationales, Autumn 2005).

Truman, Harry S. *Memoirs of Harry S. Truman* Vol. 1: *Year of Decisions, 1945.* Garden City, NY: Doubleday, 1955.

———. *Memoirs* Vol. 2, *Years of Trial and Hope.* Garden City, NY: Doubleday, 1956.

Tucker, Jonathan B. "Evidence Iraq Used Chemical Weapons During the 1991 Persian Gulf War." *The Nonproliferation Review* 4(3) (Spring/Summer1997): 114–22.

Turner, Jonathan H., and Alexandra Maryanski. *Incest: Origins of the Taboo.* Boulder, CO: Paradigm Publishers, 2005.

USSR Proposes Disarmament. Moscow: Progress Publishers, 1986.

Utgoff, Victor A. "Nuclear Weapons and Deterrence of Biological and Chemical Warfare." Occasional Paper no. 36. Washington, DC: The Henry L. Stimson Center, October 1997.

Van Creveld, Martin. *Nuclear Proliferation and the Future of Conflict.* New York: The Free Press, 1993.

van Oudenaren, John. "Deterrence, War-fighting and Soviet Military Doctrine." *Adelphi Papers* no. 210. London: International Institute for Strategic Studies, Summer 1986.

Vasquez, John A. "The Deterrence Myth: Nuclear Weapons and the Prevention of Nuclear War." In *The Long Postwar Peace,* edited by Charles W. Kegley, 205–23. New York: Harper Collins, 1991.

Wainstock, Dennis D. *The Decision to Drop the Atomic Bomb.* Wesport, CT: Praeger, 1996.

Way, Christopher, and Karthika Sasikumar. "Leaders and Laggards: When and Why do Countries Sign the NPT?" Working Paper No. 16. Montreal: McGill-University of Montreal Research Group in International Security (REGIS), 2004.

Weber, Max. *Economy and Society: An Outline of Interpretative Sociology,* edited by Guenther Roth and Claus Wittich. New York: Bedminster Press, 1968.

Webster, Hutton. *Taboo: A Sociological Study.* Stanford, CA: Stanford University Press, 1942.

Weisgall, Jonathan M. *Operation Crossroads: The Atomic Tests at Bikini Atoll.* Annapolis, MD: Naval Institute Press, 1994.

Welch, David A. "The Politics and Psychology of Restraint: Israeli Decision-making in the Gulf." In *Choosing to Cooperate: How States Avoid Loss,* edited by Janice Gross Stein and Louis W. Pauly, 128–69. Baltimore, MD: Johns Hopkins University Press, 1993.

Wendt, Alexander. *Social Theory of International Politics.* Cambridge: Cambridge University Press, 1999.

Wernicke, Günter. "The Communist-led World Peace Council and the Western Peace Movements." *Peace & Change* 23(3) (July 1998): 265–311.

Whiting, Allen S. *China Crosses the Yalu: The Decision to Enter the Korean War.* New York: Macmillan, 1960.

———. "China's Use of Force, 1950–96, and Taiwan." *International Security* 26(2) (Fall 2001): 103–31.

Wheeler, Michael O. "A History of Arms Control." In *Arms Control: Cooperative Security in a Changing Environment,* edited by Jeffrey A. Larsen, 19–40. Boulder, CO: Lynne Rienner, 2002.

Wilkening, Dean, and Kenneth Watman. *Nuclear Deterrence in a Regional Context.* Santa Monica, CA: RAND Corporation, 1995.

Wilson, George C. "Worst Case: Iraqi War Goes Nuclear." *National Journal* 34(41) (October 2002): 2992–93.

Wilson, Ward. "The Winning Weapon? Rethinking Nuclear Weapons in Light of Hiroshima," *International Security* 31(4) (Spring 2007): 162–79.

Wirtz, James J., and James A. Russell. "U.S. Policy on Preventive War and Preemption." *The Nonproliferation Review* 10(1) (Spring 2003): 113–23.

Wishnick, Elizabeth. *Mending Fences: The Evolution of Moscow's China Policy from Brezhnev to Yeltsin.* Seattle: University of Washington Press, 2001.

Wittner, Lawrence S. *The Struggle Against the Bomb,* Vol. 1: *One World or None.* Stanford, CA: Stanford University Press, 1993.

———. *The Struggle Against the Bomb,* Vol. 2: *Resisting the Bomb.* Stanford, CA: Stanford University Press, 1997.

———. *The Struggle Against the Bomb,* Vol. 3: *Toward Nuclear Abolition.* Stanford, CA: Stanford University Press, 2003.

Wohlstetter, Albert. "The Delicate Balance of Terror." *Foreign Affairs* 37(2) (January 1959): 211–34.

Wolf, Arthur P., and William H. Durham, eds. *Inbreeding, Incest, and the Incest Taboo: The State of Knowledge at the Turn of the Century.* Stanford, CA: Stanford University Press, 2004.

Wolf, Charles Jr., and Brian Rosen. "Public Diplomacy: How to Think About and Improve It." Occasional Paper. Santa Monica, CA: RAND Corporation, 2004.

Xue, Litai. "Evolution of China's Nuclear Strategy." In *Strategic Views from the Second Tier: The Nuclear Weapons Policies of France, Britain and China,* edited by John C. Hopkins and Weixing Hu, 167–89. New Brunswick, NJ: Transaction Publishers, 1995.

York, Herbert. *The Advisors: Oppenheimer, Teller, and the Superbomb.* San Francisco: W. H. Freeman, 1976.

Yost, David S. "Nuclear Weapons Issues in France." In *Strategic Views from the Second Tier,* edited by John C. Hopkins and Weixing Hu, 19–104. New Brunswick, NJ: Transaction Publishers, 1995.

———. "France's Nuclear Dilemmas." *Foreign Affairs* 75(1) (January/February 1996): 108–18.

————. "Russia's Non-strategic Nuclear Forces." *International Affairs* 77(3) (July 2001): 531–51.

————. "New Approaches to Deterrence in Britain, France, and the United States." *International Affairs* 81(1) (January 2005): 83–114.

Zakaria, Fareed. "The Reagan Strategy of Containment." *Political Science Quarterly* 105(3) (Autumn 1990): 373–95.

Zhang, Shu Guang. "Between 'Paper' and 'Real Tigers': Mao's View of Nuclear Weapons." In *Cold War Statesmen Confront the Bomb: Nuclear Diplomacy Since 1945,* edited by John Lewis Gaddis, Philip H. Gordon, Ernest R. May, and Jonathan Rosenberg, 194–215. Oxford: Oxford University Press, 1999.

Zhenqiang, Pan. "On China's No First Use of Nuclear Weapons." Paper Presented at Pugwash Meeting 279 (London, November 15–17, 2002).

Zubok, Vladislav M. "Stalin and the Nuclear Age." In *Cold War Statesmen Confront the Bomb: Nuclear Diplomacy Since 1945,* edited by John Lewis Gaddis, Philip H. Gordon, Ernest R. May, and Jonathan Rosenberg, 39–61. Oxford: Oxford University Press, 1999.

————. "Gorbachev's Nuclear Learning." *Boston Review,* April–May 2000.

Zubok, Vladislav M., and Hope M. Harrison. "The Nuclear Education of Nikita Khrushchev." In *Cold War Statesmen Confront the Bomb: Nuclear Diplomacy Since 1945,* edited by John Lewis Gaddis, Philip H. Gordon, Ernest R. May, and Jonathan Rosenberg, 141–168. Oxford: Oxford University Press, 1999.

INDEX

Able Archer crisis, 242n76

Accidents Measures Agreement of 1971, 240n48

Acheson/Lilienthal Report of 1946, 32–33, 40–41, 229n13

Adams, Sherman, 51

Afghanistan: Soviet war in, 12, 18, 79, 99–100, 145, 220n33; Taliban in, 137–38, 145, 188; US/NATO war in, 138, 139, 145, 188, 195

Africa Nuclear-Free Zone (Pelindaba) Treaty, 89, 171, 174–76

Afro-Asian Conference of 1955, 34

Algerian War of Independence, 112, 123, 144

ambiguity in nuclear policies: of France, 113, 114; of Israel, 124, 125, 130, 146, 255n3; relationship to deterrence, 11, 91, 160; of United States, 36, 83–84, 85, 89, 91, 168, 181, 212

analytical eclecticism, 13, 18, 21–37, 155, 217n2

Angola, 100

Anti-Ballistic Missile (ABM) Treaty, 81, 119, 240n48

ANZUS Treaty, 172, 173

Argentina: Falklands War, 10, 108–9, 111, 145, 149–52, 261nn24,26; and NPT, 165–66

Arms Control and Disarmament Agency, 237n10

Association of Southeast Asian Nations (ASEAN), 174

Atkinson, Rick, 153

Atoms for Peace proposal, 35, 57–58, 62–63

Attlee, Clement, 46, 48, 106, 107, 228n10, 232n46

Australia, 165, 172, 173–74

Axelrod, Robert: on cooperation and reputation, 31

Aziz, Tariq, 84, 153, 154–55, 262n39, 263n51

Baker, James, 84, 153, 154–55

Ball, George, 67; on use of nuclear weapons, 5, 68–69

Ballistic Missile Notification Agreement of 1988, 102

Baltic states, 105

Baluyevsky, Yuri, 104

Bandung Conference of 1955, 34

Bangkok Treaty of 1995, 171, 174

Bangladesh, 76–77, 132, 134

Baruch Plan of 1946, 32–33, 40, 41, 57, 94, 229n12

Bay of Pigs invasion, 65

Beilenson, Laurence, 242n78

Belarus, 103

Berlin: Blockade of 1948, 42–43, 95; Crisis of 1958–59, 57; Crisis of 1961, 65, 97, 245n1

Bin Laden, Osama, 138

biological weapons: vs. nuclear weapons, 4, 179, 220n23, 272n37. *See also* threats to use nuclear weapons, in response to chemical/biological attack

Blair, Tony, 251n83; and Strategic Defense Review, 110

Bohr, Niels, 32, 33

West Germany, 93, 98, 162, 240n54
Whalen, Richard J., 73
Wilson, Charles E., 52
Wilson, Harold, 107
Wohlstetter, Albert, 227n59
Wolfe, Thomas W., 81
Wolfers, Arnold, 34
Wolfowitz, Paul, 81
World Court, 13; World Court Project,
    267n38
World Federation of Churches, 33
World Peace Council, 33, 59, 93

Yeltsin, Boris, 102
Yom Kippur War of 1973: Egypt during,
    72, 77–78, 126, 127–28, 145, 146–49,
    247n31, 260n19; Israel during, 72, 77–78,
    126, 127–29, 130, 144–45, 146–49, 205,
    256n17, 260n19; Kissinger during, 128,
    148; Nixon during, 72, 77, 90, 128; Soviet
    Union during, 127, 128; Syria during,
    126, 127, 128, 145, 146

Zhu Chenghu, 120